SHERIDAN
The Track of a Comet

by Madeleine Bingham

Scotland under Mary Stuart

Sheridan · Portrait by J. Hoppner

SHERIDAN
The Track of a Comet

By

Madeleine Bingham

'The Track of a Comet
is as regular to the eye
of God as the orbit of a Planet.'

R. B. Sheridan

London. George Allen & Unwin Ltd
Ruskin House   Museum Street

Printed in Great Britain
in 11 point Baskerville type
by Unwin Brothers Limited
Woking and London

CONTENTS

ILLUSTRATIONS

A*

ACKNOWLEDGEMENTS

I would like to thank Professor R. D. B. French of Trinity College, Dublin and Mrs Chubb of Trinity College Library for advice and help about the career of Thomas Sheridan of the Smock Alley Theatre.

In Bath the staff of the Municipal Museum, the Public Library, and the Victoria Art Gallery, and the Assembly Rooms all helped to give me background material.

In London the Garrick Club Library and the Enthoven Collection of the Victoria and Albert Museum all supplied valuable theatrical material, as did the library of the Garrick Club.

Brook's kindly allowed me to cross their sacred portals to see the famous Subscription Room and read through their Bets Book which in itself gives a wonderful historical picture ranging as it does from bets about the American War of Independence down to sums wagered about Votes for Women.

The National Gallery in London and the National Gallery of Ireland also gave me advice with the illustrations.

Note

Certain of the quotation in this book have been slightly edited. Where this has been done, in the interests of brevity, the practice of indicating the beginning and ending of cuts by a series of dots has not always been followed, care being taken, of course, to ensure that the sense was in no way altered.

Similarly, for ease of reading, many of the capital letters for odd words have been changed to small letters, though in certain quotations thay have been retained as an example of the curiously indiscriminate way such capital letters were used.

M. B.

CHAPTER 1

The Setting and the Forebears

Richard Brinsley Sheridan is remembered for the brilliance of his comedies, which still have the magic to keep an audience laughing, after nearly two hundred years. Yet the major part of his working hours and efforts and certainly all his ambitions lay in the field of politics and the social activities which went with the politics of his era.

For him the theatre was only the means to an end, the provider of money to enable him to keep afloat in a political world where family connections and money were essentials for political advancement. It was possible to survive with one of these two, but not without either. Richard Sheridan had none of the former, and rarely enough of the latter, and when he had, he did not conserve it.

At the beginning of his career, Sheridan was, in his way, second only to Garrick in the world of the theatre. Had he concentrated on the theatre, he might have surpassed Garrick in affluence.

What went wrong? Why did this witty man relegate his true talent – playwriting – to a secondary position in his life? The answers lie largely in what he himself saw of the theatre and theatrical life and what he heard of it from his actor father, the ill-starred Thomas Sheridan – and partly in the struggle for gentility which was endemic in the family for at least three generations.

Richard Brinsley Sheridan regarded the theatre with contempt, but ironically it is through his plays that his memory still shines. To understand why he so disliked the theatre, the hazards of the century in which he lived must be considered, and also the blood and heredity with which he had to battle.

The century into which Richard Sheridan was born was one of sharp social differences – of sudden fame, of sudden fortune, and equally sudden incarceration for debt. It is difficult to understand the contrivances of his life unless these factors are taken into account. A man lives his life forward from day to day, taking the decisions which seem to be appropriate at the moment. If he has a streak of the actor in his make-up he may take foolish decisions which show him to the best advantage for a fleeting moment.

When a man's life is laid out like a journey accomplished, to record and comment on it can only induce a great humility. So many hopes which were unfulfilled, so many loves lost, so many achievements, yet in the end often so little achieved. Any man's life is a record of frailty. To read it from its hopeful beginning to its inevitable end is to be made aware of the hazards and chances which lie along the path.

It is impossible to understand the strange choice Sheridan made for his main life's work, unless his background and upbringing and the circumstances which coloured his life are used as the backdrop. Only then is it possible to understand why Sheridan so disliked the one medium in which his brilliance was unsurpassed.

The pulpit, the theatre and the House of Commons are all stages where a bubble reputation can be blown up or dissipated by a misplaced gesture or a tactless word, a wrong decision, or an ill-chosen alliance. In the pulpit, Richard Brinsley Sheridan's grandfather preached the wrong sermon; in the theatre, Sheridan's father put on the wrong play; and in the House of Commons, Sheridan allied himself with the wrong faction. In the hairbreadth differences between success and failure they were not a felicitous family.

The Sheridan ancestry is wreathed in as many mists as an Irish day. To read the various accounts of the family is like being closeted with an old relative who intones the intricacies of the family legends, part myth, part truth, and part hopeful imaginings. Sheridan ancestors are supposed to have landed in Ireland in A D 600 to found an order of learning for the Pope. Others are supposed to have become Protestant Bishops. Fairy castles are built on extinct baronies, monasteries crumbled into dust, family seats escheated to the Crown, and Jacobites who fled from the defeat of their cause – they seem to have

14

been one of those families who always trembled on the edge of gentility, only to fall by making unfortunate speeches or wrong political decisions, or by marrying the wrong women.

The seeds of Richard Brinsley's character lay in the personalities, careers and actions of his father and grandfather. They were, both of them, odd and in some ways eccentric men.

The first forebear of Richard Brinsley of whom much is known for certain was his grandfather, Thomas, the friend of Swift, who lived at Quilca in County Cavan. In books of reminiscences Quilca is mentioned as one would casually refer to Chatsworth or Blenheim. But in County Cavan its two ruined stone piers are now closed by a cattle-gate. The walls have tumbled into ruin. The huge beech trees overshadow a pasturage. Nothing remains of the house but a chimney, a wall, and a courtyard deep in farmyard mud: such is Quilca today.

Here Swift wrote part of *Gulliver's Travels*. Here Thomas Sheridan, DD, grandfather of the playwright, entertained and attempted to provide a background of solid gentility for himself. Through half-closed eyes, it is still possible to picture a time when the gate was opened for the gentry, when a neat carriage might drive up to a welcoming front door. The sunlight flickers through the trees. But as grey clouds obscure the blue sky, a doubt remains – was this ever a country gentleman's residence?

The outlines of the house seen through the sweeping branches are modest. Even the ruins are modest. They must always have been modest. Was Quilca ever more than a beginning, an attempt, and a dream? An attempt to turn a farmhouse into a 'place', and a dream of gracious living conceived by a retired schoolmaster beside an Irish lake. Perhaps his soaring imagination turned the rough ground into a sloping lawn, and the whispering reeds at the water's edge into an eighteenth century folly. It would almost seem so, because when Dr Sheridan offered to lend Quilca to the Bishop of Meath, Dean Swift said to the Bishop, 'My Lord, do you hear that vapouring scab? I will show you an exact picture of the place which he has painted in such fine colours.' He then quoted a poem of his own:

> Let me thy properties explain;
> A rotten cabin, dropping rain,
> Chimneys with scorn rejecting smoke,
> Stools, tables, chairs and bedsteads broke.
> In vain we make poor Shelah toil,
> Fire will not roast, nor water boil.

On another occasion Swift described the doctor's house as 'all torn to rags by boys and balls' and a 'chair that collapsed and let him down on his Reverend Deanship's bum'.

But in spite of all that, Swift was once content enough to be entertained at Quilca. Perhaps the good company made up for the lack of comfort, and the smoking fires were brightened by the Sheridan wit. Thomas must certainly have had some special quality which drew Swift to him and made him his confessor and confidant. When Swift's Stella died, he wrote to Thomas: 'The last act of life is always a tragedy at best.' It is likely that Thomas managed at one time to keep the tragedy at bay for Swift.

Like much to do with the Sheridans, even the date of Dr Thomas Sheridan's birth varies, but he was certainly born some time between 1684 and 1690 and died in 1738. He was said to be a true Rabelaisian: he apparently did not consider this conflicted with his ambitions in the sphere of religion, or his leanings toward erudite studies. He was certainly regarded as a great teacher of the young; he followed Milton's advice and encouraged Greek plays at his school. 'Doubtless', wrote Swift, 'the best instructor of youth in these kingdoms, or perhaps in Europe, and as great a master of the Greek and Latin languages.'

Even after Dr Thomas had quarrelled with Swift, the great writer still said, with honesty, that Thomas was 'the instiller of all the principles of honour and justice, and a man of sense, modesty and virtue, whose greatest fault is a wife and children'.

Thomas had a roving disposition; he liked comfort, but never seemed to like it enough to be able to make a real home for his family. He was erratic and witty, loved music, sports books, and philosophy, puns, and practical jokes. But the practicality was not carried beyond the jokes, and he moved constantly from one parochial living to another, and from one school to another, a prey to the feeling that the grass is always greener somewhere else. And yet his own mentality was still green, for he was constantly cheated by his friends and acquaintances. He was cheated over the farms, and as a schoolmaster he was robbed of pupils by sometime friends. Sometimes he would teach the more promising pupils for nothing, because it was in his nature to give. At the beginning of his career he earned £1,200 a year and yet, when he died, it was said he left 'more children than banknotes'. Like his grandson Richard, he must have been part lovable, and part infuriating to those who wished him well.

He misguidedly married one Elizabeth Macfadden, of Ulster, whom he nicknamed 'Ponsy'. Swift was less complimentary – he called her Xantippe, after the shrewish wife of Socrates, and presumably, when he knew her better, added to the compliment electing her 'the greatest beast in Europe'. Apparently, not content with her tribe of nine children, she inflicted numerous poor relations on her husband. They managed to eat their way through her small dowry two or three times over. While overfeeding her relatives, she managed to underfeed Dr Sheridan's pupils and waste his money. The ruin was completed by the depredation of further relatives till, in a moment of truth, Thomas Sheridan said to Swift that he was 'entirely be-Sheridaned'.

But he managed, like his grandson, to laugh away his troubles with a friend, a bottle, and a joke. In spite of his straitened circumstances, he retained a great sense of honour. For some reason he refused a headmastership from Swift, and when Stella died he refused a legacy she left him.

'You cannot make him a greater compliment', Swift said, 'than by telling him before his face, how careless he was in any affair that related to his interest and his fortune.' He went on to say that Dr Sheridan was a generous, honest, good-natured man, but his perpetual want of discretion and judgement made him act as if he were neither generous, honest, nor good-natured. This characteristic his grandson Richard was to inherit.

At Quilca, before their estrangement, the two friends laughed and joked in an atmosphere where it is said that the female Sheridans felt ill at ease. Possibly the Rabelaisian wit offended the ladies' increasing gentility, for the manners of the age were slowly changing, and growing less forthright.

Dr Sheridan was offered preferment as chaplain to the Lord Lieutenant and was asked by Archdeacon Russell to preach a sermon at Cork on the anniversary of the Hanoverian accession. For some extraordinary reason Sheridan chose as his text: 'Sufficient unto the day is the evil thereof.' Swift said Thomas was so good a marksman that he had killed his preferment with a single text. He did, however, later receive the gift of a manor from the Archdeacon, and no doubt this went the way of all his other properties. Years afterwards he tried to correct the unfortunate impression he had created by his sermon by composing odes in honour of Queen Caroline's birthday. But it was too late for odes. His original marksmanship had been too accurate.

To the end of his life Thomas Sheridan remained cheerful. He died in his fifties in a house someone had kindly lent him. When he was dying, it was remarked that the wind was blowing from the east. 'Let it blow east, west, south or north', said the dying doctor, 'the immortal soul will take its flight to the destined point.'

He must have been a jovial stoic.

*

His son, and Richard Sheridan's father, Thomas Sheridan II, was born in Capel Street, Dublin, in 1719. He was born into a Dublin which was gradually changing shape. Medieval Dublin, like so many other medieval towns, had clustered round the castle. But now it was spreading out into a grid of red-brick streets typical of the eighteenth century. Although much squalor remained elegance was coming to Dublin in the shape of neat little terraced houses on the London model. The populace was poor and violent, and many of the so-called gentlemen, although jealous of their privileges, shared that same turbulent tendency. Much of the elegance was superficial, and the greater flowering of the Town and 'ton' was to come later in the century, on the other side of the river.

Swift, who was Thomas's godfather, became his idol, and in some senses Thomas II's rigid adherence to principles which he had absorbed in his boyhood was the cause of many of his later misfortunes. The Dean was early aware of Thomas Sheridan's intelligence, and persuaded the father to send his son to Westminster at the age of fourteen. The plan was to send him on to Oxford, but like so many excellent plans in the Sheridan family it faltered for lack of money. Some fifteen months before Thomas was due to go to Oxford, Dr Sheridan could not raise the £14 to pay for the extra time at school.

It is possible that at Westminster Thomas Sheridan first became aware of 'theatre' and the acting profession. Many of the eighteenth-century crop of gentlemen actors came from the good schools of that time. These included Mossop, Coleman, Smith, the original 'Charles Surface', who was educated at Eton, and Samuel Foote, the actor, playwright, and lampooner of Garrick. This was possibly not surprising, for Westminster laid particular stress on the teaching of oratory, on dramatic productions, and on acting generally. But although Westminster may have reinforced Thomas's acting bent, the seed had already been sown before he left Ireland: he had played Mark Anthony at thirteen in Ireland, for his father was drawn to theatrical productions. Although his father was not able to produce the money necessary for an Oxford career, Thomas Sheridan II managed to make useful friends at Westminster: he met Lord George Germain and became friendly with the whole of the Sackville family, including the Duke of Dorset, who always remained a good friend as well as a patron.

Thomas Sheridan was entered at Trinity College, Dublin, in 1736. Here he did well, but Thomas – and here he was unlike his father or his son – had an inflexible character and was already, at the age of nineteen, obsessed with educational theories.

The studies at Trinity did not please him. Already buzzing about in his head were the bees of new theories of education, of elocution, of the teaching of good English instead of how to paddle in a sea of classics. The great Dean Swift, his idol, had stressed the need to write and orate in correct English, and this idea had stuck in the boy's mind.

When he left Trinity a certain antipathy to the idea of being a schoolmaster seems to have formed in his mind, despite what he said later; or possibly some small successes as an orator and actor at school and university had given him a taste for the exhilarating applause to be found in the theatre. In an 'Oration pronounced before a Numerous Body of the NOBILITY AND GENTRY Assembled at the Musick Hall in Fishamble street (and now published at their unanimous desire in 1757)', Thomas Sheridan gives his own view of why he went on the stage.

He alleges that he had decided to be a teacher like his father, but had thought he needed a greater knowledge of English; and Dr Swift had told him that if Trinity did not teach him English, or how to speak, it would have taught him nothing. To learn English, then, and how to speak correctly, he had decided 'the only way was the Stage'. But gradually he became totally involved with the theatre. 'Youth and Inexperience joined to a Temper which had more of Warmth than Prudence in it, made me blind to the difficulties which lay in my Way; alas I foresaw not then the thousandth part of what I have since endured.'

But these words were written by a chastened Thomas after he had long been battling with the public. There is little doubt that he was drawn to the world of the theatre, and the scholars of Trinity College were great playgoers. In 1742 Garrick went to Dublin where Thomas Sheridan met him, and it may have been the heady sight of Garrick's success which finally decided Thomas on his career.

The picture of Thomas in the National Gallery of Dublin was painted by Lewis, the scene painter at the Smock Alley Theatre, who later painted the ceiling at Quilca. Like the painting of the scenery for a play, the background to Mr Sheridan's picture probably had as much substance. He chose to be painted in an eighteenth-century library setting. A red velvet drop curtain decorated with gold tassels hangs beside him, as if the curtain at the theatre were being raised. He wears a blue velvet tam-o'-shanter, a house robe of blue plush lined with pink taffeta, a white lace-ruffled shirt, and an embroidered white satin waistcoat. He leans histrionically on a large leather volume of Shakespeare's plays, which rests on a heavy gilt and marble Italianate table. His face is pale, he has a long nose, brown eyes, and a high intellectual forehead. It is not the face of a fool. The eyes have a glint of humour in them: life was to eliminate this.

The theatre is a capricious mistress, and here can be found instant fame. An actress once described applause as 'heavenly rain', and this was a heavenly rain which fell easily on Thomas when he started in his chosen profession. In January 1743, at the Smock Alley Theatre, Dublin, the main part in the *Tragedy of Richard III* was performed by 'a young gentleman'. In this part Thomas Sheridan achieved an instant success, and followed this up almost immediately by *Mithridates*. He became a leading actor overnight and, without experience, he was at once rocketed to fame playing Hamlet, Othello and Brutus. From the beginning he never played small parts.

Thomas remarked to Theophilus Cibber about his instant success, 'I know not how it is, whether it be their partiality to their countrymen or whether it be owing to the powerful interest of a number of friends that I have in this city, but there never was such encouragement and applause given to any actor, or such houses since I appeared on the stage.' This was proved by the fact that when the great actor, James Quin, came to Dublin his tour was eclipsed by Sheridan. Quin went back to London in a huff, much put out by his younger rival's fame and pulling power.

The following year Thomas Sheridan was acting at Drury Lane with Garrick, and by 1745, when still only in his twenties, he was in charge of the Theatre Royal, Smock Alley. He had declined Garrick's offer to join him again at Drury Lane. In fact, he suggested to Garrick that they should join forces and play alternately in London and in Dublin. It has been suggested that this was great conceit on Sheridan's part, but at the time the offer was made, Garrick had not reached the pinnacle of success he was afterwards to attain, and Sheridan's difficulties

21

were in the future. Garrick was only three years Sheridan's senior, and at this stage not necessarily his superior. The prospect of having a theatre of his own held out glittering prizes to Thomas.

Once in charge of his theatre, Thomas set to with a will on his favourite mission in life, which was to reform the stage – and that the stage was in need of reform is an understatement. In order to appreciate some of Thomas's later troubles, and to sympathize with them, it would be as well to paint some of the almost incredible scenes and conditions with which a company had to contend in the theatre of those days, not only in Dublin, but elsewhere.

Sheridan coolly remarked that one part of the house was a bear garden and the other a brothel, nor did the audience confine themselves to the auditorium, for the stage was crowded with spectators. On Thomas's first appearance, he had requested that the stage might be cleared owing to 'the confusion a person must necessarily be under on his first appearance' if his exits and entrances were impeded 'by having a crowd to bustle through'.

Apart from the spectators on the stage, the green-room was full of servants waiting with flaming torches to escort their masters and mistresses to their carriages, and other spectators crowded into the dressing-rooms and corridors backstage.

The audience was no better served, for if an actor did not appear, his part was casually read by anyone who happened to be available, and should the house be thin, the audience would be 'dismissed'. In other words, if the actors considered that £10 in the house was not worthwhile, they would not perform that evening.

After the third act, patrons could get in at much reduced prices. As seats in the upper gallery only cost twopence, it was generally crowded, and by the end of the evening it would be crowded with drunks who had come in at half-price. Elsewhere in the theatre interruptions were caused by squabbles and battles between footmen, retaining seats for their employers, and the town mob. Beset by riots and by rival gangs, and with audiences who wandered on to the stage, got in the way of the players and refused to leave, it was not only hard to achieve an artistic production, it was sometimes difficult for an actor to be heard at all above the din of the patrons.

Apart from keeping the stage clear, and putting up the prices to keep the drunken galleryites out, the other reform that Thomas instituted was building up his own theatre wardrobe. Before that stage clothes were borrowed from friends – a Dublin lady who had bought a robe at a London auction, lent it to Sheridan for *Cato*. A bitter row broke out between him and Theophilus Cibber who took it, and Sheridan refused to appear without it. On another occasion, George Anne Bellamy (playing Cleopatra)[1] had borrowed a dress and diamonds for her part, and they were taken by the actress playing Antony's wife. When Octavia appeared, resplendent on stage, Mrs Butler (who had kindly lent her jewels) called out 'Good heaven, the woman has got on my diamonds.'

There was no doubt that Thomas's reforms were timely and, in instituting them, he did, in fact, precede Garrick by fifteen years. It could be said that these reforms were the beginning of a new theatre 'status' that was in the end to lead to stage knights and even peers. But it was done, in the beginning, at great cost to Thomas himself.

The Dublin audience did not take kindly to Thomas's reforms. It has to be admitted that he probably rode roughshod over some people, and his didactic ways and pedantic character were not to the taste of some of the Dublin audience. His productions were criticized alternately as being dull or licentious; others said that the ladies had to skulk behind their fans on hearing the bawdy remarks. The culmination of the discontents came during the winter of 1747 in what were called the 'Kelly' riots. Sheridan had incensed certain members of the audience by putting spikes at the edge of the stage to keep the spectators away, but a certain gentleman from Connemara, named E. Kelly, managed, while drunk, to climb over the spikes and make his way to the dressing-rooms. Mrs Dyer, one of the actresses, described what followed. 'He first designedly trod on her foot, put one of his knees between her legs, she protesting he would spoil her cloathes, he said he would do what her husband Mr Dyer did to her using the obscene expression.'

[1] Cleopatra in Dryden's *All for Love*.

Miss Bellamy then appeared on the scene, and tried to rescue Mrs Dyer. The drunken Kelly then pursued both the women towards their dressing-rooms. Ann Barford, the dresser, tried to stop him, and he 'abused her though she was big with child, at the same time swearing that he would have carnal knowledge of her'.

Meanwhile Thomas, who was on stage, heard the fracas, and delayed the play while he dealt with the drunk backstage, getting him taken into custody by the constables. The play continued for a while, but shortly afterwards Kelly, having escaped from the constables, reappeared in the pit and demanded an apology. Sheridan, incensed, took off the false nose he was wearing for his part of Aesop and said proudly, 'I am as good a gentleman as you are'. The evening ended with Sheridan using Aesop's oaken stick to beat Kelly soundly.

The town was then divided into those who wanted the stage reformed and those who did not. For the following two nights the riot continued, and Sheridan was warned to stay away, which he did. Presumably this was designed to keep the Kelly faction quiet. But it did not have the desired effect, for on the third night the trouble was worse than ever. The cry went up 'Out with the ladies and down with the house' and the riot commenced. The rioters managed to get on to the stage and behind the scenes: they crowded the passages, breaking down doors, tearing up clothes, running their swords through clothes' closets and chests, and even stabbing the stuffing used for Falstaff, threatening tailors, and anyone they could find backstage, in their frantic hunt for Sheridan. They forced their way into Miss Bellamy's dressing-room and even searched under her dressing table until they were satisfied that Sheridan was nowhere in the theatre. They then went up to his house, but he was prepared for them, and they went away dissatisfied.

After this final riot the theatre was closed for four weeks, but the town was now split into factions of Kellyites and Sheridanites, and for some time Sheridan went in fear of his life from Kelly's thugs. Finally Kelly, not receiving the apology he demanded from Sheridan, sued him. It was said that Sheridan had merely 'hindered' the gentleman in ravishing actresses, abusing actors, and defending himself against the outrages offered to him. Kelly insultingly declared that he had seen a gentleman-soldier and a gentleman-tailor but never before a gentleman-player. Sheridan bowed in the witness box saying 'Sir, I hope you see one now.'

It was an excellent curtain line, and he was acquitted amidst loud applause. When in turn Kelly was prosecuted, and ordered to pay a large sum, Sheridan interceded with the court and 'forgave the whole even to the expenses of the law suit'. Like his son Richard he was fond of the grand gesture.

Describing the abuses of the stage, Thomas says that a long train of management had rendered it a public nuisance and the pest of the town, adding:

'To such an absurd height had popular prejudice risen that the owners were considered as having no property there, but what might be destroyed at the will and pleasure of the people; that the actors had not the common privileges of British subjects but were actual slaves; and that neither the one nor the other were under the protection of the Law.'

He goes on to recount that after one play a gentleman took it into his head to amuse himself by cutting to pieces a scene lately painted for a pantomime. When one of the actors remonstrated, he took exception to being spoken to in this way by a mere player, drew his sword and, aided by two other gentlemen, would have killed the actor if the onlookers had not interfered.

When modern producers and actors talk of 'assaults' on the feelings of the audience, and of theatres of cruelty and violence, one may wonder if they would be enthusiastic about the intrinsic value of violence if it were used on their own theatre scenery, or if the assault would be considered so happy an outcome if it were practised on themselves.

After Thomas Sheridan had asked the authorities to remit the fines imposed on Kelly, things settled down, and for a time he became the most popular man in Dublin. A happy outcome was that through the riots he met his future wife, Frances Chamberlaine. She was amongst the fashionable ladies in the audience on the night of one of the riots, and wrote a pamphlet defending him. One critic says that Miss Chamberlaine's spirited defence of her future husband had more effect in restoring his popularity than all the explanations he wrote himself. Considering Thomas's wordy style, this is not surprising.

Frances Chamberlaine, Richard's mother, came of Anglo-Irish stock. She was a woman of undoubted literary gifts, and at the age of fifteen had written a romance. Later she wrote a comedy, *The Discovery*, which was successfully produced by Garrick, and a novel *Sidney Biddulph*, which was also well received.

Frances was described by Dr Parr, a master at Harrow as 'truly celestial', though another friend, while admitting her to be one of the three literary graces added that she was 'inclined to be lusty and had a red face'. A drawing of her shows a pale oval face and a high intelligent forehead: possibly the artist had used his licence to give a more contemplative look to her high complexion.

The romantic behaviour of 'the Manager', as Thomas Sheridan was inclined to call himself, in the theatre fracas, and his physical defence of his co-stars against the assaults and indecencies of the local 'gentlemen' caused Frances to fall in love with him; her support of his conduct brought more friends to his side, and no doubt endeared her to him.

At the begining of his career, when success was within his grasp, Thomas Sheridan must have had some of his future son's charm. Boswell remarked that 'Sheridan's well-informed, animated and bustling mind never suffered conversation to stagnate'. His future wife, Frances, wrote of him:

> If every talent, every power to please,
> Sense joined with spirit, dignity with ease,
> If elocution of the noblest kind
> Such as at once inflames and melts the mind,
> Looks strong, and piercing as the Bird of Jove,
> Address insinuating and soft as Love . . .

So the temporary triumph of Thomas over his enemies had won him a bride. They were married in 1747 and went to live at 12 Dorset Street, and for some years all was as merry as a marriage bell.

Number 12 was a neat new four-storey red-brick house in the heart of a newly fashionable area, at some distance from the theatre at Smock Alley. Possibly it had been leased from the Dorset family. The house still stands, a lone survivor of another age, flanked by a monastery and a pub. Elegance has long since left the district, but with an effort it is still possible to visualize the house as it once was – part of a polite street in which the young couple, full of hopes, began their married life. The knocker on the door is suspended from a wreath of bays and shows a hand grasping a scroll. It is appropriate – but if the laurels of fame were to fall to the lot of the Sheridan family, financial security was to elude them, in the future.

The young Sheridans attracted many fashionable friends, and at the outset the theatre brought in an income of £2,000 a year, an immense sum in the eighteenth century.

Richard Brinsley Sheridan was born at number 12 Dorset Street in 1751, four years after his parents' marriage. He was their third child. The eldest, Thomas, had only survived a couple of years and had died in 1750. In the same year, Charles Francis, Sheridan's elder brother, was born. Richard Brinsley was christened at the parish church of St Mary's on November 4, 1751. The parish register enters the christening: '1751. November 4th, Thomas Brinsley, son of Mr and Mrs Sheridan'. Whether the family had intended the third son to be christened after his dead brother is not clear. Possibly the entry in the parish register was a curious clerical error. His godfather was Lord Lanesborough, and his subsequent Christian name, Richard, by which he was known, was probably that of his uncle, Richard Chamberlaine.

This parish church, still standing in Mary Street, is a beautiful seventeenth-century building, having many affinities with similar churches in the City of London. Lined with mahogany, it has carved pews and pulpit, and an organ of elaborate woodwork decorated with cherubs; but the church is now little used, and the organ no longer plays. In its day, it was the most fashionable church on the north side of the Liffey, and the correct venue for a social event such as the christening of the young Sheridan's second son.

Thomas Sheridan now considered himself as a link between

the ruling class in Dublin Castle and the green-room, and a few years after his wedding he founded the Dublin Beefsteak Club. Here, Castle and Players met on common ground, and on one occasion Thomas even installed Peg Woffington to preside in the Presidential Chair.

But in spite of his profession and his professional associates, he was a stern disciplinarian both in the theatre and the home, a man who never missed family prayers. Before the complications of the Smock Alley Theatre overwhelmed him, he was as fond of gaiety as his father, He loved a glass of wine, and his favourite toast was 'Healths, Hearts and Homes'. His affairs were going well: the theatre had been running successfully for seven years, Thomas had managed to institute his reforms, and his prospects seemed rosy.

But resentment still smouldered. The crunch came in 1754.

CHAPTER 2

The Smock Alley Disaster

A spark can ruin a forest, a small incident start a war. The immediate cause of the wrecking of Thomas Sheridan's hopes in 1754 was the venom and vanity of an actor called West Digges.

Thomas Sheridan's popularity had been waning in the town because his Beefsteak Club seemed to some to be an outward sign that he was supporting an unpopular government, and his pretensions in consorting with the great of Dublin Castle were not well regarded by the Irish. A viceregal ball had even been given at the theatre, when the pit had been floored over, and the lighting was provided by 1,200 large wax candles, while the decorations consisted of orange trees, myrtles, bays, jasmine, trees in blossom, fruits of all sorts, tricked out with statues, rocks, grottoes, caverns, and cascades of perfumed water. All this magnificence was not calculated to endear the gentleman actor to the town.

Although Sheridan was a friend of the Duke of Dorset, there was a political slant to the final débâcle. The country was divided between the Court party and the Country party, the latter accusing the former of betraying the country 'for gold or place'.

The Irish were angry because of a clause in a finance Bill which implied that the King had power of consent over any surplus in the Irish budget, and as a result the Irish parliament had been suspended for three months.

The powder keg was primed. The spark which set it alight was Voltaire's play *Mahomet*. Sheridan had already put on this play at the theatre, and it was known by his audience. In fact, certain controversies had already raged in the press about it, especially when Mr Digges as Alcanor defended the City and the People's liberties. It was the custom of the time that

29

managers would ask their public to 'bespeak' plays, and the Country party, spoiling for trouble, not unnaturally, demanded by their requests to the box keeper the return of the play *Alcanor*.

In the interim, Sheridan had been reading the performers a curtain lecture. His account of it was later issued in a leaflet, 'The Manager called the company of Performers together and delivered to them a speech from some heads which he had wrote down.' His arguments were that actors had the right to perform which plays they pleased, and if the audience did not like the offering, they were not able, like musicians, to play out of reach of the brickbats, bottles and stones. The duty of actors 'obliged them to a post open to the battery of an incensed multitude, some of whome would show their resentment on them through malevolence or personal pique'.

So far, so good. The Manager must choose his own plays, but then came the reproach!

'To you, Mr Digges, I must particularly apply as you were the First Tragedian, I ever heard of who repeated a speech upon the encore of an audience. You have heard my arguments upon that head – if you think they are of weight, I suppose you will act accordingly; if not, remember I do not give you any order upon this occasion, you are left entirely free to act as you please.'

A mild enough reprimand, especially from Thomas Sheridan, and a gentle enough implied request, but we must suppose that it left the insufferable Mr Digges fresh from his triumph as Alcanor, seething and carefully plotting how best to have his own way.

Sheridan continues his story. 'The night after, the play *Mahomet* was to be performed, Mr Digges advanced and told the audience that he was ever ready to oblige the publick, but that he had very strong reasons against repeating the speech, and hoped and entreated that they would not insist upon this.' In fact, of course, he was hoping and silently entreating that they would so insist. He had his desire. 'At this there arose a very general cry of "No! No! The Manager! The Manager!" which continued with great clamour. The Manager heard the

whole at the side of the scenes and immediately ordered the
curtain down.' Mr Victor, the prompter, reported that Sheridan
had said 'They have no right to call upon me – I'll not obey
their call.'

Sheridan's account continues: 'He sent the prompter to
acquaint the audience that they were ready to perform the play
if it were suffered to go on in quiet. If not, they were at liberty
to take their money again. The prompter was not heard and
was obliged to withdraw.' It was a fair enough offer, but the
audience were out for blood. Possibly the manager prudently
sensed this. His own account goes on: 'The Manager then
declared his resolution of not going on the stage.' Sheridan's
friends begged him to appear, but he went back to his dressing
room, took off his make-up, changed his clothes and went home
– apparently in great agitation. It was the turning point in his
career.

The decks were then cleared for action. Sheridan's account
written in the aftermath is simple, succinct, and dramatic.
'The gentlemen in the pit desired the ladies to withdraw, tore
up the benches, pulled down the wainscot, and destroyed
everything in the auditorium, mounted the stage, set the curtain
on fire in three places, but the flame was put out, and then the
curtain was cut to pieces. All the scenery was demolished.'

The report continues as though describing a military opera-
tion:

'A party was detached to attack the wardrobe but the
precaution of the carpenters in barricading the passage, and
the resolution of a sentinel preserved it. The mob then forced
their way into the House, plundering and stealing. Others
drew the large [basket] grate in the box room from its place
into the centre of the floor and heaping the benches and
wainscot upon the Fire would soon have consumed the
House . . . had not this sight raised six of the servants belonging to the theatre to desperate courage; at the immediate
hazard of their lives they assaulted and drove the mob out
of the House, extinguished the flames, barricaded the doors
and afterwards dispersed the mob by firing out of the windows upon them.

.During this whole Transaction which lasted from eight at night till two in the morning there was no peace officer to be found in the City of Dublin; though numbers were in quest of them and though the Town Major was several hours traversing the whole town in search of one.'

Sheridan voices the inevitable questions people had been asking and gives the answers: 'Why did he perform *Mahomet* again? He did not want to lose the time and labour and money spent on it, and if he refused to play it, it seemed like an admission that it was a party play.'

He deals with the other pertinent question:

'Why did he not appear before the audience? He had heard from various quarters that there was an intention of assaulting him not only with apples and oranges but with stones and glass bottles. Mr Adderly had advised Mr Sheridan to go upon the stage and he would undertake that the gentlemen of the pit would offer no insult to him.'

Sheridan, being practical, replied that he wasn't worried about the pit, it was the mob in the galleries who would do the damage, and appealed for understanding:

'Let it be taken for granted that the manager was wrong in what he did, yet surely he cannot help thinking that the pusishment was rather too severe and in no way adequate to his crime. Suppose he had no real Foundation for his apprehensions, but from a mere panick which struck him did not care to expose himself to a danger which appeared to him imminent, and inevitable; was this a crime of so heinous a nature that nothing but the ruin of his entire fortune and loss of his life could make atonement for it? It was hard that so many innocent persons should suffer for one guilty one. That the whole company of performers and all the persons belonging to the theatre to the amount of two to three hundred should be deprived of their daily bread.'

These figures are of interest since they give an idea of the

2   Thomas Sheridan, actor. *Portrait by John Lewis*

3a. Sheridan's mother. *Portrait prob-*
ably by Lewis

3b. Sheridan's sister Elizabeth

3c. Captain Mathews. *Portrait by*
Gainsborough

3d. Mrs Crewe. *Portrait by*
D. Gardner

size and scale of Thomas Sheridan's theatre company and its staff. It was no mean affair, a mere fit-up company of strolling players. Sheridan, still smarting, adds:

'Had the theatre been consumed by fire and in consequence thereof a whole quarter of the town reduced to ashes he fears it would be no satisfactory answer to a number of families who must have thereby been reduced to want and beggary. When they enquired what was the cause of all this to say it was owing to the obstinacy of the Manager who refused to appear upon the call of an audience through a groundless apprehension that he might have his brains beat out.'

Sheridan says that his life has been defeated by one blow and the fruit of eight years' indefatigable pains blasted in a night, and concludes:

'He [the Manager] wakes as from a dream, and finds that the best and most vigorous of his years, have been employed to no purpose. He wishes from his soul that the Publick may have a better manager to conduct the theatre, and a better actor to entertain them, but he will venture to affirm that they will never find one who can serve them with more assiduity, Perseverance, and Zeal than their Ever devoted and faithful servant,

Thomas Sheridan'

The public's ever faithful servant puts the loss of the night's takings at £130, apart from the thousands lost from the wrecking of the Smock Alley Theatre.

'John Fagan of the City of Dublin came before me this day and made oath that he saw two Brick-bats thrown on the stage of the Theatre Royal, Smock Alley, on Sat. night the 2nd instant and this Deponent believes they were thrown by persons who were then in the Galleries of the Said Theatre. . . . James Lownes who was repairing the stage also swore before the justice that he had found glass bottles, stones, brick-bats and oranges.

Likewise John Wimp of the City of Dublin, carpenter, came this day before me and made oath that he is one of the carpenters employed in repairing the Theatre Royal, Smock Alley from the Havock that was made there on Saturday night, the 2nd instant, and that on clearing the stage he saw on the stage a great many brick bats, stones, broken glass bottles and oranges.'

Sheridan wrote to a friend, 'I have chosen to look upon the ruin brought upon me as if it were an Earthquake, Fire, Plague, or any other irresistible Decree of Providence.'

He put an advertisement in the *Dublin Journal* in March 1754.

'Mr Sheridan of the Theatre Royal thinks it necessary to acquaint the publick that he had entirely quitted the stage and will no more be concerned in the direction of it. He has lent the House to the performers during their benefits without any emolument to himself. Domestick concerns have so far affected him for some days past that it was impossible for him to give that attention to the subject which is required.'

The domestic concerns to which he referred was the premature birth to Frances of a child, who died in convulsions, at the age of two months. It seems likely that the child was born the week of the riots.

The Duke of Dorset, always a good friend, offered Sheridan £1,000 as reparation for his losses, a pension of £300 a year, money for new scenery. He refused all these offers because he felt it would be confirming the view of his enemies that he was in the pocket of the Court party, and this he wished to avoid at all costs. He was a proud man. Sheridan let the theatre, and retreated to England.

It is a curious trait of eighteenth-century, and even nineteenth-century families – possibly because children were born with such frequency – that they were constantly farmed out to nurses, relatives, and old servants. This happened to Richard and his sister Lissy, who were left behind in Ireland. It is possible that his insecure childhood and his humiliations at school in part explain Richard's subsequent life and career. Everything was sacrificed by the mother for the father's advancement. The children came a bad second. Later, in her successful novel *Sidney Biddulph*, Frances Sheridan describes Sir George as a man 'rather apt to overdo everything and would exert as much force to remove a feather as to lift an anchor'. This could have been a comment on her husband.

After his retreat from Dublin many lampoons were written against Thomas. One of these, printed in Dublin the same year as his ruin, mocked his ideas of stage reform: 'Rules of Accommodation. As drawn up by a Select Committee of Gentlemen, appointed for that purpose in order to establish a right understanding between the Town and the Manager of the Smock Alley Theatre.' To it was annexed a 'Number of New Toasts to be drank by the Reconcilers at their next meeting at the Phoenix Tavern'. These toasts include:

'The Royal family, not forgetting the Manager of Smock Alley Theatre.

May Ignorance never be run down in this prosperous Island.

A groan for Shakespear.

Licentiousness for ever, May Smut and Ribaldry prevail while Modesty and Good Sense are forced to hide in Corners.

No bounds to scurrility.

The Beaver's fate to the Man who does not love Whoring.

More Idleness and Less Industry.'

Thomas Sheridan had obviously bored those sections of his audience who were not inclined to uplift, or the classics.

Thomas and his wife settled in Bedford Street, Covent Garden, at the corner of Henrietta Street, for Sheridan had been offered an engagement by Mr Rich to act Hamlet at Covent Garden. But unfortunately Sheridan no longer had the drawing power in London which he once had. Garrick at Drury Lane had the edge on him. Added to which he was struggling with what he called a 'dispiriting disorder'. This is described as pains in the head, and bilious attacks, and in view of his fiery temperament, it could possibly have been migraine.

This setback to his acting career led Sheridan to think that he now saw 'the hand of heaven point out another way of life'. He turned his hand to his alleged first love, the improvement of education, writing a pamphlet on 'British Education, or the Source of the Disorders in Great Britain'.

Sheridan's theories were fundamentally good. He was against the intensive cultivation of the classics in education. 'Years were used', he wrote, 'in endeavouring to obtain an acquisition which can never be of the least use or ornament to them as long as they live.' He pointed out that the girls in the family write far better English than the boys, and that though the study of dead languages may have been of some use after the invasions of the Goths and the Vandals when 'these languages were the sole repositories of knowledge and wisdom' their usefulness was now lost.

There is no doubt that Thomas Sheridan was in advance of his time, since this revolution has only recently taken place. Meanwhile he became friendly with Dr Johnson, and in the beginning the friendship flourished. The Doctor called him 'Sherry Derry', but seems to have regarded him more as an actor than a scholar. Even his acting came in for a few scathing comments from Johnson. He said that Thomas's interpretation of the parts of Cato and Richard III were 'full of faults, some of natural deficience, and some of laborious affection'.

Like Dr Sheridan with Dean Swift, Thomas Sheridan in due course quarrelled with Johnson. It was a battle of lexicographers, due to professional jealousy. Thomas had certainly promoted in the right quarters Johnson's acquisition of a pension, for when referring to this pension, Lord Loughborough said, 'All his (Johnson's) friends assisted, but Sheridan rang the bell.' Doubtless remembrance of this aid added to Sheridan's resentment when the quarrel came.

Boswell, who had perhaps hoped to keep Thomas to his promise of frequent meetings with the Doctor, to glean good material for his books, found when he returned to London from a visit to Scotland that the two men had fallen out. The reason was simple. Thomas Sheridan had pegged away and in the fulness of time produced a dictionary of his own for which he, too, had received a pension, and for his work for the English

The Smock Alley Disaster

language. On hearing that Thomas's travails had been rewarded, Johnson remarked, 'What, have they given *him* a pension? Then it is time for me to give up mine. However I am glad that Mr Sheridan has a pension for he is a very good man.'

Unfortunately for the friendship, the remark was reported without the mitigating sentence. Boswell did his best to bring the two men together again, but Sheridan refused to be reconciled. When Johnson found that Sherry Derry was not to be wooed back into the fold, he cut him down to size in his occasionally uncharitable way. 'Why, sir, Sherry is dull, naturally dull', he said on one occasion. 'But it must have taken him a great deal of pains to become what we now see him. Such an excess of stupidity is not in nature.'

But Johnson's honest assessment of his erstwhile friend came when Garrick said 'Sheridan has too much vanity to be a good man.' To which Johnson replied:

'No, sir, there is to be sure in Sheridan something to reprehend and everything to laugh at; but sir, he is not a bad man. No, sir, were mankind to be divided into the good and bad, he would stand considerably within the ranks of the good. And Sir, it must be allowed that Sheridan excels in plain declamation, though he can exhibit no character.'

Whatever his virtues and other abilities, he seems to have been a ham actor with a monotonous style. Boswell paints in quick vignettes the picture of Thomas – talkative, intelligent, self-opinionated, and harbouring an intense jealousy of Garrick. Attacking Garrick's ability as a tragedian, putting forward his theories as to how Garrick went wrong, and then suddenly saying disarmingly that he thought Garrick the best tragic actor he ever saw. Boswell sums him up:

'Sheridan is really a fellow who knows a great deal; and his conversation is more instructive and classical than that of most people. Yet he has an Irish wrongheadedness and a positive singularity that is very disgusting; and for all that he says, I am apt to imagine that he has no real feeling of

37

poetical beauty. I take him to be a man of very great art who wants to disguise it under the appearance of nature.'

From Boswell's portrait, it is quite easy to see how Thomas irritated his fellow actors with his opinions, theories, and poetical fancies.

But whatever difficulties he had encountered in the theatre, and whatever the general public now thought of his acting, it was at that time the only profession he could follow. His grandiose ideas on education, oratory and elocution had to be set aside, and in 1756 he decided to return and try his luck with his Dublin audience again.

It was to be a new beginning. He invited Samuel Foote over, he engaged Italian dancers, and all was now to be sweetness and light, and packed houses. Unfortunately the town seems to have been as devoted to smut and ribaldry as ever, and modesty and good sense were still hiding in corners with no bounds to scurrility. Added to which Sheridan's erstwhile fellow actor, Spranger Barry, had decided to open a second theatre in Dublin.

Alarmed at this, Sheridan sent his agent, the invaluable Mr Victor, over to London to try to persuade Mr Barry 'from so strange a course'. Pushed by desperation, Thomas offered Victor good terms to act for him, for he was convinced that Dublin could not possibly support two theatres. A further worry was that Spranger Barry was now at the pinnacle of his success, a rival to Garrick in pulling power and famed for his playing of Romeo, Othello and Hamlet. Sheridan pleaded, cajoled, and even begged for kindness:

'Had Mr Sheridan shut the theatre against him and refused him entrance to it on any terms his friends might have some reason to cry out against a monopoly. He was struggling with immense difficulties to recover what he had lost; he cannot help thinking that common humanity should have rather induced Mr Barry to stretch forth a sought for hand to raise him up, than join with his enemies to trample a fallen man underfoot. Mr Barry knows well that Mr Sheridan did not deserve this at his hands.'

It was a plea to the heart with pride cast aside.

But Spranger Barry, from the lofty heights of his London successes, was in no mood to start acting under Sheridan's management again. He had gone beyond that, and his attitude was very grand. He simply proposed to lock up his Dublin theatre when he was acting in London. Spranger Barry was obviously determined to treat Dublin as a summer season at the end of the pier. If he ruined Sheridan in the process, he did not mind.

During the first year or two, while the Crow Street theatre was being built, Sheridan managed to build the theatre business up again. But he was still not certain whether he should stay in Dublin: it had too many painful memories for him. In addition to this, the usual controversies about the necessities for two theatres or one were raging, with pamphlets being written on both sides. By the time the controversies died down the theatre at Crow Street had been built, Barry had engaged his company, and Thomas had lost his fight to survive as a sole theatre proprietor in Dublin.

Again he took to his pen:

'An humble Appeal to the Publick together with some consideration on the present critical and dangerous State of the Stage in Ireland.

By Thomas Sheridan, Deputy Master of the Revels and Manager of the Theatre Royal.'

With immense labour (and verbiage) he went into the finances of the theatre, the eminence of the actors engaged, and the fact that 'it is not so easy to allure Persons from London who are well settled there as is fondly imagined'. They would, as he pointed out, only come at exorbitant prices, and he could not refrain from making a professional crack: 'The last time Mr Barry was in Dublin there were full houses on only two nights.'

Sheridan recounted some of the things which people were saying against him, how they asserted that he was jealous of all great actors, and never chose to have any of reputation appear on the Irish stage but himself. Thomas's indignation almost fizzes out of the pamphlets:

'Mr Sheridan jealous of eminent actors. He, who upon his first undertaking, invited Mr Garrick to join him.

As the date of Mr Sheridan's theatrical life in his capacity of an actor is drawing towards a period before he makes his final EXIT, lest he should not have a future opportunity he humbly begs leave to return the Publick his sincere thanks for his poor endeavours to please. They saw him overloaded with business, surrounded by difficulties persecuted by the most unrelenting malice and struggling with a most dispiriting disorder. Under these weighty pressures was he often obliged to appear before them in characters that required a vacant and unruffled mind, a perfect State of Health, and an even flow of spirits.'

But the public, he pathetically insists, 'had cheared his drooping heart with a strong cordial of the highest marks of approbation', and he appends a final word to his enemies:

'I see among you men who by an Act of the Most Outrageous violence tore to pieces my property and deprived me in one night of the Fruit of ten years incessant toil. By that single act, you deprived my four helpless children of a Property which otherwise at this day might have been worth £10,000. '*To the Publick.* Behold at your feet a faithful servant, almost worn out in the discharge of the most dangerous difficult of all employments.'

Poor Thomas signs himself the public's 'very humble and most devoted Servant'. Unfortunately, the general public, then as now, does not care too much whether a theatre flourishes or not. If they fancy an entertainment they patronise it, if not, they stay away. Thomas Sheridan had become a bore. It did not matter much to theatregoers in Dublin whether they had one theatre, two, or even none.

Sheridan was forced back to London, and about this time he said to Boswell: 'I don't value acting. I shall suppose that I was the greatest actor that ever lived and universally acknowledge so, I would not choose that it should be remembered.

I would have it erased out of the anecdotes of my life. Acting is a poor thing in the present state of the stage.' It had certainly been a poor thing for him.

In the event, Spranger Barry ruined himself by building the second theatre in Dublin. And after all the fury, the fuss, the factions, and the riots, the Smock Alley Theatre declined and finally became a warehouse.

Thomas Sheridan had been right. There had only been room for one theatre in Dublin.

CHAPTER 3

Getting on with a Bustling Life
Childhood and Schooldays

During all the stresses and disappointments of his father's theatrical ventures, Richard Brinsley Sheridan had been growing up. He was only seven and had been under his mother's guidance and care only very intermittently, when his father had made his final wordy exit from the Dublin stage. But though Richard Brinsley Sheridan was still of tender age when his father was enduring his various set-backs, and probably did not fully understand what was afoot, there is surely no doubt but that he had, from his worthy and wordy father, what may be termed in the vernacular a 'belly-full' in the years to come.

From the beginning Thomas Sheridan seems to have preferred Charles, the elder boy, to Richard. When the Sheridans went to London they only took Charles with them leaving Richard and Alicia (Lissy) behind with relatives in Ireland, first at Quilca, and then in Dorset Street, with a Mrs Knowles. During the whole of his childhood and boyhood Richard spent only eight years with his mother. His sister thought that it was this lack of guidance from a woman who had the intelligence and talent to help the boy which in part determined the course of his life. At the age of three he was left behind in Dublin with relatives, and then his mother came back to Dublin for Thomas's final theatrical débâcle. During those two years again he lived with his father and mother, only to be left behind once more when the father retreated to London after his second Dublin defeat.

During this time Richard and Lissy were sent to a 'Seminary for the Instruction of Youth' in Grafton Street, Dublin. This was run by Samuel Whyte, the natural son of Captain Solomon Whyte, Mrs Sheridan's uncle. Lissy and Richard were under the care of an old nurse, and they went to the school as day pupils at first, but afterwards, still under the care of their old nurse, they became boarders. There is something melancholy about children separated from their parents at a very early age, some deprivation which it is afterwards impossible to remedy. In many ways the children are cut off from normal life, and suffer in a way which could be equated with being orphaned. And yet in their minds is always the feeling that somewhere their parents exist, and the cheerfulness and bustle of family life is going on without them. This is especially true in families where one child is kept at home while the others suffer the separation. In the case of the Sheridans, their actions were quite understandable, harassed as they were by debts, and by the necessity of making a living in precarious ways in a harsh world where privilege took all the plums.

Mrs Sheridan was not insensible of this and she wrote to Samuel Whyte, 'How are my dear little ones? Do they often talk of me? Keep me alive in their remembrance. I have all a mother's anxiety about them, and long to have them over with me.' Samuel Whyte was a follower of Thomas Sheridan's educational theories, but Richard does not seem to have been over-zealous at studying. In fact the only way he appears to have distinguished himself was by writing lampoons and jokes. Possibly Samuel Whyte's methods reminded him too much of his father's prosy theorizing. To anyone with a sense of fun, prosy schoolmasters are a perfect target.

Thomas Moore, the Irish poet, who was also later educated at Samuel Whyte's school, writes about Sheridan's early schooldays: 'It may be consoling to parents who are in the first crisis of impatience, at the sort of hopeless stupidity which some children exhibit, to know that he (Sheridan) was by common consent both of parents and preceptor pronounced to be "a most impenetrable dunce".'

Thomas retreated from Dublin in 1758, and in 1759 Richard and his sister joined their parents in London. The family led a shifting life: they were still following the waning star of Thomas. He was now engaged in lecturing, writing dissertations on education, and planning the Dictionary for which he received his pension. Throughout his childhood Richard must

43

have been aware of his father's distresses, and must have listened to, or even perhaps eventually read, his dissertations on the plaguey state of the stage. He must also have imbibed the feeling that the stage was a precarious affair and not to be relied upon. So often children fly from the pattern of their parents' lives, only to fall into another pattern which does not give them any better chance of success. Added to which, the trials of the player constantly trying to prove that he was a gentleman was a lesson which an intelligent boy could not fail to learn.

During the summers of 1760 and 1762 the Sheridans were staying at Windsor, and here Mrs Sheridan finished her novel *Sidney Biddulph* as well as writing her one successful comedy *The Discovery*. It was this visit to Windsor which decided Richard's school. There his parents became friendly with Charles Sumner, then a young master at Eton. For some curious reason it was then the custom to appoint Etonians as headmasters to Harrow. Possibly this was with a view to improving the tone of the place, which in the eighteenth century still had the appearance of a country grammar school, with houses for boarders growing up around it. Shortly after the Sheridans met Sumner, the headmaster of Harrow died, and Sumner immediately took his place. So in 1762 Richard was sent to Harrow.

His mother seems to have taken his future career fairly lightly. Possibly in view of the increasing difficulties of her husband, the idea of again farming out at least one of her children seemed a sensible idea. She wrote, 'Dick has been at Harrow since Christmas. As he may probably fall into a bustling life, we have a mind to accustom him to shift for himself. Charles's domestic and sedentary turn is best suited to a home education.' Quiet, tractable, bookish boys are much less bother about the house than high-spirited ones. So while Richard was packed off to boarding school to prepare for his bustling life at the age of eleven, brother Charles was kept happily under the parental roof. It was not perhaps the best way to prepare for good relations between the brothers.

Two years later Thomas Sheridan's financial difficulties had caught up with him. It is exceedingly difficult to sort out theatrical finances at the best of times and in the eighteenth century, with a system which gave the backers not only numbers of free seats, but also a share of the profits, the ensuing complications were enormous. Added to which, at a time when bankruptcy laws did not exist, very often creditors managed to regain two pounds of flesh having paid for only one. In this way a man could be ruined beyond hope of recovery, and then imprisoned once he had fallen into financial complications. This is, in effect, what happened to Thomas.

From impending imprisonment, there was only one solution – flight. In September 1764 Thomas took his family, with the exception of Richard, to Blois, in the Loire valley, where they were able to live on less than a quarter of the income they would have needed in England. Richard was left to get on as best he could, alone at Harrow: he was then just thirteen, and had been at school two years.

At this time Harrow was in the process of becoming more important as a school, though it had not the aristocratic connections of Eton. It was in the main a nursery for men of the professional classes. But unfortunately, at that time actors, particularly failed actors, were not well regarded amongst bourgeoisie on their way up in the world.

Sheridan was very unhappy at school. Later in his life he remarked that it was his practice when a boy to study in the fields with no other refreshment than a sausage and a bit of bread, and the water from any brook or pond, learning a ballad from an old cobbler he met on his way.

Creevey reported Sheridan as saying,

'He was at school at Harrow, and, as he told me, never had any scholastic fame while he was there, nor did he appear to have formed any friendships. He said he was a very low-spirited boy, much given to crying when alone; and he attributed this very much to being neglected by his father, to his being left without money, and often not taken home at the regular holidays.'

To be a boarder in the eighteenth century with parents abroad was like being the child of later colonial administrators – left

45

with anecdotes about our best writers in our Augustan age.
I saw much of Sheridan's father after the death of Sumner...
I often enquired about Richard, and, from the father's
answers, found they were not upon good terms – but neither
he nor I ever spoke of his son's talents but in terms of highest
praise.'

Dr Parr says that some people had asserted that he fostered
Sheridan's talents at school, but he remarks with honesty that
this was not true. He realized that Richard had talents but
could not bring them into action. It seems the report of a
straightforward man.

Dr Parr praises Sheridan's mother. 'I once or twice met his
mother – she was quite celestial. Both her virtues and her
genius were highly esteemed by Robert Sumner.' And he puts
his finger on a cause of the dissension between Richard and
his father: 'I know not whether Tom Sheridan found Richard
tractable in the art of speaking – and upon such a subject,
indolence or indifference would have been resented by the
father as crimes quite inexpiable.' Fanatics do not always make
sensible parents.

Parr sums up:

'Let me assure you that Richard, when a boy, was by no
means vicious. The sources of his infirmities were a scanty
and precarious allowance from the father; the want of a
regular plan for some profession; and, above all, the act of
throwing him upon the town, when he ought to have been
pursuing his studies at the University. He would have done
little among mathematicians at Cambridge – he would have
been a rake, or an idler, or a trifler at Dublin – but I am
inclined to think that at Oxford he would have become an
excellent scholar.'

Presumably there spoke an Oxford man.

Richard's unhappiness at school and the reason for it are
clearly shown in the letters he wrote to his mother's brother,
Richard Chamberlaine, in 1766. This was at the time when
his whole family were in France. His uncle was a surgeon,

living in London. In character Richard's uncle is described as a pleasant little man 'with a good deal of anecdote'. He was Richard's sole lifeline during the latter's schooldays. Richard wrote:

'Dear Uncle,

'As it is not more than three weeks to the holy days, I should be greatly obliged to you if you could get me some new cloaths as soon as possible, for those which I have at present are very bad, and as I have no others; I am almost ashamed to wear them on a sunday.'

There is nothing so upsetting or humiliating for a child than to be singled out from the others by indigence. The boy goes on with resignation:

'I fancy I shall spend my holy days again at Harrow, for I have not seen nor heard from Mr Akenhead since August. Mr Sumner asked me the other day if I had heard lately from my Brother and says he has not heard from them this long time; if you have had a letter lately I should be obliged to you if you would let me know how they are, and when they come to England for I long to see them.'

Charles was, of course, with his parents at Blois. The unfortunate Richard concludes with a further plea about his clothes:

'I should be greatly obliged to you if you would let me have some cloaths as soon as possible, for when these want mending I have no others to wear. I am dear Uncle, Your Affectionate Nephew, R. B. Sheridan.'

One may wonder whether the enquiries of the headmaster about Richard's family were on the grounds of Richard's loneliness or a reflection of the non-arrival of school fees. In June of the same year, Richard was again writing about his lack of clothes:

'Dear Uncle, I hope you will not be surprised, when I tell

49

you that the cause of my present letter is partly my want of cloathes for my brown ones are quite gone and those which I have, being of a very light colour, and having mett with a few accidents, are not remarkably clean, though pretty decent. And as I have been some time obliged to wear them every day, I have two reasons for desiring new cloathes, first as I have lately got into the 5 form, which is the head of the school, I am under a necessity of appearing like the other 5 form boys, secondly as the sylver arrow is to be shot for next thursday and most of the boys having new cloaths at that time instead of August, I should be glad, if it is convenient to you, to have them likewise, and then I should be in a condition to save them very well, by having a pretty good suit at present, which I could not do, if I were to stay untill these were almost wore out.'

The exile and indigence of Richard's father was certainly the direct cause of his misery at school. But already steps were being taken about this. An Act had been passed for insolvent debtors in the English parliament and, in 1766, Thomas's friends were pressing him to profit by it. A petition, sponsored by various friends, was being put to the Irish parliament, and it was hoped that this might accomplish something without Thomas having to attend, especially as his pension from England had not been paid for more than a year.

However, as so often, Thomas was unlucky. Just as he was about to set out for Ireland to try to settle the matter, his wife died on September 26, 1766. Frances Sheridan was barely fifty. She left the erratic and whimsical Thomas with four children, an unequal talent, and a near genius for upsetting people. His main prop had fallen away. She was buried in France 'in the inclosure of a Protestant family', at night, by the light of torches, and the funeral bier was followed by many Catholics who had loved her. The coffin was even accompanied by a military escort. It sounds as if her sweet character had made her many friends in France.

Thomas was heart-broken: 'I have lost what the world cannot repair, a bosom friend, another self. My children have lost – oh, their loss is neither to be expressed nor repaired.

But the will of God be done.' Leaving his children with friends at St Quentin, in French Flanders, he went back to Dublin, the scene of his small triumphs and his vast failures. Here he managed to arrange his financial affairs. But with his usual lack of good luck the arrangements benefited his creditors more than himself.

On learning of the death of his mother Richard wrote again to his uncle Chamberlaine, once more about clothes, but this time for a sombre purpose:

Oct. 1766

'Dear Uncle,

It is now almost a week since Mr Somner told me the mellancholy knews of my poor mother's death, and as Mr Somner has not heard what time my Father will be home, he desires me to write to you about mourning. I have wrote To Riley, who, with your orders, will make me a suit of Black. I should be obliged to you if you would let me know what time you expect my Father.

You will excuse the shortness of my letter, as the subject is disagreeable.

From your affectionate Newphew,
R. B. Sheridan.

'P.S. I must also have a new hat with a crape and black stokins and buckles. I should be glad of them on Saturday.'

For some reason it has been argued that this letter indicates Richard's desire to recoil from the unpleasant side of life. While this may be true, there are two ways of accepting grief: to wallow in it like Queen Victoria, or to try to ride over it. But those who ride over it remain aware of it in their deeper selves, and a boy who had been neglected by his father must have felt at this moment of loss that the sole hopeful lodestar in his life had disappeared. Frances Sheridan was a considerable personality, loving and intelligent, and no doubt the boy's thoughts had often strayed to her during his periods of loneliness at school. Now this point of hope in his life had also vanished.

Richard was kept at Harrow for three more years. His brothers and sisters were in France, and his father was, as usual, bustling about, lecturing, orating for the nobility and gentry, and planning to reform educational systems. When Thomas returned to England he published yet another pamphlet on education entitled 'A Plan of Education for the Nobility and Gentry of Great Britain – Most Humbly ascribed to the Father of His People King George the Third'.

Thus was another bow drawn at a venture, for in his address to King George the Third, Thomas offered to give up all his other pursuits, and devote the rest of his life to education – always provided that his pension was increased. But his exhortations, and his theories, which were extremely sensible, fell on deaf ears.

Thomas's educational theories were as grandiose as his imagination, but the education of Richard was a subject on which he was less certain. Dr Parr, of Harrow, had pressed Thomas to send Richard to Oxford, but the father's finances, in their usual low state, made this impossible. So in 1769 Richard left Harrow, and joined his father in Frith Street, Soho. Richard was, as his schoolmaster put it, 'upon the town'.

His father's house was near the Pantheon, a notorious place of entertainment, and his home was in the heart of Bohemia. Here he was joined by his sisters, and his pedantic brother Charles. Richard had at last acquired a family and a friend. Alicia was to be his lifelong friend and admirer. She had been his companion at boarding school in Dublin, and now they re-found one another. She wrote:

'We returned to England, when I may say I first became acquainted with my brother – for faint and imperfect were my recollections of him, as might be expected from my age. I saw him, and my childish attachment revived with double force. The same playful fancy, the same sterling and innocuous wit that was shown afterwards in his writings, cheered and delighted the family circle. I admired – I almost adored him. I would most willingly have sacrificed my life for him.'

Here in London, surrounded by distractions, Richard

resumed a somewhat scrappy education. Nearby, at Carlisle House, Angelo ran a riding and fencing school, and Thomas Sheridan seems to have swopped talents with Angelo. While Angelo taught the boys fencing and riding, Thomas gave Angelo's son Henry lessons in his usual subjects of oratory and pronunciation. Richard had also to submit to his father's educational theories, while a Mr Lewis Kerr, a physician who could no longer practise – from 'loss of health' – taught Richard maths, and Charles Latin. It was possibly during this time that the seeds of Richard's difficulties with his father really took root. There is nothing so cramping to the personality as being instructed by a relative. Nor were Thomas's educational obsessions likely to make a student of a lively, witty young man.

At the end of the year 1770 Thomas removed with his family to Bath. This was to be Richard's university of pleasure.

CHAPTER 4

To Bath—A Province of Pleasure

Bath in 1770 was in the high summer of its fashionable heyday. The two Woods were rebuilding the city in the classical manner, and had already laid out many of its charming squares and streets. It was becoming a sophisticated town of beautiful houses, its streets and squares not adorned with trees but having fine large spaces, cobbled and enhanced with obelisks or some central classical decoration.

Bath was a city round which the countryside lapped on all sides, and though fashionable people would stroll through the pasture-land which edged the town, the country and country pursuits were regarded with some contempt. The *Bath Guide* gives a cursory, practical, and patronizing glance at the country surrounding its elegancies, mentioning that the herbages are the best for sheep, and that fresh butter comes in from the country every day. The roads are said to be safe and pleasant, and casually, *en passant*, it is mentioned that 'access to the hills is either on horseback or in carriages'.

It is described as a province of pleasure, but it was a province where good breeding demanded that everyone follow a set of careful rules, which were laid down by the Master of Ceremonies. When the Sheridans descended from the coach at Bath in 1770, this high office was held by Captain Wade. His term of office had begun on April 18, 1769, on which date he 'officiated at a numerous and splendid ball when the greatest satisfaction was expressed by all the company'.

Captain Wade drew up his list of rules which included very detailed instructions as to what his ladies and gentlemen should wear. No hats in the public rooms in the evening, ladies who dance minuets to be dressed as they would be at St James's, with a full trimmed sack with lappets (a small lace head-dress) and large hoops. On the other hand, ladies who danced country dances must not wear hoops. Whether the ladies decided which dances they were going to join in before attending the Assembly Rooms, or whether they periodically took off their hoops, is not explained.

Captain Wade also laid down careful rules for gentlemen, who must wear their hair in small neat black silk bags. They must not wear boots in the public rooms in the evening or spurs in the morning. He also made it chillingly clear that very few people would be sitting down: 'No bench will be called for at the Balls for any lady under the rank of Peeress.'

This was a closed society where parvenus were looked down on, where the rules of etiquette were followed rigidly, and consequently it was a society where only the outstandingly gifted would be able to cross the lines. But there were places where the fences could be scaled – public balls took place twice weekly, and there were plays at the theatre in Orchard Street three times a week. The fashionable and wealthy gathered at one of the assembly rooms every evening. Mornings were given over to health at the Pump Room, for Bath water 'possesses that milkiness, Detergency and middling heat so friendly adapted to weakened constitutions'.

John Wood had planned his city so that all the new streets should be 'but a sixpenny fare of a chair' from the principal public buildings, and Bath was to become a place of elegant idleness, of strolling, gambling, dancing and gossiping, of taking tea in the Spring Gardens, or sipping the waters of the Pump Room to restore those weakened constitutions. Doubtless the young Sheridans, like Miss Austen's heroine, were 'all eager delight, as they approached Bath's fine and striking environs'.

Fortunately or unfortunately for Richard Sheridan, his father's talents needed patrons, the press of fashion and public acclaim. Thomas needed the crowds in the Rooms, and the Sir Plumes sipping the waters. They were his audience and his subsistence. Here Thomas began to perform again. This time he devised a series of 'Attic Entertainments'. These were a mixture of Thomas lecturing and declaiming, interspersed with music and singing. He had found a good venue for his bustling and orating, his family had found a home, and they were soon to have a circle of friends and acquaintances. If money was short, diversions were many.

It was a curious atmosphere into which to bring a young family with no mother, and as far as the boys were concerned, one with little education and which held no particular plans for their future. Like all such fanatics Thomas had his eyes on education in general, and the particular boys under his roof were over-looked for general theories.

It must have been difficult for his young family to be poor in the midst of so much luxury. For at a time when it cost 1s 2d a week to keep a pauper in the Bath Hospital, one visit to the Spring Gardens, open during the summer season for public breakfasts with music, cost 1s 6d. In the evening a mere 6d admittance would entitle you to anything at the bar to that value.

In 1770, Richard Sheridan was only nineteen. He was high spirited, and the world of Bath was before him. A letter he wrote to Mrs Angelo, addressed to Queen Square Court, Soho, on October 13th of that year, gives the feeling of ease and humour which was one of the wellsprings of his character:

'May it please your Majesty,

At a meeting of the Sheridanian society, in Parlour assembled, the following resolutions (amongst others of great importance) were determined on, and I appointed to give your Majesty information of them.

Thomas Sheridan esqr. in the chair. R.B.S. Sec.

1) Resolved—that we are all alive. N.B. this pass'd nem con.

2) Resolved – that her majesty be acquainted thereof.

3) Resolved – that R.B.S. be honoured with that commission.

Therefore I take the first opportunity of remitting to your Majesty these important, and interesting particulars, in obedience both to the resolution of the society, and (what are still more binding) your Majesty's commands.'

He asked Mrs Angelo to stay with them, as 'it will be much to the benefit of Your Majesty's Health and Spirits'. Richard goes on to make fun of the *Bath Guide:*

'But I have likewise another embassy to your Majesty; this is from King Bladud, who (as the Bath Guide informs us) reigned in England about 900 years before Christ, and was the first discoverer of the springs at Bath. This King keeps his state on a fine rotten post in the middle of the water decorated with a long account of his pedigree. His Majesty whispered me the other day that having heard of your fame, he had long wished to see you; he says that, except his sister of Orange, he has not seen a royal female for a long time; and bid me at the same time assure your majesty, that tho' in his youth, about 3,000 years ago, he was reckoned a man of Gallantry, yet he now never offers to take the least advantage of any lady bathing beneath his Throne, nor need the purest modesty be offended at his glances. So says his Majesty of Bladud; and in justice I must acknowledge that he seems to be as demure, grave and inoffensive a King as ever sat upon a – post.

We have got a very neat house, pleasantly situated and very cheap. To describe it prettily, I should tell you that the River Avon runs not 200 yards from our door; but t'is a female river I fancy, for it is so exceedingly shy and modest and holds its head so low, that we can't get a glimpse of it even out of our windows.

Bath is by no means full yet; but there are however on some nights enough to make it tolerably disagreeable . . . but the Ladies are still in great hopes of being so crowded so as not to be able to walk.'

He considers that most of the ladies he had seen are as 'ugly as lions'. At this time in his life Richard was described by his sister Alicia. 'He was handsome not merely in the eyes of a partial sister, but generally allowed to be so. His cheeks had the glow of health, his eyes, the finest in the world, the brilliancy of genius, as soft and tender as an affectionate heart could render them.' He was slim, of medium height, with wavy brown hair powdered in the current mode, and his brilliant eyes were grey blue. His mouth was curved, almost girlish, and ever ready to smile. In later portraits the chin seems to fall away a little, but in the drawing attributed to

Gainsborough the youth reclining in his chair has a modish if watchful air, and in his plain buttoned coat and tight hose he seems the very picture of a fashionable beau of the period.

This was the youth who was to discover, in Bath, his university and his inspiration. Bath was the background for his comedies, and the well-spring of his characters. Here the observant youth could watch and laugh at the foibles and follies of the passing monde, but he could laugh without malice, and comment with wit. The romantic attachments of Bath (and its ensuing duels) were the basis of *The Rivals*, and the gossiping tongues of the ladies of Bath formed the ideas which gave birth to *The School for Scandal*.

At the time of his settling in Bath, Thomas Sheridan was no longer a draw as an actor. Gone were the days when people would flock to his Cato, King John, or Hamlet. His Attic declamations needed some extra interest to draw the town. He found this fillip in Eliza Linley, a young girl of sixteen.

*

Her father, the musician Linley, was the son of a carpenter who had settled in Bath to follow his trade when the classical streets were being built. But the son had a great talent for music, and came to the attention of Chilgot, an organist. By virtue of his outstanding talent Thomas Linley was already, when he married at the age of nineteen, a professional musician. He had twelve children, and Eliza Linley was his eldest daughter, and second child. She was generally acknowledged to be the most beautiful. At the age of sixteen, when she joined in Thomas Sheridan's entertainments, she had been a professional singer for four years, for Thomas Linley believed in utilizing the talents of his 'nest of nightingales', while they were still fledglings.

Famous and eulogized, Eliza was as virtuous as she was beautiful. All her contemporaries combine to hymn her praises both in verse and in prose, while artists preserved her classical profile on canvas, in sculpture and in stained glass. Sir Joshua Reynolds painted her twice as St Cecilia, she was the model for Charity in the window at New College, Oxford, and Our Lady in a picture for the Nativity. Her beautiful oval face, clouds of dark hair and lovely figure in its softly flowing garments, in some way seem to encapsulate the spirit of the age.

Even that old voluptuary John Wilkes was moved to lyricism after dining with her family, and remarked that although Eliza was exposed to the rude gaze of mankind, she remained the 'most modest, pleasing and delicate flower in Nature's garden'. Thomas Moore's succinct account of the beautiful Eliza not only gives a contemporary account of her charms, but with its period flavour of snobbishness outlines the ambiguous nature of her profession at the time:

'The young Maid of Bath appears indeed to have spread her gentle conquests, to an extent almost unparalleled in the annals of beauty. Her personal charms, the exquisiteness of her musical talents, and the full light of publicity which her profession threw upon both, naturally attracted round her a crowd of admirers, in whom the sympathy of a common pursuit soon kindled into rivalry, till she became at length the object of vanity as well as of love. Her extreme youth, too, must have removed, even from minds the most fastidious and delicate, that repugnance they might justly have felt to her profession, if she had lived much longer under its tarnishing influence, or lost, by frequent exhibitions before the public, that fine gloss of feminine modesty, for whose absence not all the talents and accomplishments of the whole sex can atone.'

But Eliza's position was difficult in spite of family support. At this time actresses were considered as no better than prostitutes, or at best fillies to be looked over as possible candidates to be taken in keeping by the gentlemen about town. Eliza, however, had intelligence, and in addition to her hymned spirituality, she also had character and wit, in spite of her frail constitution. And yet she was known to be as unconventional as she was sweet and had once, for a joke, fought a sham duel with her sister at a picnic.

When the Sheridans came to Bath in 1770, the Linley and Sheridan families had become acquainted. They were all young, they were all high-spirited and to both Charles and Richard, as to the rest of the town, Eliza was a magnet.

Mr Thomas Sheridan, on the other hand, considered the Linleys beneath him. With a carpenter grandfather, and a mother who was as vulgar as she was money-grubbing, Sheridan père considered his family almost to be slumming by mixing with the Linleys. Like so many gentlefolk who have a hard job to make ends meet, he hung on to his gentility like a dying soldier clinging to a tattered regimental flag. He was prepared to employ Eliza as a draw to his entertainments, but he was not so prepared to accept the Linleys socially. Yet both families lived in the same kind of small three-storey town houses which clustered near the river in Bath, and as far as money was concerned, the Linleys, thanks to the popularity of their music at concerts and the Assembly Rooms, were better off than the Sheridans, and eventually moved to a larger house round the corner from Pierrepont Street, where Eliza had been born. This house, although modest, has decorative pineapples still embellishing its façade, and one wonders whether Mrs Malaprop's pineapple of perfection was taken from these. Subsequently, with the building of the New Crescent, nearer to the Upper or New Assembly Rooms the Linleys moved again to an even more modish district.

The Sheridans at this time were not living in nearly so fashionable a part of the town. But Thomas Sheridan was not going to let his social standards slide. If he had nothing else, he had the knowledge of being a gentleman. He did not consider the Linleys good enough for his children; moreover Eliza had already been the centre of a Bath scandal. It was not a scandal which had been of her own choosing. Presumably her money-minded mother, and possibly both her parents, had decided that the time had come to marry her off. In the usual eighteenth-century way, they cast about them for a monied suitor who would be prepared to make a settlement in exchange for Eliza's beauty.

Thomas Moore cuts through the drama in his prim way:

'She had been, even at this early age, on the point of marriage with Mr Long, an old gentleman of considerable fortune in

Wiltshire, who proved the reality of his attachment to her in a way which few young lovers would be romantic enough to imitate. On her secretly representing to him that she never could be happy as his wife, he generously took upon himself the whole blame of breaking off the alliance, and even indemnified the father, who was proceeding to bring the transaction into court, by settling £3,000 upon his daughter.'

At a time when girls were regarded as property by their fathers, and Eliza's singing was worth a thousand pounds a year to the family, any transaction is credible. No doubt her pure celestial voice and soft presence in the concert hall was the means of providing the rest of the family with their less celestial bread and beef. The match seems to have been engineered by the mother, and the settlement garnered by the father. Eliza was bound to her father like an apprentice until she came of age, and if the family was going to lose her services as a singer when she married, they were determined to be compensated by a comfortable settlement. In the event, they kept the girl and got the money.

Samuel Foote, the comedian, made use of the story, a classic eighteenth-century plot, in a play called *The Maid of Bath*. In this the innocent girl is sold by the mother to an avaricious old lover, Solomon Flint, who tells the Fair Maid that her family is low, and her fortune nothing at all. But the mother, no less a trafficker in flesh than the madam of a brothel, says, 'Would you refuse an estate because it happened to be a little encumbered? You must consider the man in this case as a kind of mortgage.' Whatever the facts of this dubious trans-action, Eliza came out of it with credit.

It was not long before the fires of love burning at her altar were to involve her in an even more complicated situation. Amongst her admirers and pursuers were Nathaniel Brassey Halhed, a school friend and literary collaborator of Richard, and Richard's own brother, Charles Sheridan, the paragon of the family. Making up a trio was a so-called 'Captain' Mathews. The Captain was married, but whether Eliza knew this or not is in doubt. He had been a friend of her family for some years, and had known her as a child when she had sold programmes from a flower basket for the family concerts. Mathews was a handsome man, even allowing for flattery by Gainsborough. By some Mathews is described as 'a pleasant man of pleasure', other contemporaries used stronger words, while a satirist writing about him in old age makes Mathews say, 'There was a time, indeed, when I made a figure with the sex, and could select from my list of conquests a fair specimen of every degree of rank from the duchess to the spouse of the squire.' Mathews married an heiress, in the careful eighteenth-century manner, some time during the fateful year of 1770; but the Linley family were allegedly unaware of this.

There is no doubt that it had become the mode to fall in love with the beautiful Eliza Linley, and when she sang at Oxford she seems to have had much the same effect as Max Beerbohm's Zuleika Dobson. Halhed, having heard the charmer sing at Oxford in the Oratorios, wrote to Richard: 'I am petrified, my very faculties are annihilated with wonder; my conception could not form such a power of voice, such a melody, such a soft yet so audible a tone. Oh, Dick, I wished myself hanged for not being able to commit my ideas to paper.' But Richard himself was now moving quietly with devotion (and with verses) towards the woman he loved.

Thomas Moore in his sly way records the progress of the courtship:

'But in love as in everything else, the power of a mind like Sheridan's must have made itself felt through all obstacles and difficulties. He was not long in winning the entire affections of the young "Syren" though the number and wealth of his rivals, the ambitious views of her father, and the temptations to which she herself was hourly exposed, kept his jealousies and fears perpetually on the watch.

With a mind in this state of feverish wakefulness, it is remarkable that he should so long have succeeded in concealing his attachment from the eyes of those most interested in discovering it. Even his brother Charles was for some time wholly unaware of their rivalry, and went on securely indulging in a passion, which it was hardly possible, with such opportunities of intercourse to resist, and which survived long after Miss Linley's selection of another had extinguished every hope in his heart but that of seeing her happy. Halhed, too, who at that period corresponded constantly with Sheridan, and confided to him the love with which he also had been inspired by this enchantress, was for a length of time left in the same darkness upon the subject and without the slightest suspicion that the epidemic had reached his friend.'

Thomas Moore was never inclined to give Sheridan the benefit of the doubt. It is possible that Richard concealed his feelings as much because he was not sure of winning the girl, as from intentions to deceive his rivals. In Sheridan's writings are signs of his hopes and fears:

> Is her hand so white and pure?
> I must grasp it to be sure.
> Must I praise her melody?
> Let her sing of Love and me.
> If she choose another theme
> I'd rather hear a peacock scream.

Be that as it may, he could be practical in action, as we see from a fragment of comedy:

'I took this part of his character from a little trait of my own. You must know, gentlemen, that my system of courtship is never to be whining and dangling after a woman for months together. No, damme! My process is only this – a military plan – first a surprise – a summons – an escalade – an assault. Simply this, if I want a favour of a woman, I ask her for it.'

Nevertheless it has been said of Sheridan's character that he always seemed to achieve his ends by stealth. This may be understandable in a young man who was always living on the fringe of things – on the fringe of gentility, on the fringe of wealth, and for long on the fringe of finding a way to use his abilities. There can be frustration in seeing the rich and foolish, to whom the plums of life fall without effort, enjoying ease and rich pleasure. To the gifted youth, on the outside looking in, this could have held a particular bitterness. Yet bitterness does not seem to have been a part of Sheridan's character. He turned the hardships of life into a joke.

At the end of the summer of 1771, with Eliza Linley being openly wooed by some, and quietly stalked by Richard, Thomas Sheridan went on the bustle again. He had written a play, *Captain O'Blunder*, which he was about to produce in Dublin, and so he set sail leaving his children to their own devices. At this time Richard was barely twenty, Charles a year older, Alicia just seventeen and Elizabeth only thirteen. To leave a young and impressionable family at Bath, in the ferment of youth was asking for trouble. But Thomas had to prop up his tottering fortunes as best he could.

That same autumn the New Assembly Rooms, or Upper Rooms as they were called, were opened with great éclat. The opening function was called a Ridotto, which was a general entertainment with music, dancing and liberal refreshments. One thousand two hundred tickets were sold at one guinea each, to admit one gentleman and two ladies. Single tickets for gentlemen cost half a guinea. Amongst the gentlemen at half a guinea was Richard Sheridan; and the ladies included Eliza Linley, whose father directed the music.

The rooms were indeed magnificent – the finest in Europe, it was said – with a ballroom over a hundred feet long, with pale walls and magnificent chandeliers, a card room, a great Octagon Room, a forecourt for the setting down of the quality in their sedan chairs, arcades to shelter the carriage folk from the weather, and an elegant tea room. What was less elegant was that the tea room, not being entirely devoted to tea, had a side staircase down which footmen could propel gentlemen who had been over indulging. In the basement they were hustled into a plunge bath in an attempt to restore them to a state of fitness to join the ladies.

Sheridan wrote a skit on the grand opening for the *Bath Chronicle*.

> Two rooms were first opened – the long and the round one
> (These Hogstyegon names only serve to confound one)
> Both splendidly lit with the new chandeliers,
> With drops hanging down like the bobs at Peg's ears;

4b. Elizabeth Linley as St Cecilia. *Portrait by Reynolds*

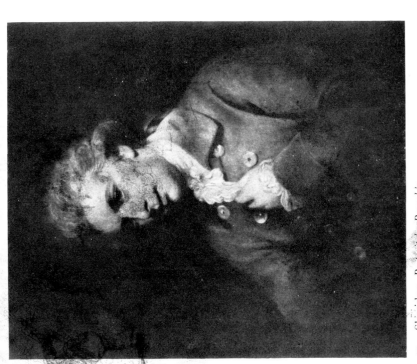

4a. Sheridan. *Portrait by Reynolds*

5a. Thomas King

5b. John Palmer

5c. Miss Pope

5d. Mrs Abington

He goes on to describe a mixed company of Miss Spiggots, Miss Tapes and Miss Sockets together with Mrs Soaker, adding, 'I believe there *were* some beside quality there.' Captain Wade, the Master of Ceremonies, had not entirely succeeded in keeping out the Mrs Malaprops.

Sheridan's skit became so successful that Crutwell, the editor of the *Bath Chronicle*, published it as a separate pamphlet, and so, with the opening of the new Assembly Rooms, came the first scent of fame to the young Sheridan.

The Upper Rooms set the seal on the life of fashion at Bath, and the daily round of pleasures were centred about it. Here the gentlemen read their journals in the morning, the young danced, the gamblers lost their money, and the tipplers tippled. If this was, as has been said, Sheridan's university, it was a university which had a brittle, ephemeral quality. Here Eliza Linley sang and here she was ogled and quizzed by the young bloods from all over the country who found in Bath a new hunting ground for prospective females.

But with the Sheridan father absent, the plots around the 'Saint' thickened. Captain Mathews, in spite of his prudent marriage, was still pursuing Eliza. Amongst his other methods was the threat of suicide – for he is supposed to have brandished a pistol in front of her. When this did not produce the desired effect, he then threatened that he would blacken her character in the eyes of the world. It was a small world, and Eliza had already suffered the brush of scandal with her pseudo-engagement to the old gentleman Mr Long and the play *The Maid of Bath* was still fresh in people's minds. As a performer she could not afford to lose her reputation, in an age in which female virtue was an all-paramount passport to acceptance in polite society.

An added worry was that she was afraid of her father. It seems certain that he was a mercenary man, though he seems to have been fond of his daughter. But a daughter was merely a piece of property to be used as a father thought best. When he had been asked by Garrick if she could sing at his theatre, Linley had refused, and he had sent a similar refusal to Colman at the Haymarket Theatre:

willing to sacrifice her life. Eliza later said that Mathews had written to her saying that 'she had given him so much trouble that he had the greatest inclination to give me up, but his vanity would not let him do that without gaining his point. He therefore said he was resolved the next time I met him to throw off the mask. He then said he would sufficiently revenge himself for all the trouble I had given him; but if I changed my mind and would not see him, he was resolved to carry me off by force. The moment I read this horrid letter I fainted.'

The authenticity of this account has been doubted, but in spite of its high romantic tone, and the dramatic circumstances it recounts, it seems to fit in with much that followed. Unless there had been actual threats from Captain Mathews why did the girl become so frantic? It was not certainly in her interests to run away from her troubles unless there was some pressing and disastrous reason for it. Yet this she soon contemplated. Eliza at this point was tired of her way of life, and tired of being pursued by men most of whose intentions, except those of the elderly suitors, do not seem to have fallen into the category of honourable.

She was probably tired of performing because she does not seem to have been the kind of girl who enjoyed public acclaim, her health was not strong, and the grip which her father had on her talents from the age of twelve had worn her out. This is borne out by Alicia who says, 'Miss Linley, now completely disgusted with a profession she never liked, conceived the idea of retiring to a convent in France, till she came of age, meaning to indemnify her father by giving up part of the money settled upon her by Long.' This plan of retirement to a convent was well in the vein of the romanticism of the age. To shut oneself up in a cloister, away from the persecutions of men, had a fine dramatic ring of renouncement of the world about it. And so, through the winter, the hurried conferences and plans went on.

*

Meanwhile Thomas was writing from Dublin:

'My dear Richard,

How could you be so wrong headed as to commence cold

bathing at such a season of the year, and I suppose without any preparation too? You have been paid sufficiently for your folly but I hope the ill effects of it have been long since over. Pray what is the meaning of my hearing so seldom from Bath? Six weeks here, and but two letters. You were very tardy; what are your sisters about? I shall not easily forgive any future omissions.'

There are very many good reasons why the young Sheridans were not in the writing vein, but Richard replied on February 29, 1772:

'I could scarsely have conceived that the winter was so near departing, were I not now writing after Dinner by day-light. Indeed the first Winter season is not yet over at Bath. They have balls, Concerts, etc. at the Rooms from the old subscription still. Mr Linley and his whole family, down to the seven year olds are to support one set at the new Rooms, and a band and Singer at the old.'

It is certain that old Thomas Sheridan was not in need of news about the Linleys, or about music. He disapproved of musicians in particular and music in general. Of music Thomas said, 'It often draws persons to mix in such company as they would otherwise avoid.'

But while the father was absent, happily imagining his brood engaged in improving pursuits, the plots and counterplots went on.

CHAPTER 5

The Elopement

The idea of fleeing to a convent seemed to the romantic young families to be the most sensible plan. And who better to think of ways and means but Richard, Richard who had warned off the threatening Mathews. Richard must be the one to assist beauty to flight.

So Alicia and Richard in hurried consultation took their decision. The sister says she thought it 'meritorious to assist a young person situated as Miss Linley was in getting out of the difficulties that surrounded her, and offered to give her letters of introduction to some ladies she had known in France, where she had resided some years, and Sheridan offered to be her conductor to St Quentin, where these friends lived. The arranging the whole plan, of course, produced frequent meetings between the young couple, and tho' Sheridan was then strongly attached to Miss Linley, he claimed only the title of friend.' In her remembrance of the elopement there still, perhaps, lingers in Alicia's account a slight trace of a feeling that she too had been deceived.

So the plan of beauty being rescued from the Beast, and a reputation unsullied, was set *en train*. The field was clear, because the prudent Charles had decided to conquer his passion for Miss Linley. He realized that a portionless wife of seventeen was no match for a young man with his way to make in a world, where the great need was for patrons. He took what his sister says was a formal leave of the charmer and went off to a farmhouse in the country to wrestle satisfactorily with his useless passion. 'I have totally got rid of my very ridiculous attachment', he wrote, 'which had before made me very unhappy and which was the more absurd as I could possibly have no view in it, and that I was at the same time conscious to myself that I was indulging a passion which

70

could only make me acquainted with the pains of love but never taste its sweets.'

Richard had different views, but he still moved stealthily. It is quite clear that Eliza at this time thought of him merely as a friend, for she later wrote: 'You are sensible that when I left Bath I had not an idea of you but as a friend. It was not your person that gained my affection. No, Sheridan, it was that delicacy, that tender compassion, that were the motives which induced me to love you.'

On the night of March 18, 1771, scarcely more than a fortnight after Richard had written to his father telling him nothing that mattered, the great adventure began. The Linley family were performing at the Assembly Rooms, and Eliza had made her excuses because of illness. The Linleys' tall house in the Crescent was empty, when Richard Sheridan arrived with a sedan chair. It was a desperate step for the young girl to leave the shelter of her father's house and set off on such a journey. But Sheridan had carefully arranged for a post chaise, with a duenna to act as chaperone.

It is possible that at this point Sheridan had confessed his love, or maybe hinted at his hopes; the song from his opera *The Duenna* is supposed to have been written at this time:

> Had I a heart for falsehood framed,
> I ne'er could injure you;
> For though your tongue no promise claimed,
> Your charms would make me true.

The song also speaks of 'acting a brother's part'.

The story as recounted by the sisters leaves many questions unanswered. Journeys, hurried or otherwise, cost money, and the coaches which reached London in one day were not cheap: 'Flying machines set out from the Greyhound in the Market Place at 11 p.m. and arrived in London the next evening – Greyhound (Bath) to Belle Sauvage, Ludgate Hill £1 8s od. Any luggage above 10 lbs weight was charged at 1½d a mile. Who supplied the cash for this journey of the distressed maiden, her protector, and the chaperone? Was it the maiden herself, or did the devoted sisters manage to find the sum from their meagre housekeeping money? It was never explained. Pre-

71

sumably they caught the evening coach flying along the Bath Road through Melksham, Marlborough, via Newbury and Maidenhead, and reaching London along the Kensington Road. The first stage of the rescue of the Maid of Bath had been accomplished.

A way had been found, a beginning made, and now it was necessary to seek out the means to continue. It was said that first of all Sheridan went to see a relative in the City, a Mr Ewart, who commended him for his prudence in escaping with 'an heiress who had consented to be united to him in France'. But Mr Ewart, although approving the flight in general, does not seem to have supplied money for the rest of the project. The young couple then went at night to seek another source of help. This friend has been described as 'an old gentleman in Holborn', and also as 'the son of a respectable brandy merchant in the city'. Probably they were father and son.

In the account given by Alicia she says:

'He suggested the idea of their sailing from the port of London to Dunkirk, to which place his father had a vessel ready to sail immediately. This plan, as making a pursuit more difficult, was immediately adopted, and the old gentleman, not being entirely let into the secret, accompanied the young couple on board his ship, recommending them to the care of the captain as if they had been his own children.'

This family is supposed to have been called Field.

The fleeing couple sailed from the Port of London having now not only some money but also letters of introduction to their benefactor's correspondent at Dunkirk, where they were given recommendations to several people at Lille. But the passage, though easily arranged, was not pleasant. A great storm blew up, and when one thinks of the smallness of the cross-channel sailing boats at this period, it must have been a terrifying experience for Eliza, whose health at the best of times was exceedingly frail. Sheridan is supposed to have despaired of her surviving, and said later that 'his love for her was such that, had she expired, as once he feared she might, he would assuredly have plunged with her body to the grave'.

Eventually they arrived at Dunkirk. Then all the chronicles become blurred. Here Sheridan met a school friend who recommended Miss Linley immediately to a convent where she could stay. This is corroborated by his sister Alicia, who says that Eliza immediately secured an apartment at a convent, where she was resolved to remain until either Sheridan came of age, or till he was in a situation to support a wife. From the sister's account it seems as if Sheridan had already managed to persuade Miss Linley that his feelings, though honourable, were not those of a brother.

En route to the recommended convent, the young couple stopped at Calais, and here Sheridan saw two French officers ogling his beautiful companion; taking into account Sheridan's admitted jealousy this must have had some great effect on his emotions. Whether as a result of this incident, or because of a change in Eliza's emotions, or merely as a form of protection, they decided on a clandestine form of marriage. Beauty in distress is ever inclined to take a tender view of a lover who is prepared to aid. Afterwards Sheridan was to write in *The Duenna*, 'in the heart's attachment, a woman never loves a man with ardour till she has suffered for his sake'.

Elizabeth Linley and Richard Sheridan were married, at the end of March 1772, at a village near Calais by a priest well known for his services on such occasions. As they were both under age, the ceremony was invalid. Perhaps they knew this, or maybe Sheridan hoped that some form of ceremony would bind Eliza to him, or serve as a protection to her, or both. In any case, they were accompanied by Miss Linley's chaperone, and there has been no suggestion from any biographers or from his family that Sheridan's intentions were other than honourable. In an age when a woman's honour involved not only chastity but commerce with regard to marriage, this is of paramount importance.

When she arrived in Lille Eliza fell ill. A letter from a Dr Dolman addressed to 'Monsieur Sheridan, Gentilhomme Anglais a l'Hotel de Bourbon sur la Grand Place' runs, 'Dear Sir, it will not be improper to give one of the powders in a glass of white wine twice a day – morning and evening. Don't wait supper for me. I have sent the recipe to the apothecary.'

Linley did not behave like a father robbed of his child. Alicia, who should know, says:

'After some private conversation with Mr Sheridan he appeared quite reconciled to his daughter, but insisted on her returning to England with him, to fulfil several engagements that he had entered into on her account. The whole party set out together the next day, Mr Linley having previously promised to allow his daughter to return to Lille when her engagements were over.'

That has the authentic ring of the practical Mr Linley. Contracts were contracts, and once he was satisfied that virtue was no longer in danger, and had indeed been preserved, then it was on with the Oratorios.

But Mathews had not been idle either. For on April 8, 1772, he had sent a letter to the *Bath Chronicle*.

'Mr Richard S—— having attempted, in a letter left behind him for that purpose, to account for his scandalous method of running away from this place, by insinuations derogating from *my* character, and that of a young lady, innocent as far as related to *me* or *my* knowledge; since which he has neither taken any notice of letters, or even informed his own family of the place where he has hid himself; I can no longer think he deserves the treatment of a gentleman, and therefore shall trouble myself no further about him than, in this public method to post him as a l—— and a treacherous s——.'

When Alicia remonstrated with Mathews for attacking her brother in the public press, Mathews, who seems, to say the least, to have been a gentleman who preferred to spread the blame about if he possibly could, immediately said that Charles was privy to it. At this point the two abandoned lovers of Miss Linley fell out. Charles indignantly denied that he had anything to do with this public 'posting' of his brother in the *Bath Chronicle*, and was then within an ace of calling Mathews out.

Meanwhile the runaways, with accompanying father and presumably duenna, had arrived in England. Sheridan's account of his actions written after the event ran:

'Mr T. Mathews thought himself essentially injured by Mr R. Sheridan's having co-operated in the virtuous efforts of a young lady to escape the snares of vice and dissimulation. He wrote several most abusive threats to Mr S., then in France. He laboured, with cruel industry, to vilify his character in England. He publicly posted him as a scoundrel and a liar. Mr S. answered him from France (hurried and surprized) that he would never sleep in England till he had thanked him as he deserved.'

Eliza and her father at this point thought that Sheridan, having left them at their London hotel, would be going back to Bath. But it was not in Sheridan's nature to take insults lying down, whether bound by Mr Linley or not. He had gone off to find Ewart, and discovered that Mathews was in lodgings kept by a man called Cocklin in the Crutched Friars. Not only that, he learned from Ewart that Mathews was threatening violence against him saying that he would adivse 'his friend not even to come his way without a sword, as he could not answer for the consequences'.

Sheridan's answer to this was to provide himself with a pair of pistols, and hurry round to the lodgings in the Crutched Friars, arriving there about midnight. But when Mathews found an angry, armed, reckless young man outside his door at midnight he prudently did not let him in, and when Sheridan went on banging at the door, he pretended the key had been lost. This did not satisfy Sheridan, who stood outside the house banging and shouting till two o'clock in the morning when Mathews eventually let him in – due, we may imagine, to complaints from the neighbours.

Sheridan says that Mathews showed himself to be a coward at this point. He dressed himself, and called Sheridan his dear friend and one with whom he would be particularly unhappy to have any differences. On catching sight of the pistols he invited Sheridan to sit down, complained of being cold, and in short showed himself to be a complete poltroon. Sheridan adds, for good measure, that 'never had he seen a man behave so perfectly dastardly'.

During the course of what must have been a very heated conversation Mathews was relieved to discover that Sheridan had not yet read about the actual letter in the *Bath Chronicle*. This gave him a breathing space, and he said that he had never meant to quarrel. 'His behaviour', said Charles Sheridan later, 'was so very condescending that Dick let him off for a very small concession to be made in the Bath paper.' So long as Sheridan's name was cleared on the home ground he would be satisfied. The two men laboured for hours discussing the exact wording of the explanation and apology. In the grey dawn Sheridan left, somewhat calmed down.

Two days later the Linleys and Sheridan departed for Bath, and the first visit Sheridan made was to the publishers of the *Bath Chronicle*. There he discovered the full extent of Mathews' insult and his treachery. There seems at this point to have been a temporary quarrel between the brothers, presumably because of the blame which had been laid at Charles' door by Mathews. But eventually this was smoothed out. Charles admitted that he had let out a few angry words on first hearing of the elopement, but as for the rest this had been a distortion of Mathews.

Both brothers were now agreed that it was impossible to put up with these public and private insults and that unless Richard avenged the insult to his honour he could never show his face in public again. Charles would back Richard up, literally, to the hilt. This seems to have been the one and only time when Charles behaved with a certain dash. He had already obtained a post as secretary in the Legation in Sweden, and he was awaiting the return of his father from Dublin in order to tie up the remaining formalities and make his preparations for departure. But the insult to the family honour came first.

The sisters were not told of what had occurred and had been decided. But at night the brothers travelled post to London, and the following morning when the sisters rose they found the brothers had disappeared, and immediately jumped to the wrong conclusion. Moore says:

'On the following day (Sunday) when the young gentlemen did not appear the alarm of their sisters was not a little increased, by hearing that high words had been exchanged the evening before, and that it was feared a duel between the brothers would be the consequence. They had instant recourse to Miss Linley, the fair Helen of all this strife, as the person most likely to be acquainted with their brother Richard's designs, and to relieve them from the suspense under which they laboured.'

But at her father's house in the Crescent Miss Linley knew no more than the sisters. 'Their mutual distress being heightened by sympathy, a scene of tears and fainting fits ensued, of which no less remarkable a person than Dr Priestley, who lodged in Mr Linley's house at the time happened to be a witness.'

By that Sunday morning the brothers were in London: bent on avenging honour, they were losing no time. First they drove off to find the son of Mr Ewart, who had agreed to act as second. Then Charles Sheridan carried the challenge to Mathews, though even at this late date Charles attempted to get Mathews to apologize, arguing with him for two hours. But Mathews would only propose compromises and never an outright apology. Every means of avoiding a conflict had been tried. The duel was fixed for six o'clock on Monday evening in Hyde Park.

Mathews had decided on swords, but to make assurance doubly sure, a case of pistols was also brought. Accordingly, on May 4th, at six o'clock in the evening, in Hyde Park, Sheridan, attended by his second, Ewart, met Mathews and a Captain Knight, his uncle, who was acting as his second. A chaise and four was kept waiting at the turnpike, presumably to take care of the wounded in the event of any disaster. The opponents walked to the Ring (Rotten Row). Sheridan is said to have made a final effort to get Mathews to give him a full apology but Mathews refused.

There ensued a series of farcical happenings which took the edge off the drama. Sheridan chose the ground for the encounter. Mathews countered by appealing to his second, claiming that it was uneven. The four warriors then crossed the Ring and found a flatter piece of ground behind a building. Sheridan had drawn his sword, when his second saw someone watching them. The party then found another place, but this time it was Mathews who alleged that there were spectators, though Sheridan said they were very far off. Mathews then suggested that they should go back to the Hercules Pillars at Hyde Park Corner. Here Sheridan again unsheathed his sword. This time Mathews objected to an officer who seemed to be observing them, and though Ewart gave his word that nobody should intercept those who might need the chaise, Mathews remained obstinate, and actually proposed to defer the duel till the following morning.

Sheridan described all this, with some reason, as trifling work, wanted no more delay and went up to the officer who was supposed to be watching, and the latter 'politely retired'. But by this time Mathews had retreated to the gates of the Park. Even allowing for the fact that Sheridan's account must have been coloured by anger and frustration, Mathews could hardly be said to have been spoiling for the fight. Eventually, the Castle Tavern at the corner of Henrietta Street and Bedford Street was the agreed venue, and here a room was engaged for the conflict. By this time it was dark.

After the duel Sheridan wrote a long letter to Captain Knight explaining the conflict in detail. It is difficult to understand why all these details had to be clarified unless it is clearly understood that the nice points of duelling were interconnected with the conduct of a gentleman, and were therefore of the utmost importance to Sheridan. Apparently, according to Richard, he had Mathews at his mercy and could have run him through but Mathews called out two or three times 'I beg my life'.

At this point Knight, Mathews' second said, 'There, he has begged his life and now there is an end of it.' But still Mathews would not give an apology, and Mathews flung down his sword which Sheridan promptly and angrily broke. Then Mathews became indignant and having first said 'he would never draw a sword against the man who had given him his life', he decided that the breaking of the sword was another insult. The quarrel was on the point of erupting again, but the protagonists were smoothed down. 'I then', wrote Sheridan, 'asked Mr Mathews if it did not occur to him that he owed me another satisfaction.'

By 'satisfaction' in this context Sheridan did not mean another duel, but a clear public apology. But despite all the fracas with broken swords and broken promises which had already taken place, Mathews still would not agree. Sheridan's letter continued, 'It was in his power to do it without discredit, I supposed that he would not hesitate. This he absolutely refused unless conditionally; I insisted on it, and said I would not leave the room till it was settled. After much altercation and with much ill grace, he gave the apology which afterwards appeared.'

The apology ran: 'Being convinced that the expressions I made use of to Mr Sheridan's disadvantage were the effects of passion and misrepresentation, I retract what I have said to his disadvantage and particularly beg his pardon for my advertisement in the *Bath Chronicle.*'

Honour had been somewhat laboriously satisfied and the two Sheridan brothers then sped back to Bath by flying coach, and were able to show the apology to the frightened sisters. Sheridan went straight round to the local newspaper, and contradicted the rumours about the duel that had appeared in it so that when Mathews did appear in Bath, he was cold-shouldered by everybody, even though he had not been inactive himself, and had managed to convince the important and powerful master of ceremonies, Captain Wade, that in some way Sheridan's duelling manners had lacked the finesse demanded on such occasions.

In the midst of all these deeds of partial derring-do Thomas Sheridan returned from Dublin.

*

Already angry because of the elopement, he was outwardly even more furious at the publicity of the duel. But it was represented by Charles that the family honour had to be vindicated, and that purely on this account Richard had acted honourably, if quixotically. That Charles was on Richard's side in the affair is proved by a letter he wrote to his uncle, Richard Chamberlaine:

'I suppose you will acknowledge it was impossible to have put up with these publick and private insults; every gentleman we were acquainted with thought it incumbent upon Dick to resent this properly, otherwise he could never show his face. But Dick's spirit did not require that the opinion of others should teach him what to do; Dick disarmed his antagonist; made him beg his life and also sign an apology to be put in the Bath paper of his own inditing; thus is the affair concluded highly to the honour of Dick, who is applauded by everyone.

I am my dear Uncle, your affectionate and dutiful nephew, Charles Francis Sheridan.'

Thomas Sheridan may have secretly applauded his son's conduct in the vindication of the family honour, and possibly the old actor, in his heart of heart's, appreciated the happenings for the intrinsic drama which they represented. But there were other things which did not please him so much. Alicia says, 'He [Thomas] also had some cause of displeasure with respect to the numerous debts his son had contracted to carry on his various plans.' Obviously flying coaches, post chaises, cases of pistols and accompanying ammunition, besides swords, trips to France, putting young ladies *en pension* with nuns, paying for lodgings in London, and hiring upstairs rooms in coffee houses for duels all cost good money, which in the Sheridan family was, as always, in short supply. But apparently old Sheridan was finally mollified, and paid up his son's debts on the promise of more prudence in future.

But while Thomas Sheridan may have forgiven Richard for his rash elopement and subsequent duel, he was quite opposed to mixing with musicians. Any idea of Eliza and Sheridan making a match of it was out of the question, even if it had been openly mooted. Nobody seems to have told him of the clandestine 'marriage'. Mr Linley was also opposed but for a different reason. He wanted a richer husband than Sheridan for his beautiful daughter.

But there is nothing more inspiring to young love than opposition, and unlike the buds in spring, foul weather can make love burst into further blossom. The couple met in secret. It was the custom at this time for lovers to adopt classical names: Richard had become Horatio and Eliza transformed to Delia. The romance grew in intensity, fostered by the opposition of the Roman fathers. Horatio and his Delia were meeting in secret, and Sheridan wrote a poem hymning their romantic rendezvous:

> Uncouth is this moss-covered Grotto of stone,
> And damp is the shade of this dew dripping tree,
> Yet I this rude Grotto with rapture will own,
> And Willow, thy damps are refreshing to me.

For, says 'Horatio', 'this is the Grotto where Delia reclined, and this is the Tree kept her safe from the wind, as blushing she heard the grave lessons I taught.'

Eliza replied:

'I will call you Horatio, that was the name you gave yourself in that sweet poem. Write to me then, my dear Horatio, and tell me that you are equally sincere and constant. My hand shakes so at this moment, I can scarce hold the pen. My father came into my room this moment, and I had just time to stuff the letter behind the glass.'

On another occasion she wrote:

'Eleven o'clock. Though I parted from you so lately, and though I expect to see you again so soon, yet cannot I keep my fingers from the pen but I must be plaguing you with my scrawl. Oh, my dearest love, I am never happy but when I am with you. I cannot speak or think of anything else. When shall we have another happy half-hour? I declare I have not felt real joy since I came from France before this evening.'

Then even the beautiful Eliza shows herself not free from the pangs of jealousy:

'Perhaps now whilst I am writing and amusing myself by

expressing the tender sentiments which I feel for you, you
are flirting with Miss Waller or some other handsome girl
or making fine speeches. No, my life and Soul, I love you
to such a degree, that I should never bear to see you (even
in joak) show any particular attention to another.'

The subterfuges to which the lovers were reduced become
plain:

'If you do speak to that woman, I think we might contrive
to send our letters there, directed under feigned names. I
could easily frame some excuse for getting them. Till then
I shall expect you will write your letters, and give them
yourself – for I do insist on hearing from you, for I am sure
it is nothing but laziness that prevents you.'

Even in the heat of his love for Eliza, Richard was averse to
writing letters. Action was what he preferred.
Apart from fathers there were other watchful eyes. Eliza
says:

'I really think Charles suspected something this evening.
He looked amazingly knowing when I came down. Deuce
take his curious head. I wish he would mind his own business
and not interrupt us in our stolen pleasures. Is it not amazing,
my dear love, that we should always have so great an inclination for what is not in our possession?'

Richard and Eliza were in the plight of the innumerable
lovers in the romances of the period. Secret meetings in
grottos, correspondence carried on in feigned names, hostile
fathers, suspicious brothers, and a secret, if invalid marriage
by a priest of the Roman persuasion. No set of circumstances
could have been better calculated to fan the flames of fervent
romance. The parties and receptions which they attended in
common, while pretending to be 'just friends' added a spice of
danger to their plight. This is made clear by another letter,
'For fear I should not be able to speak to you, I write to tell
you I shall be at Mrs Lyn's this evening. Don't tell Lissy that
you know of my being there, as I promised her I would not

tell you. Only think of Captain Hodges! I am frightened out of my wits.'

After a party Elizabeth writes again to her Horatio:

'Twelve o'clock. You unconscionable creature to make me sit up this time of the night to scribble nonsense to you, when you will not let me hear one word from you for this week to come. Indeed my dearest love, I am never happy except when I am with you, or writing to you. Why did you run away so soon tonight? Tho' I could not enjoy your conversation freely, yet it was a consolation to me that you was so near me. I gave up my cords the moment you left me, as I could not play with any patience. Upon my knees, half nacked [*sic*], once more I am going to tire you with my nonsense. I could not bear to see this little blank without filling it up. I do insist that you write to me, you lazy wretch, can't you take so small a trouble? I can receive your letter by the same method. My sister is very impatient that I don't come into bed, but I feel more happiness in this situation, tho' I am half froze, than in the warmest bed in England.'

Her father, in the guise of manager and agent, was again moving forward. Too much time had been wasted in activities which did not bring in returns, and she adds, 'My father and I had a long conversation this morning. He wanted me to go to a private concert at Dr Davenport's but I availed myself of his promise [possibly made at the time of the elopement] and excused myself as I am resolved not to go so much to those kind of meetings.'

It has been suggested that some of the concerts – 'those kind of meetings' – were on a Gentlemen Only basis, or were given in private houses where she could not be sure that she would be treated with 'delicacy'. Eliza goes on, 'He says he shall have a concert for my brother's benefit in a fortnight, and he shall expect my performance without any objections. You know I could not refuse him; but I am resolved never to go into public but on these occasions.' Nevertheless the lovers were to be parted by Miss Linley's father and her public. It had been arranged that she should sing at Oxford, and before going 'Delia' was writing to her 'Horatio' again:

'Wednesday night, 12 o'clock. The anxiety I felt whilst in my dear Horatio's company tonight would not let me feel the pains of separation, but now that I am retired, and at full liberty to give way to my own unpleasing ideas, I cannot describe what I feel to be so long divided from you. Oh, my love, how vain are your doubts and suspicions; believe me, if I thought it possible for me to change my present sentiments of you, I should despise myself. Never shall you have the least reason to suspect my constancy or my love. I am in a very gloomy disposition tonight, but I will not give way to it. I will try to forget every disagreeable circumstance, and only look forward to those happy hours which I hope are still in store for us. With what rapture shall we meet, when we may do so without constraint, when I may lie in your arms without the fear of parents, or the ill-natured world. I could write to you without ever leaving off, but my sister insists on my coming to bed.'

It was certainly not easy for Horatio and Delia to correspond, surrounded as they were by large families, and watched by suspicious fathers. But like the Montagues and the Capulets, the fathers only helped to push the romance forward. The orchard walls may have been hard to climb but determined lovers were never deterred by obstacles, and the streets of Bath with their many little alleyways, full of bonnet shops, mantua makers, jewellers, and print shops must have given many opportunities for 'chance' encounters. And there was always Spring Gardens, where people rowed over by boat, or Sydney Gardens with the Avon running softly at its edge.

It has been said that Eliza's letters largely reflect the raptures and romanticism of the period, but to read them after two hundred years certainly makes this ardent girl herself come alive, as she sits half 'nacked' in her bedroom, scribbling while her sister complains and tells her to come to bed.

Eliza left to fulfil her engagement at Oxford; but the male rivals had not yet finished with each other.

CHAPTER 6

The Duel (Second Act)

When Mathews returned to Wales, he discovered that the reputation he had garnered in Bath had followed him, and he found himself universally shunned. It was said that apologies could be a proof of courage or they could be proof of cowardice, and Mathews' neighbours were inclined to take the view that his apology proved his fear.

At this point a gentleman called Mr Barnett bustled forward. He had recently moved to Wales, and seeing the way in which Captain Mathews was being treated by his neighbours, he decided to lend him a hand in restoring his character, with, says Moore, 'a degree of Irish friendliness, not forgotten in the portrait of Sir Lucius O'Trigger'. Mr Barnett re-roused Captain Mathews' fiery sentiments, and offered to be his second. Mathews accepted Barnett's offer and the two men proceeded to Bath to re-kindle the fires of the fight, convinced that a second duel was the only way to wipe out the shame of the abortive first duel, and Mathews' subsequent apology. Mr Barnett was the bearer of the challenge, which he had the cruelty to put into Miss Sheridan's hand, saying it was a note of invitation for her brother. This, in a sense, it was.

Thomas Sheridan was in London, making preparations for Charles' departure to his diplomatic post in Sweden, and was quite unaware of the new warlike preparations. He had only been persuaded with the greatest difficulty to forgive Richard for the first duel, and was not likely to tolerate a second with its subsequent scandals and publicity.

Mr Barnett bustled round Bath trying to find Sheridan, who appeared to be absent from home a great deal. It is not known for sure whether this was because at first he shunned a second duel on account of the difficulties he had had with his father. A letter from Barnett written from his lodgings in Bath explains his trials as a harbinger of battle. It is dated June 30, 1772:

'I had ere this hoped for the pleasure of seeing you. I find by the servant it is uncertain when you will be here. I have taken the liberty of handling this line to request the favour of you to let me know where I shall meet you this evening, and when. If equally agreeable to you at the White Hart. As I am very tender on my feet the Stones are not very pleasant walking on. Pray excuse this scrap of paper, as it is what the servant gave me. From your most obedient servant,
W. Barnett.'

The cobblestones planned by the architect Wood to set off his squares and streets obviously had their disadvantages. This curt letter infuriated Sheridan with its veiled suggestion that he was avoiding an encounter. It was not yet a challenge, merely a prelude. Mathews then drew up an account of the first duel, and the interfering Barnett then duly went round on his tender feet to get Sheridan to sign it. It was this paper which caused the second duel.

The *Bath Chronicle*, always the first with in-depth reporting of the local news, was later to say: 'The Duel between Mr Mathews and Mr Sheridan was occasioned by Mr S's refusal to sign a paper testifying the spirit and propriety of Mr M's behaviour in their former encounter. This refusal enduced Mr M. to send him a challenge.'

This refusal is corroborated by Sheridan's own account, reported by Creevey. 'Accordingly a messenger arrived from Mathews to Sheridan with a written certificate in favour of Mathews' undoubted honour in the former affair to be *signed* by Sheridan, or else the messenger was to deliver him a second challenge.'

Luckily Eliza was completely ignorant of this new threat to their happiness. Sheridan wrote letters to his father and his sisters and, putting Eliza's miniature round his neck, went out to face his enemy for the second time. He was prepared to lay down his life for Eliza, and in fact had written to his friend Thomas Grenville:

'I hope you have seen her. Tell me she is happy; if she is otherwise tell her to be so. O upon my soul, if it were the part of an angel to come down from Heaven to watch over her and reconcile her mind to peace. I wish dying could assure me of the power to come from Heaven to her with that happiness which I fear she will never know here. It is impious to say it, but I believe I should exchange a Robe of Glory for *her* livery.'

Sheridan chose a different second, a Captain Paumier. This was not wise, for Paumier was a very young man with no experience of affairs of honour, and in the event was to prove a very broken reed indeed.

At three o'clock in the morning on July 1, 1772, the opponents and their seconds met at the White Hart Inn. They then drove off into the summer night in two post chaises, through Bathford, down the Bradford-on-Avon road, to Kingsdown, a common high above Bath. It must have seemed bleak and lonely to the young Sheridan, with its uneven turf and the odd thorn trees dotted about. It was not a good spot for duelling because there was no flat ground.

Mathews, certainly seeking for some advantage over his young opponent, wished the encounter to take place with pistols. But before they reached the Down, Sheridan had decided on swords. With his usual virtue of hindsight Charles said this was sheer folly, for he was no match for one who had learnt fencing in France and was considered very skilful in that science. Doubtless the same remark could have been made about pistol shooting, since Mathews had favoured pistols.

As with the first duel, the opponents started the proceedings by arguing, adding an occasional polished insult. Mathews said that he preferred pistols because he feared a repetition of the former ungentlemanly scuffle at the encounter in London. Sheridan replied tartly that had he known at the first meeting what his opponent's theory of a gentlemanlike scuffle was, he would certainly 'have put the chance out of his power' – in other words, killed him. Further argument ensued between the four men as to whether pistols should be used. Mathews later said that Sheridan cut short the proceedings and advanced on him, flourishing his sword and calling upon him to draw.

Again the duel, if this shambles can be thought worthy of such a name, seems to have degenerated into a free-for-all. Mathews' second, recording the proceedings later, says:

'Mr Mathews advanced fast on Mr Sheridan; upon which he retreated, till he very suddenly ran in upon Mr Mathews, laying himself exceedingly open and endeavouring to get hold of Mr Mathews's sword. Mr Mathews received him on his point, and I believe disengaged his sword from Mr Sheridan's body, and gave him another wound.

Mr Mathews, I think, on finding his sword broke, laid hold of Mr Sheridan's sword-arm and tripped up his heels; they both fell; Mr Mathews was uppermost, with the hilt of his sword in his hand, having about six or seven inches of the blade to it, with which I saw him give Mr Sheridan, as I imagined, a skin-wound or two in the neck – for it could be no more, the remaining part of the sword being broad and blunt; he also beat him in the face either with his fist or the hilt of his sword. Mr Sheridan's sword was bent, and he slipped his hand up the small part of it, and gave Mr Mathews a slight wound in the left part of the belly; I that instant turned again to Captain Paumier, and proposed again our taking them up [stopping the fight]. He in the same moment called out, "Oh! he is killed – he is killed!"

'I as quick as possible turned again, and found Mr Mathews had recovered the point of his sword, that was before on the ground, with which he had wounded Mr Sheridan in the belly; I saw him drawing the point out of the wound. By this time Mr Sheridan's sword was broke, which he told us. Captain Paumier called out to him, "My dear Sheridan, beg your life, and I will be yours for ever." I also desired him to ask his life: he replied, "No, by God, I won't".'

Naturally, as with the first duel, the accounts of the opponents, the opponents' seconds, and the opponents' friends and enemies were all different. One takes one's choice. It was afterwards alleged that Mathews had some kind of body armour which had caused Sheridan's sword to break. Another account says that at first Sheridan had the advantage and seems to have bent his sword by thrusting at Mathews, but as they rolled on the sloping ground, the older and stronger man found himself uppermost, hitting Sheridan's face with the hilt and hacking at his neck with the six or seven inches of his broken blade, which eventually stuck in the earth.

Once Sheridan was on the ground his courage was not in doubt. Asked if he would beg his life, his reply 'By God, I won't', was a conscious choice of likely death to dishonour.

The established facts are that Mathews had Sheridan at his mercy, that some of these blows caused flesh wounds in the neck, and that Sheridan managed to ward off others with his hand, which was cut. Yet other thrusts cut his coat, injured his chest and stomach, and shattered the miniature of Eliza which he wore round his neck. The frame was found with one of Sheridan's sleeve buttons in a mess of blood after the fight.

Whatever the rights and wrongs of the duel, and whatever the nice points of duelling, this seems to have been a very untidy affair. Certainly Paumier does not seem to have helped Sheridan as he lay unarmed on the uneven ground, being hacked and sliced by the furious Mathews. The second apparently panicked, and allowed Mathews to go on hacking and stabbing without effectively trying to stop the conflict. In the end, with Paumier panicking, Barnett claimed: 'I desired he would assist me in taking them up. Mr Mathews most readily acquiesced, first desiring me to see Mr Sheridan was disarmed', a precaution for which in the circumstances he can hardly be blamed.

Barnett's account makes the whole thing seem as if it were done in a very gentlemanly way, for it ends: 'Mr Sheridan and Mr Mathews both got up, the former was helped into one of the chaises, and drove off for Bath, and Mr Mathews made the best of his way to London.'

The facts were slightly different. As Sheridan lay bleeding on the ground, Mathews certainly rattled off in his carriage, but the younger man's plight was desperate. He had been wounded in several places, and thought his last hour had come. He was helped into a shepherd's hut where he was given water, and rested for a while until he was a little recovered. One of the postillions then helped him into the post-chaise and he was driven to the White Hart in Bath. The best surgeons in Bath, Lee and Ditcher, were immediately sent for, and his wounds were dressed.

While Sheridan lay wounded at the White Hart Inn, 'Captain' Mathews was making his way to the coast, to escape to France until the whole thing had blown over. Sheridan had been set against an experienced opponent who had acted with more cruelty than courage. Had Mathews considered his own conduct of a chivalrous nature he would hardly have decided to take off for foreign parts immediately afterwards. The word duel was a misnomer. It was a simple fight between two males about a female.

*

For the rest of the day, while Sheridan lay wounded in the White Hart, news of the duel was reviving all the gossip occasioned by the first one. The news sheets were predicting his imminent death, but after a few days Richard was back at home recovering. His sisters had removed him from the inn because of the noise and heat. Soon he was sitting up in bed reading the newspapers because, he said, he wished to know whether he was alive or dead. With his resilience and high spirits he had begun to see a comical side to the affair, but the anticipated paternal explosion inevitably occurred.

The news duly reached Thomas and Charles Sheridan in London, and Thomas reacted in his usual impetuous way. First, he threatened to sue Mathews. Then he was furious with Richard for indulging in a second duel. Later, when he found that his son had become a wounded hero in the eyes of Bath and the world, he softened towards one who had defended the family honour in this magnificent way. Finally, having run the gamut of these various and typically Thomasonian emotions, he refused to speak to Richard, and forbade all friendly comings and goings with the Linley family.

Charles' reaction was also typical, He wrote a long, very Joseph Surface-ish, letter to Richard:

London July 3, 1772.

'Dear Dick,

It was with the deepest concern I received the late accounts of you, though it was somewhat softened by the assurance of your not being in the least danger. You cannot conceive of the uneasiness it occasioned to my father. Both he and I were resolved to believe the best, and to suppose you safe, but then we neither of us could approve of the cause in which you suffer. All your friends here condemned you. You risked everything, where you had nothing to gain, to give your antagonist the thing he wished, a chance for recovering his reputation. Your courage was past dispute: he wanted to get rid of the contemptible opinion he was held in, and you were good natured enough to let him do it at your expense.'

Charles finally weighs in with matters nearer his heart, namely financial arrangements.

'I am exceedingly unhappy at the situation I leave you in with respect to money matters, the more so as it is totally out of my power to be of any use to you. Ewart was greatly vexed at the manner of your drawing for the last £20 – I own I think with some reason.'

Meanwhile Eliza's father had somehow kept her in ignorance of the duel, despite the reports of Sheridan's wounding which were in all the Oxford papers. As a good manager-agent he wanted to be sure that the show would go on, and continue to go on. She ends one letter by saying: 'If I find you well and happy on my return I shall be content. If my prayers are granted, I shall once more embrace my Horatio, and convince him how sincerely I am his Eliza.' So she would, but it was a near thing.

So Eliza innocently went on singing, and Sheridan's friend Grenville, who was then an undergraduate at Oxford, mentions the effect this had upon her audience:

'Miss Linley's appearance on that day inspired the greatest

interest in the company present. As her ignorance of the duel
and its consequences were known to every person, and her
beauty joined to the effect of her truly enchanting powers
could not fail of exciting a degree of sympathy in young and
susceptible minds when they thought of the heavy calamity
that hung over her.'

Soon after, they all drove back to Bath.

A few miles outside the city, the family were met by a
clergyman called Mr Panton, who managed to prevail upon
Mr Linley to let Eliza join him in his carriage so that he could
gently break the news about Sheridan. But nobody could really
soften the blow, and the sudden tidings had a most unexpected
effect, for Alicia says that Eliza's feelings 'were so taken by
surprize that, in the distress of the moment, she let the secret
of her heart escape, and passionately exclaimed "My husband,
my husband!" demanding to see him, and insisted upon her
right as his wife to be near him day and night'.

This may have been the dearest wish of her heart but it
certainly was not the dearest wish of Thomas Sheridan's heart,
since he had forbidden all communication between his daughters
and the Linley family. But the faithful sisters still managed to
convey messages between the wounded Richard and Eliza.
Both the fathers still thought their reasons good for opposing
the match. Linley's was self-interested and financial, old
Sheridan's social and snobbish. Alicia puts it more delicately:

'Through some of his friends R. B. Sheridan found out that
Miss Linley's assertion of her marriage had answered no
end but suggesting the idea to both Fathers of breaking the
the match, Mr Linley to secure to himself the advantage of
her talents, and Mr Sheridan from a high spirit of honour,
which made him very averse to his son's forming a connexion
with a Person whose name had been so much the subject
of public discussion. Many traps were laid for both parties,
but they contrived to evade them, attributing what she had
uttered before Mr Panton and others to mere agitation of
mind.'

Eventually, through Alicia's intervention, Thomas Sheridan,

condescended to speak to Richard again; but he remained adamantly against marriage.

Finally Eliza was packed off to relations in Wells. From there she wrote to Richard:

'Believe me, I have not been in my senses for two days, but the happy account of your recovery has perfectly restored them. Oh! my dearest love, when shall I see you? I will not ask you to write, as I am sure it must hurt you. (This was because of the wounds on his hand.) Oh! my Horatio, I did not know till now how much I loved you. Believe me, had you died I should certainly have dressed myself as a man and challenged Mathews. He should have killed me, or I would have revenged you and myself.

God in Heaven bless you, my dearest Horatio, and restore you once more to health, to happiness, and the arms of your Eliza.'

This was the one thing both fathers were determined to prevent.

Linley, displeased by Sheridan's snobbishness towards his daughter, tried to make Eliza seriously promise never to marry Richard Sheridan, while Thomas Sheridan made Richard promise never to correspond with Eliza. Even the lovers themselves fell prey to doubts and suspicions. Forgetting his wounded hand, Eliza wrote, 'For God's sake write to me'. and in an excess of suspicions signed herself coolly his 'sincere' Eliza. Shortly after this they met at some reception in Bath, and Eliza's conduct provoked jealousy on the young man's side. Afterwards she wrote:

'How can you, my dear Horatio, torment yourself and me with such unjust suspicions? If I was prudent, it was my father's conversation made me so. He declared he would sooner follow me to the grave than see me married to you as you would ruin me and yourself in a short time by your extravagance. I know he watched us last night; t'was that which made me cautious. I never can think of another. I do not know how to see you. My situation at present is very disagreeable. I am not suffered to go out without my father

95

or mother, and I am so watched that I can scarce find a moment to write.'

*

Then, as at other critical moments in his life, Thomas Sheridan suddenly obtained an engagement to act in Dublin. His idea was to take the whole family with him, and not leave them alone this time, to get into mischief without him. Then he abruptly changed his mind, and decided to pack them all off to France, which would not only put them out of harm's way – and the Linleys' way – but would also be more economical. The sisters, Alicia and Betsy, should be put in Richard's care.

Then, just as abruptly, he changed his mind again. It would be most unwise to leave two girls of tender age in the charge of such an incorrigible fellow. He was, said Thomas, unworthy of such a charge, unworthy, Sir, to prove a guardian to his young and virtuous sisters.

At this point old Sheridan lost all patience with the problem, and simply packed Richard off to Waltham Abbey in Essex, under the care of some friends called the Parkers. Richard was set to study for the Bar, far from the loved charmer, and from his sympathetic sisters. A good course of repentance, serious study, and a ban on writing and receiving letters would best serve the cause of all concerned.

On August 27th, Richard arrived at Waltham Abbey and wrote dutifully to his father: 'I arrived here on Friday evening. I am very snugly situated in the Town; tho' I should have liked it better to have been out of it.' He goes on, perhaps deceptively, to allay his father's suspicions about his supposed double dealing in the romantic and heroic episodes in which he had been involved, and adds: 'I can now have no motive in solemnly declaring to you that I have extricated myself, and that on this subject you shall never again have the smallest uneasiness. I intend to call on Mr Adams tomorrow when I shall arrange my studies.' It appeared that he had decided to forget Eliza.

He seemed set to become the model pupil. But there still remained a few minor difficulties consequent upon his fussing

6 *a*: Elizabeth Linley when young. *Portrait by Gainsborough. Pennsylvania Museum.*
   b: Elizabeth Linley and her brother Thomas

7   *Above:* Bath: the Assembly Rooms. *Below:* Bath: the Lion Hotel,
Guildhall and Abbey Church

and feuding with Mathews. As tactfully as he could he refers to his debts of 'folly and extravagance, some of them contracted later than they should have been, tho' to get rid of obligations of a former date'.

But by the same post he wrote a much less reformed letter to his sister Betsy:

'This letter is wholly *entre nous* and your Sister if you will. Let me remind you, if you have not done it to call on Miss D'Oily for my bill. William, I believe will give you one of Mrs Purdie's. Will you instruct William to prevent Evill's giving his bill to my father, as my Note which he has is sufficient, and as my Father will discharge that, there is no occasion for his knowing the Particulars.'

It is no wonder that Richard wanted the details of Evill's bill kept from his father. It was full of the kind of trifles which no father likes to finance.

Bath, November, 1771.
Bought of William Evill
In the Market Place.

	To 1 pair neat Foyls		10	6
Dec. 12	To 1 pair ,, ,, ...		10	6
Jany. 23/72	1 neat Toothpick case	4	4	0
June 10	To 1 neat Hair Locket	1	11	6
	To 1 neat fancy ring	2	12	6
	To 2 do. Seals		9	0
	To fitting a picture in a case. . .		3	6

The neat hair locket must have contained the picture of Eliza. The total bill, which also included garnet buttons, gold seals, and German hollow blades to swords with vellum scabbards came to a total, as far as Mr Sheridan senior was concerned, of £15 12s 6d. Richard added that he would mention the bill to his father 'in his own way'.

But although Richard was studious and apparently repentant, the newspapers had not forgotten him, and the *Public Advertiser* of November 19, 1772, was still getting the details wrong, including the duelling weapons: 'Mr Sheridan jnr, who last summer fought a duel with Captain Mathews about the Maid of Bath, is entirely recovered of his wounds but has lost the use of his right arm from receiving a shot between the bones at the joint.'

In mitigation of Thomas Sheridan's opposition to the match, there is no doubt that Mrs Linley was a vulgar and parsimonious woman, while Mrs Sheridan had been a cultured and charming lady. In the context of old Sheridan's fierce pride in his status as a gentleman, his opposition can be excused. Indeed it is underlined by Richard's own attitude towards his friend Grenville, to whom he wrote frequently during his exile at Waltham Abbey. His letters show how great was the gulf between the nobility and ordinary folk who considered themselves to be gentlemen. He writes that he wishes to make it clear that 'my connexion is with Mr Thomas Grenville, if you should by any accident cease to be that Gentleman (i.e. inherit a title) you must not be surprised if I think our correspondence dissolved'.

He speaks of passing two days in excessive melancholy, 'and I am perfectly convinced that that unfortunate being called a Lover, if a true one, would better bear a separation from her he loves in a Desert than a Paradise'. Suffering from all the obvious pangs he says 'When I see a pair blest in peace, and in each other Let me say "Why am I shut out from this forever?" and 'tis torture. Let me sit in a beautiful scene I exclaim "What would her presence make this?" and 'tis worse than a wilderness. Let me hear musick and singing "I cannot hear her sing and play" and the notes become the shrieks of the Damned.'

He was not always playing the role of the despairing lover. On the same day he wrote to his sister Betsy in a much more cheerful vein. 'By the way, I thought Mrs Bowers seemed more alarmed about the money than was necessary. 'Tis all for flowers.' Unfortunately nosegays for ladies have to be paid for. He then adds, 'Take care of all the things I left behind me. There is an old Muff which I shall seriously be obliged to you if you will put by for me.' He notes that a Miss Peake wanted him to teach her a dance called the *Allemande*.

In spite of his despairing sighs, he was not above treading a measure or two with other young ladies. Or possibly they were not averse to treading a measure with him. Richard was a volatile young gentleman who veered from duels and despair, to muffs and allemandes according to his mood. He had a very Celtic temperament.

Yet there seems little doubt that at this period he was genuinely torn in his feelings for Eliza, perhaps because of his dependence on his father and the assurances he had given. He wrote in the autumn of 1772 to Grenville:

'But what shall I say of this attachment! To hope for happiness from it, I must agree with you, 'tis and must be impossible. I have received a letter from her, since I wrote to you counterband (i.e. illicitly) filled with the violence of Affection, and concluded with prayers, commands, and entreaties that I should write to her. I did not expect such a Desire, as she had acquiesced to my determination of not corresponding. Indeed, as we had always other subjects to employ us when together, she hesitated less in agreeing to a distant mortification, and I by that had less occasion to explain properly to her the Necessity of it. I cannot now do it: for to tell her *why* I am right is to plunge into the wrong: to tell why I did *resolve*, is to break my resolution, yet to deny her and not excuse my denial is a hard mortification. I am determined not to write; not from the conviction of the necessity of such a determination, but I cannot break my solemn Promise. How strange is my situation: if I consult my Reason, or even one half of my feelings I find conviction that I should wish to end this unfortunate connexion – what draws the knot, rejects the influence of reason, and has its full moiety of the feelings (dearest, tenderest) with the Passions for its hold. Perhaps then it is best that there is an artificial but powerful bond that keeps me to the other Party.'

He is possibly referring here to his secret marriage.

He was only twenty-one and the whole of his life was before him. He goes on to say to Grenville, perhaps projecting his own thoughts and fears towards the hypothetical troubles of a friend: 'I should obey the dictates of my reason, and I could with propriety, warn *you* not to indulge a passion which must be equally fatal to you . . . need I say that were I free and saw you advancing towards my present situation I should try to hold you back as from a Precipice.' But he was enmeshed in love as he expressed it:

> But when enraged I number
> Each failing of her mind,
> Love still suggests her beauty,
> And sees – while Reason's Blind.

That he had a delicacy in his passionate feelings is proved by his explanation to Grenville:

'There is one point you misunderstood me in with regard to perils and probabilities. I did not mean anything as to Miss Linley, nor hint at any peril in particular. I meant only that a young man of a warm constitution, and of a generous temper must in general run some risque, and probably get into some difficulties from his intercourse with women. I do not mean with those of a low kind, for the inconveniences which mere passion brings a man into are what he deserves. I allude only to the embarrassments of the heart, which I believe will always be perilous where there are passions, and at the same time too much delicacy to relish their gratification with prostitutes.'

He had, at bottom, the romantic sentimental nature which leads into scrapes, yet tries to preserve its picture of the world as a beautiful place untarnished. But that he was tempted is proved from a letter addressed from the Bedford Coffee house in London in November:

'I write now from a coffee house in London, being just come from the play. Whenever I have been at an idle and irrational amusement, whenever I have been in company with fools and coxcombs, I return with the strongest sensations of disgust, and if I have no real friend on whom I can turn my thoughts, I am extremely wretched. Through this only, I have taken a pen to scribble to you. The principles of love are the same. A love (a true one) shall fly with rapture, from the society of courtezans to contemplate but the picture of his mistress. I am interrupted – '

What interrupted him? A woman, a bet, or a joke?
But the deeply romantic streak was endemic to his character. He recommends Grenville to read Sir Philip Sidney's *Arcadia*.

'If you have not read it and ever read romances, I wish you would read it. For my own part, when I read for entertainment I had much rather view the characters of life as I would wish they *were* than as they *are*: why should men have a satisfaction in viewing only the mean and distorted figures of Nature? Whatever merit the painter may have in his execution, an honest mind is disgusted with the design.'

He was a man of his time. This feeling for charm was part of the mentality which produced arcadian poetry, which inspired Fragonard and Watteau: gods, goddesses, pierrots, and masked ladies and gentlemen who could frolick eternally in bosky picnics undeterred by the mundane everyday things of life. Would it not be charming if it were summer all the year round and flowers grew under our feet?

But Miss Linley was still writing her impassioned letters to Sheridan, and unfortunately for the two fathers Miss Linley's engagements included touring the country. Every time the sound of oratorios and recitals approached London or Essex the elder Sheridan became nervous. He even contemplated packing Richard off to Scarborough. 'He proposes that I should retire a few hundred miles northward – that all the counties in the neighbourhood of London were within the magic circle of a certain formidable enchantress who was to keep her Lent there.'

But in spite of the enchantress, there was a Mrs Lyster, wife of a neighbouring surgeon, who seems to have found him bold and amusing, and an anonymous Miss C. fell in love with him and returned to Bath burning with jealousy and full of scandal. It was unlucky that Miss C. came from Bath. The rumours of her undying passion soon reached Miss Linley. Eliza was not a girl to turn a deaf ear to all this:

'I have been deceived so grossly by you, and by every one that it has almost deprived me of my reason, but I have paid too, too dear for my experience ever to put it in your power, or anyone's to impose on me again. I did not expect you to attempt to vindicate your conduct. You cannot to me. Think – oh, reflect on what I have suffered, and then judge if I can consent to risk my life and happiness. For God's sake, Sheridan, do not endeavour to plunge me again into misery. Consider how much your persisting to refuse my letters will distress me. Reason, honour, everything forbids it. This is not a sudden resolution, but the consequence of cool deliberate reflection. You are sensible it is not from caprice, but when I tell you that I have lately had some converstaion with Mrs L. and Miss C–y, you will not suppose I will be again deceived.'

While Eliza was hurt and despairing, Sheridan's moods varied; if at one time he had been writing in the correct despondent strains of the despairing lover, by November his animal spirits seem to have come uppermost. Cheerfulness is breaking through the lover's complaints. He asks Grenville to come over and visit him, and offers some few rural delights: 'I wish you could on any pretence come and spend a fortnight in Essex. You shall hunt and shoot and study in the prettiest rotation imaginable. At night you shall go on stargazing parties, and with ladies two, and conclude the Day with very good wine, and Pipes if you choose them.'

But while Sheridan was proposing wine and pipes, and stargazing parties, Eliza soon was again beset by suitors. Whether as a result of this, or because of her anger with Sheridan, she wrote to him to try to get her letters back. But Sheridan had vowed to her that he would never give the letters up unless she told him she loved another man. 'Do not distress me so much as to continue in that resolution', Eliza wrote. 'Believe me I am incapable of loving any man. They [the letters] cannot be of any use to you. Do not think I shall alter my resolution, or that I am to be terrified by your threats. I will not think so basely of your principles as to suppose you meant anything by them.'

The suggestion was that he had threatened when he heard of other suitors to give away the secret of their marriage. She adds ominously: 'There are unsurmountable obstacles to prevent our ever being united, even supposing I could be induced again to believe you.' There was now a very large rift in the lute of love.

> 'Know then that before I left Bath, after I had refused Sir T. Clarges and other gentlemen of fortune on your account, who I found had given up all thought of me, in the anguish of my soul, which was torn with all the agonies of remorse and rage, I vowed in the most solemn manner upon my knees before my parents that I would never be yours by my own consent, let what would be the consequence.'

There follows a description of a scene from any play of the period where the minor is being forced for financial reasons to bestow her body on the first gentleman with the money to support her in luxury:

> 'My father took advantage of my distress and by upbraidings mixed with persuasions, prevailed on me to promise that I would marry the first man (whose character was unexceptionable) that offered. I repented that I had made this promise afterwards, for though I resolved never to be yours, I had not the least intention to be another's.'

Eliza said that she had comforted herself that no one would seek her in marriage. But a gentleman manager of her father's pushing nature was hardly likely to let such a property go unsought. Soon another firm offer was on hand. Eliza described him as not a young man,

> '... but I believe a worthy one. When I found my father so resolute, I resolved to acquaint the gentleman with every

circumstance of my life. I did, and instead of inducing him to give me up, he is now more earnest than ever.

I have declared it is not possible for me to love him, but he says he will depend on my generosity – in short there is nothing I have not done to persuade him to leave me but in vain. He has promised not to take my fortune, and you may be assured this circumstance will have great weight with my father.'

If woman was a physical chattel, her body to be disposed of to the highest bidder, equally her property was at the disposition of father or husband. When Mary Wollstonecraft wrote her passionate pleas against the subjection of woman she had much to plead against. It is not perhaps surprising that woman 'in keeping' were more amusing, wittier, and more free than their married sisters. So long as they acted with reasonable discretion, and made sure that their careers of gallantry were rewarded by something in the funds, they were not fettered like their virtuous sisters.

Eliza, beset by the importunities of lovers, prospective husbands, and a stern father was less fortunate:

'You see how I am situated. If this was not the case, I could never be your wife – therefore once more I conjure you to leave me and cease persecuting me. My father has this minute left me. He knows I am writing to you, and it was with the greatest difficulty I pacified him. He was going immediately to your lodgings. He has given strict orders to Hannah to bring every letter to him. You will make me eternally miserable if you persist after what I have told you. Be assured I will not open any letters of yours, nor will I write again. If you wish me to think my happiness is dear to you, return my letters. If not I cannot compel you, but I hope your generosity will not permit you to make an improper use of them. For God's sake write no more. I tremble at the consequences.'

The letters which Eliza so urgently reclaimed have disappeared. Possibly Sheridan returned them and Eliza destroyed them.

The Duel (Second Act)

With Eliza under his tutelage, and a prospective suitor with well-lined pocket in the offing, old Linley again toured with his singing troupe – to Gloucester, Winchester, and back to Bath. No doubt the marriage rumours which followed his principal star did not detract from the interest of the audience. By Lent of 1773, the Fair Maid of Bath was singing in London for the first time.

The *London Magazine* heralded her appearance saying she had been sung by bards and fought for by heroes, and Fanny Burney gushed over her in her diary:

'She is believed to be very romantic. She has been very celebrated for her singing, though never till within this month has she been in London. She has met with a great variety of adventures and has had more lovers and admirers than any nymph of these times: she has been addressed by men of all ranks – I dare not pretend to say honourably, which is doubtful; but what is certain is that whatever were their designs she has rejected them all. She is really beautiful, her complexion a clear, lovely animated brown, with a bloomy colour on her cheeks, her nose that most elegant of shapes, Grecian – fine, luxurious, easy-sitting hair, a charming forehead, pretty mouth and most beautiful eyes.'

On April 2, King George III, who was a lover of oratorios, was recorded by our old friend the *Bath Chronicle* as having listened to the Linley music:

'April 2nd, Mr Linley, his son and eldest daughter (Elizabeth) were at the Queen's concert at Buckingham House; Miss Mary Linley, being ill, could not attend. The King and Queen were particularly affable; His Majesty told Mr Linley that he never in his life heard so fine a voice as his daughter's nor one so well instructed: that she was a great credit to him and presented him with a hundred pound bank note.'

The report went on to record that no one attended the concert but their Majesties, the children, and one lady, that it continued for five hours, and that no one sat, except the two performers who played on the harpsichord and the violincello, which seems to prove that the audience as well as the performers had stamina. If Eliza was not enamoured with the idea of being a performer, it was possibly because it demanded too much of her both emotionally and physically. A five-hour performance might have tired even a dray horse.

There were other disadvantages. Horace Walpole says that the King 'ogles her as much as he dares in so holy a place as an oratorio and at so devout a service as Alexander's Feast'. With the lovers estranged, the oratorios in full voice, it seemed as if true love would never triumph over its adversaries, good sense and prudence.

CHAPTER 7

Lovers' Meetings

As so often with the doings of Sheridan, his actions in the next part of the story are cloaked in mystery. There were rumours that, although he had kept his promise to his father not to see Eliza or communicate with her, he had in fact been slipping up to London and hearing her sing at Drury Lane – even, it was said, dressing up as a hackney coachman in order to drive her home after the performance – which is certainly in keeping with his dashing character and his lifelong liking for practical jokes and japes.

Her performances seemed to have reached their peak at this time when Fanny Burney wrote about her:

'She has performed this lent at the Oratorio of Drury Lane under Mr Stanley's direction. The applause and admiration she has met with, can only be compared to what is given to Mr Garrick. The whole town seems distracted about her. Every other diversion is forsaken. Miss Linley alone engrosses all eyes, ears, hearts.'

Against this background of admiration and a stream of hard cash, it was no wonder that Linley père viewed the sighs of the lovers as a threat to family prosperity. Marriage for Eliza was only to be with a man who could offer a decent percentage on the corporal capital invested. Yet love can laugh at locksmiths, foil the plans of managing fathers, abate the jealous rages of estranged lovers, and one melting glance can alter the firmest of resolutions to part forever.

Thomas Moore succinctly records the facts:

'Whatever may have caused the misunderstanding between her and her lover, a reconcilement was with no great difficulty effected, by the mediation of Sheridan's young friend Mr Ewart; and, at length, after a series of stratagems and scenes which convinced Mr Linley that it was impossible much longer to keep them asunder, he consented to their union, and on April 13, 1773, they were married by license. Mr Ewart being at the same time wedded to a young lady with whom he also had eloped clandestinely to France, but was now enabled, by the forgiveness of his father, to complete this double triumph of friendship and love.'

The young Mr Ewart seems to have had some taste for romance, since he it was who helped Sheridan to elope in the first place to France. Possibly like Lydia Languish he had a penchant for the products of circulating libraries. But at least Ewart had had the prudence to elope with an heiress. Sheridan still had his way to make in the world.

Richard Sheridan was entered at the Middle Temple on April 6, 1773, so it was possibly a promise that he could carve out a career for himself as a barrister which had caused the final collapse of Linley's objections. Added to which, Sheridan had foregone some part of Eliza's settlement from Mr Long. The rest was wisely tied up for her in Consols.

But if Mr Linley finally swallowed his financial hopes and softened, the same could not be said of Thomas Sheridan, bustling about in Dublin. He was appalled. Appalled or not, the romance was concluded with various press announcements. The *Gentleman's Magazine* was brief: 'Mr Sheridan of the Temple to the celebrated Miss Linley of Bath.' The *Morning Chronicle* three days after the wedding went into more detail:

'Tuesday was married at Marylebone Church by the Rev. Dr Booth the celebrated Miss Linley to Mr Sheridan. After the ceremony they set out with her family and friends, and dined at the Star and Garter on Richmond Hill; in the evening they had a ball after which the family and friends returned to town, and left the young couple at a gentleman's house at Mitcham to consummate their nuptials.'

Amor Omnia Vincit, including fathers, finance, and snobbery.

*

So at the age of twenty-two, Richard Sheridan had become the husband of a bride of twenty, and they settled down to honeymoon in Buckinghamshire. A month after the wedding Richard wrote to his good friend Grenville:

'I should inform you first that I have for some time been fixed in a grand little Mansion situate at a place called East Burnham about 2 miles and a half from Salt-Hill; which as an Etonian you must be acquainted with. Had I hunted five years I don't believe I could have hit on a place more to my mind, or more adapted to my present situation: were I in a descriptive vein, I would draw you some of the prettiest scenes imaginable. From my account of East Burnham you will say that Paradise was but a kitchen garden to it.'

East Burnham, although very close to industrial Slough, manages to keep a country atmosphere to this day. Beech and oak woods are interspersed with narrow twisting lanes, and the fields surrounding it can still boast a lowing herd or two. Like the enchanted honeymoon of so long ago, the name of the cottage has disappeared. But the roads down which they must have driven in their gig under the fresh spring trees remain, and the names are evocative — Thompkins Lane, Malt Cottage, East Burnham Well, and perhaps their solitary horse pulled them up Pumpkin Hill. Married lovers on fifty pounds a year can imagine that any pumpkin could turn into a rich coach, and that to a couple as well endowed as they know themselves to be, fortune could be waiting around every corner. Sheridan's letter to his friend reflects his happy and idyllic mood:

'On the whole I will assure you, as I believe it will give you more pleasure, that I feel myself absolutely and perfectly happy. As for the little Cloud which the peering eye of Prudence would descry to be gathering against the Progress of the Lune, I have a consoling Cherub that whispers me, that before They threaten an adverse Shower, a slight gale or two of Fortune will disperse them. But when a Man's married 'tis time he should leave off speaking in Metaphor. If I thought it would be entertaining to you I would send you an account of the arrangement of my Household which I assure you is conducted quite in the manner of plain Mortals, with all due attention to the Bread-and-Chesee-Feelings – I have laid aside my Design of turning Cupid into a Turnspit's Wheel, and my Meat undergoes the indignity of a Cook's handling. I have even been so far Diffident of my Wife's musical abilities as to have Carrots and Cabbage put into the Garden Ground and finding that whatever effect her Voice might have upon the Sheep on the Common, the Mutton still obstinately continued stationary at the Butchers.'

But when one is twenty-two, newly married with a beautiful wife, and it is spring, butchers' bills can be ignored. Even a day away from the beloved is too long:

> Teach me, kind Hymen, teach – for thou
> Must be my only tutor now –
> Teach me some innocent employ,
> That shall the hateful thought destroy,
> That I this whole long night must pass
> In exile from my love's embrace.

Although they remained secluded at East Burnham throughout the long summer, the world was already beating at their cottage door. Contracts for thousands of pounds for Eliza to sing were flourished temptingly in front of them. But both Richard and his bride had their faces firmly set against her singing again, and had refused to let her fulfil her former contracts. Sheridan makes plain his understanding of Eliza's position in writing to his father-in-law: 'Nor (as I wrote to Mr Isaac) can you (Linley), who gave the promise, whatever it was, be in the least charged with the breach of it, as your daughter's marriage was an event which must always have been looked to by them as quite as natural a period to your right over her as her death.' Commenting later on Sheridan's refusal to let his wife sing in public, Dr Johnson was approving. Like Sheridan, Johnson had a high sense of preserving his own dignity. 'He resolved wisely and nobly to be sure. He is a brave man. Would not a gentleman be disgraced by having his wife singing publicly for hire? No, Sir, there can be no doubt here.'

A cynic could say that with the sharp distinction which was then made between gentlemen and ladies, and mere performers, in refusing to let his wife sing to pay the bills, Sheridan had his eye on his own glittering future. He had suffered in his schooldays as being a poor player's son, and he was not going to become a mere singer's husband. He felt in himself the surge of talent, and that single handed he could pit his wits against the world, and win.

Although Eliza would have been quite willing to use her talents to augment the family exchequer, she had never liked being a performer, and was only too happy to retire. What of the two furious fathers?

Old Linley seems speedily to have decided not only to make the best of an impecunious son-in-law, but genuinely to have taken a liking to him. They were immediately engaged in friendly correspondence, even about the bills in connection with the wedding. 'Some unforeseen delays prevented my finishing with Swale till Thursday last', wrote Sheridan. John Swale was a solicitor who had arranged the details of Eliza's marriage settlement. His account came to twenty-five pounds to which Sheridan, in his usual way, managed to add another fifty which he borrowed from Swale. 'When everything was concluded', wrote Sheridan, 'I likewise settled with him for his own account, as he brought it to me, and for a *friendly* bill, it is pretty decent.' The *prix d'ami* is not always as cheap as it seems.

The other father was in Ireland, and by no means inclined to be placated. Typically, he had once more refused to have anything to do with Richard. Thomas seems all his life to have reacted in similar forms to all his distresses, either by suing people or refusing to speak to them. He wrote to his adored Charles a week after the wedding, 'I consider myself now as having no Son but *you* and therefore my anxiety about you is the greater.'

He flatly refused to meet Eliza as his daughter-in-law. Linley did his best to effect a reconciliation, but old Sheridan remained adamant. He had no use for love matches unbacked by money, and still considered that someone who taught elocution to the sons of the nobility and gentry, and had even cured a stammer in the son of an Earl, could hardly be said to be on the level of mere fiddlers and singers.

He was finished with Richard. His sisters must no longer consider him as a brother. As he wrote: 'Your sisters, too, know of no other brother, and would therefore naturally expect an increase of attention.' What the two girls Lissy and Betsy thought of the idea of losing their loved and amusing brother was not considered.

*

Spring and summer passed idyllically at East Burnham, only marred by the fact that the young couple possessed no more than a mere fifty pounds a year. There hovered the necessity of tearing a living out of a world in which privilege ruled, where gentility was precariously balanced between debts and duns, beyond which poverty yawned. Although Richard Sheridan had an ebullient optimistic nature, his was not the character to make a slow progress through the intricacies of the law. There must be some other way to make a quick profit. Almost in spite of himself, he was forced by his necessities into the profession of his father and his mother. It was not a taste for the theatre which drove him into writing plays, but the stark fact that the sheep stayed on the common unless the butcher was paid.

He had toyed with quick ways of making money from writing for some time. Before being packed off to Waltham Cross by his father he had written part of a comedy, *Jupiter*, based on a classical theme, with his friend Halhed. The solemn Mr Moore publishes extracts from this farce, with clear explanations of jokes which unhappily serve only to flatten them. Since that time Tom Moore's voice has been joined by many others. Professors and critics have burned the midnight oil, lengthily engaged on explaining jokes. Large tomes have been written, with expositions of Sheridan's method of working. Intricate exposés of the constructions of his comedies have been piled like Pelion on Ossa. There is nothing like a trowel for flattening a soufflé.

Comedy is a mood, a way of looking at things, a combination of good sense, misplaced logic, and above all, high spirits.

No one who has ever written a comedy could delve into such explanations, and nobody who has worked in the theatre could ever take the examination of a comedy seriously. This is not how a comedy is made. It is a thing of gossamer and good nature. It is a form of writing which is produced for quick effect. The plan of action, the wit, the people in the play, the fun, are things of a moment's thought. It is to wake up one morning and suddenly see the tragic as the comic, and turn the dross of life into laughter. This is something which is in the nature of the writer. It is not something which is laboured over. The original idea of a comedy is a quick picture, a sudden burst of interior laughter. And, hey presto, the characters take shape, the action is imposed on them, and in a matter of days a comedy is born.

Sheridan's nature was perfectly suited to the writing of comedies. He had a quick brain, and a ready wit. If he despised the theatre as being beneath the contempt of one who was born a gentleman, he did know the vicissitudes of the theatre and the way that plays were made. His mother had written comedies his father had written a comedy, and from his early childhood he had heard talk of comedies and tragedies and stage effects. There are some things which people do not have to learn. They know them in their bones. For comedy and tragedy and all the effects produced in the theatre are instinctive things, and the appeal of the theatre comes from the stomach, which produces tears and laughter.

A comedy is a tragedy turned upside down. But it takes a man of good humour and wit to see how this can be done, so when Sheridan sat down to make some housekeeping money, the first thing which occurred to him was to turn his own life into comedy. He remembered the duels, the sighing of the lovers, himself and Eliza, and out of them he constructed *The Rivals*. In due course the experts have got to work on this comedy. They have proved to their own satisfaction that he took Mrs Malaprop from a comedy of his mother's, *A Trip to Bath*; that Sir Lucius O'Trigger was taken from a play of his father's; that Lydia Languish was not supposed to be Eliza, that Julia was; that this character and that were plagiarized from this literary source and that.

In his preface to *The Rivals* Sheridan wrote that he had not read many plays and went on:

'Yet I own that, in one respect I did not regret my ignorance; for as my first wish in attempting a play was to avoid every appearance of plagiary, I thought I should stand a better chance of effecting this from being in a walk that I had not frequented, and where, consequently the progress of invention was less likely to be interrupted by starts of recollection; for on subjects on which the mind has been much informed, invention is slow of asserting itself. Faded ideas float in the fancy like half forgotten dreams; and the imagination in its fullest enjoyments becomes suspicious of its offspring, and doubts whether it has created or adopted.'

This passage has been singled out as showing Sheridan's duplicity, as an attempt to spike the critics' guns before they were fired.

Whether he remembered the characters in his mother's *Trip to Bath* is irrelevant. The comedy of *The Rivals* was the love affair of Sheridan and Eliza. Lydia and Julia were both Eliza, as Jack Absolute and Faulkland are both Sheridan himself. By splitting the characters down the middle Sheridan, with great skill, managed to put all the aspects of his love affair into four characters.

When Faulkland says, 'Oh Jack! When delicate and feeling souls are separated, there is not a feature in the sky, not a movement of the elements, not an aspiration of the breeze, but hints some cause for a lover's apprehension', Sheridan is making fun of his own feelings. 'What! *happy* and I away!'

His father was transformed into Sir Anthony Absolute, and all the comings and goings at Bath were made, with the witchery of wit, into brilliant and immortal comedy. He made things as he would have wished them to have been. Lydia was an heiress, Sir Anthony forgives his son, the sabre rattling is all in fun, the duel has no serious consequences and does not end in blood or threatened death as the real duel did. Once married to Eliza, Sheridan could afford to find the whole thing funny, for it had had a happy ending. All journeys should so end in lovers' meetings, that is one essential of a comedy.

Sheridan could almost have had later analysts and critics in mind when he made one of his characters say: 'It *is* a grave comedy – it was ever my opinion that the stage should be a place of rational entertainment; instead of which, I am *very* sorry to say, most people go there for their diversion.'

Comedy has been much more enduring than tragedy over the last two hundred years. Very few tragedies have survived. The suffering heroines and noble heroes have mostly been thrown into the theatrical prop basket, but Sheridan's comedies come up as fresh and bright as if they had been written yesterday.

*

In the winter of 1773, the young Sheridans left East Burnham and went up to London. For some time they lodged with Stephen Storace, a composer, and in the spring of 1774 they moved into their own house in Orchard Street, Portman Square. Mr Linley, who had by now been completely won over to the side of the young couple, furnished the house for them, and it was about this time that Sheridan wrote *The Rivals*. On November 17, 1774, he wrote to his father-in-law:

'If I were to attempt to make as many apologies as my long omission in writing to you requires, I should have no room for any other subject. One excuse only I shall bring forward, which is that I have been exceedingly employed and I believe very profitably. There will be a comedy of mine in rehearsal at Covent Garden within a few days. I did not set to work on it till within a few days of my setting out for Crome, so you may think I have not, for these last six weeks, been very idle. I have done it at Mr Harris's (the manager's) own request; it is now complete in his hands, and preparing for the stage. He, and some of his friends also who have heard it, assure me in the most flattering terms that there is not a doubt of its success. It will be very well played, and Harris tells me that the least shilling I shall get (if it succeeds) will be six hundred pounds. I shall make no secret of it towards the time of representation, that it may not lose any support my friends can give it.'

The notoriety which Sheridan had gained over his duels and despair were an asset. Anyone who had been mentioned in the public prints was cash to a theatrical manager. But real life can always break through comedy, and in the same letter Sheridan says, 'I must ease my mind on a subject that much more nearly concerns me than any point of business or profit. I must promise to you that Betsy (Eliza) is now very well, before I tell you abruptly that she has encountered another disappointment and consequent indisposition.'

It was not surprising that Sheridan approached the subject of Eliza's miscarriages with caution, for in a letter of June 26th, his father-in-law had warned him about her delicate health and mentioned her 'seminal weakness'. Linley had reinforced his message by adding starkly: 'You must absolutely keep from her, for every time you touch her, you drive a Nail in her Coffin. This must have been a terrifying message for a young man who was passionately in love with his wife. But it was a harsh age which accepted infant mortality, the sudden of the young, and the incessant pregnancies of wives, as all part of life. A beautiful wife was a gift from the gods to Sheridan, but it was a beauty which was essentially fragile.

In London the Sheridans were already being drawn into the life of fashion. Crome, which Sheridan mentions in his letter, was the house of the Earl of Coventry. And in Orchard Street the young Sheridans attracted many new friends and admirers. Although Sheridan objected to his wife singing in public, he had no objections to her singing for friends and soon his wit, and her enchanting voice, had made their house a centre of gaiety. This modish circle of friends was likely to prove an asset to Sheridan's plays.

Apparently *The Rivals* was produced anonymously, although Sheridan had not been averse to letting all his friends and acquaintances know that he was the author. Possibly it was one of those well-kept open secrets which can produce more publicity than a play with the author's name on the programme. The first night of *The Rivals* was on January 17, 1775, at

Covent Garden, and the following was the cast of the characters
on the first night:

Sir Anthony Absolute	Mr Shuter
Captain Absolute	Mr Woodward
Faulkland	Mr Lewis
Acres	Mr Quick
Sir Lucius O'Trigger	Mr Lee
Fag	Mr Lee Lewis
David	Mr Dunstal
Coachman	Mr Fearon
Mrs Malaprop	Mrs Green
Lydia Languish	Miss Barsanti
Julia	Mrs Bulkeley
Lucy	Mrs Lessingham

'This comedy', says the prim Mr Moore, 'as is well known
failed on its first representation, chiefly from the bad acting
of Mr Lee in Sir Lucius O'Trigger. Another actor, however,
Mr Clinch, was substituted in his place, and the play being
lightened of this and some other incumbrances, rose at once
into that high region of public favour, where it has continued
to float so buoyantly and gracefully ever since.'

Behind those clear, simple sentences how many theatrical
tantrums and how much green-room drama must lurk: the
sacked actor, furious at being bereft of his part: the furious
re-writing and cutting of dialogue by Sheridan, working by
candlelight. For with the fluttering of fans and bright conversation of an impateint audience, a play could be damned
and never seen again.

If eighteenth-century audiences were more restive it is not
surprising. They sat on benches without backs, and as the
house lights could not be dimmed there was a much more
intimate rapport between the actors and the audience than
there is in modern times, when a captive audience sits in the
dark. Not only could the audience see the actors, but the
actors were much more conscious of the audience. And the
audience was not disinclined to give the actors a piece of their
mind if they felt so inclined, as old Thomas Sheridan well

PERFORM'D BUT ONCE.

At the Theatre-Royal, Covent Garden,

This present WEDNESDAY, JANUARY 18, 1775,
Will be presented a NEW COMEDY call'd

The RIVALS.

The CHARACTERS by
Mr. W O O D W A R D,
Mr. S H U T E R,
Mr. L E E,
Mr. L E W I S,
Mr. Q U I C K,
Mr. L E E L E W E S,
Mr. D U N S T A L L,
Mr. F E A R O N,
Mrs. G R E E N,
Miſs. B A R S A N T I,
Mrs. L E S S I N G H A M.
And Mrs. B U L K E L E Y,
With a PROLOGUE and EPILOGUE.
And N E W S C E N E S and D R E S S E S.
To which, By Particular Desire, will be added, (the THIRTY-FIFTH TIME)

The DRUIDS.

With the ALTERATIONS, the LAST NEW SCENE and
ADDITIONAL PERFORMANCES.
Signor R O S S I G N O L,
Being his TENTH APPEARANCE HERE.
The CHARACTERS of the
PANTOMIME and DANCES as USUAL,
With NEW MUSIC, SCENES, MACHINES, HABITS and DECORATIONS.
The MUSIC composed by Mr. FISHER.
The Scenes painted by Messrs. DALL, RICHARDS, and CARVER.

☞ NOTHING under FULL PRICE will be taken.
NEW BOOKS of the Songs, Choruses, &c., will be sold in the THEATRE.

118

knew, added to which the comings and goings in the side boxes did not help the actors to maintain the illusion.

The evening's entertainment started at six or earlier in winter. As there were no numbered seats, it was the custom in London, as in Dublin, for footmen to keep the seats for the nobility and gentry until they deigned to arrive. But if the seats were not filled by the time the curtain rose then anyone who was waiting for seats could take them. This led to open disputes, with others in the audience joining in the fray about who had priority. Some of the boxes had three tiers of benches which were hinged. Dresses could be torn and hands injured by a quick twist of the wrist, and the constant banging of the seats, and muttered imprecations, was no help to the more tender passages of a play.

Should a play prove popular and all seats be filled, the doors to the pit were screwed up, irrespective of fire dangers, to prove to the disappointed customers that there was positively no room either standing or otherwise. One uncomfortable denizen of the pit who had been trapped in this way yelled out to Mrs Jordan, playing Rosalind in *As You Like It*: 'Ma'am, you lady, in boy's clothes, pray order the door to be opened or by God I shall be squeezed to death.' As late as 1798 the *Gentleman's Magazine* said, 'The spectator is obliged to ask his neighbour's leave to move his own arms and legs.'

Another disadvantage to the actors was the fashionable audience in the boxes, for as their names were written in the 'Box Book' at the entrance to the theatre, it could be referred to by any passer-by, and often the spectators were as great a draw as the actors. Notice would be taken of the dukes, duchesses, nobility and gentry who were to be present at the evening's performance. Should the play fail to hold the audience's attention, society ladies could be observed chatting and greeting their friends in their boxes. The ladies were gently illuminated by candles or lamps so that their toilettes and jewels could be seen by the *hoi-polloi*, and the actors on the stage in a shaky production thus had a good deal of competition from the feathers and furbelows in the stage boxes.

As many of the spectators could have been waiting for more

than two hours, firstly in the street for the doors to be opened, and then jostling in the entrances to buy their un-numbered tickets, by the time they had finally fought their way to their seats they were in no mood for second rate entertainment.

A German traveller remarked:

> 'Before the doors are opened, there is generally for an hour and longer such a crowd, and such a mobbing, that many a one, who perhaps is inclined to see a play performed, stays away, because he does not like to be jostled about for such a length of time, among a multitude where the least politeness is entirely out of the question and where pickpockets are extremely busy.'

An additional hazard to success was that the theatres were unheated in the winter, and unventilated in the summer. It was not until 1796 that an elegant fireplace was introduced into the Royal Stage Box at Covent Garden Theatre 'to the great surprise and no less comfort of their Majesties', said the *Morning Herald*.

Against this background it was not surprising if the success of Sheridan's first comedy trembled in the balance. After the first night, the critics were divided. One said that the 'very imperfections of the play showed the man of genius, the gentleman and the scholar'. But others voted it a bungle, and insufferably tedious. Some critics took exception to the natural dialogue, and Mrs Malaprop was voted 'an exotic beyond the wilds of nature'. One correspondent called it a 'gulph of malevolence'.

The actors did not come off much better. Lydia was informed she was a mere 'mimic'; Lewis, who played Faulkland, was said to have 'struggled with a very difficult character'. Shuter (Sir Anthony) forgot his lines, and Woodward (Captain Absolute) was flattered by being told that he had 'often appeared to greater advantage'. The actors who played Lucy and Acres 'exhibited their accustomed pert maid and country bumpkin'. But the main fury of the critics was against Sir Lucius O'Trigger. This was 'an affront to common sense, and so far from giving the manners of our brave and worthy neighbours (the Irish) that it scarcely equals the picture of a respectable Hotentot' [*sic*].

On the second night the part of O'Trigger was given to Clinch. But this had little effect at first, and Sheridan in despair wanted to withdraw his piece. But in one of those last minute conferences which are, and always will be, part of theatre life, Harris, the manager, persuaded Sheridan that with a little cutting and revision the play could get by, and the *Morning Chronicle* smugly recorded that the author, 'willing to show his obedience to the will of the town, withdraws his comedy that he may prune, correct and alter it, till he thinks it worthy of the public favour'.

Eliza was at Slough when the news of the disaster reached her. Her reaction was curious:

'My dear Dick, I am delighted. I always knew that it was impossible that you could make anything by writing plays; so now there is nothing for it but my beginning to sing publickly again, and we shall have as much money as we like.'

The usual offers for Eliza to sing were immediately forthcoming, but Sheridan was still adamant. 'No', he said. 'That shall never be. I see where the fault was; the play was too long and the parts were badly cast. I profited by his (Harris's) judgment and experience in the curtailing of it – till, I believe, his feeling for the vanity of a young author got the better of his desire for correctness, and he left many excrescences remaining because he had assisted in pruning so many more. Many other errors there were which might in part have arisen from my being by no means conversant with plays in general, either in reading or at the theatre.'

The hurried changes were made, and the play reappeared on January 28, 1775. It was played on the same night as a 'new musical entertainment called *The Two Misers*'. It should here be explained that an evening's entertainment at the theatre at this time commenced with what could be called a warm-up with a 'good band of musick'. They usually played two or three selections. If the audience did not like their choice of airs, they would call for something which was more to their taste. After the music came the prologue, then the main play which had two intervals of approximately ten minutes, and then a two-act afterpiece. The afterpiece could be a comedy, a farce, a burletta (an entertainment with music and dancing) or even at times shortened versions of Shakespeare's plays, either tragedies or comedies. Luckily for Sheridan his piece did not have to compete with a slice of *Measure for Measure* or *Romeo and Juliet*.

After the cuts in obedience to the will of the town, the critics changed their tune about *The Rivals*. Although they were still complaining about Lydia, and the attacks on lending libraries, they were even disposed to regret some of the cuts he had made, including Lydia's idea of real love: 'How often have I stole forth, in the coldest night in January, and found him in the garden stuck like a dripping statue! And while the freezing blast numbed our joints, how warmly would he press me to pity his flame and glow with mutual ardour! Ah Julia, that was something *like* being in love.'

The comedy ran for fourteen nights, which was a very long run. Sheridan's name and reputation were made, but as often with plays, it had been touch and go. Eliza's favourite sister, Mary Linley, wrote to her about the family's hopes and fears:

'My dearest Eliza,
We are all in the greatest anxiety about Sheridan's play – though I do not think there is the least doubt of its succeeding. I was told last night that it was his own story, and therefore called *The Rivals*, but I do not give any credit to this intelligence.'

Possibly the family were bored with scandals about Eliza's suitors, and the human mind is always inclined to believe what it wants to believe. Mary added more practically, 'I am told he will get at least £700 for his play.' After the productions and the revisions she wrote again:

Bath, January 1775.
'It is impossible to tell you what pleasure we felt at the

receipt of Sheridan's last letter, which confirmed what we had seen in the newspapers of the success of his play. The *knowing ones* were very much disappointed, as they had so very bad an opinion of its success.'

An author can always rely on a circle of friends for discouragement.

'After the first night we were indeed all very fearful that the audience would go very much against it. But now, there can be no doubt of its success, as it has certainly got through more difficulties than any comedy which has not met its doom the first night.'

Later, presumably after reading the play in Bath, she wrote again in a high state of excitement.

Bath, February 18, 1775.
'What shall I say of *The Rivals*! – a compliment must naturally be expected; but really it goes so far beyond any thing I *can* say in its praise, that I am afraid my modesty must keep me silent. When you and I meet I shall be able better to explain myself, and tell you how much I am delighted with it. We expect to have it here very soon; it is now in rehearsal. You pretty well know the merits of our principal performers.'

But she gives the cast with pertinent comments on some of the actors whose work, perhaps, her sister did not know:

'Faulkland . . . Mr Diamond (a new actor of great merit, and a sweet figure).
'Miss Lydia . . . Miss Wheeler (Literally a very pretty romantic girl of seventeen).'

This last was obviously a nice piece of contemporary type casting.
After the production, Mary reported delightedly:

123

'I waited the success of Sheridan's play in Bath; for, let me tell you, I look upon our theatrical tribunal though not in *quantity*, in *quality* as good as yours, and I do not believe there was a critic in the whole city that was not there. But, in my life, I never saw anything go off with such uncommon applause. There was a very full house, nor did I hear, for the honour of your Bath actors, one single prompt the whole night; but I suppose the poor creatures never acted with shouts of applause in their lives, so that they were incited by that to do their best. They lost many of Malaprop's good sayings by the applause; in short, I never saw or heard any thing like it; – before the actors spoke, they began their clapping. There was a new scene of the North Parade, painted by a Mr Davis, and a most delightful one it is, I assure you. Everybody says that yours in town is not so good. Most of the dresses were entirely new, and very handsome. We only wanted a good Julia to have made it quite complete. You must know that it was entirely out of Mrs Didier's style of playing.'

As Mr Didier was playing Captain Absolute, he had obviously wangled a part for his wife to the detriment of the play. These are the hazards of comedies. Many a good one has doubtless foundered becasue the manager put his mistress in a key part. The startling success of Sheridan's comedy had the effect of adding impetus to the young couple's social success in London. Thomas Moore says:

'The celebrity which Sheridan had acquired as the chivalrous lover of Miss Linley was, of course, considerably increased by the success of the Rivals; and gifted as he and his beautiful wife were with all that forms the magnetism of society – the power to attract, and the disposition to be attracted – their life, as may easily be supposed, was one of gaiety both at home and abroad. Though little able to cope with the entertainments of their wealthy acquaintance, her music, and the good company which his talents drew around him were an ample repayment for the more solid hospitalities which they received.'

Moore only hints that in return for musical parties at Orchard Street, their wealthy friends asked them for long visits to their country houses. As a country house visit could then last a month or two, these long stays must have been some relief to the family exchequer, as well as propelling the young Sheridans into the society which Richard coveted.

The *Morning Post* of February 4, 1774, was more explicit, and reported that they were 'fitting up a music room where concerts would be given twice a week for the nobility'. Sheridan's sister wrote:

'Mr and Mrs Sheridan gave some private concerts at their house in Orchard-street, Portman Square as a return for the civilities and hospitality they received from many persons of fashion and consequence. A music-room was accidentally annexed to their house, and it was the least expensive entertainment they could give; the performers consisting entirely of Mrs Sheridan's family. But these concerts were given as the discharge of a debt of civility already incurred. No money was ever received, nor were any such concerts given at Bath.'

There was a vast 'gulph' between taking money for singing, and paying back country house visits with a concert given at home.

In the context of the hectic social life into which they were gradually being drawn, Eliza's letter expressing delight at the original failure of the play is understandable. Possibly she realized that once drawn into the great world her life with Sheridan would be totally transformed. In spite of her dislike of 'coming before the publick', she was prepared to sing if shi could preserve their life together. She seems to have known instinctively that public success would produce a change in their relationship. She also knew, in spite of her love for him, Sheridan's weaknesses, his procrastination, his sudden fits of melancholy which contrasted with his gaiety. She must also have feared the impact of the large rich world, of the town palaces and country houses, on someone who had not the means to back up his pretensions. But she loved him and believed in him, and knowing his dangerous ambitions she yet bowed to them. As Sheridan saw it, this was only a start, a way of making money, and at a time when precedence and place led to patronage and jobs, it was also a way of making useful friends, who might lead him to a life of politics which would lift him out of the theatrical rut of a 'mere player's son'.

As he wrote to Grenville, 'I shall one of these days learnedly confute the idea that God could ever have intended individuals to fill up any particular Stations in which the accidents of Birth or Fortune may have flung them. The Track of a Comet is as regular to the eye of God as the orbit of a Planet.' That he saw himself as a comet is not in doubt. But the track of a comet, although it gives a brilliant light, can be temporary. However, when a man is young, clever and in love, there are no ends to his ambitions, and Sheridan saw ambition as a virtue not a vice.

'It has been an everlasting Fashion to declaim against the Pursuits of Ambition, and the expectation of Happiness in the scenes of publick life. Yet, may we not with some justice attempt to prove, that there is to be found a surer Foundation to build on, than in any of the most captivating roads of private, and comparatively solitary Enjoyments. Envy is the attendant on Greatness – a Prince's Smiles are not to be depended on – The association of Men in Power is full of Jealousy and Distrust. The voice of the People is inconstant – True – But does malice never reach a private Station? Are the smiles of Friendship never deceitful? Do we never meet with ill-will from our Companions – and does the syren voice of Love never turn to Discord, or court other auditors?'

He went on to say that if a man based his life on his wife, mistress, or friends, then they might die, and 'the calm and secluded mode of his Living, which formed one of its chief comforts, must in that case be one of the chief causes of his extreme disquiet'. But true ambition, he declared, could never be disappointed, it hoped most when most oppressed, Eliza had a formidable rival to her charms in Ambition, as outlined by Sheridan writing from deep conviction to his friend, in 1772.

There was no doubt that their life together 'trembled upon the edge of perilous possibilities'. Sheridan's comedy completed the fame brought by Eliza's voice, and Orchard Street became a magnet. Apart from the Earl of Coventry with whom they stayed at Crome, there was a rich Mr Coote, at whose musical parties Eliza frequently sang, accompanied occasionally by the two little daughters of Mr Coote, who were the originals of the children introduced into Sir Joshua Reynolds' portrait of Eliza as St Cecilia. Apparently it was her voice which had been the original attraction for Sir Joshua; but their acquaintance had started badly.

Sir Joshua had planned a musical party, at which he expected Eliza to sing. As she was to be the star attraction of the evening he had invited a large company, and even bought himself a new pianoforte in anticipation of the musical treats in store for his guests. Having first asked the Sheridans to dinner, and presumably installed his new piano, Sir Joshua then let drop a heavy hint to Sheridan that Eliza was supposed to sing. The young man's pride was immediately touched. Even if it were true that, as a couple, they were expected to sing for their supper, it had to be done more tactfully. He gave Sir Joshua a dusty answer, saying that with his assent she had resolved never to sing again in a public company.

Presumably social etiquette drew a fine distinction between singing in her own home, and performing at the houses of others. Sir Joshua, pardonably annoyed at the purchase of the piano, and the dashed hopes of his guests, said, 'What reason could they think I had in inviting them to dinner, unless it was to hear her sing? – for she cannot talk.'

But Eliza was not apparently as touchy about her singing as her husband. Mr Rogers, a contemporary, wrote:

'Hers was truly "a voice of the cherub choir", and she was always ready to sing without any pressing. She sung here a great deal, and to my infinite delight; but what had a peculiar charm was, that she used to take my daughter, then a child, on her lap, and sing a number of childish songs with such a playfulness of manner, and such a sweetness of look and voice, as was quite enchanting.'

However, when Sir Joshua had recovered from his musical huff, he became a great friend of the young couple. It was then he captured forever on canvas that picture of Eliza singing to the children which is painted in words by Mr Rogers. But already the finger of the future was pointing the way of success to Sheridan, and Eliza was to sing for money no more.

In 1775, Dr Johnson had published his pamphlet on America called 'Taxation no Tyranny', which supported the government in its attitude to American taxation. Moore says this pamphlet is a work 'whose pompous sarcasm on the Congress of Philadelphia, when compared with what has happened since, dwindle into puerilities upon the great tide of events are even the mightiest intellects of this world'.

Drawn towards politics as he had always been since his first attempts at writing, Sheridan began an answer to Dr Johnson. Sheridan apparently intended to attack Dr Johnson on the ground that his reasoning was coloured by his acceptance of a pension from the government, and that therefore his opinions were distorted by venality. 'It is hard', he wrote, 'when a learned man thinks himself obliged to commence politician. Such pamphlets will be as trifling and insincere as the venal quit-rent of a birth-day ode. Dr J's other works, his learning and infirmities, fully entitled him to such a mark of distinction. There was no call on him to become politician.' Sheridan adds, 'Men seldom think deeply on subjects on which they have no choice of opinion: they are fearful of encountering obstacles to their faith (as in religion), and so are content with the surface.'

One of Johnson's opinions to which Sheridan objected was a sentence where he says, 'As all are born the subjects of some state or other, we may be said to have been all born consenting to some system of government.' Sheridan dismisses this as a most slavish doctrine. Johnson supported the right of conquest, on which opinion Sheridan remarked: 'This is the worst doctrine that can be with respect to America. If America is ours by conquest, it is the conquerors who settled there that are to claim these powers.' But Sheridan's pamphlet was never published; it remained merely a fragment.

Some critics of Sheridan have said that his duplicity was

8 *Above:* Bath: the Pump Room. *Below:* Bath: the Royal Crescent

9   Mrs Sheridan and Mrs Tickell. *Painting by Gainsborough*

again shown in his dealings with Johnson, for after refuting the Doctor's arguments in the strongest terms he afterwards wrote a prologue to Savage's play, *Sir Thomas Overbury*, in which he referred to Johnson's *Life of Savage* in flattering terms. It is undeniably an unattractive trait to condemn in private and flatter in public, but it could be that Sheridan's view of Dr Johnson was in the first instance coloured by the fact that Thomas Sheridan regarded him as one of his many enemies. Equally it could be said that it is possible to disagree politically with a man, and admire him in other ways.

CHAPTER 8

Annus Mirabilis

The Rivals was produced at the beginning of the year 1775, and in May of the same year, Sheridan wrote *St Patrick's Day*, a short farce. It was written as an act of gratitude to Clinch, the actor who had saved the day as Sir Lucius O'Trigger, and was given as a benefit for him. Clinch had a large and needy family, and Sheridan was determined that the actor should profit considerably from his benefit.

It should perhaps be mentioned here that benefit nights formed an important part of the theatrical scene at this time. Actors and actresses sold tickets personally to their distinguished friends for these occasions, and when it came to fixing salaries, the possibilities of earning larger sums from personal benefits were taken into consideration by the management. When Sheridan's father was arranging with actors to come over to Dublin, he mentions over and over again that he must pay higher salaries in Dublin to attract the actors otherwise they would not come, for they must have some compensation for the loss of their benefit nights.

When the principal actors and actresses called politely on their friends the tickets were often neat little engravings in the taste of the period, adorned with classically draped ladies, cupids playing on pipes, or carrying torches. One card with pink, blue and gold painted edges says merely, 'Admit two to boxes. S. Siddons.' The actors very often gained large sums from 'waiting on' their friends, and grand hostesses often paid several hundred pounds for benefit boxes, so presumably the actor, even if he were forced to play tradesman, had a tradesman's reward.

Even the workers had their benefit nights. 'Mr Clanfield the fireworker most respectfully entreats the kind assistance of his friends on the present occasion and humbly hopes they will be punctual in having his tickets as the only method to render him essential service.'

Sometimes most of the proceeds of the sale of tickets went to the actor concerned, with a proportion to the management; and at other times, depending on the drawing power of the actor, they took a smaller proportion. *St Patrick's Day* was in this context a big 'thank you' present from the grateful playwright. The farce was written at great speed, and like most of Sheridan's work for the stage, it has a fresh liveliness.

The soldiers agree to 'argue in platoons', and their grumbles about the pubs could have been written yesterday: 'The Red Lion an't half the Civility . . . the two Magpies are civil enough; but the Angel uses us like devils, and the Rising Sun refuses us light to go to bed by.'

When the girl, Lauretta, defending her right to love a soldier says, 'No, give me the bold upright youth who makes love today and has his head shot off tomorrow,' Mrs Credulous replies, 'Oh, barbarous! to want a husband that may wed you today and then in a twelvemonth to have him come like a Colossus, with one leg at New York and the other at Chelsea Hospital.' And when Justice Credulous says, 'I won't die', and his wife replies, 'Psha, there's nothing in it', the reply has a fine flavour of Sheridan: 'Aye, but it leaves a numbness behind that lasts for a plaguey long time.'

The farce was a great success, and Sheridan went on to an even greater success with *The Duenna*. By the autumn of 1775, the play was written and Sheridan was in active correspondence with his father-in-law about the music for it. These letters give an insight into the mind of a man who was now at home in his medium, and who knew his audience, and its limitations. The remarks are swift, sure, and pertinent, and in strange contrast to his letters to social and political friends which seem to reveal a mind which is striving primarily for effect. To Thomas Linley, he wrote:

'Dear Sir,

We received your songs today, with which we are exceedingly pleased. I shall profit by your proposed alterations. but I'd have you to know that we are much too chaste in

NEVER PERFORM'D

At the Theatre-Royal, Covent Garden,

This prefent TUESDAY, November 21, 1775,
Will be prefented a New COMIC OPERA, call'd

The D U E N N A :

OR THE

DOUBLE ELOPEMENT.

The PRINCIPAL CHARACTERS by

Mr. M A T T O C K S,

Mr. Q U I C K,

Mr. W I L S O N,

Mr. D U B E L L A M Y,

Mr. M A H O N,

Mr. WEWITZER, Mr. FOX, Mr. BAKER,

AND

Mr. L E O N I.

Miss B R O W N,

Mrs. G R E E N,

Mrs. M A T T O C K S,

The MUSIC partly NEW and partly selected from the most EMINENT COMPOSERS.
With a NEW OVERTURE, SCENES, DRESSES, and other DECORATIONS.

End of Act II. a new SPANISH DANCE

By Signor & Signora ZUCHELLI, & Mr. DAGUVILLE,
Signora V I D I N I, &c.

To which will be added (not acted here these Ten Years)

The LYING VALET.

Sharp (First Time) by Mr. L E E L E W E S,
Gayless by Mr. D A V I S,
Justice Guttle by Mr. BOOTH, Dick by Mr. JONES,
Beau Trippet by Mr. W E W I T Z E R,
Meliffa by Miss A M B R O S E.
Mrs. Gadabout, Mrs. POUSSIN, Trippet, Mrs. MASTERS,
Kitty Pry by Mrs. P I T T.

BOOKS of the SONGS in the OPERA to be had at the Theatre.
The Doors to be open at Five o'clock, to begin exactly at Six.

[*Vivant Rex et Regina.*

London to admit such strains as your Bath spring inspires. We dare not propose a peep beyond the ancle on any account; for the critics in the pit at a new play are much great prudes than the ladies in the boxes.'

Sheridan had clearly learned his lesson from the first production of *The Rivals*, and was determined to go all out to charm and please, and to leave any dubious passages out of his plays in the future. Reading between the lines of the current taste it could be said that Victorian prudery was casting its first shadow in the late eighteenth century. The striving for good taste and good manners which is so apparent in Jane Austen, and in Sheridan's own adaptation and bowdlerization of *The Relapse* (*The Trip to Scarborough*), had already begun. And good taste demanded that all jokes which could be regarded as near the knuckle were to be rejected, and nothing which would bring a blush to the cheek of a girl could now be permitted in the theatre. Sheridan implored his father-in-law to come to town:

'In short, unless you can give us three days in town, I fear our Opera will stand a chance to be ruined. Harris is extravagantly sanguine of its success as to plot and dialogue, which is to be rehearsed next Wednesday at the theatre (Covent Garden). They will exert themselves to the utmost in the scenery etc. but I never saw anyone so disconcerted as he was at the idea of there being no one to put them in the right way as to music. He entreated me in the most pressing terms to write instantly to you, and wanted, if he thought it could be any weight, to write himself.

As to the state of the music, I want but three more airs, but there are some glees and quintets in the last act, that will be inevitably ruined, if we have no one to set the performers at least in the right way.'

Sheridan said that they were hoping to have a rehearsal of the music at his house in Orchard Street, 'tomorrow se'nnight', but he added, 'Every hour's delay is a material injury both to the opera and the theatre.' A few days later he wrote again, and his letter gives an interesting sidelight into the methods of composition, for it seems as if Linley had not read the whole play before composing the music, or possibly had not read any of it.

Sheridan referred to the actor, Leoni, who was to play Don Carlos, in *The Duenna*:

'I cannot briefly explain to you the character and situation of the persons on the stage with him. The first, a dialogue between Quick and Mrs Mattocks, I would wish to be a pert, sprightly air; for though some of the words mayn't seem suited to it, I should mention that they are neither of them earnest in what they say. Leoni takes it up seriously, and I want him to show himself advantageously in the six lines beginning "Gentle maid". I should tell you that he sings nothing *well*, but in a plaintive or pastoral style; and his voice is such as appears always to be hurt by much accompaniment. I have observed too, that he never gets so much applause as when he makes a cadence [cadenza].'

These are the observations of someone aware of his audience. He ends:

'I like particularly the returning to, "O the days when I was young!" We have mislaid the notes, but Tom [Eliza's brother] remembers it. If you don't like it for words will you give us one? And it must be *funny*.'

Part of the success of the music for *The Duenna* was due to the fact that Linley (and Sheridan) had skilfully used well-known airs, in some instances with new words. 'How Merrily we live', and 'Let's drink and let's sing' are to be sung by a company of friars over their wine. 'The words will be parodied, and the chief effect I expect from them must arise from their being *known*; for the joke will be much less for these jolly fathers to sing any new thing than to give what the audience are used to annex the idea of jollity to.'

Richard Sheridan had no ear for music but he had an instinctive understanding of the effect he was seeking as a playwright. It was here that his wife's exquisite taste in music and deep knowledge of the musical art was of enormous benefit to him. There is no doubt that at this point in his career, and indeed later, she helped him in many ways.

There is a pathetic little appeal from Eliza, written as a postscript to one of Sheridan's letters, urging Thomas Linley to come to London. 'Dearest father, I shall have no spirits or hopes of the opera, unless we see you. Eliza Ann Sheridan.' Thomas Linley may have been a hard taskmaster to Eliza in her singing career, but she obviously had a high regard for his musical abilities and talents, and now that the troubles of his disapproval of her marriage had been satisfactorily resolved, and son-in-law and father had been reconciled, she relied on his musical judgment implicitly. Linley and Sheridan seem to have made at this time an excellent and practical theatrical team, and to have brought out the best in one another without fuss or temperament, a tribute to their characters, which seem to have been without conceit when it came to the theatre.

Another insight into the slapdash way of writing and composing for the contemporary theatre is given by Sheridan's off-hand remark about the verse: 'For the other things Betsy [Eliza] mentioned, I only wish to have them with such accompaniment as you would put to their *present* words, and I shall have got words to my liking for them by the time they reach me', which has a touch of tin-pan alley about it.

But at this time Sheridan was in the first flush of his energy and his success. He was practical, sensible, and hard working. Yet in spite of all the rush and excitement, he had time to think about his family. Thomas Sheridan was still sulking in his theatrical tent, although he was still acting: '*Cato*, by Mr Sheridan being his first appearance on the stage these sixteen years.' But in the midst of the hurry and bustle of his own Covent Garden production, Richard referred to his father's work. 'My father was astonishingly well received on Saturday night in *Cato*. I think it will not be many days before we are reconciled.' But there the forgiving son reckoned without the father's obstinacy. There is no doubt that Richard felt his father's estrangement deeply, for not only was he cut off from him, but also from his much loved sisters.

During the run of one of Richard's plays, he heard from an old family servant that his father was taking his two sisters, Betsy and Lissy, to see the play. Sheridan watched them in their box from the wings during most of the play. When he returned home he was so overcome with melancholy at his remembrances of the past that he burst into tears. Eliza, who had not previously seen the really dark side of his nature, questioned him as to why he was so overcome with sadness in the midst of his success and reported, 'He owned how deeply it had gone to his heart to think that *there* sat his father and his sisters before him, and yet that he alone was not permitted to go near them or to speak to them.' At the time of his elopement, duels, and marriage, they had been partners in his confidences and part of his life. Yet now at this time of success they were as far away from him as they had been when he had been sent to school. The child who wept in his solitude at Harrow was father to the man who wept bitterly at his own triumph.

Everyone likes to share success, and Sheridan at this point in his life might have been pardoned for thinking that an actor who knew how hardly theatrical success was won might have spoken a word of praise to his son who had won it.

The year 1775 was the *annus mirabilis* in Sheridan's life. In January *The Rivals* was produced, on May 2nd his farce *St Patrick's Day* won acclaim, and in November, four days before *The Duenna* opened to equal success, his son Tom was born. *The Duenna* proved to be the greatest money-maker of the three plays. It played for seventy-five nights on its first run, and became even more successful than the *Beggar's Opera*. Money was now pouring in to replenish the young Sheridans' coffers. Owing to their rich friends and lavish style of living it was pouring out just as quickly. But Sheridan's sanguine temperament had already set his eyes on fresh fields to conquer: Garrick, owner of the Drury Lane patent, was about to retire. The two patent theatres of Covent Garden and Drury Lane had the monopoly of producing straight plays, and on this account the owner of a patent had a lucrative property.

Garrick with good and careful mangement, and the drawing power of his own genius, had made a considerable fortune from Drury Lane. He had won an equally great reputation for parsimony. But running a theatre is like housekeeping, it has to be done with prudence. Small things make all the difference between profit and loss, and the small things had been attended to by Garrick. As a result the profits went up under his management. In 1771, on an expenditure of £26,410, the income was £32,548, netting him a profit of over six thousand. By the end of his time at Drury Lane the income had risen to nearly £38,000 and though the expenses were running at over £33,000, there was still a fine profit. This was achieved by paying attention to details such as fruit and sweetmeat concessions, leasing out the vaults under the theatre to wine merchants, making the collection of candle ends part of the housekeeper's salary, and even melting down the tarnished gold lace on used costumes in order to recover the gold. Other sources of revenue were the sale of old costumes, and fines paid by actors for non-appearance.

The expenditure on new scenery and costumes could be considerable, for the audience at this time demanded spectacle. This in its turn necessitated a considerable number of people being employed at the theatre. At Drury Lane there were nearly a hundred actors, actresses, singers, and dancers, as well as nearly forty 'house servants', numerous barbers, dressers, and charwomen, as well as scene painters, fireworkers and scenemen. Garrick's payroll at the time of his retirement was over £500 a week, a large sum at a time when a servant could be paid a few shillings a week.

Apart from other difficulties a theatre manager had to contend with the exorbitant demands of leading actors. Under Garrick's management actors like Spranger Barry, Charles Macklin and John Lee could demand up to one-third of the night's receipts. Spranger Barry at the height of his success demanded a third of the nightly receipts above £80. On his benefit night he did not even pay the usual house charges, which meant that the theatre had to stand the expenses while he cleared the profit. This famous Romeo had a greater eye on the box office than he had on Juliet.

While it might be said that a profit of £4,000 on an outlay of £38,000 was a reasonable profit to make, being over ten per cent, this profit was only obtained with great difficulty and cheeseparing, and Rich, at Covent Garden, had found it just as easy to make a loss. Added to his profit on the theatre, Garrick also netted £400 as an author, £800 as an actor, and £500 as manager, each year.

A sharp eye was kept on the money which actually came in. To this end tellers were employed whose job it was to check the number of people in the house with the money taken for the various seats, and a constant reckoning took place. There were three offices for this, a 'Box Office' for the sale of boxes, a First Gallery Office, and an Upper Gallery Office. Each had two men to look after them, a Keeper and an Assistant. These in their turn were supervised by others described as Cheques. There were Cheques on the Box Office Keeper, the First Gallery Office Keeper, and on the Upper Gallery Office Keeper, as well as two 'numberers' counting the people in each house. There was little chance of seat money disappearing, and nobody trusted anybody.

The method of taking profit at the end of the season was simple. The manager paid all the bills and pocketed the sum left over. The following season the theatre started again from scratch with such income as they had left over from the sale of costumes, candle ends, and fruit concessions. Sometimes the cash in hand only just met the expenses of scene painting, and the buying of new costumes, so the season would start with a deficit. Consequently the actors' salaries had to be met out of the money which came in to the box office.

It was into this world of candle ends and hardly-gained profits that Sheridan proposed to launch himself, and found his fortune. His hopes ran high, for Garrick had been impressed with the young man's gifts, and the idea of handing over Drury Lane to a successful playwright seemed to have advantages.

Suddenly, from being a penniless young man of twenty-five, Sheridan found himself likely to be launched into the great London entertainment world on a managerial level, and with his sanguine temperament he began to treat the large sums involved in the purchase of the theatre in much the same lofty way that he had written to his sister Betsy about Mr Evill's bill for neat foils and lockets. He wrote to Thomas Linley, indicating that Garrick was a wise and wily bird:

'According to his [Garrick's] demand, the whole is value at £70,000. He appears very shy of letting his books be looked into, as the test of the profits on this sum, but says it must be, in its nature, a purchase on speculation. However, he had promised me a rough estimate, of his own, of the entire receipts for the last seven years. One point he solemnly avers, which is, that he will never part with it under the price above-mentioned. That is all I can say on the subject till Wednesday, though I can't help adding, that I think we might *safely* give five thousand pounds more on this purchase than richer people. The whole valued at £70,000, the annual interest is £3,500; while this is *cleared*, the proprietors are *safe*, but I think it must be *infernal* management indeed that does not double it.'

There spoke the tyro. It always seems simple to make a theatrical profit when one does not have to do the theatrical accountancy. Sheridan's eyes were not on candle ends and actors' benefit nights. He was looking forward to many golden campaigns, as he put it, should the negotiations with Garrick succeed.

Sheridan was busy in other directions, for he adds at the end of the letter: 'I am finishing a two-act comedy for Covent-Garden which will be in rehearsal in a week. We have given *The Duenna* a respite this Christmas, but nothing else at present brings money. We have every place in the house taken for the next three nights, and shall, at least, play it fifty nights with only Friday's intermission.'

At this time Garrick was still acting, and by a stroke of irony revived Sheridan's mother's play, *The Discovery* at Drury Lane, in which he played the principal part, in order to try to find a draw equal to *The Duenna*. It was said that the old woman, the Duenna, would be the death of the old man, Garrick.

But Garrick was determined to retire and so the negotiations for the purchase of his patent began to wind their tortuous way to a close. Most of Sheridan's contemporaries found it incredible that a penniless young man should have suddenly been able to raise an immense sum, and within a few short months find himself the virtual owner of Drury Lane. Later, when friends asked him how he had done it, he was accustomed to mutter something about the 'philosopher's stone'.

But his philosophers' stone was simply an enormous and delicate superstructure of loan piled on loan, of mortgage on mortgage, and promised annuity on promised annuity. Everything had been flung into the melting pot on the promise of future profits, and Sheridan himself had only needed to raise some £1,300. This sum he had attempted to secure with the aid of his wife's jointure, but fortunately without success.

The purchase of Drury Lane was in fact achieved by a most complicated system, borrowing from both Peter and Paul, and promising to pay interest to both. If *The Rivals* was written about Sheridan's fighting and wooing, and *The Duenna* founded on his elopement, the scenes in *The School for Scandal* where Charles Surface deals with the money-lender were to be equally well-rooted in fact.

Sheridan's purchase of Drury Lane was not entirely plain sailing for a new purchaser, the actor George Colman, appeared on the scene. But he wanted the whole patent or nothing, and Garrick had been in partnership with a man called Lacy, whose son Willoughby Lacy had inherited his father's share in the patent. Willoughby Lacy, a rich, idle young man was not prepared to sell, which left Sheridan free to buy himself into management.

On January 4, 1776, Sheridan wrote to Linley: 'I meet Garrick again tomorrow evening, when we are to name a day for a conveyancer on our side to meet his solicitor.' At this point in his career Sheridan gave the impression of being a good business man and in his letters about the sale he writes about limitations of patent, tenures of house and adjoining estate, and repair of premises with ease and expertise. Being a man of quick intelligence he was able to seize the essential points, and impelled by the idea of the profits to be made from such a sound proposition as the Drury Lane patent, he gave his whole energies to the end in view.

There is no doubt that he had impressed Garrick as a man

of the theatre who would valiantly carry on the work which had been so successfully conducted for so many years. An old man retiring at the pinnacle of his success likes to hand over to someone who is going to appreciate and foster his life's work. Garrick was like an old farmer who has manured and tended his fields for many years and, reaching an age when his energies are fading, hands over to a younger man who has the vision and strength to keep the fields fertile. When the negotiations were at the point of being concluded Sheridan wrote to Linley: 'We should, after this, certainly, make an interest to get the King's promise, that, while the theatre is well conducted he will grant no patent for a third – though Garrick seems confident he never will. If there is any truth in professions and appearances G. seems likely always to continue our friend and to give every assistance in his power.'

The financial division was: Ewart (Sheridan's old friend who had helped him at the time of his elopement) to take £10,000; Mr Linley, £10,000; Richard Sheridan, £10,000, and a Dr Ford the remaining £5,000. Kitty Clive, the long time comedy partner of Garrick, was excessively amused at the list of the patent purchasers. 'What a strange jumble of people they have put in the papers as the purchasers of the patent! I thought I should have died with laughing when I saw a man-midwife (Dr Ford) among them: I suppose they have taken him in to prevent *miscarriages*! I have some opinion of Mr Sheridan, as I hear everybody say that he is very sensible: he has a divine wife, and I loved his mother dearly.'

In a very short time, just a few months, the scenery of Sheridan's life had been struck, and from love in a cottage, the background had been transformed – £10,000 here or there was a bagatelle, £5,000 was a trifling sum which could be raised in this way or that but not a sum which anyone needed to give too much thought to.

Linley himself had raised his £10,000 from an 'anonymous person' who let him have the money at four per cent. Linley's £10,000 share was, in fact, raised by giving Garrick, the 'anonymous person', a mortgage on property which he had in Bath, as well as a lien on the share in the theatre. There is no doubt that then, as now, financial affairs in the theatre, or anywhere else for that matter, were like a cat's-cradle. As long as the strings hold it is useless to enquire how it is managed.

*

With the coming of Richard's success, Thomas Sheridan was beginning to allow himself to be won over. To an actor and erstwhile manager, a son, however recalcitrant, who had one of the London patent theatres in his pocket was no longer an asset which could be ignored. Swallowing his pride, he offered his services to the new management on their own terms. Sheridan took note, and was also engaged in trying to persuade Thomas Linley to seek his fortune solely in London, expressing surprise at any hesitation on the part of his father-in-law.

The city of Bath, the university where Richard had learned about life, had loved and won his wife, was already a small backwater in his life. The young man with all before him holds out glittering prospects to his elder statesman in the theatre, and writes to give him the courage and élan which he feels in himself:

'You represent your situation of mind between *hopes* and *fears*. I am afraid I should argue in vain (as I have often on this point before) were I to tell you that it is always better to encourage the former than the latter. It may be very prudent to mix a little *fear* by way of alloy with a good solid mass of *hope*; but you, on the contrary, always deal in *apprehension* by the pound, and take *confidence* by the grain, and spread as thin as leaf gold. In fact, though a metaphor mayn't explain it, the truth is, that, in all undertakings which depend principally on ourselves, the surest way not to fail is to *determine to succeed*.'

The tide was about to be in flood and was to lead on to fortune, not only for himself but for all those around him.

Meanwhile, old Thomas Sheridan was not selling himself short when it came to giving his son the benefit of his services. He agreed to come for a year just to give Richard the benefit of his experience, while naturally expecting just reward for his trouble. Had Richard thought deeply at this point what a train of theatrical disasters the elder Sheridan's experiences had been he must have thought twice about considering them an asset. Perhaps he did think twice and his desire for a reconciliation and a reunion with his sisters was too strong.

Richard, writing to Linley, goes on to say, 'My father must certainly be paid for his trouble, and so certainly must you. You have experience and character equal to the line you would undertake; and it never can enter into anybody's head that you were to give your time or any part of your attention gratis, because you had a share in the theatre.' There were to be profits and pickings for everybody in this golden enterprise.

Sheridan's was the temperament of a salesman, the sky was filled with pie, and there were no possibilities which were to be neglected for the generous benefit of everyone. His father-in-law would have a good return on his money, an income from his musical talents, and at the same time he could get further monies from pupils as well as acting as a talent scout for the theatre. His own father would have a job. Eliza, too, was put to some useful purpose in the enterprise.

'I have had a young man with me who want to appear as a singer in Plays or Oratorios', Richard told Linley. 'He is not one-and-twenty, and has no conceit. He has a good Tenor Voice – very good ear and a great deal of execution, and of the right kind. He reads Notes very quick and can accompany himself. This is Eliza's verdict, who sat in Judgement on him on Sunday last. You mustn't regard the Reports in the Paper about a third Theatre – that's all nonsense.'

But the idea of a third patent theatre was always a constant threat, and it was in particular a deadly threat to the purchasers of Drury Lane; for all their hopes and plans and all their golden profits, not to mention such minor details as the re-payment of vast loans, mortgages, and annuities, depended on their keeping the monopoly between themselves and Covent Garden.

By the middle of 1776 the negotiations were nearly con-cluded, and the prize was within Sheridan's grasp. Colman, who had wanted all or nothing, was out of the way. Lacy kept his half of the patent, and the other half was divided between

Richard, Linley, and Dr Ford. But now that the sanguine hopes of owning the glittering prize were realized, it was necessary to give some attention to exactly what was going to be put on at the theatre. The golden campaigns had to start without delay.

Richard's idea was to engage Thomas Sheridan as manager, but he set himself against allowing his father to act. The result might have been expected by anybody but the good-natured and optimistic Richard. Thomas Sheridan exploded. Smarting under the insult he did the usual thing. He left for Dublin – to play Hamlet. But Thomas Linley was appointed director of music which must have pleased Eliza, who had such great confidence in her father.

The realities of running a theatre produced their usual crop of problems of thespian temperament, particularly on the part of Mesdames Yates, Abington, and Younge. This trio of actresses dispensed charm on stage, and behaved like the furies off stage. But during the course of his first season at Drury Lane, Richard worked with great industry and patience. He sought out new performers, and his was the hand which revised old plays and looked for new ones. Eliza helped him by sifting through the manuscripts of aspiring authors, which must have been a very hard task.

In December, a musical play was produced, *Selima and Azor*, with scenery by the famous scene designer De Loutherbourg. Mrs Baddeley was enchanting as Selima. It was said she looked like an angel and sang the flower song like a siren. The music was composed by Eliza's brother Thomas, and directed by Thomas Linley père.

Five days later, on December 10th, Perdita Robinson appeared on the stage for the first time, as Juliet. Her mentor and producer was none other than Garrick himself. It is reported that during the rehearsals he frequently went through the whole part of Romeo until he was dropping with fatigue. On the first night Perdita Robinson had Sheridan encouraging her from the wings, while Garrick sat amongst the orchestra whence, to quote 'his keen and penetrating eyes, darted their lustres'. It was an auspicious début for all concerned, and justly successful, although the part of Juliet was announced on the bills as being played by an anonymous 'young lady'.

A continuing minor headache for Sheridan at this time was tragedy and tragedy writers. The vogue for classical tragedies was still at its height. Elviras and Zaras suffered and swooned on battlements in pentameters of indifferent verse. But Sheridan with his high spirits and genius for mockery does not seem to have taken this gloom and despondency seriously. He remarked in one of his letters to Linley that he had been saddled with a tragedy left over from Garrick's management, and prayed to be excused from giving an opinion on another tragic bard, 'being already in disgrace with about nine of that irascible fraternity'. The tragedy he had been saddled with was *Semiramis* by Captain Ayscough, a former schoolfellow of Sheridan's, and a friend of Perdita Robinson's husband. It is depressing to think of a comedy writer being besieged by a despondent group of determined tragedy writers sometimes slipping out of Drury Lane pursued by an angry posse of men armed with sheaves of paper thick with metric gloom.

Sheridan sensed that there were too many classical tragedies being written, for the great draw at this time was the large spectacular production. Just as the modern film industry was compelled by television to spend more on lavish outdoor films, so the two great patent theatres were now compelled to vie with one another in providing lavish settings and costumes to astonish the town.

In the same letter to Linley, Sheridan spoke of a species of pantomime to be shortly put into production, calculated to 'draw all human kind to Drury Lane. This is become absolutely necessary on account of a marvellous preparation of the kind which is making at Covent Garden.' The Covent Garden spectacle was called *Harlequin's Frolics*.

The small non-patent theatres specialized in music and dancing, and now the patent theatres had to provide straight plays, music, dancing, and also spectacle. The small theatres were more in the genre of music halls and could not afford to spend large sums on costumes and scenery, so the worry of the managers of Drury Lane – described in Sheridan's letters as 'self and partners' – was to keep an eye on Covent Garden.

And Covent Garden was now firmly sold on spectacle as a way of attracting the public.

These spectacles necessitated the employment of skilled craftsmen or 'machinists' to produce the props for the illusions, transformation scenes, and grand processions. One of these machinists, called Johnstone, apparently went as a spy to see what the rivals were doing at Covent Garden. Johnstone was justly celebrated for his skill in producing flying chariots, triumphal cars, palanquins, wooden children to be tossed over battlements and straw heroes and heroines to be hurled down precipices. Further specialities of his were wickerwork lions and pasteboard swans, and he was in fact the constructor of a general theatrical menagerie. In the two shilling gallery at Covent Garden, Johnstone and a friend had an unpleasant surprise. A real elephant came clumping down centre on the stage.

'This is a bitter bad job for Drury', hissed the friend. 'Why, the elephant's alive! He'll beat you hollow. What do you think on't?'

'Think on't?' said Johnstone, in the contemptuous tone of a true craftsman. 'I should be very sorry if I couldn't make a much better elephant than that at any time.'

Apart from choosing between spectacle, comedy, or tragedy, a theatre was a business. There were people to see, plays to be chosen, singers and actors to be engaged. Sheridan was prepared to brush tragedy writers from the doorstep, Eliza could audition singers, and his father engage actors, but there were still letters to be written: and Sheridan hated to write letters. Even when a certain Captain Ormsby sent him a candlestick, described by Sheridan as a silver branch, its reception was mixed. 'This will cost me, what of all things I am least free of, a letter', he wrote dolefully, and remarks that he wishes it had been anything but a candlestick as he cannot fit candle, candlestick, or snuffer into a metre. But he added that 'as the gift was owing to the muse [*The Duenna*], and the manner of it very friendly, I believe I shall try to jingle a little on the occasion; at least, a few such stanzas as might gain a cup of tea from the urn at Bath-Easton.' This was harking back to the past. At Bath Easton lived a literary lady who gave breakfast parties and all the company had solemnly to place their poems in a Roman urn. The writer of the best poem was crowned with a wreath of myrtle, but Sheridan had gone beyond the myrtle wreaths of literary ladies at Bath. That was part of his youthful past.

His tenderness for his wife and son is shown in the same letter, where he says 'Betsy [Eliza] is well, and on the point of giving Tom up to feed like a Christian and a gentleman, in other words of weaning him'. The child was then ten months old. In an age when the children of the rich were put out to nurse it says much for the maternal devotion of this delicate girl that she had breast fed him herself and for so long. 'As for the young gentleman himself, his progress is so rapid that one may plainly see the astonishment the sun is in of a morning at the improvement of the night.' Richard had an enchanting and graceful way of putting over tenderness with a pleasant joke. He was a man of sentiment but not of sentimentality, and like all good humorists he could include himself in the joke.

Although he had carried out a managerial *coup de théâtre* in gaining control of Drury Lane, there were legacies other than tragedies which he had inherited from Garrick. One of these was Willoughby Lacy. His father had been a partner of Garrick's, and when he died old James Lacy had left his share of the patent to his son. Willoughby Lacy seems to have been a pleasant if dissolute man. He was said to live in a spendthrift style, had a town house and a country house, and to have married a great beauty, driving her to church in a splendid coach and four. Sheridan does not seem to have been averse to spending jovial evenings with him. Angelo, son of the man who had given Sheridan fencing lessons describes a party of pleasure down at Isleworth, where Lacy lived:

'Our orgies lasted until day (with the exception of a few of the more sober guests, who departed earlier), when about five o'clock our party of bons vivants sallied forth to the garden, it being a bright summer morning. Sheridan and I had a fencing match; and Jerry Orpin, the brother of Mrs Lacy, for a wager jumped from the lawn, his clothes on, into the stream and swam backwards and forwards across the Thames.'

But it was a different matter when Lacy, long on fun and short on funds, in 1776 tried to raise the wind by selling part of his share to two other people. His share had been mortgaged to Garrick, and Garrick wanted the money paid back. When Sheridan found out that Lacy was negotiating behind his back he refused to act as manager at Drury Lane. The result was total confusion. Not only Sheridan, but the actors and actresses also went on strike, including the famous Mrs Abington, afterwards to perform so brilliantly as Lady Teazle. Other actors, according to Sheridan, were seized with a sudden plague: 'The manner too in which they are seized, I am told, is very extraordinary – many who were in perfect Health at one moment, on receiving a Billet from the Prompter to summon them to their Business are seized with sudden Qualms, and before they can get thro' the contents, are absolutely unfit to leave their rooms.' Lacy was faced with a situation in which he had no manager and few actors.

Had he been a man experienced in running a theatre it might have been possible for him to obtain substitutes from other theatres. Eighteenth-century actors worked hard, and were expected to be able to switch plays in mid-stream if required to do so. They were expected to be able to memorize up to fifty different parts, and indeed entire plays, and if asked to appear at a moment's notice in a well-known play, it was taken for granted that they could do this. One actress at Covent Garden appeared on 153 nights in 37 different parts.

Sometimes a play was substituted for another right at the last moment, should a leading actor be ill. The management relied on their actors being able to give a substitute performance, but generally it was not in the same play because certain actors were expected to act in certain plays. If they could not appear the play would be given at a later date.

It was simpler to stage an impromptu straight play at that time, for in straight plays the production itself was simple. The actors tended to stand formally, and as the furniture was kept at a minimum there were no troubles with plotting the action between actors and scenery and props. A German traveller remarks that the actors seldom approached each other rapidly, 'nor do they unnecessarily touch each other'. It was obviously a form of theatre which relied very much on the words and the gradations of tone for dramatic effect, and because the actors were used to team work, and very often had worked with one another for upwards of twenty years, these last minute substitutions were not as hair-raising as they might have been.

However, it is recorded that, on one occasion, when it was too late to print handbills about the change of play, the actors are said to have had only one copy of the play between them, and it was one they had not learnt. They read it using a candle, passing the single copy of the play from one to the other. Finally they arrived at a passage in the manuscript which was so heavily revised that they could not read it at all. The audience began to hiss. One of the actors civilly explained their difficulty to a gentleman in the pit, who examined the manuscript and ceremoniously informed the audience that the speech was unreadable. Satisfied that the actors were doing their best the audience cheered, and the actors were given permission to leave the passage out.

So with a strike of management and actors on his hands, Lacy now tried some substitution which is mentioned by Sheridan in a letter to Garrick:

'At night, and again on Sunday morning, Lacey sent by Hopkins to entreat I would return to the management and that he would do everything in his power to procure matters to be settled to my satisfaction, and would give up the point if he could prevail on them. As I was aware of this, and felt on what secure ground I stood I still declined hearing anything on the subject – so that after changing their Play several times, they were reduced to playing "The Committee" and after Tuesday, they had not one Play which they could perform. This appeared to have a great effect in settling the matter.'

As indeed it might. Garrick was on the side of Sheridan in the dispute, and eventually it was settled, although some discordant voices were raised against Sheridan for his light-minded attitude towards his responsibilities in allowing his own actors to strike in a dispute which largely concerned himself.

At the beginning of 1777, Sheridan put on, as a stop-gap, his cleaned-up version of *The Relapse*, called *A Trip to Scarborough*. Mr Moore was uncompromising in his opposition to the new version. He was struck with surprise that Sheridan should 'be able to *defecate* such dialogue, and at the same time, leave any of the wit, whose spirit is in the lees, behind. The very life of such characters as Berinthia is their licentiousness, and it is with them, as with objects that are luminous from putrescence, to remove their stain is to extinguish their light.'

Moore's judgement was correct, Sheridan's version was tame compared to the original, but he had to play to the tastes of his audience. As Vanbrugh wrote in *The Provoked Wife*: 'I'd have men talk plainly what's fit for women to hear without putting 'em either to a real or an affected blush.'

In spite of complaints that Sheridan had produced nothing of note, the play seems to have had a reasonable success. A contemporary critic said:

'In the first place the piece cost him no trouble; in the next it was well fitted for his company, by whom it was excellently performed; and in the next it gave an opportunity for producing, in one night, three most remarkable actresses, Mrs Abington, Miss Farren and Mrs (Perdita) Robinson – the first at the very top of her profession for comic humour – the second of surpassing loveliness and elegance – and the third, one of the most beautiful women in London. It was a temporary expedient, and as well as I can remember, successful.'

Sheridan's charm for the ladies came in useful in managing such a cast. As he says in a letter to Garrick, 'I mean to be vastly civil to female talent of all sorts'. Then, as now, leading actresses expected a little incense to be burned to their talents, and a manager with charm was able to dispense this with little labour and, equally important, no expense.

Sheridan's trouble with Lacy was not the major difficulty with which he had to contend. Thomas Sheridan, the old leopard of so many disastrous campaigns at the Smock Alley Theatre, Dublin, had not changed his spots. After hiving off to Dublin in high dudgeon because he was not allowed to act, he had eventually loomed upon the scene once more, doubtless attracted by the smell of good meat. He was as touchy, tactless and self-important as ever, given to upsetting the actors, and on one occasion he even snubbed Garrick. Thomas Sheridan had always been jealous of Garrick and alleged that it was because Garrick feared his talents that he had been banned from the stage of Drury Lane for so many years.

Thomas was invariably his own worst enemy. He hated Johnson for his fame over his Dictionary, certain that he himself had written a far better one. He considered himself to be Garrick's equal as an actor. And he was certain that, had he been given the chance, he could have reformed the entire educational system in England and Ireland. He was a man of some skills, but the troubles and disasters which he had undergone in Ireland had warped his character; and the early loss of his wife removed an influence which could, perhaps, have softened his view of the world. By 1778 although he had somewhat recovered from his huff and did join the company, he still smarted from the ban on his acting.

Thomas's bitterness at this period is well reflected in a letter to his son Charles, written some time after the events had occurred. But even after the lapse of time, Thomas shows himself to be still crackling with fury at the insult to his talents:

'At length a scene opened which promised better days. Garrick's retiring, whose jealousy had long shut the London theatres against me, such an opening was made for me, both as manager and actor as might soon have retrieved my affairs, and in no long space of time have placed me in easy circumstances. But here a son of mine steps into possession, whose first step was to exclude me wholly from having any share in it.

Afterwards, when by extreme ill-conduct they were threatened with ruin, he agreed to put the management into my hands upon condition that I should not appear as a performer, and in this he got his brother managers to

join him with such earnestness that merely to gratify him
I acquiesced.

I desire to know whether if the theatre of Drury Lane
had fallen into the hands of the worst enemy I had in the
world, determined upon ruining me and my family, he
could have taken more effectual means of doing it than those
which have been pursued by my own son?'

In view of what Richard knew of his father's temperament,
it was a kind but foolish act to put the irascible gentleman in
charge of anything at all. Thomas Sheridan had suffered much
but had learned nothing. Seamen thought it was unlucky to
shoot an albatross, but it is obviously just as unlucky to engage
a live one as manager in as delicate an enterprise as a theatre;
Thomas was one of the worst albatrosses in the business, even
though nobody shot him. In his account of his troubles he
forgot the manner in which he had treated Richard, he forgot
cutting him off from his sisters; and Richard's miserable
schooldays and unpaid schoolbills had equally and conveniently
faded from his mind. Thomas was quite sure where the faults
lay, and they were not in his own heart.

But in 1777, in spite of his initial difficulties with Lacy and
his father, Richard's star was in the ascendant. In May of
that year his masterpiece *The School for Scandal* was produced.
For nearly two hundred years the literary moles have been
busy on the origins of this comedy. Every speech, every
witticism, every stage direction, and each *coup de comédie* has
been turned upside down and inside out. It has been allegedly
proved that Sheridan wrote a sketch with a similar plot, before
The Rivals; that this character and that were taken from other
people's comedies.

Dr Watkins writing in 1817, admitted that this comedy
'elevated Mr Sheridan in the public esteem as the first dramatic
writer of his day, and he was complimented with the appella-
tion of being the younger Congreve'. But having well larded
his opening paragraph on the subject of the comedy, Dr
Watkins LL.D then goes on to say that many people thought
Mrs Sheridan had written the comedy, and that an even
stronger rumour 'asserted that the play was written by a

young lady, the daughter of a merchant in Thames Street; that, at the beginning of the season, when Mr Sheridan commenced his management, the manuscript was put into his hands for his judgment, soon after which, the fair writer, who was then in a state of decline, went to Bristol Hot Wells, where she died.'

The idea of a young person in a deep decline managing to write a brilliant comedy which is then stolen by a wicked management is worthy of a place in a play by Sheridan. Sheridan had, in fact, taken great pains with the polishing of this play until every line was faceted to shine brilliantly. But in his usual way, he was still at work cutting and changing while rehearsals were under way. The play was not finally finished until the date of the first night had already been announced. Meanwhile, the actors fretted in the wings waiting for all the last minute revisions to be finished. On the last page of the manuscript is written, 'Finished at last, Thank God! R. B. Sheridan.' To which the harassed prompter added a coda: 'Amen. W. Hopkins.'

The original cast was as brilliant as the play. The key part of Lady Teazle was played by the difficult Mrs Abington. It was said that three actresses drove Garrick from the stage and one of the three was Mrs Abington. Certainly Garrick hated her personally, and wrote that she was as silly as she was false and treacherous. But it was also admitted that no one could deliver a smart speech with such severity, that she had been pitched out of the dregs of the town, and lived for years as a tavern girl, and that it was infinitely to the credit of her tact and esprit that she should have raised herself and, like Woffington, have learned refinement and accomplishments. Her manner was bewitching, and no one apparently could play a fan so delightfully.

Other critics mentioned that she had great elegance, her address was graceful, and her looks animated and expressive. The tones of her voice were not naturally pleasing to the ear, but her incomparable skill in modulation rendered them agreeable, and her articulation was so exact that every syllable she uttered was conveyed distinctly and harmoniously. Another comment was, 'She, I think, took more entire *possession* of the stage than any actress I have seen. She was always beyond the surface; untwisted all the chains which bind ideas together, and seized upon the exact cadence and emphasis by which the point of the dialogue is enforced.'

She seems to have had exquisite taste in dress, and it was said that she was consulted about dress by ladies of distinction. There was no doubt that Sheridan was well served in his first Lady Teazle. The only sour comment came from Horace Walpole: 'Mrs Abington can never go beyond Lady Teazle, which is a second-rate character.'

Sir Peter was played by Thomas King, whose acting was said by Lamb to leave 'a taste on the palate both sharp and sweet like a quince; with an old, hard, rough withered face, like a john apple puckered into a thousand wrinkles; with shrewd hints and tart replies'.

Mr Moses was played by Robert Baddeley, the ex-pastry cook who is still remembered when the Baddeley cake is eaten each year. He left money for a cake, with wine and punch, to be distributed in the green-room on Twelfth Night, to make the future sons and daughters of Thespis remember an old friend and member of the profession.

The cast on the first night was as follows:

Sir Peter Teazle	Mr King
Sir Oliver Surface	Mr Yates
Joseph Surface	Mr Palmer
Charles	Mr Smith
Crabtree	Mr Parsons
Sir Benjamin Backbite	Mr Dodd
Rowley	Mr Aickin
Moses	Mr Baddeley
Trip	Mr Lamash
Snake	Mr Packer
Careless	Mr Farren
Sir Harry Bumper	Mr Gawdry
Lady Teazle	Mrs Abington
Maria	Miss P. Hopkins
Lady Sneerwell	Miss Sherry
Mrs Candour	Mrs Pope

NEVER PERFORMED.

At the Theatre Royal in Drury Lane,

This prefent THURSDAY, the 8th of May, 1777,
Will be prefented a NEW COMEDY call'd THE

School for Scandal.

The PRINCIPAL CHARACTERS by

Mr. KING,

Mr. YATES,

Mr. DODD,

Mr. PALMER,

Mr. PARSONS,

Mr. BADDELEY, Mr. AICKIN,

Mr. PACKER, Mr. FARREN,

Mr. LAMASH, Mr. GAUDRY,

Mr. R. PALMER, Mr. NORRIS, Mr. CHAPLIN,

And Mr. SMITH.

Mifs POPE,

Mifs P. HOPKINS,

Mifs SHERRY,

And Mrs. ABINGTON.

The Prologue to be fpoken by Mr. KING,
And the Epilogue by Mrs. ABINGTON.
With NEW SCENES and DRESSES.
To which will be added

The MAYOR of GARRATT.

Major Sturgeon by Mr. BANNISTER,

Sir Jacob Jollup by Mr. WALDRON,

Mr. Bruin by Mr. WRIGHT,

Lint by Mr. WRIGHTEN. Heeltap by Mr. BRANSBY,

Jerry Sneak by Mr. BAKER,

Mrs. Bruin by Mifs PLATT,

Mrs. Sneak (firft time) by Mrs. DAVIES,

The Doors will be opened at Half after Five, to begin exactly at Half after
[Six o'clock.

All the players lived up to the play. Mrs Pope was said to
be type cast as Mrs Candour. It was said that she behaved in
exactly the same way in the green-room. Even Lamash, who
played Trip, had the right character for his part. 'He was
naturally a fop', it was said, 'though not a *polished* one; he
could not assume the gentleman, but the gentleman's gentleman fitted him like his clothes; one would have thought his
mother had been waiting woman to the Duchess of Kingston
and his father the duster of Lord Chesterfield's clothes.'

Joseph Surface was John Palmer. His asides to the audience
were said, by downright acted villainy, to give a glimpse into
the depths of his personality. Palmer, like Mrs Candour, was
playing in character. Indeed when he had been genuinely
feigning illness on one occasion, he had adopted a supposed
humility. Putting his hand on his heart he said to Sheridan,
'If you could but know what I feel at this moment – *here*!'
Sheridan stopped him in mid-stream: 'Why, Jack, you forget
that *I wrote it*!' Sir Benjamin, played by Dodd, was said to be
'the prince of pink heels and empty eminence'.

Sheridan personally supervised the rehearsals and saw to it
that each line was given its right balance and timing. He even
corrected the formidable Mrs Abington. When she spoke the
line, 'How dare you abuse my relations?' he said, 'That will
not do, it must not be pettish. That's shallow, shallow! You
must go up the stage with, "You are just what my cousin
Sophy said you would be", and then turn and sweep down on
Sir Peter like a volcano: "You are a great bear to abuse my
relations! How *dare* you abuse my relations?" ' The source of
this anecdote is Ellen Terry's *Story of My Life*, and the tale is
supposed to have been handed down by an ancestress of
Charles Reade, who told it to Ellen Terry. It has the ring of
an authentic rehearsal scene.

Apart from his own innate wit and intuition, when it came
to the staging of the comedy and the putting over of the
dialogue Sheridan had the help of David Garrick in super-
intending the rehearsals and writing the prologue to the play.

Over the years the people in *The School for Scandal* have been
as well dissected as the jokes. As for Thomas Sheridan he
could not forbear to make one of his usual acid remarks:

'Talk of the merit of Dick's comedy – there's nothing in it! He had but to dip the pencil in his own heart, and he'd find there the characters of both Joseph and Charles Surface.' Superficially this may seem to be true. Sheridan had traits which were not as straight as the proverbial die. But his sisters and others were well aware of the material on whom he had based Charles and Joseph Surface. The characters were not based on himself alone. They were based on himself and his brother Charles.

In some of the girls' letters they refer to Brother Charles's conduct as being 'Surface-ish'. And in old prints of the play, Charles is depicted holding a bottle, while Joseph has his nose in a book, which in quintessence is the picturization of the two brothers. In the eyes of father Thomas, they were the idle and industrious apprentices. Richard was good enough to go ahead with his bustling superficial life, while Charles had always been the industrious apprentice, ever ready to listen to father's homilies and to drink in his theories. The unfortunate fact was that the idle apprentice was now the owner of a theatre, and publicly acclaimed as the writer of the best opera and the best comedy of the time. The golden boy, Charles, the industrious apprentice, was simply a minor diplomat.

Surely in the stage character of Charles, Sheridan drew the real Richard, his own portrait as he saw it, as it appealed to him, as he wished it to be, delineating the good-hearted rake, the *homme moyen sensuel*, who even if he whores a little, drinks a good deal, and gets into debt yet, at heart, is the best of fellows, a cheerful clubbable man who is also well liked by the ladies.

Perhaps the choice of the name Surface for his most successful pair of comedy characters was deliberate. It was on the surface that he preferred to live, ignoring the dark, melancholy side of his personality. It was said of him that beneath a thoughtless exterior lay a solitary and unhappy soul. Among people of Celtic blood it would not make him unique. Sheridan often quoted the sombre words of Dryden:

> Vain men! How vanishing a bliss we crave,
> Now warm in love, now withering in the grave;

157

Never, oh, never more to see the sun;
Still dark in a damp vault – and still alone.

But thanks to the successful life he had achieved in less than
six years, the dark side of existence could temporarily be
forgotten.

The School for Scandal was a nasty turn-up for Thomas
Sheridan's book. It is difficult not to come to the conclusion
that old Thomas was jealous of his son. If he was, it would
be harsh to criticize him. Looking back over his own life and his
disappointments both as an actor and as an actor-manager, it
must have been hard for him to accept that of his two sons,
the one who had seemingly made so little effort should suddenly
find himself at the summit of his profession. An even more
bitter pill to swallow was that Richard had become the friend
of Sheridan père's old enemy, Garrick.

*

When it came to the actual casting of *The School for Scandal*,
Sheridan had wanted the beautiful Perdita Robinson to play
Maria, the ingenue, but as we have seen, the part was taken
by another. Later, Perdita herself wrote:

'Mr Sheridan acquainted me that he wished me to perform
a part in *The School for Scandal*. I was now so unshaped by
my increasing size that I made my excuses, informing Mr
Sheridan that I should probably be confined to my chamber
when his since celebrated play would make its first appearance. He accepted the apology and in a short time I gave
to the world my second child, Sophia.' Mrs Robinson must
certainly have been very near her time of confinement,
because pregnancy was not a state which seems to have
worried eighteenth-century actresses, who would cheerfully
play noble virgins while six or seven months pregnant.

There was a last minute hitch in the production, not this
time due to theatrical troubles, but to the Lord Chamberlain. On May 7, 1777, the day before the first night, Sheridan
wrote to 'The Licencer of Plays':

'Sir, If the following comedy call'd *The School for Scandal*
meets with the approbation of the Lord Chamberlain we
shall have it perform'd at The Theatre Royal in Drury
Lane.

R. B. Sheridan. For self and partners.'

The Licencer refused approval, on government advice. The
background was political. An election was in progress in the
city for the office of Chamberlain. John Wilkes was the anti-
government candidate. His opponent was a money-lender,
nicknamed appropriately, 'Vulture' Hopkins, but no relation
to the prompter at Drury Lane. He was a man who had founded
his fortune on lending money to minors at exorbitant rates
of interest. The government, fearful in case any satire on usury
might favour Wilkes, came down against the play. But Sheridan
went at once to the Lord Chamberlain himself, Lord Hertford,
who found this storm in a political tea-cup as ludicrous as did
Sheridan, and at once granted the licence.

On May 8, 1777, all difficulties resolved, the play opened
to a brilliant audience. The famous beauty, Mrs Crewe, and
the even more famous Duchess of Devonshire, were in the
boxes as well as all the fashion and *ton* who had come to see
themselves mirrored on the picture frame stage. To later
audiences *The School for Scandal* encapsulates all the manners
and modes of the later eighteenth century, but whereas present-
day audiences perhaps find the edge of its satire overlaid with
the charm of the pictured past, the contemporary audience,
while admiring Mrs Abington's gown and the play of her fan,
found the topical satire sharper, the wit more stabbing.

Amid the universal acclaim there were few discordant voices
raised against the play. Only Cumberland, a writer of turgid
tragedies, is alleged to have pinched his children, saying,
'There is nothing to laugh at, my little angels; keep still, you
little dunces.' Cumberland may have been carping, and old
Thomas Sheridan sour, but the comedy took the town by
storm. Angelo, Sheridan's old fencing master, tells how a friend
was passing by Drury Lane when he heard a loud and sudden
noise like an explosion, and was unable to place what it
could possibly be. He approached the Theatre Royal and

found that the sudden noise which had startled him was the prolonged applause at the falling of the screen in the fourth act of *The School for Scandal*.

Garrick, apart from attending rehearsals, was said to have 'never been known to be more anxious for a favourite piece'. On the first night, Sir George Beaumont met him in the lobby, 'and with sparkling eyes, I remember, he expressed his admiration of the play, and particularly praised the fourth act'. The old actor had a nose for successful theatre, but like the careful manager he was, Mr Garrick was still keeping an eye on the play a few days after the first night:

'Mr Garrick's best wishes and compliments to Mr Sheridan. How is the Saint today? (Mrs Sheridan)
A gentleman who is as mad as myself about ye school remarked that the characters upon the stage at ye falling of the screen stand too long before they speak; I thought so too ye first night: he said it was the same on ye 2nd, and was remark'd by others; tho' they should be astonished and a little petrify'd yet it may be carry'd at too great a length. All praise at Lord Lucan's last night.'

There was 'all praise' everywhere, in effect, and the falling of ye screen had consolidated Sheridan's success.

10a. Thomas (the Elder)

10b. His wife

10c. Thomas (the Younger)

10d. Ozias

10e. William

10f. Samuel

The Linley Family

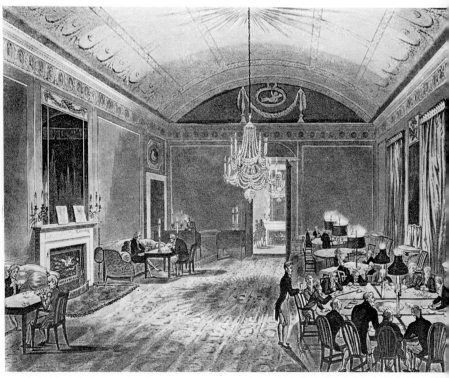

11 *Above:* A Rout in the Pantheon (*Rowlandson*). *Below:* The Great
Subscription Room at Brooks's (*Rowlandson*)

CHAPTER 9

Golden Campaigns

If the sky had once been cloudless at East Burnham, it was equally so at Drury Lane, during Sheridan's honeymoon period with this famous theatre.

Garrick was in a mood of pristine delight with his successor at Drury Lane. To a flatterer who said, 'To you, Mr Garrick, I must say, the Atlas that propped the stage has left his station.' Garrick replied, 'Has he? If that be the case he has found another Hercules to succeed in the office.' The down to earth friend retorted: 'This was but a single play, and in the long run will be but a slender help to support a theatre', a remark of a kind well calculated to lose friends rapidly.

But the thin wail of such a Cassandra could be disregarded, for night after night the theatre was full to overflowing, and presumably night after night the pit was screwed up to keep out the milling but enthusiastic crowds in the street. During the seasons 1777 to 1779 it was played seventy-three times, and made £15,000 which was over twenty per cent of the money invested in the theatre itself.

As a result of the success, money was pouring into the pockets of Sheridan and into the coffers of the theatre. In the theatre accounts it is recorded that it 'damped' every other piece, even the old favourites, such as *The Tempest* and *The Old Bachelor*. Sheridan attempted to vary the fare by reviving his mother's comedy, *The Discovery*, and even placated the tragedy writer Cumberland by playing *The West Indian*. It was to no avail. The *School* was the only play which the public wanted to see. It was equally successful in the provinces, and expecially in Bath, where Sheridan went to superintend the rehearsals.

The accounts at this time of his attention to the details of his play seem to belie the stories of his general carelessness.

But when it came to his plays he always did pay the greatest attention to the very smallest details, realising rightly that the art of comedy is a precise art, like that of miniature painting on ivory, demanding that each gesture and each intonation should be balanced, or the feather-light airiness of the good humour and fun would be dissipated.

Speaking of Sheridan rehearsing the Bath production, Bernard, who played Sir Benjamin, said:

'Nothing could have been more pleasant or polite than his manner. In his sensitiveness as an author he never lost sight of his propriety as a gentleman. The person who gave him the most trouble was Edwin, who was continually forgetting business. Sheridan, with the utmost good humour, put him right every morning.'

At the very last rehearsal before production, Edwin, who was well known for his drinking, was suffering a hangover from a punch supper, and finally Sheridan lost patience and cried: 'Good God, Mr Edwin, there you go again! You've lost your situation!' Edwin apparently was one of those actors who liked to improvise, and said his method when he got a new part was to study how 'to turn it about and about, as an artist drawing from a bust, in order to find the points which might give him the most power over his audience'. In short, he was the kind of actor who threw a sharp comedy entirely out of balance. But apparently Sheridan managed to make him toe the line, and the play was claimed to have been an even greater success in Bath than in London.

This may have been local boasting, but possibly certain Bath characters recognized themselves and their ways, for Richard had started the play when he had been still living in Bath, and the nodding heads and whispering tongues behind the fans in the Pump Room had originally sparked off his hatred of malicious gossip. It was gossip which had now been fined into the pure gold of comedy.

The coda was spoken by Sheridan, who said that the night after the first performance he was so drunk in the street that he was nearly taken up by the watch: Charles Surface always had his weaknesses.

*

But if Sheridan being nearly taken up by the watch represented the weak side of his nature, the ladies in the boxes equally beckoned to the poor player's son as a mode of life which it was his ambition to join.

Eliza's voice had acted like an incantation to unlock the drawing rooms of the great to him, and his own fame as a playwright had thrown them wide. The Duchess of Devonshire, while at first demurring at the impropriety of entertaining a couple with such humble backgrounds, was won over. Mrs Crewe, the beautiful 'Amoret', was one of Sheridan's fervent admirers, and even, it was said, had encouraged and applauded the final versions of *The School for Scandal*, so a copy of the play, finely bound, was forwarded with a set of laudatory verses to Amoret:

> Graced by those sign which truth delights to own,
> The timid blush and mild submitted tone:
> Decked with that charm, how lovely wit appears,
> How graceful science, when that robe she wears!
>
> A taste for mirth, by contemplation schooled,
> A turn for ridicule, by candour ruled,
> A scorn of folly which she tries to hide,
> An awe of talent which she owns with pride.

The verses end: 'Thee my inspirer and my model – Crewe'.

What Eliza thought of these delicate verses as she toiled away at the accounts of Drury Lane, or read through the effusions of frustrated and aspiring playwrights, is not recorded. There is no doubt that she had rightly feared the impact of the great world on Sheridan's personality. But he had already been drawn into it, and even before his success with *The School for Scandal* his exploits had troubled her. Mrs Crewe was an essential part of her worries – as far back as the production of *The Rivals*.

At this time Amoret Crewe was at the height of her beauty and her wit. It was said that there was something dove-like about her which was much more powerful than a bolder charm. Sheridan wrote:

> The softer charm that in her manner lies
> Is framed to captivate, yet not surprise;
> It justly suits th'expression of her face
> 'Tis less than dignity and more than Grace.

Amoret was the daughter of Mrs Greville, and was at the peak of her social eminence. In the year when *The Rivals* was produced she gave a famous fête to which Sheridan was invited: it seemed his fame had at last broken down the remaining social barriers for him.

In 1777, when his theatrical success was still fresh and new, Eliza had gone to stay in Bath with her father and mother. A press of business kept Richard at the theatre, but he had time to attend Mrs Crewe's fête. It was a splendid occasion and all the famous beauties of the age were there, the Duchess of Devonshire, the Countess of Jersey, Lady Craven, and, above all, Amoret herself of course, the hostess. From London, Richard, alias Silvio, sent Eliza, alias Laura, a set of graceful verses which hymned the beauties of the Spring and ended: 'Pardon (said Silvio with a gushing tear) 'Tis Spring, sweet nymph, but *Laura is not here.*'

The verses were accompanied, perhaps tactlessly, by a description of the grand party he had attended. The beauty of the women, as well as their flattering attentions to himself, were touched on, but Eliza, alias Laura, did not see the affair in the same way as her Silvio. She replied at length, and in verse. One verse ran:

> To other scenes doth Silvio now repair,
> To nobler themes his daring Muse aspires;
> Around him throng the gay, the young, the fair,
> His lively wit the list'ning crowd admires.

Nor were the charms of Mrs Crewe unknown to the absent Laura, who wrote:

> His voice awards what still his hand denies,
> For beauteous Amoret now his eyes pursue.
> With gentle step and hesitating grace,

Unconscious of her power, the fair one came;
If while he view'd the glories of that face,
Poor Laura doubted – who shall dare to blame?

It was understandable that the caressing voices of the grand Whig ladies should have gone to Richard's head. For one thing, and very importantly, he did not regard himslef as a mere poor player's son. He considered himself as a cut above that, as a gentleman, and the son of a gentleman, even if a poor gentleman, and as one who was at last coming into his rightful place in society. Furthermore he had always known that he had it in him to shine and to sparkle. He was witty, and cleverer than the people he had watched from the wings, and now that he had achieved a leading part in the raree show for himself, why should he not enjoy it? If failure is hard to bear, success is equally difficult to weather. As he said, to succeed it is necessary to determine not to fail, and he had so determined.

Staying at the top needs certain qualities, a grasp of essentials, particularly financial essentials, an attention to practical detail, and a clear head in the morning. These were qualities which the young playwright found dull. The writing of plays is a sudden thing, with a few swift strokes the effort can be carried to fruition. Producing a play which 'smells of the lamp' does not as a rule succeed so easily. The qualities which make the polished actor, the quick wit which makes the good comedy writer, are not often allied to the qualities which make for the smooth running of a big theatre.

Unfortunately the theatre itself represented Sheridan's security and his stake in the great world. Without the theatre he had no income and no means of supporting his social graces – or even his family. He found finances dull, he found letter writing even duller. And although Eliza read the plays – and presumably placated the furious, frustrated playwrights, and tested would-be singers, and kept the accounts, she was only a presence waiting back stage to field the pieces and smooth his path.

As might have been expected, the actors and actresses seem to have behaved worse under the relaxed discipline of Sheridan, than they did under David Garrick, and poor Hopkins, the prompter, had a very hard row to hoe. It should here be explained that the prompter at this period was not a man who just sat in a cubby hole giving cues to actors who had 'dried'. His duties were many and various. He was responsible for seeing that the actors were called to the theatre, he had to decide on the forfeits or fines appropriate to such actors as did not appear, and write out the playbills. Amongst his other duties were supervising stage properties, keeping a note of stage business, keeping music and band cues, and, in case he had any time left, to write the 'puffs' which appeared in the news-sheets.

Very early under Sheridan's management at Drury Lane, Mr Hopkins, the prompter, was in trouble:

'I have been silent thus long in hopes to have sent you an account of the new pantomime, which is again obliged (on account of the scenery's not being ready) to be deferred till Friday. This delay has been attended with very bad houses, having nothing ready to perform but the common hackneyed plays, as you will see by the papers. We played last night *Much Ado About Nothing* and had an apology to make for the change of the three principal parts. About 12 o'clock Mr Henderson sent word he was not able to play. We got Mr Lewis from Covent Garden, who supplied the part of Benedick. Soon after Mr Parsons sent word he could not play. Mr Moody supplied the part of Dogberry; and about four in the afternoon Mr Vernon sent word he could not play. Mr Mattocks supplied his part of Balthazar. I thought myself very happy in getting these wide gaps so well stopped'

and he had every reason to feel he had avoided disaster.

By May 1778, the theatrical honeymoon was fraying at the edges. Garrick had received a letter saying that in the future the interest on his investments, £2,200, could not be paid to him until the debts and charges on the theatre had been met. Garrick, not unnaturally, replied that he wanted his money, or he would be obliged to foreclose. Thomas Linley's answer was to cause several catty paragraphs about Garrick to appear in newsprint. This led to a further exchange of sharp letters. Finally, Linley was obliged to write from his house in Norfolk

Street, Strand, confessing that he had written the paragraphs. He gave the lame excuse that it all was meant to be a humorous reply to a previous attack on Garrick, and that unless the words were perverted from their true meaning there was nothing that conveyed any idea that did not show Garrick to advantage.

Linley's wordy explanations received very short shrift indeed from Garrick, who replied succinctly enough:

August 16, 1778.

'Gentlemen,

The rudeness of your letters, which is always the sign of a bad cause, I shall pass over with the utmost contempt; but as you have proposed to my friend Mr Wallis, and my brother, an arbitration, I cannot as an honest man refuse to meet you upon any ground. I therefore desire that your attorney will, without delay, in concurrence with Mr Wallis settle, and prepare this matter, and that all other correspondence may cease between you and

Your humble servant
D. Garrick.'

Garrick's claims were settled – but only in part – when he died his heirs were still the creditors of the theatre.

*

Like all other theatre proprietors, Sheridan was forced in the end to attend to small details. There is extant a long if somewhat rambling run-down on theatre expenses in Sheridan's handwriting. This refers to all the details from disputes between actors about dressing rooms, to the general running expenses of the theatre, and from it we see that he, as others before him, had now been reduced to worrying about candle ends: 'The Dressers have had a perquisite of the Candles left in their Rooms (this custom ought to be abolished as many bad consequences may arise from it).'

He asks how the fruit women and shops are billed, complains that dancers have been charging up their stockings, and says that they must provide their own white stockings as they have to do at Covent Garden. Buff gloves and hats are to be

returned to the wardrobe, and stockings are to be stamped with
the actor's name. And surely one porter would be sufficient to
call the actors to rehearsal?

The account sounded very businesslike. It listed all the
expenses such as rent, taxes, oil, coal and candles, which had
to be paid regularly. It stated that obviously carpenters,
printers, lamplighters, bill stickers, tailors, and mantua makers
bills must also be met regularly. It was all sane, sensible, and
sound, except that it was written by a man who never even
opened a letter if he could avoid it. Plans about finance were
made, and economies were suggested: 'Costly after-pieces
should not be made common as the Extra Expences are great.
A list of the properties should be delivered and often overlooked
(i.e. looked over diligently) as neglect and Embezzlement are
liable to creep on this Department.'

In the end, Sheridan asked himself and his co-owners the
vital question: 'If with this plain account before us we are
inattentive or extravagant, shall we not deserve the Ruin which
MUST follow?' The economies were suggested but seldom carried
out.

It had been at this point that the stormy petrel Thomas
Sheridan was brought in as manager. Possibly Richard thought
that his father, being at least administratively experienced in
running a theatre, could attend to all the details which so
bored him, and that he himself could get on with general plans
and projects.

In his usual way, Thomas Sheridan immediately set about
putting cats in every available pigeon loft and, like Linley,
upset Garrick. This was inexcusable in the circumstances, for
Garrick had been kindness itself to Richard. He had promoted
and fostered his management and attended the rehearsals, to
the detriment of his health. But Garrick, who was not a small-
minded man, weathered even the petty spite of Thomas. He
wrote in a conciliatory vein to Richard, after one incident:

'Pray assure your father that I meant not to interfere in his
department: I imagined (foolishly indeed) my attending
Bannister's rehearsal of the part I once played, and which
your father never saw, might have assisted the cause, without

giving the least offence. I love my ease too well to be thought an interloper, and I should not have been impertinent enough to have attended any rehearsal, had not you, sir, in a very particular manner desired me. However, upon no consideration will I ever interfere again in this business, nor be liable to receive such another message as was brought me this evening by young Bannister. You must not imagine that I write this in a pet: let me assure you, upon my honour, that I am in perfect peace with you all, and wish you from my heart all that you can wish.'

Thomas Sheridan was becoming a liability to his son, as he had been to himself. The same qualities which had infuriated and amused the Dubliners of long ago were still present in his character. He was still pompous and self-important, but he now added unkindness to his other traits.

Taking their cue from the managers some of the actors were now encouraged to treat Garrick, the retired lion, with rudeness and even contempt. At a Theatrical Fund Dinner he was studiedly neglected. Thomas King, one of the Drury Lane actors, wrote a rambling letter to Garrick proferring some kind of excuse. Garrick replied in a bantering way, but his words reveal a deep wound. He had done Old Drury proud, and he had not deserved to be insulted.

'You are a male coquette, Mr Thomas, but have such winning ways with you, that we readily forget your little infidelities. I must confess that my reception at the Fund Dinner was as surprising as it was disagreeable and un-expected. I seemed to be the person marked for displeasure and was almost literally sent to Coventry. Though I ventured among you after a very severe illness, and had dressed myself as fine as possible to do all the honour I could to the day and the Committee, I never was more unhappy for the time; however, let it be forgotten, and when we meet, let not a word be said of what is past. Poor Old Drury! It will be, I fear, very soon in the hands of Philistines.'

Thomas Sheridan was jealous of his reputation as a gentleman. Now Garrick had shown himself to be one. The picture of the old distinguished actor, dressing himself very fine, in spite of his illness, and making the effort to appear at the dinner, only to be cold shouldered, is distressing and makes the heart sick.

In 1779 Garrick died. Richard Sheridan, as the chief mourner, followed him to the grave, and wrote a monody to his memory, which was spoken from the stage at Drury Lane. This was given on March 12, 1779, and written by Sheridan. A monody seems to have been a mixture of verse and music. The scene is described in a contemporary account, which says there was an air of awful solemnity and woe about the occasion, and that the scenery consisted of a thick grove of bays and cypress in front of which was the funeral pile of Mr Garrick. The figures of tragedy and comedy in *basso relievo* were surmounted with the figure of fame mounting to the skies with a medallion of Mr Garrick and little cupids weeping over his urn. 'Before a pyramid Mrs Yates with dishevelled hair and in a flowing robe of purple satin spoke the monody.' Mrs Yates seemed to have a penchant for dishevelled hair for an earlier notice said, 'We cannot however regard Mrs Yates' sudden entrance with dishevelled hair after she has but a moment before left it with her hair in perfect order as other than a mere stage trick.'

This time the dishevelled hair seems to have been well received for the critic says, 'The monody was received by the audience with a sort of pleasing melancholy,' and added, 'Mr Sheridan however last night proved that it is possible for the same mind to possess the most admirable talents for sprightly scenes of comedy and the happiest genius for the most delicate poetry.'

> The throng that mourn'd as their dead favourite pass'd
> The grac'd respect that claim'd him to the last;
> While Shakespeare's image from its hallow'd base,
> Seem'd to prescribe the grave and point the place.

Mr Moore does not seem to have taken a very good view of Sheridan's valedictory verse on Garrick, and remarks that it was more remarkable, perhaps, for refinement and elegance than for either novelty of thought or depth of sentiment. This is probably a fair criticism, for Garrick himself had expressed his feelings about himself and his profession so much better:

> The painter's dead yet still he charms the eye,
> While England lives his fame can never die;
> But he who struts his hour upon the stage,
> Can scarce protract his fame through half an age
> Nor pen nor pencil can the actor save;
> The art and artist have one common grave.

The theatre king was dead. The mourning coaches had passed. But Sheridan, the new wearer of the crown, did not find it sitting as easy on his head as he had hoped. Running a theatre was hard. Yet in the beginning his flair and his talent for managing people produced reasonable results. He worked strenuously, writing his own plays, adapting other people's, and placating his actresses. Like all clever if sudden people, he found the beginning of anything exciting, a challenge, full of difficulties to be overcome, and tricks to be learned. Having lived on the fringe of theatre business all his life, Sheridan had learned the tricks with the instinct of one born to the job which, although he did not like to think so, he had indeed been. But after Garrick's death, the old order at Drury Lane had passed completely. There was no one now who could watch carefully from the wings, and give hints on the falling of ye screen. Sheridan was on his own.

Now his co-helpers were the two quarrelling fathers, Thomas Linley and Thomas Sheridan. They had made his life tiresome as an aspiring husband to Eliza. In the theatre, they had both on different occasions insulted Garrick. Thomas had always been touchy, and Linley had become so. Only Eliza represented some sort of order and stability. But she was frail and a woman. There was no mettle to hand to withstand so much disorder. What Sheridan lacked at this moment was a strong stable man behind him, someone to seize the reins at Drury Lane, and keep the two fathers in some sort of good order. Harmony, with Thomas Sheridan around, would have been too much to expect.

The manner in which theatre finances continued to be

conducted at this time was not conducive to economy. In Garrick's day each season began with a small fund of £200 or £300, which was money scraped together from odd receipts from the previous season, such as income from the usual candle ends, second-hand clothes, and fines. The heavy expenses of the theatre, actors' salaries, benefits to leading actors, and scenery and costumes still had to be met as the money came in at the box office. For a man of Sheridan's happy-go-lucky temperament the possession of a till to dip his fingers into was to prove a fatal temptation to his own solvency and that of the theatre.

To add to his natural extravagances, he was now moving in a society which was dedicated to show, which built palaces in town, and mansions in the country, where display was considered to be part and parcel of leading a life of fashion. A young man with a beautiful wife and the world at his feet could be pardoned if he felt tempted. Where he had once run up bills for neat foils and coach journeys, he now ran up bills for houses, carriages, horses, servants, and lavish entertainments.

Garrick did not live to receive his capital back, and the mortgage was, in fact, not paid off till fifteen years after his death, and by the time the settlement came, the claims of the Garrick estate amounted to £30,000. But in spite of the load of his current debts Sheridan, nothing daunted, decided that he wanted to become sole proprietor of Drury Lane. This ambition added further loans and interest on loans to his original debts. It was a fatal mistake.

Willoughby Lacy, equally mistakenly, had decided that he wanted to become an actor, and no doubt with a view to financing this unwise scheme, he finally sold his share in the theatre to Sheridan. Richard, in his usual way, propped up his complicated finances by selling off some of his original shares – to Ford, the man-midwife, and to his father-in-law Linley, at a profit. There were still to be golden campaigns.

Sheridan played with the shares of the theatre as if they were cards in a gambling game; but although he always seemed to have a couple of aces up his sleeves, some of the cards were invariably absent. He probably thought that the other players would not notice this, while the game was noisy and in progress, and that with luck he would be able to replace the missing cards before the game was finished. His charm would smooth away all difficulties.

It was about this time that he met Fanny Burney, the author of *Evelina*, and her description of him at a party underlines the reasons for his popularity:

'Mr Sheridan has a very fine figure and a good though I don't think a handsome face. He is tall, and very upright and his appearance and address are at once manly and fashionable without the smallest tincture of foppery or modish graces. In short, I like him vastly, and think him in every way worthy of his beautiful companion.'

Sheridan took the trouble to flatter Miss Burney by asking her to write a comedy, and pressing her father whenever he met him to let him see what she had done. But by the time Miss Burney had done some work on it, he had forgotton all about it. Her account, 'I have actually now written the fourth act, but Mr Sheridan has not yet called.' It had, after all only been a party conversation, and a quick way of charming an eminent young lady.

In October of 1779, the year that Garrick died, Sheridan wrote his last original play, *The Critic*.

*

Several biographers of Sheridan have made it clear, by laboriously studying parallel texts of *The Rehearsal*, by George Villiers, Duke of Buckingham, that Sheridan lifted whole paragraphs from this farce and incorporated them into his own play. This is probably true. But Sheridan took Buckingham's old play and made of it something shining, new and eternally funny. As Richard himself wrote in the play: 'Two people happened to hit upon the same thought, and Shakespeare made use of it first, that's all.' The fact is that *The Rehearsal* in which Garrick had played the principal part of Bayes, was never seen on the stage again from the time *The Critic* was first produced.

This play is as good a comment on theatre manners today as it was on the day it was written. Every line has the ring of observation. When Puff says, 'Sir, shall I trouble you to die again?' an actor's inevitable indignant expression springs immediately to the mind. And how many playwrights have not suffered at the cutting of their lines as Puff did: 'The description of her horse and side saddle? Zounds, I would not have parted with the description of the horse!'

Actors still cry, in effect, 'Don't interrupt us just here, you ruin our feelings!' or, 'I thought, sir, I wasn't to use my white handkerchief till heartrending woe.' Stage managers and producers still have the same backstage problems of which Sheridan made fun: 'The carpenters say that unless there is some business put in here before the drop, they shan't have time to clear away the fort, or sink Gravesend and the river.'

Modern producers could say with sneer, 'I am quite of your opinion Mrs Dangle the theatre in proper hands might certainly be made the school of morality: but now I am sorry to say people seem to go there principally for their entertainment!' By substituting the word 'concern' for 'morality', the comment is as pertinent as it ever was.

Many people at the time questioned whether it was wise for Sheridan to ridicule in this way his alternative form of bread and butter, for from the time the play was seen, it was difficult to sit through the woes of the Elviras without laughing. On the night of one performance of *The Critic*, the tragedy writer Cumberland was sitting in a box, and Sheridan asked if he had been seen to laugh. The reply was in the negative. 'Why then', said Sheridan 'that was cursedly ungrateful in him, for during his last tragedy I laughed confoundedly at every scene.' Behind every poetic tragedy there now trembled the laughter produced by *The Critic*.

Smyth, the tutor of Sheridan's son, says that he wrote some verses which he took to Sheridan, who of course did not read them, but in his usual kind way said, 'Now, my good Smyth, if you can write poetry, go you and write a tragedy, and you may then make you own fortune and mine, too.' It is always fatal for theatre managers to encourage writers, and in this case it also did not serve, for poor Smyth said that no one would ever write a tragedy if he once became as conversant with *The Critic* as he was.

The cast, as was only right for a 'managerial comedy', was handpicked. Parsons acted Sir Fretful, to the discomfiture of Cumberland, the tragedy writer. Thomas King played Puff; Mrs Pope played Tilburina, the heroine – stark mad in white satin – and John Palmer, the former Joseph Surface, played Sneer. It is said that Sheridan, in one of his mischievous moods, had type cast the role of Lord Burleigh, giving the part to Mr Moody, a very stupid actor with 'looks profound'. Sheridan said that the actor could not possibly make a mistake. The prompter's directions clearly said: 'Mr Moody as Lord Burleigh will advance from the prompter's side – proceed to the front of the stage – fall back to where Mr Waldron stands as Sir Christopher Hatton – shake his head, and exit.' The story goes that a friend made a bet with Sheridan that Moody would blunder in some way. So Sheridan, to add to the hazards of the bet, would not let the actor rehearse. On the night, instead of shaking his own head, the actor went over to Sir Christopher, took *his* head in his hands, shook it from side to side, slowly and made his exit with a look of great satisfaction.

As usual, Sheridan had not finished the piece when it was already in rehearsal. Thomas King, who played Mr Puff, was so worried that he had not the final scenes in his hand that he devised a way to make Sheridan finish the play. While a rehearsal was going on, King told Sheridan he had something to discuss with him, and ushered him into a room with a blazing fire and candles ready lit. On the table were laid anchovy sandwiches and wine. Here Linley was waiting, and both King and Linley told Sheridan that it was imperative that the play should be finished at once. They managed to get Sheridan to the table, then locked him in with the sandwiches and the wine to finish the farce.

It was a great success and the beautiful Georgiana, Duchess of Devonshire, said it was one of the funniest she had ever seen. The play appeared with a fulsome preface by Sheridan addressed to Mrs Greville, the mother of Amoret. What Eliza thought of this is not recorded.

*

Sheridan had now conquered the theatre, and the town. At twenty-eight he was at the summit of his stage achievement. He had the heritage of Garrick in his hands, with the bonus of his own inimitable wit. He had only to keep the horses trotting, giving a touch to the reins now and again, and the carriage wheels could have been kept rolling merrily along for many a year. But the bread-and-butter finances of a theatre were not likely to have any appeal to a temperament such as Sheridan's as a permanent way of life.

Since his father had fallen out with everyone he decided to turn the management over to Thomas King. The theatre would not now represent anything more than a quick way of bringing in an income – which would enable him to live like the gentleman he felt himself to be, both by inclination and by descent.

It could be said that he had been lucky, but the luck had been preceded by many hopeless and hapless days in his early youth. Now, if he reached further and higher for the good things in the world which he craved, it need not be a matter for surprise. He had the happy knack of seizing a golden opportunity and making the best of it. He had done this with Drury Lane. But for Sheridan the curtain was always up and he was always on stage. He was now looking for a larger stage.

He had his eyes on Westminster: but this was a stage where he had no experience and where the cards were not in his hands to deal. His century was par excellence a century of contrasts: when walking round a Palladian house, or looking at the exquisite follies and bridges in one of Capability Brown's gardens, it is easy to picture the brocade-clad ladies, eyes enlarged with bella donna, above their fans, and the men, polished and witty, with that touch of Roman stoicism which endured into the nineteenth century, to be lost in our own day. It is harder to remember that underneath the polished comedies of the period there lay the hard concealed truths of girls sold into marriage, of settlements in which property figured more prominently than people, and to realize that Hogarth pictured the life in the streets better than Rowlandson.

In this uneasy century Sheridan had all the attributes of the fashionable gentleman except the two essentials: the right relations, and a secure financial backing. They were two necessities for a budding politician which he decided to ignore. He had already made his way brilliantly in the murky waters of the theatre, why should he not succeed equally brilliantly in the larger sphere of politics? There was some knack to it, and he would find the clue, as he had found the knack of writing plays, and becoming the owner of a theatre.

Sheridan had a temperament which felt alive only when it had an audience. There are some people who are only themselves when they are not themselves. Hazlitt said that an actor was not himself except when 'he was beside himself'. Maugham in *Theatre* makes the actress's son say to her that if she went into a room alone and looked into the mirror she would find that she did not exist. This was true of Sheridan. The chameleon character of the actor is such that his ability can take on the protective colouring of a Lord Foppington or a Charles Surface. This strange amorphous quality Sheridan possessed.

Writers often despise the things which they do with ease. They throw off the trappings of the art which they can practise with élan and enter the great world of politics or social life only to trivialize their talents and to fail in their ambition to correct the shifting values of the world. Politics seem to be played on a great stage, but posterity does not favour most politicians. Who remembers Lord Bute now except for the boot which was thrown at him? It is, however, easy to understand how passionately the poor player's son wanted to escape from his background. Lord Holland said on one occasion, 'Sheridan assured me at the same time that his treatment at school had created in his mind such an aversion for the stage that he had never seen a play when he wrote *The Duenna*; that he engaged in that work from absolute indigence; and that throughout his life he had never seen a representation from beginning to end, except for his own pieces at rehearsals!' Lord Holland found this incredible, but later at the Marquis of Abercorn's private theatre, Sheridan said 'he did not remember ever previously sitting out any play in his whole life'.

He was already on friendly terms with the great Whig ladies of Devonshire House. He had met Burke at Dr Johnson's club, and was soon to become the intimate of Charles James Fox.

Lord John Townshend claimed that he was the first to bring the two men together at a dinner at his house. Fox had been told that all the notions he might have conceived of Sheridan's talents and genius from the comedy of *The Rivals* would fall infinitely short of the admiration of his astonishing powers which he would entertain at the first interview. Townshend said:

'The first interview between them there were very few present, only Tickell (afterwards to be Sheridan's brother-in-law) and myself, and one or two more, I shall never forget. Fox told me after breaking up from dinner that he had always thought after my uncle Townshend Hare the wittiest men he ever met with, but that Sheridan surpassed them both infinitely. Sheridan told me next day that he was quite lost in admiration of Fox and it was a puzzle to him to say what he admired most, his commanding superiority of talents and universal knowledge, or his playful fancy, artless manners, and benevolence of heart which showed itself in every word he uttered.'

There was no doubt that the two men had dazzled one another, and they were to become, and remain for many years, the closest of friends and boon companions.

Sheridan had been drawn to politics long before he started to write plays, and there exist fragments of various political essays which were written before he wrote his comedies. A long and complicated scheme for starting a school for the daughters of impoverished gentlefolk was addressed to Queen Charlotte and presumably never sent. A fragment of some article intended to form part of a periodical called *Hernan's Miscellany* in which Sheridan aged twenty, tries to write as if he had the long grey beard and wisdom of a senior politician. Politics had always been at the back of his mind, and plays were merely a quick way to turn an honest few thousand to support his beautiful wife.

He was sitting at the summit of fame and fortune, and he was still only twenty-eight. It could be said 'he walked in silver slippers in the sunshine' and listened to constant applause.

CHAPTER 10

The World of Whigs

All Sheridan's friends were in the Whig camp and he attached himself to their cause. The spirit of reform was in the air and Sheridan, with his ideas of liberty and equality, fell in with those who favoured it.

His first appearance on the political scene was when he took part in a great demonstration as a member of the Westminster Association. Charles James Fox presided over this meeting of more than three thousand people in Westminster Hall. The sponsors included many members of the nobility and gentry, including the Dukes of Richmond and Portland, the Grevilles, the Cavendishes, and also took in less privileged mortals such as John Wilkes and Alderman Sawbridge. The programme was ambitious. It demanded annual parliaments and universal suffrage.

These necessary reforms were to lead to the promised land. It seems that Sheridan regarded parliamentary reform as a fairly distant prospect. He is said to have remarked, 'Whenever anyone proposes to you a specific plan of Reform always answer that you are for nothing short of Annual Parliaments and Universal Suffrage – there you are safe. Edward III said a parliament shall be holden every year once, and more often if need be. For my part, I am an oftener if need be.' It was perhaps unwise to make jokes on serious subjects, but it was Sheridan's nature to seize any joke on the wing. He was now swimming in deep and difficult waters. It was not easy to become an MP in the days of the rotten borough.

Charles James Fox had become an MP under the patronage of his father, Lord Holland, who was allied by marriage to the Richmond and Gordon family; he also had the blood of Charles II in his veins. Added to which his father had made many millions as Paymaster General during the Seven Years

179

War: some fifty millions had passed through Lord Holland's hands, a good deal of it had stuck, and nine years after his death the Treasury were still trying to prize some of the remaining loot from the hands of his executors. So Fox, although only two years Sheridan's senior, had the background of money and family which gives a man not only confidence in himself but the feeling that he is born to lead, and deserves his place in the world as of right.

Sheridan had no patron, so that particular means of entry to Parliament was barred. The second way was to buy a borough, and then represent it either in person, or by proxy. It was said that the Nabob of Arcot could depend on seven faithful members of parliament known as the Bengal Squad, to support his views with their votes. The third way to get into Parliament at this time was to make a play for the votes of self-styled independent electors who were not under the sway of a definite patron. The so-called independent electors regarded free dinners, ale and a five guinea sweetener no bar to their independence and made this mode of entry also fairly expensive. It was this third means which Sheridan chose.

He first tried for Honiton in Devonshire; this was a corrupt borough in the pockets of the Younge family. Ozias Humphry, an old friend of the Linleys from the Bath days lived there and Sheridan was soon in hot correspondence with him about the wisdom of choosing this as a seat. In spite of the expense and labour needed, the number of candidates in the field made Honiton seem more like a steeplechase than a serious political contest. The ramifications of independent patronage are outlined by Ozias writing to Sheridan:

'Mr McLeod is nephew to Mr Bacon, who was formerly an unsuccessful Candidate to represent the Borough. Mr Fox is in treaty for a considerable estate – if he makes the purchase it will give him command of near fifty additional voters, beside the present candidates two or three others hold themselves ready to propose.'

Sheridan's comment was, 'They are damn'd Fellows if they think to mend themselves by choosing a Scotsman and a Mac too!'

In spite of his uncle's ill-success, Alexander Macleod was returned, and that was the end of Sheridan's hopes of Honiton, though later, in his usual optimistic way, he wrote to Humphry: 'Upon my soul I believe you were wrong about Honeton (*sic*) as I have been close to it – but tho' wanted was obliged to go to another place I am after.'

Mr. SHERIDAN and Mr. MONCKTON prefent the Bear-er with a DINNER & SIX Quarts of Ale.

No.

E. S

July 6th.

DREWRY, PRINTER.

Mr. MONCKTON and Mr. SHERIDAN prefent the Bearer with a DINNER and SIX Quarts of Ale.

No.

E. S.

July 6th.

His hopes were soon fulfilled. Through the influence of the Spencer family, and fighting under the colours of the Duchess of Devonshire, he was elected for Stafford. The election cost Sheridan over a thousand pounds cash. This included ale tickets at £40, swearing in young burgesses at £10, subscription to the infirmary at five guineas, and Ringers (town criers) four guineas. Clergyman's widows came fairly cheap at only two guineas.

This was only the initial payment, there were also annual running expenses, and doubtless burgesses and clergyman's widows had not only to be made sweet but kept sweet. It was said that some kind gentleman had lent Sheridan the money, that the election was paid for by a share in Drury Lane, and that many of the voters had been purchased by being offered free seats at the theatre. Nor were the legislators any less corrupt than the voters. Sir Nathaniel Wraxall in his *Posthumous Memoirs* mentions that the chief clerk in the Navy Office, although his salary was only £250, received in gifts up to £2,500 yearly. There were other small perks, a member of the Board of Trade ordered dozens of pewter inkstands which he changed for a nice piece of silver for himself. On another occasion the same man ordered lengths of green velvet 'for the ostensible purpose of making bags to contain office papers'. He was afterwards seen resplendent in a suit of the same green velvet, and many years after he had left his post was still writing to his friends on the office writing paper. The Post Office joined in the fun: 'Game of every description was sent up to the Secretary of the General Post Office in Lombard Street as a sort of feudal homage from the provincial postmasters scattered about the Kingdom.'

In the contemporary circumstances to become an MP was not a poor man's game, but to Sheridan it seemed that a theatre in his pocket was as good as money in the bank.

Sheridan was elected at the same time as his friend the Hon. Edward Monckton, the figures being: Monckton 258, Sheridan 247, Whitworth 168 and Drummond a mere 46. The winners penned a splendid missive to those who had elected them:

'We have found you men of your words – we will deserve the continuing of your friendship. If we deceive you, you will have no difficulty in turning us out again, as we shall deserve. Independent candidates will no more be afraid to offer themselves, for you will have made it appear that you

are the masters of your own rights, and that you are determined to hold them in your own hands, and to keep your
Borough free.'

How free it really was is questionable, for Sheridan wrote
to the Duchess of Devonshire a few days later:

> September 19, 1780.
>
> 'Madam, I am entirely at a loss how to thank your Grace
> for the Honor and service which your Grace's condescending
> to interest yourself in my election at Stafford has been to
> me. Having sent the Recommendation which I had the
> Honor to received from Lady Spencer to his Lordship's
> agent, I profited by the Permission allow'd me to make
> use of your Grace's Letter as my first and best introduction
> to Lord Spencer's Interest in the Town.'

The rumble of a Duchess's coach wheels could set other wheels
turning, had done so, and he was humanly elated. He said
that after dinner on the day of his election he 'stole away by
himself to speculate upon those prospects of distinguishing
himself which had been opened to him, and that this was the
happiest moment of his life'. He had indeed come a long way
since he was a shabby schoolboy at Harrow.

Once elected, the next goal was to become a member of
Brooks's, the exclusive Whig club. Apparently the manager of
Drury Lane was not regarded by some members as being fit
material for St James's. It was said that among the opponents
to Sheridan's election were the Earl of Bessborough and
George Selwyn, who were determined to exclude him. As
elections had to be unanimous, they were able to do this by
being present on every occasion when his name came up for
election, in order to blackball him. The ballot took place
between eleven at night and one in the morning when members
were possibly in a mellow mood.

There is a story that eventually Sheridan and his friends
caused a message to be sent to Selwyn saying that his daughter
had been taken suddenly ill, while the Earl of Bessborough
received a note saying that his house was on fire. As soon as

they were out of the club, Sheridan was elected, and when they came back, having discovered that they had been hoaxed, it was too late to do anything. Although the story is supposed to be apocryphal, it has the right ring of the cruel practical jokes in which Sheridan and his friends delighted.

Unlike the serious Pitt, Sheridan plunged into the life of Brooks's with a will. He had found a place where he was supremely at home, where in the large beautiful rooms wine, play and wit held sway, and living seemed high, wide and handsome. The basis of the Whig philosophy at Brooks's was aristocratic, and they held public opinion in contempt. There was something in this attitude which had an immense appeal for Sheridan, added to which he was drawn to Fox as a friend and fellow wit. Fox was a gambler, too, who would risk a fortune or his reputation at a throw in the Great Subscription Room and had been known to lose £11,000 in one evening. This was a dramatic attitude to life with which Sheridan was in complete agreement. Other men could fuss and fume, and consult their interests, but a sudden idea, a quick coach journey, a joke at the expense of an opponent, could do as much business and provide more amusement.

Sheridan was returned for Stafford on September 12, 1780. He made his debut about the same time as that other young man, nearly nine years his junior, William Pitt. Pitt, the son of Chatham, had been born and educated to be a leader in the House of Commons. He had never set his sights on any other career except that of Parliament.

Sheridan first spoke in the House of Commons on September 23, 1780. Although it was said that he was heard with particular attention, and that the house was uncommonly still while he was speaking, his speech was not regarded as a success. It was thought that his manner of address was too complicated and flowery, and that he was at too much pains to prove that his theatrical background was now behind him. The speech was a successful defence of his own election, and a protest against a petition to unseat him for bribery. Obviously ale, tickets, and small payments to supporters were not considered as bribery in the true meaning of the term. These are nice points between which it is difficult to differentiate. Possibly real bribery was considered to be money paid in large sums to one person, and not in small amounts to a number of electors.

Mr Woodfall, the most celebrated of Parliamentary reporters, describes how Sheridan came up to him after his first speech and asked his opinion. Woodfall was the expert critic in the art of parliamentary oratory. In those days it was forbidden to take notes in the House of Commons. Woodfall, known as 'Memory' Woodfall, was constantly at his post, listening and recording everything he heard. Whatever the hour, he was to be seen in the gallery in his usual place, chin on gold headed cane, ready for the debate, and ready to memorize what was said.

Woodfall's answer to Sheridan was devastating: 'I am sorry to say I do not think that this is your line – you had much better have stuck to your former pursuits.' Sheridan rested his head upon his hand, and then said vehemently, 'It is in me, however, and by God, it shall come out!' Sheridan's instinct to turn to the expert, to consult his opinion is very much the instinct of the actor to ask how the play had come over that evening.

Certainly the House of Commons at this period provided in many senses a good field for Sheridan's talents. It was intolerant of bores. It was indispensable that a member should look and conduct himself as a gentleman. Wit was a shining asset, which could lift a man out of the rut; and wit, delivered at an opponent with a smile, was an attribute which Sheridan had in abundance. Always good humoured, and always ready with an amusing shaft at the expense of others, he knew that he could shine. Perhaps in this first speech he had shown too much determination to escape from his past.

On November 2, 1780 Sheridan, seconded by Mr Fitzpatrick was finally elected to Brooks's, which thereafter became his second home.

At the outset he took his duties as a Parliamentarian seriously, as he had done with the management of his theatre. But from the very beginning his theatrical background was a disadvantage to him in the House of Commons, although he needed the money which came from it. It was the sole means of support for himself and his family, and yet this fatal connection was constantly being used against him. He was regarded in the House as an adventurer – and, what was worse, an Irish adventurer. He had come into politics without the solid backing of birth and parliamentary ancestors which favoured the careers of Pitt, Fox, and Windham. It was generally felt unsuitable that the manager of a theatre should find a place in the House of Commons.

When Sheridan reproved Mr Courtenay for the tavern wit with which he had ridiculed the opposition, he ended by saying 'that the most serious part of the argument appeared to him to be the most ludicrous'. Courtenay, not disinclined to hit below the belt, said that the Honourable Gentleman was an enemy to mirth and wit in any *house* but his own. The Old Boys in the Old School House were watching the new boy and judging him by his background. Pitt was the son of a former brilliant pupil, he was at once accepted and listened to with respect.

Sheridan was not. He had to fight all the way. He was expected to behave like Charles Surface, and Members were surprised to find that he was untiring in his attendance at the House, that his ideas were practical, that what he said was never irrelevant, and that much common sense was interspersed with wit. The great asset which Sheridan had was his real talent as an orator, whatever 'Memory' Woodfall said about his début. The eighteenth-century House of Commons appreciated oratory. Like the Romans, Sheridan's contemporaries regarded oratory as an end in itself. The policies and the debates went on as they always do in Parliament, but at this particular time the manner in which the policies were put forward, the weighing of the words, the balance of the sentences, working up to a peroration, were savoured as other men savour fine wines.

It is hard for a generation like ours when the stage, and screens, both large and small, are so often illumined by actors conversing in grunts, to understand the aesthetic pleasure which the eighteenth century took in listening to words used, as a painter would use his colours on a palette, to conjure up pictures. These pictures were built up like the paintings of the period, with an eye to general effect, yet each little detail was carefully limned, and every telling adjective and simile was appreciated by the audience.

His opponents agreed that Sheridan was to the manner born, but he was not: he was trained in it. Sheridan had been reared on oratory by his father, and while some of the instruction may have gone over his head in seas of boredom, the lesson had been learned.

Pitt's first speech, unlike Sheridan's, was received with rapture by his fellow parliamentarians. Pitt was only twenty-one when Burke said of him, 'He is not a chip of the old block, he is the old block itself,' and in the beginning Fox's reaction was equally enthusiastic. Pitt had been elected to Brooks's and everything in the Whig garden seemed to be coming up Parliamentary roses – except that the Whigs were in opposition.

The election had been occasioned by the Gordon Riots which had caused general panic. Lord George Gordon had managed to set a great part of London alight by bringing out the old cry of 'No Popery' when the emancipation of the Catholics had been mooted. For a week the whole of the city had been a prey to rioting and drunken mobs, who burned the chapels of the Catholic Ambassadors, and the prison of Newgate, threatened the Houses of Parliament, and laid siege to the Bank of England.

William Hickey, the diarist, who returned from India on leave in the summer of 1780, says:

'From my sister I learnt of the horrors of the riots that had occurred three weeks prior to my arrival, which from their novelty and violence paralysed the inhabitants of the metropolis from one extremity to the other, and from the consequences of which they had not yet recovered. I saw, upon entering the City, some of the effects and large parties of military, both horse and foot, upon duty in different places, especially at the Bank and in St Paul's Churchyard.

Apart from noting the military patrolling the streets, Hickey noticed the smoking ruins of houses, distilleries, and churches. In his usual chatty way he consulted his cab driver as to how such excesses could have been committed in the heart of

London. The coach driver said that twenty resolute men might have dispersed the mob but when they found they were in control they were joined by mixed bands of pickpockets, housebreakers and thieves of all kinds ready to join in the fun.

By the time the flames had been put out and the mob driven back, the general run of the population were in a Tory non-reforming mood. The King himself had spent over £80,000 to make sure that his friends were elected. So Pitt, Fox, Burke and Sheridan were all at this moment in opposition; but although the riots had given the population a temporary fright, the government was not in a strong position.

Sheridan spoke in a very practical way about the aftermath of the Gordon Riots. The great Whig fear at this time was that once the military were out on the streets, they could seize power – and keep it. They would then be able to curtail the liberty of the people. The military represented danger from the King. Therefore Sheridan asked why the same magistrates and policemen who had proved themselves to be so futile in an emergency were still in control. They were, he said, 'Men of proved imbecility and convicted depravity'. Had they been left at their posts because the government wanted the 'protection of the bayonet to continue in repute', and so make it necessary to use the military again because the civil authorities were unable to keep order? He suggested that inaction might deliberately breed an excuse for oppression.

In his first session in Parliament Sheridan opposed his friend Fox in his attempt to reduce the ages under the Marriage Act. It was proposed that young persons should now be allowed to marry at sixteen. He said that his honourable friend who brought in the Bill appeared not to be aware that, if he carried the clause enabling girls to marry at sixteen, he would do an injury to that liberty of which he had always shown himself the friend, and promote domestic tyranny which he could consider as little less intolerable than public tyranny. If girls were allowed to marry at sixteen they would be abridged of that happy freedom of intercourse which modern custom had introduced between the youth of both sexes, and which was, in his opinion, the best nursery of happy marriages. Guardians would in that case look on their wards with a jealous eye from a fear that footmen and those about them might take advantage of their tender years and immature judgement and persuade them into marriage.

Sheridan, with a backward glance, was probably thinking of the happy meetings in Bath with Eliza, and imagining what could have happened if she had been allowed to be married off at sixteen to a rich old man. Moore, the poetical trimmer, did not take a kindly view. He described the speech as youthful and romantic: but underneath the alleged romanticism, Sheridan's view had a streak of common sense.

When it came to opposing the American War of Independence, Sheridan and Fox were as one. England was at this time still waging her unsuccessful campaigns. The Whig tendencies were for liberty, and the support of free men everywhere. In Sheridan's day 'liberty' was a word which stood for something specific, a beacon in a dark world, and the King and the King's friends were still considered a threat to free men everywhere. As the Whigs saw it, the government was carrying out a vindictive war against America, and the stupidity and obstinacy of the King and Court were allied to apathy on the part of the great mass of the electorate. Between folly and apathy, Liberty, that proud banner, was likely to be cast into the dust.

Moreover England was not only battling against the liberty of the Americans, but also carrying on wars of aggression, in the Whig view, against both the French in India and the Indian people. Fox and Sheridan were seen, and saw themselves, as torch carriers for Liberty, preserving the Constitution from the slimy hands of the oppressors.

Thundering against the American War, which had become both unsuccessful and unpopular, was a way to court popularity and votes, and this, combined with a bias towards parliamentary reform, gave much power to Fox and Sheridan in opposition at this time. Their hopes of office were riding high on the public execration of Lord North and his administration.

Sheridan declaimed thus about North: 'A deliberate body of so uncommon a form would probably be deemed a kind of State Monster by the ignorant and vulgar, they would probably approach it with as much reverence as Stephano does the monster in *The Tempest*. What one body and two voices! – a most delicate monster, a very shallow monster, and particularly a most poor credulous monster.'

On one occasion he said that while most of his political opponents went about inveighing against the government, in private, and acknowledging its total incapacity, yet when they went to the House of Commons they voted as if they believed them to have every virtue under heaven. He remarked sarcastically that 'Some gentlemen, as Mr Gibbon, for instance, while in private they indulge their opinion pretty freely will yet in their zeal for the public good even condescend to accept a place in order to give a colour to their confidence in the wisdom of the Government,' adding that the patient was dying of the doctor not of the disease.

Things do not change much over the centuries.

*

Although Lord North carried the brunt of the censure for pursuing the foolish policies of George III, he was not seen by his contemporaries as the prize fool he has since become. Even his Whig foes admitted that some of the worst aggressions against the colonies had been committed long before he came to power. But he was an easy-going man, and possibly the idea of the Divine Right of Kings died hard in his mind. If times had been easier he would not have achieved the reputation with which his name is now synonymous. His friends and co-Parliamentarians saw him as a man of playful wit and unvarying good humour. These characteristics were in total contrast to the seeming harshness and stupidity of his policies.

He was, perhaps, one of those men who are pliant when they should be firm, and immovable when they should concede. Unfortunately for him, insulting words when flinging the Tea Duty in the face of the Americans – 'a total repeal of the Port Duties could not be thought of till America was prostrate at the feet of England' – set the seal on his reputation as a foolish oppressor.

When Sheridan entered Parliament the star of Lord North was already in its decline, it was bright morning for the opposition, and for Sheridan the opportunities looked limitless.

The horizon of his ambitions seemed to have opened up, and his career seemed to show extraordinary promise, despite his socially unfortunate theatrical connections. He conducted himself with seriousness and with sagacity, and his talent for oratory was before long well regarded on both sides of the House.

Lord Brougham said of him, 'Sheridan has a warm imagination, a fierce, dauntless spirit of attack, familiarity acquired from his dramatic productions, with the feelings of the heart; a facility of epigram and point; the more direct gift of the same theatrical apprenticeship; an excellent manner not unconnected with that experience; and a depth of voice which suited the tone of his declamation.' It was said that although his wit occasionally descended to farce, the wit was not the inspiration of the argument.

However, in view of the prejudice against his background, it was going to need hard work and application to shake off his disadvantages. But he had the quick brain of a barrister, and the ability to marshal his arguments in due order. Given time, and luck, he was doubtless confident that he could shake off his unfortunate family connections.

Sheridan saw the great world of ambition as an anodyne against private griefs. Before he had married Eliza, he had expressed this point of view to his friend Halhed. He put forward the idea that if a man depended on purely private happiness, then a change of feelings on the part of the loved one, or the cold hand of death, could disturb that happiness.

Sheridan, with his Celtic streak, feared the hand of death, and he saw ambition as an aid to side-step sorrow and the ills to which the flesh is heir. 'True Ambition', as he had said, 'can never be disappointed – it hopes most when most oppressed.' At last he had found a way to combat sorrow, or some sorrow, and to develop to the full the talents which he knew he possessed.

He was set on a course, then, which among other rewards should keep the dark at bay and bury the sombre side of his personality. As he had said to the pessimistic Woodfall – it was in him, and by God, it was going to come out.

CHAPTER 11

The Friend of Liberty
and Member of Brooks's

It is difficult to simplify the tortuous politics of another era. The shifting bases of power, the different pressures on human beings battling through their lives, lend different emphasis to abstract ideas. Politicians writing their reminiscences can take an over-optimistic view of their own motives. Moments when they have sunk their nobler sentiments without trace, or much regret, to secure governmental posts are conveniently forgotten. Speeches which they made when moved by spite or envy become perorations in the cause of liberty. Wrong policies which may have been conceived after a drinking bout become mistakes caused by the pusillanimity of others. The cowardice of political friends becomes prudence, while the prudence of foes becomes blindness and crass folly.

When Sheridan entered Parliament it was under the wing of the Whig oligarchs, the great families who had curbed the power of the Hanoverians, and broken an attempted stranglehold of the monarchy. But over the years the power which the Whigs held as their right had been encroached upon by the King. Using a system of patronage he had built up during the lax government of Lord North and his Tories, George III had increased his personal power. This was inevitably seen as a threat to the liberties of the people, and the Whigs, intent on regaining their powers against the King, and in spite of their aristocratic attitudes and the complicated grapevine of marriages and political connections which held them together, were again posing stridently as the champions of liberty. They welcomed the new ideas coming out of France, and hailed the French revolution as a new dawn and, like Wordsworth, they felt it was bliss in that dawn to be alive, and to be young was

12 *Above:* The Prince Regent, Mrs Fitzherbert, Sheridan (*Gillray's* view of suspected intrigue). *Below:* The Faro Table at Devonshire House in 1791 (*Rowlandson*). *Metropolitan Museum, New York*

13   *a:* 'The Falling of Ye Screen'.   *b:* Drury Lane Theatre on fire

very heaven. They could foresee neither the bloody outcome
of the ideas of Rousseau, nor the decline of liberty into the
welter of blood under the sway of the Jacobins, nor the exten-
sion of the powers of the people into the dictatorship of
Napoleon.

The American War had now declined into what was called
a policy of harassing America. It was, however, more harassing
to the government at home, and to George III in particular.
It was rapidly getting to the point where if the war were not
stopped, and the power of the King curbed, then there was
going to be a choice between keeping the peace and keeping
the King, a point made, in effect, by Pitt later, in a different
way.

Sheridan has been called by some an imperialist democrat
or a patriotic radical. But as regards the American War he was
always in total opposition to the foolish and intemperate
policies which had been pursued. About it he said that it was
impossible to separate contempt from resentment and ridicule
from indignation, and when Lord John Cavendish moved a
vote of censure on Lord North's administration, and Rigby
made what was called an insolent speech full of levity, Sheridan
cut him down to size: 'Undoubtedly', he said, 'if the degree of
offence which speeches gave was to be considered as the
criterion of eloquence, the right honourable gentleman must
be looked up to as the Demonsthenes of that assembly.'

Then he pricked a weak spot in the government's defence.
Rigby believed, he said, that as a Member of Parliament, as a
Privy Councillor, as a private gentleman, he had always
detested the American War as much as any man, but he had
never been able to persuade the *Paymaster* that it was a bad war,
and unfortunately it was the Paymaster who always voted in
that House. Rigby was both Paymaster and Privy Councillor.

The North administration tottered towards its close, and in
1781 the British Army surrendered to Washington at York-
town. King George III was baldly told by his subjects of the
City of London: 'Your armies are captured. The wonted
superiority of your navies is annihilated. Your dominions are
lost.' Although the news of the defeat in America had already
reached London two days before Parliament opened, King

George III in his opening speech to Parliament still seemed to persist in the policies which had led to so many disasters.

But there was not long to wait. Pitt made his remarkable speech in the House of Commons, and ended by saying that it was a simple question of whether the King would change his ministers and keep the Empire, or keep his ministers and lose the kingdom. George III was treading on the dangerous ground which had driven other Kings from England.

The government fell, and on April 8, 1782, the Marquess of Rockingham became Prime Minister. Shelburne and Fox were both Secretaries of State. Burke became Paymaster General of the Forces, and Sheridan became Under-Secretary of State for Foreign Affairs. After only two years in Parliament he was already in the government. It had been a brilliant rise. He had made his mark before the most sophisticated audience in the kingdom.

Sheridan wrote to his brother in April of 1782:

'Tho' I have time only to send you a very few lines to Night, I will not omit to convince you how very much a man of business I am become, by acknowledging the receipt of a letter from you this Day—I take it for granted that you know from our Newspapers that it is the Under Secretary of State who is become thus punctual. I wanted to force myself into Business Punctuality and information. The want of attention or knowledge of Business shall not positively be an objection to me in anything I may aim at hereafter—as you shall see and hear—and so also will you hear of Mr Secretary Fox.'

Brave words, but in the small affairs of day-to-day business Sheridan was negligent. It was one thing to shine before an audience in the House of Commons and quite another to be sitting at a desk mulling through mounds of paper. Wags said that during this period there was a notice attached to Sheridan's door: 'No application to be received here on Sundays, nor any business done during the remainder of the week.'

Walpole said of Fox at this time, 'Mr Fox already shines as greatly in place as he did in Opposition. He is now as in-

defatigable as he was idle. He has perfect temper, and not only
good humour, but good nature and more common sense than
any man, with amazing parts that are neither ostentatious nor
affected.' It was not surprising that Sheridan, who shared so
many of these admired qualities, was his friend. But unlike
Charles Fox, he was not the spoiled child of a rich man. Richard
Sheridan had a background which in many ways he wished to
forget, and relatives who once he had achieved some eminence
were in turn not likely to forget Richard Sheridan.

*

As might have been anticipated, just as Sheridan's old
father had reappeared on the horizon as soon as he had become the proprietor of a theatre, so his brother Charles became friendly as soon as Richard was in the government.
Charles Sheridan was now living permanently in Ireland: he
had become an Irish MP in 1776, and had been called to the
Bar in 1780.

Although Charles' character was that of a plodding place-
hunter, it has to be admitted that the scoldings and advice
with which he was disposed to interlace his letters to Richard
showed some horse sense, and were doubtless the less welcome
for that reason. Indeed one may imagine that Richard's heart
sank at the mere sight of a letter from Charles, fearing such a
one as he received soon after his appointment: 'But as you may
now be in a situation in which you may obtain some substantial
advantage for yourself, for God's sake improve the opportunity
to the utmost', wrote Charles, 'and don't let dreams of empty
fame (of which you have had enough in conscience) carry you
away from your solid interests. I return you many thanks for
Fox's letter—I mean for your intention to make him write one
—for your good intentions always satisfy your conscience and
you seem to think the carrying them into execution a mere
trifling ceremony. I will forgive you, however, on condition that
you will for once in your life consider that though the will alone
may perfectly satisfy yourself, your friends would be a little
more gratified if they were sometimes to see it accompanied
by the deed'—here he comes to the nub of the matter—'and
let me be the first upon whom you try the experiment.' Charles

goes on to make a careful suggestion as to his own future: 'I think I may rely upon you that whoever comes over here as Lord Lieutenant, I shall not be forgot among the number of those who shall be recommended to them.'

Interspersed with wisdom and demands for help in his place-hunting, Charles casually mentions that he resents having to pay his uncle an annuity which is a great drain on his exchequer, and ends by saying that he cannot pay 'dear Dick' the fifty pounds he owes him.

But Sheridan, good-hearted as always, does not seem to have harboured any real resentment against his brother, and he managed to get Charles appointed Secretary for War in Ireland. Charles, being of sterner yet more pliable stuff than Richard, always managed, like the turncoat Vicar of Bray, to keep afloat. He was one of those useful men whom nobody particularly likes to engage, but equally, once in office no one likes to dismiss.

There was great busy-ness in this administration. Peace proposals were mooted with France and Holland, and independence was to be accorded to America. But the seeds of dissolution were dormant in the ministry from the beginning, and unfortunately for Sheridan, it was short-lived, surviving only eight months. It has been said that the quarrels of the Whigs at this juncture represented a form of political Protestantism, and paid a similar price for the freedom of its doctrines in a multiplicity of opinions, whereas Toryism, like the Roman Church, held its followers together by the common doctrine of the infallibility of the throne, and took care to repress any schism inconvenient to the general interest. This may have been a good defence, but it was not justification for the quarrels which were largely based on personal animosities. For one thing, Shelburne and Fox disliked each other.

The actual political cabals between the different wings of the party were mostly concerned with the independence of America. Shelburne and his friends saw the granting of independence to the States as a humiliation to England. Fox and Sheridan saw it as the dawn of a new era, and an urgent matter, before France gained yet more credit in America.

Not content with quarrelling at home, they were even sending different envoys abroad. Fox and his friends, including Sheridan, had their own envoys in Ireland, while in Paris Shelburne had as envoy a Scotsman called Oswald, and Fox had sent Thomas Grenville. There was no unity even in these foreign negotiations, and in Paris two conflicting fronts were shown towards France.

The administration managed to keep going on an uneasy basis until July 1782, when the Prime Minister, Rockingham, died. The King sent for Lord Shelburne to form a new Ministry. Unfortunately, Sheridan was one of Fox's sincere followers, but Shelburne was the arch enemy of Fox. It was an inherited dislike. Fox's father, Lord Holland, had described Shelburne as a 'pious fraud', and he had been caricatured as Malagrida, or the 'Jesuit'.

The facts were that Shelburne was clever, hard working, and assiduous in his attention to detail, unlike both Fox and Sheridan. It was said that Shelburne knew more about finance than the Chancellor of Exchequer, and more about foreign affairs than the Foreign Secretary. He was not a boon companion, and not an intimate of the clubbable fellows at Brooks's. When in Opposition Fox and Sheridan were reeling out of the club in the early hours, he would be hard at work with his staff at Lansdown House, examining accounts, weighing up the consequences of fiscal policies, and preparing for office.

Unlike Fox and Sheridan, he had no charm—he was a well-balanced, smooth man, and Fox disliked him and was determined not to serve under him. Fox, the spoiled child, was no different now from the indulged boy he had once been. 'Young people', Fox's father had said, 'are always in the right, and old people in the wrong. Let nothing be done to break his spirit.' If Charles wished to break up a gold watch, wash his hands in cream at the dinner table, or throw his father's office correspondence in the fire he was allowed to. He still did not like to be thwarted, and he would have none of Shelburne.

He decided to resign. Sheridan followed Fox into the wilderness of Opposition. This resignation of Fox and his followers in the middle of the peace negotiations with France and America was not well regarded in the country. It was the beginning of Fox's slide from power, for Shelburne chose William Pitt to be his Chancellor of the Exchequer. Fox may have regarded himself as a man of the people, but William Pitt was the first minister to realize that the basis of power rested with the rising middle classes. He was not interested in the complicated cabals of the old-time Whigs. He would appeal above their heads to the great mass of his countrymen. Although they did not know it, the day of the Whig families dividing the spoils of power and office between themselves and their hangers-on was over.

Sheridan had chosen the wrong side. The charm of Fox and of the aristocratic ladies who surrounded him had been too attractive a background for a man such as Sheridan to resist. He was now in the middle of the magic circle which once he had read about in the news sheets. Fox was his friend and the claims of such a friendship were sweeter than those of office. Besides, would not the shifting tides of politics bring Fox's ship into harbour again with fame and fortune on board? 'And so', wrote Sheridan to Grenville, 'begins a new Opposition but wofully thinned and disconcerted, I fear.' The sweets of office had not lasted long.

Fox and Sheridan were freer and friendlier than ever, and loud in their condemnations of the Jesuit of Berkley Square, Lord Shelburne. He had been, as they saw it, the cause of the downfall of the ministry. Had Fox at this point consented to serve with Shelburne he would have made a greater mark in history than he did, but personal piques and personal loyalties continued to prevail. Sheridan justified their going out of office by saying, 'Those who go out are right, for there is really no question, whether having lost their power, they ought to stay and lose their characters.' The attitude of Fox and Sheridan was perfectly consistent, perfectly understandable, and absolutely misguided.

The hubris of Shelburne and Fox, who both refused to play second fiddle to the other, split the party. Jointly they could have kept the King and the King's friends in check, but they remained devoted to keeping their old animosities alive. Soon the plots and counterplots thickened again. At the beginning of 1783 the peace treaty of Versailles had been concluded with

France, and the provisional treaty with America was laid before the House. A vote of censure on this was carried, and the ministry of Shelburne fell, beaten by a mere seventeen votes.

More plots, cabals, and corridor politics then followed. For nearly six weeks England was without a government. Pitt had refused the King's offer to form a ministry. It was said that he wished to give Fox enough rope to allow him to destroy himself. North was called back, but North suggested the Duke of Portland. On hearing *his* name, the King merely said, 'Then I wish you good night!'

An impasse had been reached. It was like a nursery quarrel. Shelburne wanted Pitt; North could favour Shelburne; Fox wanted Pitt but his pride would not let him serve under him. A certain amount of Dutch auctioning went on. Finally the unthinkable was thought of—and Fox and North formed a coalition. Fox had seen this as the only road which would lead him back to power. He excused this new alliance by saying that it was only the American War which had caused him to execrate the name of North, and brand him as an enemy to free men all over the world. At this point, eating his words seemed a simple matter to Fox.

Sheridan was supposed to have been against the coalition, and it was said that he warned Fox of the folly of allying himself with his old enemies. But Lord John Townshend, writing to Lord Holland long after the events said:

'Well, Sheridan, do you know, instead of being adverse to the Coalition, as I dare say you have often heard the vapouring rogue declare, was on the contrary I assure you one of the most eager and clamorous for it. His hatred of Pitt, and his anxiety to get into office were motives sufficient. It is true he had no hand in carrying the measure into effect for nobody had any sort of confidence in him. Think of his impudence afterwards in boasting that he had always deprecated the Coalition and foretold its disastrous consequences.'

Lord Holland reports:

'Upon my acknowledging that Sheridan had cajoled me

into a belief that he had strenuously deprecated the Coalition Lord John sent me the following reply: "I have laughed heartily at your account of Sheridan's having duped you into a belief of his noble sacrifice of judgment and opinions to the wishes of others, by his acquiescence in the Coalition and handsome support of a measure he originally disapproved. In his great wisdom it seems he foresaw, for foretell he certainly did not, all the ill consequences of the imprudent step. These secret thoughts, however, he kept carefully locked up in his own breast, never uttering a syllable of disapprobation of the measure in the course of it to Mr Fox, to myself, or to any one of his intimate friends till more than a 12 month afterwards; when I allow he was one of the loudest in his lamentations and condemnations, though I don't think he had the impudence even then to say that he had been prepared for the events that followed.'''

It may have been that Sheridan did foresee the rashness of Fox's move, but he was loyal to Fox, his friend, to the point of ignoring his own interests. Unlike his brother, Charles Sheridan, Richard was not a dedicated place hunter. He was fond of devious negotiations, and was easily carried away on the tides of emotion, but he was never his own best friend in a worldly sense.

Retired politicians writing to one another long after their old conquests are like aged courtesans: they will never admit that they have been wrong or rejected. Nor do a few calumnies of their former rivals or associates bother them over-much. From the manner of his behaviour during his career in Parliament, the picture of Sheridan as being over-eager for place – and the word over-eager must be stressed – seems to be out of character.

Moore, in his Journal, says that Sheridan paced up and down for hours trying to persuade Charles Fox that he was making a mistake, and that Sheridan pointed out that the middle classes, whom he highly respected, would condemn the coalition on its first appearance merely because it was composed of men who had long been political enemies. On these grounds, 'full of apprehension for the character of his right honourable friend' he most certainly had advised against the coalition. This has been denied by Sheridan's denigrators.

In mitigation it must be said that to Sheridan, friendship and good fellowship were paramount. All his life he was to prefer old friends to new ones, and Fox was his friend, both in Parliament and out of it.

When Fox's party first came back to power the ordinary people of England had been with them. The hopes of the people from the new government were extravagant. They expected peace with France, and with America, on honourable terms; the reform of Parliament, the cutting down of place-hunters everywhere, and a general atmosphere of permanent happiness and prosperity, because electors are forever optimists.

But Fox's coalition with his former enemies was not well-regarded. Only a year or so before he had been inveighing against North:

> 'From the moment I shall make any terms with one of them, I shall not rest satisfied to be called the most infamous of mankind: I could not for an instant think of coalition with men who in every public and private transaction, as ministers, have shown themselves void of every principle of honour and honesty; in the hands of such men I would not trust my honour even for a minute.'

His honour seemed pliable, for now he was sitting side by side with them on the front bench. The public saw men who had calumniated and abused one another now seemingly happy as allies. Since it was not felt that a coalition was justified except in times of national peril, the populace regarded the spectacle of this particular coalition as unsavoury, a number of politicians dividing up the spoils of office between them.

Lord North handled Home Affairs, and Fox was Foreign Secretary. Sheridan, with Burke's son, was a secretary to the Treasury, a curious post for someone who had not the faintest idea of how to handle money, either public or private. Burke himself was Paymaster of the Forces.

The beginning of the Ministry was not auspicious for the

King, who hated Fox and was threatening to return to Hanover. 'Sulky Nobbs', as Eliza Sheridan called him, turned his back on Fox when he kissed hands. It was said that he looked like a shying horse at Astley's just before it kicked off its rider with turned-back eyes and ears.

*

The Ministry was certainly not on a sound basis and yet it was at this difficult period of the proceedings that Fox decided to introduce his India Bill. Considering the delicate balance of the Ministry both in the House of Commons and the country, the decision to bring in a controversial Bill at this juncture was unwise in the extreme.

The background to the disorders which had grown up in India was the extraordinary position of the East India Company. Originally it had been a few trading stations engaged in bringing goods like tea and rice to Europe, but the India of the Moguls was a collapsing Empire, and the East India Company gradually became drawn into raising private armies and making and breaking princely empires. India itself became a happy hunting-ground for younger sons of upper-class families seeking their fortunes. The East India Company paid very badly. Clerks drew a mere five pounds a year, and to compensate for their miserable salaries the employees of the company at all grades were expected to augment their salaries by judicious trading on the side. It was inevitable that the trading became more important than the job, and many of the employees returned as so-called 'nabobs'—retired ex-India millionaires who, with peppery complexions and health often destroyed by heat and fever, returned to die in England. Although the servants of the East India Company were filling their pockets, the Company itself did not prosper.

However, the nabobs, on retiring with their lakhs of rupees, normally managed to buy the goodwill of a number of Members of Parliament, who could then be guaranteed to vote to leave things in India as they were. People in England saw and were jealous of the returning nabobs. But it is only fair to say that they did not see the dangers which these men had been through, or count the numbers who had never returned.

For India was not only a place where squalor and riches lived side by side, but one where death could strike literally from one hour to the next. William Hickey, who sailed to India in 1769, describes the hot and evil wind which below off shore as he arrived, and how the ship's carpenter 'a strong-made vigorous man' died within an hour of being seized with violent cramps. On another occasion he rides along the shore to spend a happy weekend with a friend, and on reaching the bungalow finds the man and all his servants dead.

There were disadvantages to the pursuit of a fortune in the East, but the picture looked different from England, and Warren Hastings, then Governor General of Bengal, was considered an oppressive tyrant, from whom power must be wrested. Although it was on the subject of Indian affairs that Sheridan was later to make his mark on the House of Commons, and to prove that he was the orator he felt himself to be, his was not the moving hand or brain behind the India investigations. The prime instigator behind the rooting out of abuses was Burke. One of his distant relatives, William Burke, had failed miserably to retrieve his fortune in India, and he acted as informer. Another of Burke's informants was one Philip Francis, an implacable enemy of Warren Hastings, who had been wounded when fighting a duel against the Governor.

Hickey, who usually takes a fairly lenient view of most people, described his first meeting with Francis. Hickey had been bidden to a breakfast to present his letters of introduction. Francis opened the first letter and then burst out laughing, saying that 'it struck him as superlatively ridiculous for Mr Burke to imagine that he could be of the smallest use to an attorney'. Hickey remarks that he felt 'extremely mortified at his impertinent manner, especially before so large a company'.

If Hastings was to be indicted for high-handedness, Philip Francis does not seem to have been far behind in such behaviour, and if jealousy of Hastings is included in the character package-deal, then Burke was listening to a very biased witness. But Burke was on the war-path, and once he had collected his facts, his fervent imagination was unleashed. He was generally considered to be intellectually intemperate: Burke raved like a Bedlamite for two hours, said one eye witness. Nor was he averse to using disgusting images once his spirit was roused. He spoke of 'a foetus in a bottle', of 'foul and putrid mucus in which are engendered the whole brood of creeping ascarides'. The Governors in India were excrement, vermin on a carcase, offal on which fattened the kites, and he referred to Sir Elijah Impey, one of the Chief Justices, as having a fox smell. Unlike Mrs Malaprop he was not 'nice' in his derangement of epithets.

There is no doubt that many of his facts were true, even if some were exaggerated or crudely expressed. Sheridan's hand in Indian affairs was more equivocal. He was following a middle path. Sentimentally he was on the side of the oppressed Indian masses, his heart melting at the outcry about 'trampled Hindostan', and he would have been glad to see the humbling of the nabobs who flaunted their Eastern plunder. But he did not deal in the extremes of idealism as did Burke, nor was he as over-optimistic about the outcome.

Once political passions are unleashed it is difficult to adopt a middle road without being accused of chicanery by political allies. Whatever happened later, in the beginning Sheridan was against too much energy being used to pursue and confiscate the wealth of the East India merchants. On the whole, although he supported the India Bill, idealism and the pursuit of oppressors could be carried too far.

Ironically, it is possible that had things turned out differently Sheridan himself might have been driven to seek his fortune in the East. His friend, Nathaniel Halhed, a rival for the hand of Eliza in the past, had sailed for India, and had become one of the lieutenants of Warren Hastings, and a great scholar versed in Eastern languages. Halhed helped Warren Hastings in a translation of the Hindu law to prove, as the Governor himself said, that the inhabitants of that land were not in the savage state in which they had been unfairly represented. The Hindu princes and the eighteenth-century administrators had in fact some things in common, such as a certain culture and an eye for riches.

Sheridan thought that if the government in England could remedy the worst abuses, then there was no need for drastic action, or for sacrificing an exceptional man like Warren

Hastings – whose appointment had been confirmed by a government which had refused to accept his resignation. But if Parliament would not remedy the abuses then Warren Hastings should be brought home, and the whole issue enquired into in the proper form.

It was here that Sheridan's attitude was perhaps questionable, for he seems to have acted as a go-between. The 'Bengal squad' had many supporters in the House of Commons, because the lakhs of rupees had done their work well. They could wreck Fox's Bill, and bring the Ministry down. Whether at the instigation of Fox, or on his own initiative, Sheridan consulted his old friend from Harrow, Halhed, who was on leave from India, and it seemed sensible to sound him out about Governor Hastings' recall, and to find out what were the opinions of Governor Hastings from someone recently arrived from India who would have direct information. Subsequently, under Fox's aegis, Sheridan found a friend, his old schoolmaster, Dr Parr, who was prepared to canvass the views of Major Scott, the agent of Warren Hastings.

Like his acquisition of Drury Lane, an air of mystery hangs over these negotiations. The stories woven about the encounters are many and various. Sheridan's enemies suggested that he had been asked by Fox to put forward the suggestion that the impeachment of Hastings would be given up, if the Bill were enabled to sail smoothly through the House of Commons.

Later Sheridan said that the India Bill had been mentioned, but merely as a matter of conversation, and not as a proposition, that there had not been the slightest idea of bartering with Hastings for his support of the Bill, and that he had only sent his friend to know whether Warren Hastings would come back if recalled. Major Scott subsequently agreed that this was the truth about the interview. But a doubt remains.

It certainly did look as if Fox were trying to get the East India magnates on his side. Had he received some encouragement from Major Scott, via Sheridan, possibly Warren Hastings would never have been impeached. But as in so much political accommodation everything hung poised, floating like a feather tossed by currents of air, and the delicate suggestions

made over a glass of wine in a drawing-room looked different
later when dragged out into the light of day by enemies.
Burke was not for accommodation, the dung heap must be
cleaned up, and Fox came to share this uncompromising point
of view. Armed with the facts carefully collected by Burke,
Fox decided that the government of India was to be put into
the hands of seven commissioners. The names of these commissioners were announced: four were followers of Fox, and
the other three were creatures of Lord North, one of them his
own son.

Then the great storm broke about the heads of the Whigs.
Pitt said that the pretended relief to Asia was grounded on
injustice and violence in Europe, and that, 'property was
menaced', a sentiment which at once rallied the middle
classes. The country squires sounded a view-hallo of alarm.
Leadenhall Street and its merchants were equally appalled.
One merchant was said to have dropped dead of apoplexy at
the very idea. It was death by descending dividends, or the
fear of them.

The Opposition saw the taking away of the charter of the
East India Company, not only as an injustice in itself, but as a
threat to all charters everywhere. This hit at the roots of many
contracts and was not a simple matter. It was also considered
a way of putting jobs worth vast sums at the disposal of Fox.
He was caricatured as the Great Mogul Carlo Khan riding on
an elephant (Lord North) with Burke as his accompanying
trumpeter.

It was at this point in his career that the evil reputation of
his father, Lord Holland, came to haunt his future. He was
now regarded as a true son of his father, and the idea that he
should be given so large a slice of patronage appalled every
right-thinking man in the country. There had been echoes of
his father's peculations which still disturbed the Ministry.
Under Lord Shelburne, Barré, who had been awarded the
Pay Office, had found that Lord Holland's accounts as Paymaster, though eighteen years overdue, were still hanging fire,
and there was a small matter of £100,000 still owed to the
Exchequer. Handling these was an old minion of Lord
Holland's, one Powell. This man Powell had been accustomed

to manage the Holland interests, and also the non-interests, for his stint included dealing with Charles Fox's debts. Powell had not forgotten to line his own pockets and Barré dismissed him; but Burke, who was sorry for him, put him back in his job. Pitt seized hold of these facts to discredit both Fox, who wanted to forget how the family fortune had been built up, and Burke, who had been foremost in deciding on reforms and a clean up of these little nests of corruption. Fortunately for the embarrassed protagonists Powell cut his throat, and thus also several Gordian knots.

However, none of this deterred Fox from pursuing his Indian reforms. It was obvious that there were fantastic abuses in India, but they were not, of course, confined to British activity. Much oppression and bribery went on among Indians, including Indians in the vast areas over which the British had no control. If they joined in for their own ends, this was no doubt deplorable but not altogether surprising. It was an age of corruption everywhere. There was even a small item in the accounts for the First Minister which said, 'private stationery—£1,300', which either meant that some firm had shown amazing patience over a long period, or that the First Minister's letter writing was on a most remarkable scale.

But *coûte que coûte*, Fox was determined on his Bill and went forward with it. Sheridan's negotiations with the agents of Warren Hastings, if they were admitted to be negotiations, had come to nothing.

Warren Hastings, against whom in the end all the venom of Fox and his 'Fox Hounds' was to turn, was an able administrator, carrying out an almost impossible task in conditions which were fraught with many and complex difficulties. Apart from the disordered state of India, there was the double standard of English and Hindu laws, and the minor wars which necessitated the servants of the East India Company serving as soldiers one minute and traders the next. Hickey, for example, left his first position in India because he was expected to take part in the wars.

Some of the men who had preceded Hastings in the government of India had returned to their native land with vast fortunes. But Hastings was not one of them. After his first tour in India, which lasted fourteen years, he came back to England in 1763 with very little money. He spent four years at home, and was then forced by poverty to seek another situation in India: and there he stayed until 1783.

As seen from the House of Commons, the Indian landscape looked uniformly ugly, and highly coloured oratory had free rein. Burke said that Fox was treading the road that all heroes had trod before him. Wilberforce, who was against the Bill, compared the seven managers and eight assistants to 'seven physicians and eight apothecaries come to put the patient to death', while Lord Eldon brought out the Book of Revelations and compared Fox to the seven crowned beast rising up out of the sea 'to whom there was given a mouth speaking great things. Alas, the great city, wherein were made rich all that had ships, in one hour is made desolate.' There was no lack of mixed metaphors or hyperbole.

Wraxall says that in this debate no individual distinguished himself more throughout the whole progress of the proceedings than Sheridan, 'whose matchless endowments of mind, equally adapted to contests of wit or of argument and even under the control of imperturbable temper, enabled him to extend invaluable assistance to the minister'.

But in spite of all the oratorical fervour, and the fact that the Bill was carried in the Commons, the end was in sight. The Foxites attempt at the reform of India failed. The King was against it, the Lords were against it, and after various pieces of political jobbery, Fox was compelled to go to the country.

Pitt was returned with a majority of over two hundred. One hundred and sixty of Fox's followers, now called Fox's martyrs, lost their seats. Fox was returned for Westminster partly with the aid of the Duchess of Devonshire, who dressed herself in the buff and blue of Washington's uniform, but inevitably the election was not without incidents. Pitt, on his return from receiving the freedom of the City of London, was preceded by a triumphant mob who, on turning down St James's Street, tried to force the members of Brooks's to illuminate their windows in celebration. A counter-attack by members and club servants was mounted. Shouting, 'Fox and popular government!' they demolished the carriage of the Prime

Minister, while other fervent patriots, shouting, 'Pitt and the Constitution!' broke all the windows of Brooks's. Pitt beat a retreat to White's.

Fox said he had had nothing to do with the fracas. He had a perfect alibi: 'I was in bed with Mrs Armistead, who is ready to substantiate the fact on oath.'

Sheridan managed to scrape back for Stafford with the aid of more ale tickets and a further expenditure for clergymen's widows; but Sheridan and the 'Fox Hounds' were out of office, and it was the beginning of a very long haul in opposition.

Pitt had triumphed, and Pitt was not entirely the friend of Sheridan. They had already had one passage of arms. At the beginning, like the others who sat in the House of Commons as of right, Pitt had not taken Sheridan seriously. As Chancellor of Exchequer he had said:

'There is no man, sir, who admires more than I do the abilities of that honourable member, the elegant sallies of his mind, the pleasing effusions of his fancy, his dramatic turns, and his epigrammatic allusions. If they were only reserved for the proper stage, they would no doubt ensure the plaudits of his audience.'

Sheridan replied to Pitt that whenever he might think proper to repeat such allusions, he would meet them with perfect good humour. 'Nay, more, encouraged by the ecomiums bestowed on my talents, should I ever again engage in the occupations to which he alludes, I may by an act of presumption attempt to improve on one of Ben Jonson's best characters, the Angry Boy in *The Alchemist*.' *Angry boy* was a current slang term meaning vapourer. When it came to oral rapier work the two men were evenly matched, but it did not make them friendly opponents.

Sheridan did not only return to the Commons, he also had to return to the theatre, to get its affairs in some sort of order and make an income. Like Fox he was out of favour, and out of place. Unlike Fox, he had no financial support other than what he could earn for himself.

CHAPTER 12

Parliament and Theatre—A Double Bill

Although Parliament provided a splendid audience for Sheridan, always in the background to his public life and apparent social insouciance there was the Theatre Royal, Drury Lane. He was like an acrobat riding two horses at once, each of them mettlesome and likely to throw the rider.

His sister-in-law Mary Linley, who had married Richard Tickell in 1780, comments in her shrewd way on Sheridan's manner and modes of conducting what he was pleased to call business. 'Sheridan seems full of business', she writes in 1784, 'yet in good spirits, so I hope he hasn't many plagues, tho' there's no judging by his manner. For, like Charles in *The School for Scandal*, his spirits and distresses generally rise together, I think.'

She had obviously fallen under Richard's spell, for she says, 'I in particular am one who think you cannot ever be half kind enough to Sheridan.' But Mary and Eliza were under no illusions about his failings. 'I hope you will beg Sheridan to open all his letters. You know as well as I that Sheridan's days are generally weeks.' One of his visitors seeing a mêlée of coronetted letters unopened on his desk remarked ruefully, 'We are all treated alike.'

His wife said that anything in his hands was irrecoverable. It is hard to see how a man of such disorganized habits managed to keep so much business going at the same time, but it was mostly done by disappearing when things became awkward, and leaving things to others. His colleagues at the theatre and his relations at home were constantly writing to one another announcing his imminent arrival. 'Sheridan is expected in town everyday', writes Mary Tickell, 'so it is to be hoped he will set matters in a little better train at Drury Lane; for at present Tickell says the receipts are dismal to a degree of ruin;

that my father [Linley] however seems contented with the quiet of King's management.'

Anything would presumably have been quiet after the management of Thomas Sheridan, who had once more taken himself off from Drury Lane, but not without leaving a string of complaints behind him. He had, as usual, made himself extremely difficult. Betsy Sheridan, Richard's younger sister, poor girl, was living with her father and wrote in her journal: 'My father declared himself much displeased with my conduct in not having joined in his resentment to Richard instead of proposing a reconciliation.' But this time even the noble son Charles was also out of favour. 'He then went into his usual complaints of the ill-conduct of both his sons and even hints as if he may be driven to appeal to the world if they persevere in denying their assistance.'

He was quite determined to banish Richard from his sight again, and Betsy had to bear the brunt of his evil humour. She writes to her sister Lissy, in Dublin: 'My father says he has no objection to *my* seeing Dick and his wife. But for his part *he* never will.'

Sheridan had given his mother-in-law, Mrs Linley, the job of wardrobe mistress at Drury Lane, which was admirably suited to her very parsimonious nature. Betsy does not seem to have liked the look of her: 'Mrs Linley is grown older than anyone I have met. She has lost all her teeth and looks a compleat Witch. Dick sat by me and asked me a thousand questions about Ireland that made me smile as one would have supposed that I had come from the farthest part of America.' Sheridan had not been in the country of his birth since he had left it at the age of seven, and it had now become for him part of a misty and provincial past, somewhere to be enquired after, like a well-loved old relative.

Later at Drury Betsy remarked. 'Dick sat behind me the the whole night, and often renew'd the subject of my father. He [Richard] is I think greatly altered, he is altogether a much *larger* man than I had form'd an idea of—in his manner very kind but rather graver than I expected, indeed I should rather say melancholy than grave.'

Richard was only thirty-three, yet the description is of a

much older man. The stress of doing too many things at once
was beginning to tell. He even complained to his sister of
Charles's neglect and said he wished for some correspondent
in Ireland who would have written to him at length on the
state of that country. Presumably Charles, the trimmer, was
not going to commit himself on paper to someone who was now
in opposition and not likely to be of use for some time to
come.

These family quarrels and difficulties did not make life any
easier. Thomas Sheridan flatly refused to see him, and would
not even receive Eliza and Mary Tickell. He was still brooding
sulkily on the fact that King had been given the manager's
job at Drury Lane instead of him. Old Surly Boots, as Eliza
called him, was not to be wooed. But Surly Boots had done
Richard one good turn, he had talent spotted Sarah Siddons at
Bath. She had previously come to London under Garrick's
management, but her first appearance had not been a success
and she had returned to touring. Eventually, possibly due to his
father's enthusiasm, Mrs Siddons had been engaged with her
brother John Philip Kemble to act at Drury Lane.

In an age when noble classical heroines were dominant on
the stage, the dignified Sarah fitted the bill and filled the
boxes. But Richard does not seem to have taken Sarah, whose
prudishness was proverbial, as seriously as she took herself.
Mrs Siddons herself said that one night as she stepped into her
carriage to return home from the theatre, Sheridan suddenly
jumped in after her. 'Mr Sheridan', she said, 'I trust you will
behave with all propriety: if you do not, I shall immediately
let down the glass, and desire the servant to show you out.'
Sheridan *did* behave with all propriety. 'But', continued
Mrs Siddons, 'as soon as we had reached my house in Marlborough Street, and the footman had opened the carriage door
– only think! – the provoking wretch bolted out in the greatest
haste, and slunk away, as if anxious to escape unseen.' Sheridan
was always ready to have a joke at someone else's expense, and
as a result of Mrs Siddons' prim remark, he seems to have been
behaving like a clandestine lover in a French farce.

She was a very formidable lady, and carried her decla-
matory style into private life: when contemplating calico in a

warehouse she paralysed a shopman by declaiming 'In God's name, sirrah, will it wash?' in ringing tragic tones. At one dinner she declaimed, 'I am very ignorant, but I *thirst* for information—pray what fish is that?' But farce occasionally broke in even on Mrs Siddons. On one occasion, the night was hot and she sent a boy out to get her a pint of porter, but by the time he reappeared she was on stage. Unfortunately the boy carried out his commission meticulously, following Lady Macbeth round the stage with the pint pot, until several quelling looks from her flashing eyes sent him scurrying off-stage, beer and all. It was an incident which would have done very well for *The Critic*.

She was obviously not the kind of light conversationalist with whom Richard would have been at home, nor were his relations with her and her brother Kemble improved by the fact that salaries were not paid regularly at Drury Lane. But here Sheridan could use his charm. With the audience arriving, and Mrs Siddons refusing to answer the prompter's call, he would appear at the eleventh hour, and although no money or arrears of salary were forthcoming, he would eventually hand her into his carriage and drive her, now in the best of humour, to the theatre—a remarkable *tour de force* on Sheridan's part, since he said of her that she was a 'magnificent and appalling creature to whom he would as soon have thought of making love as to the Archbishop of Canterbury'.

Some of his foreign performers did not take so benevolent a view of his financial aberrations. Pachierotti, the opera singer, talked of the slippery manager Sheridan and described him as the object of his 'particular despise'. The days of good husbandry under Garrick had gone for good.

But behind Sheridan was Eliza, gentle, charming, intelligent, and helpful, reading the plays with her sister, Mary Tickell, interviewing performers, and no doubt using her soft talent to soothe the ruffled feathers of the actors at the theatre. It was not an easy life to live. In addition to the constant knowledge that they were living far above their income, there were added the uncertainties, the fluctuations of fortune at the theatre. She was also involved in a hectic social round of visits to Sheridan's grand friends. Eliza had all the necessary qualities of beauty, brains, and charm, but her spirit was stronger than her health.

She wrote graceful sentimental verse, and some of her lively amusing letters show not only her deep abiding love for him, but also her good humour. But although he loved her, in a jealous possessive way, the attractions of the great social world now took him away from her constantly, and then she wrote to him regularly. Some of her letters are heartbreaking in the love she shows for him, the desperate longing for his presence, the agony caused by separation from him. In the pathetic desire for his continued company, even in a humble cottage, she reveals not only her devotion but also, perhaps, an intuitive knowledge that her life span was not destined to be a long one, and therefore her chances of the type of happiness she craved were limited by time.

If these letters, and some of her sensible suggestions, had a deep effect on Sheridan it was not noticeable. Though it may be unjust to suggest it, it could be that sometimes they lay for a period among all his other unopened letters. It is one of the less attractive aspects of Sheridan that he does not seem to have appreciated the glory of Eliza's devotion until it was too late. It does not make him unique, but it was sad for her.

In one letter, she wrote:

'I am writing in my bed half asleep, Sir. I did not know Edwards was going to Town till I was quite undressed going to bed, when he knocked at my dressing-room door to know if I had any commands. My poor Dick! I am grieved to hear that you should be vexed and disappointed, and wish to my soul I could remove the difficulties which tire you. I still hope to see you for I have such faith in your conquering all the obstacles which oppose you in any way, that I think nothing impossible for you. God bless thee, my dear Dick. I am half blind with sleep.'

And again:

'My dearest love, nothing can equal my disappointment on receiving your note. We expected you last night, and sat up till two this morning, and waited dinner till five today. I wish that instead of Ned you had sent the horses, that we might have come to you, for I almost despair of seeing you tomorrow at Heston. Do you *really* long to see me? And has nothing but *business* detained you from me? *Dear, dear* Sheri, don't be angry. I cannot love you and be perfectly satisfied at such a distance from you. I depended upon your coming tonight, and shall not recover my spirits till we meet.

But don't fret, my dearest, for let what will happen we must be happy if I may believe your constant assurances of affection. I could draw such a picture of happiness with you that it would almost make me wish the overthrow of all our present scenes of future affluence and grandeur.'

She looked back to their beginnings, felt instinctively that they were taking the wrong path, and had an idea that they should take a cottage in Flintshire, and Eliza had been to see the house:

'My idea originally you know was to give up our house in Town entirely, and then the money we should get for our furniture there would pay for what we should want here.

When you were obliged to be in town, a ready furnished house would do as well as another for us, and would be trifling expenses in comparison with Bruton Street. I wish to God you would reconcile yourself to this. Suppose people should say you could not live in so large a house, where would be the disgrace, and what *can* they say more than they do at present? You never will persuade people you are very rich, if you were to spend twice as much as you do, and the world in general would applaud you for it. Do think of this, my dearest Dick, and let me have a little quiet *home* here that I can enjoy with comfort. I am now going to bed. God bless you. Good night.'

She also tried to get him to make some solid provision for their future, perhaps to obtain some sinecure which would take care of their expenses. 'Tell me all about your affairs, my

dearest Dick, and tell me honestly whether we ought in
prudence to indulge our inclinations for a country life. Have you
done anything in regard to the Prince of Wales, which you said
you would?'

However Sheridan did not like to ask favours for himself.
He would speak for others, but he made it a point of honour
to accept nothing politically for himself. He might keep his
own actors waiting for their money but somehow that was a
different matter. Jobbery was something which he would have
no part in. There was a touch of old Thomas's pride in his
character. What was more difficult—he had always so much
disordered business on hand that he was impossible to pin
down, or even to find, and this hurt her, too:

'My dearest love, I shall call at the theatre for the chance of
seeing you, though I am afraid it will be in vain; but I
write again to beg you will come to us in the evening, for
indeed my dear Sheri I am never so happy as when you
partake my amusements and when I see you cheerful and
contented with me. Your note had a tinge of melancholy in
it that has vexed me, because I know my own heart and that
it has not a thought or wish that would displease you, could
you see it. I shall not therefore enjoy this party tonight unless
you are of it.

I don't suppose it is necessary to be drest, but if the House
sits late and you cannot come at all, at least send me one
little kind line to make me feel happy for the rest of the night.
If by accident the coach should miss you, Mrs N. lives in
Portman Square. God thee bless, my dear one; believe that
I love thee and will love thee for ever.'

Footmen and coaches constantly pursued the elusive Sheridan
from the theatre to the House of Commons, and from the
Commons to Brooks's. And always in the background was
Eliza, waiting, encouraging, advising, and hoping:

'Dear Sheri, let me see you soon tonight – good-natured and
happy – for upon my soul and life, I love you, dearest,
better than my soul and could be happier with you in some

little cottage under the alps than with the whole world beside.

Your own true Poush.'

Nor was she without insight as to the dangers of Sheridan's political career, and would chide him affectionately for being what she called a sanguine pig. On one occasion she writes: 'I am more than ever convinced we must look to other resources for wealth and independence, and consider politics merely as an amusement – and in the light it is best to be in Opposition, which I am afraid we are likely to be for some years again.'

Eliza was quite right about Sheridan's pig-headed optimism. Underneath her charm and good humour she had a sensible intelligent approach to things, was infinitely more down to earth than Sheridan, and was not inclined to take events or people at their face value. Sheridan himself found it impossible to resist anything in the way of new propositions. He put money into the Pantheon, which was to produce operas, and lost it, and was forever over-extending his options only to find that he had not enough ready cash even to meet the commitments which he already had. Always full of projects, ever unwilling to think that they could possibly fall to the ground. Richard was in this way, too, like his father, and Eliza was constantly trying to get him to achieve some practical result from all his comings and goings. She wrote to him when he was staying with the Duke of Bedford:

'I hope you will reap some advantage from being bored with his horses and bets. If he would but do what I mentioned in my last letter, it would make our fortunes I'm sure, and what would it do to him? Why don't you talk with Charles [Fox] on the subject and get him to propose it as a good thing to the Duke of Bedford. Do, my dear Dick, sacrifice a little of your *false delicacy* (which no body has but you) to our future happiness, and manage this matter. I am sure it could be done if you would.'

But it is difficult for a man, or at least for Sheridan, who has come up from nothing, who is mixing with people richer

and grander than himself to broach the matter of obtaining
a place, of putting money into a project, or of lending a
little patronage. There is usually the point when the eyes
of the patron cloud, and the suppliant knows that he is losing
esteem by asking for something for himself. It is simpler, and
more agreeable to make witty remarks, to entertain, and to be
regarded as a good fellow. Why upset one's friends with
appeals for help? Something will turn up. A new theatre
project will make a fortune and then all will be well. Tomorrow
is another day, and next week will bring a better enterprise.

But Eliza did not share his sanguine hopes, and was often
right. 'I can't make out what business you are settling with
Harris. Is it good or bad plagues? I have no opinion of Mr H.
nor ever had. He is selfish, that is, quite a man of the world. Of
course *you* are no match for him; but I trust you do not deceive
me when you say you shall settle things *well*, though (as the
poor sailor said) I'll be hanged if I see how, for you seem all
poor and pennyless, I think, not able to play Whist when the
fine ladies wanted you, nor nothing.' One cannot grudge her
this touch of exasperation and cattiness, and in her distrust of
Harris, Eliza was quite right. Harris's theatrical swan turned
out to be worse than a goose. It failed, and Mr Harris sailed
from England's green and pleasant land to Boulogne leaving
Sheridan with the debts.

Sheridan's was indeed a hectic but disorganized life, and
merely to read about his activities is to feel exhausted by their
multiplicity and their complications. He would get up at four
o'clock in the morning, light a large number of candles around
him, and eat toasted muffins while he worked. Sometimes
totally unprepared for his next day's speech in the House of
Commons, he would work at break-neck speed, his desk always
littered with unopened letters. To open them might only un-
leash another crop of plagues. Actresses like Miss Farren might
want money:

'Miss Farrens compts to Mr Sheridan and informs him She
cannot think of playing to night till he has given an order
for their returning the money She has had so unjustly stopt
from *her* this day for not attending rehearsals. She comes out

to night at the danger of her life, has been extremely ill the whole week, and inclined as she always is to do her best to save the managers She cannot but look on their behaviour as the greatest of cruelty and *contempt* she ever knew.'

Miss Farren was a draw and would have to be placated. So poor Mr Peake down at the theatre must be written to immediately, not that this was out of the ordinary, because Sheridan was constantly penning frantic letters to him from different parts of the country. On one occasion, detained at an inn, he wrote a brief note: '*Undone for the want of £10!*'

The creditors were not backward in coming forward to wait on his doorstep, or the duns to sit in his house to collect money due to them. A certain Mr Fozard, from the livery stable, physically prevented him going out on one occasion. Unabashed, with the utmost composure, Sheridan sat down and both he and the livery stable keeper went through his unopened letters. Little by little £350 was discovered in the unopened mail.

'Lucky dog, Fozard, you've hit it this time,' he said. Fozard, like many other importunate creditors, managed to make a profit on the bill. This very often happened. It was easier, as he had once written, to pay the bill than to look for the receipt. It is hard to understand how so much disorder could have been productive of anything except an increasing inability to concentrate. Yet in a remarkable way he did manage to make some sort of sense out of some of his activities, though not enough. His seat in Parliament cost him money, and necessity was forever inducing him to risk more and more in theatrical ventures. Yet when he retrieved some money he found it hard to keep. In 1782, he managed to get rid of his share in the Opera House, but almost immediately risked his money in the abortive Pantheon venture. However, he never missed a first night at Drury Lane, and was always interested in the minutiae and technique of acting. Mrs Siddons makes his intense interest in the production of *Macbeth* clear:

'Just as I had finished my toilette and was pondering with fearfulness my first appearance in the grand fiendish part, comes Mr Sheridan knocking at my door, and insisting, in spite of all my entreaties not to be interrupted at this to me tremendous moment, to be admitted. But what was my distress and astonishment when I found that he wanted me even at this moment of anxiety and terror to adopt another mode of acting the sleeping scene!

He told me that he had heard with the greatest surprise and concern that I meant to act it without holding the candle in my hand; and when I argued the impracticability of washing out the damned spot that was certainly implied by both her own words and those of her gentlewomen, he insisted, that if I did put the candle out of my hand it would be thought a presumptuous innovation, as Mrs Pritchard had always retained it in hers.'

In some things, Sheridan was a stickler for the stage conventions. But Mrs Siddons stuck to her point, and acted the scene to her own taste. She says, 'Mr Sheridan himself came to me after the play, and most ingenuously congratulated me on my obstinacy.'

It is hard to understand why a man who wrote so well for the theatre, and who understood so instinctively the feelings of the players, and the interest they took in the smallest points of staging, could have killed the talents which he so clearly had in order to orate about estimates and taxes and engage in the scoring of points at Westminister. Yet, in a sense, he had excelled too easily in the theatre. He had written plays which had at once succeeded beyond his highest expectations. It was all too easy, and he pined for a larger and more stable audience. He also liked the great world, and wished to prove that the O'Sheridans were a match for it. As indeed in many senses they were, and more than a match. But he knew the basic flaw in his own character better than anyone else, except perhaps Eliza. It was vanity.

He once said to Lord Holland:

'They talk of avarice, lust, ambition, as great passions. It is a mistake; they are little passions. Vanity is the great commanding passion of all. It is this that produced the most grand and heroic deeds, or impels to the most dreadful crimes. Save me but from this passion, and I can defy the others. They are mere urchins, but this is a giant.'

It was the need for money to keep Eliza which had led him into the theatre, but it was the killing passion of vanity which led him into the House of Commons. There he knew his wit could shine brighter than that of others, which it did, and there he would have the power of swaying men's minds and hearts to great decisions. But all this he could have done in the theatre, which in his heart he despised. He had seen what it had done to his father and he knew how the burden of being a player's son, and a poor player's son at that, had affected his own life, and how often his pride and vanity had been wounded as a result. It was the siren call of vanity he recognized, but which he could not conquer, which led him to the boon companions at Brooks's, and it was vanity which led him away from Eliza towards the admiring eyes of the ladies at Devonshire House and Crewe Hall. And to vanity was added a taste for constant movement and excitement, to shut out the sorrow of the world and his attacks of melancholy. The admiration he craved, and which had become necessary to him, was shutting him away from himself, too, and was changing his character.

There is no doubt that he was unfaithful to Eliza, but in an age when male infidelity was regarded as a peccadillo, and part of a man's life beyond the home, this was not perhaps the worst of the damage he was doing to his chances in life. His drinking friends, Tickell, Richardson, Charles James Fox were a constant audience for his wit, and what better way to pass an evening than with wine and wit, and the caress of laughter sweet to the ears like applause in the theatre. Eliza was well aware of the siren voices, including that of wine:

'Thank you, Sir, for your fiff (family language for small note) and still more for the journal you promise me to morrow. I see you are ever so affronted with me, but upon my life without the least cause. I have never had one *cross* feel towards you since you left Crewe, but I must say whatever is in my mind to say on all subjects, you know, and when you tell me how vexed and grieved you was at not being able to speak that Monday, on account of your making yourself so ill on Sunday, would you have me say drinking to that excess is *not an abominable habit?* And where I see *idletons* as Jack Townshend can overcome all your good and strong resolutions mustn't I think that London and its inhabitants and their ways do alter people whether they will or no?'

While Sheridan was wasting his time drinking and laughing with the idletons, Eliza was sometimes playing cards and losing money to her rich friends at country houses. Like all players who hope to make much needed money and cannot afford to lose, the gambling does not seem to have been much of an amusement to her, to judge by one petulant letter she wrote: 'If it goes on I shall soon be on the debtor's side of Mrs Crewe's book. It is the abominable Whist they make me play, and they beat us every game. I lost one and twenty guineas last night and fifteen the night before.'

Even Eliza with her commonsense contrived to feed his vanity with her loving remarks, and wrote to him:

'There was a Mr Thurby here yesterday. I did not see him, but Mrs Bouverie said he was very warm in his politics, and in talking of *you*, he said, "Oh, a leading man, Ma'am, a leading man, solid, quick, lively, nobody like him, Ma'am a leading man!" There's for you, Sir. We laughed for an hour, Mrs B. and I at him, not for saying you was a *leading man*, Sir, but at his manner.'

The unknown Mr Thurby, whose admiration so delighted Eliza, was only one of the thousand voices which drew Sheridan towards the applause he craved, but now unfortunately the adjective 'solid', as applied to Sheridan in the House of Commons, in the theatre, or in his private life was inaccurate. His quick brain enabled him to tear the salient points out of any problem and give the impression of knowing the subject in depth. This is the talent of the playwright or the painter, who can seize a quick impression of life, transfer it to stage or canvas, and implant a fleeting feeling in the minds of others. It is not the talent of the dedicated politician. In the eighteenth century, politicians were not so well served as today, with a posse of civil servants and statisticians to produce instant facts and figures. More homework had to be done, and for Sheridan, with so many other activities, homework was tiresome.

Sheridan, like Byron, was a man of two conflicting characters. Although Byron was born later, they were both men of the early eighteenth century, men of reason and wit, who lived on into a more solid century. Sheridan's comedies looked backwards to Congreve and Wycherley, and although he had bowdlerized *The Relapse*, he did not approve of his own bowdlerization. It was something which he had done to bring in the customers and pander to the popular taste.

Like most people he was a prisoner of the conflicting currents of his own age. When he wrote verse it was tinkling, pleasant verse, the literary equivalent of Fragonard or Boucher, and as with Fragonard there was a *fin de siècle* melancholy at the core of his being. If only the lovers could always be setting sail for Cytherea, if only the music and the swish of brocades across the grass could always be heard and the bright eyes could never grow dull or skins become wrinkled.

Even the attentions of Amoret, Mrs Crewe, had palled:

'She has asked me a thousand questions of various kinds, to all which I have answered as I would to the town Cryer if I was questioned by him. I believe she feels that my heart is shut against her, and behaves accordingly; but I dare not complain, nor would it be of any service to me if I did; she is of an unhappy disposition, and there are moments when, in spight of her behaviour, I feel inclined to pity her.'

People should not become unhappy or boring. It is upsetting. It is not amusing.

In August 1786 the Sheridans and the Tickells went on a journey to Weymouth and Plymouth. Sheridan had been to the rocky shore to see a wreck:

'I saw many carry off the prizes, some humanely looking to

the living wretches, exhausted yet clinging to the wreck. I
alone remained. I looked on the Sea and Sky and thought of
the feelings of those who had thus lost friends. My soul was
awed by the scene, and I resolved to bury the officer left,
and as far as my memory recollected, to perform the rites of
Sepulture. I dug a grave. I, on my knees, began to say,
Hast thou no mother – who is the dearest friend that will
regret the loss? – if it be thy Parents, speak in this glory, this
shade – if thy Brother——. At that name I thought I heard
a whisper in the glade. Is it thy Lover – a Cupid appeared,
a pale, a meagre form, no laughing roses on his cheek. He
said, 'I am Love, a ghastly figure, the lying cheat in me
beyond. Ask me no more, I hear her tears that would
embalm his grave." I closed the turf and said, "O God be
not angered with that Love. I stand here to bury this dead
man," and I turned the sand upon his Tomb!'

This was a passage which could have been written by Byron,
after the death of Shelley – melodramatic, self-absorbed,
strange, and melancholy.

The great world had carried Sheridan and Eliza away from
one another in spite of themselves. Thomas Grenville once
heard Richard murmuring, 'Sad, that former feelings should
have so completely gone by. Would anything bring them
back? Yes – perhaps the gardens at Bath and the cottage at
East Burnham might.' For Richard it was impossible to go back,
though Eliza would have liked to do this. 'It is in times of
trouble and distress that the real feelings of the heart are
known', she wrote to him. 'You, who think me given up to
folly and dissipation put me to the proof. Say, I am ruined, will
you prefer going with me to the farthest part of the globe and
to share with me there the misery of solitude and poverty, to
staying in the world and to be still flattered and admired? and
see if I hesitate a moment. Believe me, my dear Dick, you *have*
resource if you really love *me* better than your ambition. Take
me out of the whirl of the world and place me in the quiet
and simple scenes of life I was born for, and you will see that
I shall be once more in my element, and if I saw you content
I should be happy.'

But it was hard to forgo the wit and the applause, it was hard to leave a scene where any moment right bring a new and exciting triumph. Eliza's gentle voice called him back but he blocked his ears.

Apart from the financial disorder at the theatre, there were uncertainties about their homes. Eliza's plea for a permanent little *home* was a *cri de cœur*, for they were always moving. In London alone Sheridan lived in Orchard Street, Cavendish Street, Frith Street, George Street, Grosvenor Street, Hertford Street, Jermyn Street, Lower Brook Street, Norfolk Street and Wimpole Street. There is nothing so worrying as an unstable background for a woman who longs to make a real home for her family, and this Eliza was never allowed to do. At first they moved so as to be in more fashionable districts, later it was to avoid debts and duns. In Bruton Street, Sheridan had to get his silver out of pawn for a dinner party. He also asked a bookseller called Beckett to fill his bookshelves for the evening. The bookseller agreed, on one condition: two of his shopmen had to be dressed up in livery to serve a dual purpose – to wait at table, and to keep an eye on the stock. Poor Eliza's little safe home drifted farther and farther away. In the end no more was said of the cottage in the country. It had become a sentimental dream of the past, and had nothing more to do with real life.

Betsy Sheridan, Richard's sister, gives a vivid chatty description in her journal of the life of the family at this time, noting especially Eliza's attempts to heal the breach between Dick and his father. Eliza very often came round to see Besty with this end in view, but Thomas was not to be placated at being deprived of his managership of Drury Lane. Besty also makes shrewd comments on the bustling social life which the Sheridans were leading. Writing to her sister Lissy, Betsy says, 'In the evening I had a very long visit from Mrs Sheridan. She enquired kindly for you, but did not seem well, complained much of her head, but indeed the life she leads would kill a horse, but she says one must do as other people do.'

She puts her finger on the disadvantages of being a Sheridan in the context of the life Richard and Eliza were trying to live, saying that there can be no pleasure in society unless 'you feel you have a *right* to your place in it'. This was something which Richard did not admit even to himself, for he was a passionate believer in the equality of man, and a career open to all the talents. He had no wish, as Betsy had, to spend the days among the middling sort of people.

Although Richard had suffered from his lack of independent means, most of his schemes, and his failures, were due to a wish to achieve sudden and easy wealth. His brother had adopted a more cap-in-hand approach, and in this way was able to keep his desires and his means trotting in double harness.

Meanwhile poor old Thomas was now reduced to living on his small pension in lodgings with Betsy, but he was still full of schemes for reforming Irish education. He was trying to get patrons to subscribe to this grandiose project, and apparently Betsy had some hopes from Richard: 'Dick talks stoutly of assisting my Father – God send he may not again disappoint him.' Considering the muddle all his own financial affairs were in, doubtless Richard's sanguine nature could not see any particular obstacle to agreeing to help his family. What was one more commitment among so many?

Apart from the vivid sketches of old Thomas in his decline, the picture which Betsy's journal builds up of Sheridan and his wife at this time, is of a couple leading a hectic social life, and only on the off-days, when they are not out and about sparkling and amusing their fashionable friends, having the leisure to let down their hair and realize that things are not as rosy as they seem on the surface. Betsy paints a picture of Richard when he is 'off stage': 'Dick very dull from not being well and fancying himself worse.' Eliza was crying at parting with Tom, whom they were sending to be tutored by Dr Parr. Tom, the Sheridans' only child, was much cherished and spoiled by both his father and mother, and as Dr Parr had once taught Sheridan himself, presumably Sheridan thought that private tuition would be a solution to the boy's education.

But on stage, children and financial worries had to be forgotten. While the charmers are in motion, letters can remain unopened or pursue one around the country, actors' importunities can be forgotten, and debts can be pushed into the back of the mind. But when the party was over it was necessary to come home.

Betsy was right to say that it was better and more comfortable to live amongst the 'middling sort of people' for both she and Eliza realized that this was the way to achieve peace of mind. This was not a situation to which Richard was prepared to submit, however. Middling meant that one was failing, slipping from the summit. It was impossible to sit back while there were still new worlds to conquer, and fresh audiences to enchant. Women had little idea of what could be achieved in the world. There was always some way out of every difficulty. A plodding life among the middling people was not to be thought of, or considered. A fresh triumph could always be around the corner.

CHAPTER 13

Fair Fame Inspires

Were there one whose fires
True genius kindles, and fair fame inspires;
Blest with each talent, and each art to please
And born to write, converse, and live with ease.

Pope

At the time of the downfall of so many of Fox's Martyrs, Sheridan had managed to be returned for Stafford because he was liked by the electors, mainly, it was said by one of his critics, because he appealed to the lowest sections of the community. A witty candidate whose quick repartee could make the voters laugh, and was hail fellow well met with all classes was welcomed back as an old friend.

Fox's re-election at Westminster was not so simple. The King had strained every nerve to prevent his success, even to administering what he called 'gold pills' to the voters and ordering 280 of the Guards to vote for his opponent, Sir Cecil Wray. Horace Walpole comments on this rustling out of the military vote that 'it was an act which his father in the most *quiet* seasons would not have dared to do'.

There followed a bout of objections, chicanery, plot and counter-plot in an effort to prevent Fox taking his seat in the House, and by the other to ensure that he did, which at times bordered on farce. The High Bailiff of Westminster alleged that Fox had not been lawfully elected, and instituted an enquiry into the voters, called the Westminster Scrutiny. Meanwhile Fox was elected for the Kirkwall Boroughs and he and Sheridan were able to attack the Ministry from the Opposition benches.

Sheridan was particularly effective in defence of his friend, and during the debates, Beacroft said of him that 'he had the quickest penetration and the liveliest and readiest wit he ever knew a man possess', adding that his attacks were well calculated to throw ridicule on the administration, and the jobbery which had taken place between the King, Pitt and the sensitive conscience of the High Bailiff of Westminster. Eventually after a year, and a cost of over £18,000, Fox's majority was reduced by a mere two votes. When it came to bribery and corruption there was nothing to choose between one side and the other, except the means they used.

It was during this session that the affairs of India once more exercised the House. The Indian background to this debate has already been briefly described in connection with Fox's India Bill, but although the Bill had been dropped, the repercussions rumbled on, and Burke was still busy collecting his evidence, and marshalling his facts, if facts they could be called, for his main well of information, Philip Francis, was a tainted source.

Francis's main aim from the time of his going to India was to blacken Warren Hastings' name and replace him. There is little doubt that any ruler in India at this time would have been forced into deeds which would not have borne investigation in the clear light of day. But Hastings had helped to fight the French, intent on driving the British out of India, the Mahratta marauders, intent on despoiling the Indians, his own council, intent on driving him home, had managed to save the East India Company's finances and had kept his part of the country as stable as was possible in the circumstances: it was no small achievement.

Francis had been attacking Hastings directly and indirectly for ten years, and Hastings himself had written: 'There are many gentlemen in England who have been eye-witnesses to my conduct. For God's sake call upon them to draw my true portrait, for the devil is not so black as these fellows have painted me.' He had written this in 1775, but by 1786 his name was to become even blacker.

The strands of the web being woven against him were complicated in the extreme. Even his enemies admitted that he had not enriched himself as others had done, but political complications in England, and the wealth to be gained in India, had made him a pawn. At the beginning, Pitt had been inclined to protect the useful and experienced Governor General, and to gloss over the charges against him, but gradually the political chameleons were beginning to change colour.

There were possible political advantages to be gained from investigating the charges against the Governor. It has been variously suggested that Pitt was jealous of the increasing influence of Hastings at Court, and that the King, softened possibly by gifts of diamonds, was thinking of appointing Hastings President of the Board of Control. The disadvantages to the envisaged impeachment were that the public were not not on the side of Hastings' accusers, and that Hastings' administration had been largely successful, and success always has charms.

Suddenly Pitt changed his mind. Fox, Sheridan, and Burke made a formidable combination against him. If their talents could be diverted into attacking Warren Hastings, then Pitt would have a freer hand in his own policies. This diversion of what have been called restless and powerful spirits could act as a lightning conductor, rendering these spirits less harmful to the administration. Burke's was the hand which had gathered the evidence, but his eloquence was not sufficient to push the accusations home. Moore says of him, 'in vain did his genius put forth its superb plumage glittering all over with the hundred eyes of fancy, the gait of the bird was heavy and awkward, and its voice seemed rather to scare than attract'.

His delivery was bad, and when he originally introduced his charges about the depredations in India, it made so little impression that Pitt and Grenville went on chatting and were inclined to take no further action in the matter. It was at this point that Burke decided to enlist the oratory of Sheridan on his side.

Many of Sheridan's biographers have said that at first he was against the impeachment of Hastings: but Burke was determined that if he were to succeed in his attack on Hastings he must at all costs have Sheridan. He was aware of Richard's power to move the hearts and the emotions, and wrote to Eliza:

'I am sure you will have the goodness to excuse the liberty

I take with you when you consider the interest which I have and which the Public have in the use of Mr Sheridan's abilities. I know that his mind is seldom unemployed but then, like all such great and vigorous minds, it takes an eagle flight by itself, and we can hardly bring it to rustle along the ground, with us birds of meaner wing, in coveys.'

This was perhaps the siren voice, indicating a triumph to be won in oratory, the appeal to vanity, the killing vice, which pushed Sheridan into a course of action which cool justice might have sought to avoid. He had often advocated the middling course in politics, but now he chose the path of Burke's immoderate attacks, for it presented that chance to shine which he had been waiting for. What better case for an orator than the defence of two Eastern princesses whose sufferings, properly presented, could move stones, and make the rocks weep? Add to it injustices, wars, depredations, rapes, rapine, taking place under the burning skies of Bengal, and it was an opportunity not to be missed for the imagery of the writer orator.

According to their political persuasion, writers have delineated the Begums of Oude as suffering saints or old harpies, as princesses despoiled of their wealth by the rapacious British, or relatives keeping a grip on millions to which they were not entitled.

Suja-ud-Dowlah, the Rajah of Oude, had been an ally of Hastings, and had paid the East India Company for the forces used in protecting his territories from invasion. There was no doubt that this was to the advantage of the Company as a way of protecting their trade. But when Philip Francis arrived in India he tried to break the treaties with the Rajah under the threat of withdrawing the British forces. The Rajah had regarded Hastings as a personal friend, and before he died, possibly from shock at this sudden withdrawal of British support, he implored the Governor General to extend his friendship to his son, Adaf-ud-Daula.

It was here that the British became imbroiled in purely domestic quarrels, for the new Rajah's troops were mutinying due to arrears of pay, and the new British Controllers including

Francis, were insisting on their pound of flesh, demanding that all the arrears due from himself and his father should be paid. According to some accounts, as a means of getting himself out of his difficulty, he shut up his father's widow and her mother at the palace of Fyzabad until they disgorged the money he needed for paying his troops and for paying off the arrears due to the British for their former garrisons.

Other accounts say that the allegedly helpless youth was forced to surrender to his father's widow nearly the whole of the two millions which the deceased Rajah had saved up for just such an emergency. The Queen Mother, it was stated, had no claim to this money, already had £50,000 a year, which should have been enough for her modest needs, and was now claiming another two millions under a will which was never produced, and that Bristow, Francis's agent, had forced the unfortunate prince to sign away his patrimony under duress.

Other accusations were that the two Begums were protected only by two faithful eunuchs, who were seized and maltreated till the moneys were paid to the East India Company; that the eunuchs were, in fact, loaded with irons and starved until half a million had been wrung from them. The defenders of Hastings, for their part, said the Begums, in order to keep a firm grip on the money, had joined in an insurrection with Cheyt Singh to attack the British.

It was not a story which reflected credit on anyone, least of all on Philip Francis, who, on balance, seems to have decided to play several games at once. He wished to gain credit for himself by keeping the moneys due to the East India Company, but at the same time to contrive to discredit Hastings; to ruin his policies of partial pacification through alliances, and yet to brand him as an instigator of unjust wars. It was a complicated game of chess nicely calculated to bring glory to Francis and discredit to Hastings.

In the purlieus of Westminster and the plotting drawing-rooms of the politicians, little was to be heard on the credit side, and now the whole weight of the attack was to be put into the hands of Sheridan: he was to use it well.

*

On February 7, 1787, the House of Commons debated whether Warren Hastings should be impeached. There were over five hundred members present when Sheridan rose to speak.

It was an astonishing performance. He spoke for five-and-a-half hours. He held his audience enraptured, orating with great rapidity, yet with a clarity which carried his voice to all parts of the house. No exact transcript remains of this speech, which was to be referred to by all the leading men of his day as a triumph of oratory; but such shreds and patches as remain give an idea of an attack in the style of an old-fashioned counsel for the prosecution.

Although it is hard to judge the words without the fire of the speaker, the flash of his eyes, or the modulations of his actor's voice, there is no doubt that against Hastings he was hard, incisive, sarcastic, and uncompromising, and made great play about the 'sanctity of the Zenana' having been violated, a subject which certainly appealed to his romantic notions of veiled eastern beauties behind their latticed windows:

'I profess to God I feel in my own bosom the strongest personal conviction of the facts charged against the conduct of Mr Hastings towards the Begums of Oude. There are many gentlemen now in the Committee who have avowed to me the same conviction of his guilt. It is in this conviction that I believe from my heart that the treatment of these illustrious women comprehends every species of human profligacy.'

Referring to the 'sanctity of the Zenana' he said:

'still he (Hastings) recurs to Mahometism for an excuse, as if there was something in the institution of Mahomet that made it meritorious in a Christian to be a savage; that rendered it criminal to treat the inhabitants of India with humanity or mercy; that even made it impious in a son not to plunder his mother. Where is the British faith? What has become of that awful sanction which has proved the consolation of so many nations, and the glory of our own?

I declare, Sir, from my conscience, that the system which Mr Hastings then followed in his Government of India may be termed a series of unparalleled cruelty, oppression, and plunder. He acted diametrically opposite to the command of Parliament and the East India Company; and the Committee of the Commons have frequently reprobated his principles.'

These latter sentiments were nicely calculated to appeal to the dignity of the Commons and to draw attention to the fact that they were being overruled. He went on to demolish Hastings' defence:

'But, says Mr Hastings, "Look not back to the records, weigh not the enormities of my past crimes. Listen to my own defence. I will prove that every article of peculation, rapine and murder, ascribed to my measures, proceeds from the antipathies of my enemies." Poor, unfortunate gentleman! He happens to have his tranquil moments annoyed by the cries of injured innocence! I am ashamed to trouble the Committee with more facts; and were I not sensible that a very considerable majority of my auditors were already satisfied I declare to God, Sir, that I would sit down at this moment without proceeding one single step farther . . . '

He did not, of course, sit down, but went on for a further few hours, but it was a nice theatrical stroke. Naturally, as Hastings had his defenders, Sheridan had to demolish his qualities, as well as drawing attention to his depredations:

'There is undoubtedly something about him either of parts or property which for a number of years has exercised a most fascinating influence.

We see nothing solid, or penetrating, nothing noble or magnanimous, nothing open, direct, liberal, manly or superior in his measures or his mind. All is dark, insidious, sordid and insincere. . . . The serpent may as well abandon the characteristic obliquity of his motion for the direct flight of an arrow, as he can excuse his purposes with honesty and fairness. He is all shuffling, twisting, cold and little. There is nothing in him open or upright, simple or unmixed. There is by some strange, mysterious predominance in his vice, such a prominence as totally shades and conceals his virtues. There is, by some foul, unfathomable, physical cause in his mind, a conjection merely of whatever is calculated to make human nature hang its head with sorrow or shame. His crimes are the only great thing about him, and these are contrasted by the littleness of his motives. He is at once a tyrant, a trickster, a visionary, and a deceiver.'

Dundas had remarked that the 'greatest defect in the politics of India was that they were uniformly founded on mercantile maxims'. This gave Sheridan a sweep of metaphor of which he took the greatest advantage:

'It was in this manner that nations have been extirpated for a sum of money, whole tracts of country laid waste by fire and sword, to furnish investments; revolutions occasioned by an affidavit, an army employed in executing an arrest; towns besieged on a note of hand, a prince expelled for the balance of an account, statesmen occupied in doing the business of a tipstaff, generals made auctioneers, a truncheon contrasted with the implements of a counting house; and the British Government exhibited in every part of Hindostan holding a bloody sceptre in one hand and picking pockets with the other.'

When it came to notes of hand, and balances of accounts unpaid, Sheridan's metaphors were allied to facts of which he was only too well aware on the home front. He talks of

'. . . a ruined prince, a royal family reduced to want the wretchedness, the desolation of kingdoms, or the sacrilegious invasions of palaces, within this dismal and unhallowed labyrinth it was most natural to cast an eye of indignation over the wide and towering forest of enormities, all rising in dusky magnificence of guilt, yet it became not less necessary to trace out the poisonous weeds, the baleful brushwood, and all the little, creeping, deadly plants which were in quantity and extent, if possible, more noxious.'

There was no doubt that the hot winds of India had certainly produced a rush of metaphors to the head, and the actor in Sheridan had contrived to take advantage of a unique opportunity to dazzle and amaze. Sheridan had proved that it 'was in him and by God it would come out!'

The effect of the speech is well illustrated by a Mr Logan, who was the author of a defence of Hastings, and who came in to the House to listen, with all his prejudices ranged well on the side of the innocent and unjustly accused, as he thought. 'All this is declaration without proof', he said to a friend after the first hour of oration; 'This is a most remarkable oration', he admitted at the end of the second hour; 'Mr Hastings has acted very unjustifiably', he conceded after Sheridan had been speaking for three hours; 'Mr Hastings is a most atrocious criminal' he burst out when the fourth hour had run; and finally, 'Of all monsters of iniquity the most enormous is Warren Hastings.'

Pitt remained quite unmoved during the oration, and coolly remarked, 'An abler speech had, perhaps, never been delivered.' Charles Fox was overcome. 'Eloquent indeed it was, so much so, that all he had ever heard – all he had ever read, when compared with it, dwindled into nothing, and vanished like vapour before the sun.'

Horace Walpole writing to the Countess of Ossory said it was not only a speech which had turned the vote, but turned everybody's head as well. He went on:

'One heard everybody in the streets raving on the Wonders of that speech; for my part I cannot believe it was so supernatural as they say – do you believe it was, Madam? How should such a fellow as Sheridan who has no diamonds to bestow, fascinate all the world? – Yet witchcraft, no doubt there has been, for when did simple eloquence ever convince a majority? Mr Pitt and 174 other persons found Mr Hastings guilty last night. Well, at least there is a new crime, *sorcery* to charge on the opposition!'

The outburst of praise which greeted Sheridan was universal, flattering, and heady. Wraxall, one of Sheridan's opponents, had to admit that the oration was the 'most splended display of eloquence and talent which has been exhibited in the House of Commons during the present reign. Sheridan neither lost his temper, his memory, nor his judgment throughout the whole performance, blending the legal accuracy of the Bar when stating facts or depositions of witnesses with the most impassioned appeals to justice, pity and humanity.'

Sir Gilbert Elliott writing to his wife describes how he was overcome with emotion so that 'the bone repeatedly rose in my throat'. The House was worked up to an intensity of emotion, especially as Sheridan reached the climax of his peroration 'indeed his own feelings were wound up to the utmost pitch' and when he sat down 'there was a universal shout . . . every man was on the floor and all his friends throwing themselves on his neck in raptures of joy and exultation.'

The Earl of Chatham wrote, 'Everybody is full of Sheridan's speech on Mr Hastings business. I really think it, without any exception one of the most wonderful performances I ever heard and almost the greatest imaginable exertion of the human mind.'

His triumph was complete, but it was an actor's triumph. Even Pitt had to admit that it was impossible to 'vote with perfect calmness' while the intellect was swayed by Sheridan's oratory. The House adjourned till the next day in order that the sensibilities of the Commons could be reduced to a less highly charged state of emotion. The debate was resumed the following day. Philip Francis, Hastings' enemy, who did not like Sheridan, said 'he wished to pay his tribute of applause to that wonderful performance at the moment when the impression of it was strong upon him'.

If Sheridan had triumphed, so had Philip Francis. The motion was carried by 175 votes to 68. Warren Hastings was to be impeached, and Burke, Fox and Sheridan were appointed to be the managers of the trial.

It need hardly be said that Charles Sheridan was not slow to add his congratulations, dated from Dublin Castle a week after the speech: 'My dear Dick, Could I for a moment forget that you were my brother I should merely as an Irishman think myself bound to thank you for the high credit you have done your country.' Charles had already profited by Sheridan's rapid rise in the world, who knows there might be further pickings to come? Lissy, Sheridan's childhood playmate, wrote with affection, pride and sincerity: 'I rejoice in your success. May it be entire! May the God who fashioned you and gave you powers to sway the hearts of men and controul their wayward wills, be equally favourable to you in all your undertakings, and make your reward here and hereafter!'

Even old Thomas who was then living in Dublin found that some of his son's fame had brushed off on to himself, and was mollified by it. For Lissy said in her letter to Richard: 'My father is, in a degree that I did not expect, gratified with the general attention you have excited here: he seems truly pleased that men should say "there goes the father of Gaul".'

Warren Hastings' seven-year-long torture had begun. That was the other side of the coin of the oratorical triumph, for the monster painted by the fervid metaphors was an able administrator in the context of the disorders in which he was able to operate. The terrible oppressor was the same man who had encouraged Sheridan's friend Halhed to translate the Hindu laws, who upheld the ancient civilizations of India, and who disapproved of missionaries. He held that the 'Hindoos' and the 'Mohommedians' had their own religions of equal worth to the Christian religion, and that missionaries were better kept out of the country. In this latter opinion he was probably in advance of his time.

Philip Francis boasted that even if Warren Hastings were acquitted, he would be a ruined man. It was a mean sentiment expressed by a mean mind.

It could be said that Sheridan's part in this first indictment against Hastings, was simply that of a barrister taking advantage of a good brief. He saw himself merely as an advocate. In a scribbled note he remarked: 'The counsel is not only not bound to ask his conscience, but he is bound *not* to do it. He has a duty and a trust which ought to receive no aid from conviction. What I am saying may sound derogatory, but it is not so.' Until Sheridan made his great speech in the House of Commons about the suffering Begums of Oude, there had been little public interest in the affair. It was this speech which turned the scales, and projected the affairs of the Governor of India into a *cause célèbre*.

Pitt and his colleagues, having started the great war machine in motion against Hastings, lost interest in it. Dundas was asked for help by one of the managers of the trial who said 'You cannot be indifferent to our success'. Dundas is said to have replied 'Troth am I. Ye hae done what we wanted. I shall gie myself nae trouble aboot what comes of ye.' It was a cynical attitude to the attack on one man's life's work.

To Sheridan, the prosecuting and glittering counsel fell the same task as before, describing the sufferings of the two Princesses of Oude. Just before the trial Burke had written to him:

'Well, it will turn out right – and a half of you or a quarter is worth five other men. I think that this cause which was originally yours, will be recognized by you and that you will again possess yourself of it. The owner's mark is on it, and all our docking and cropping cannot hinder its being known and cherished by its original master.'

The laurels were being carefully apportioned. Burke adds in a footnote, 'I feel a little sickish at the approaching day. I have read much – too much, perhaps, and in truth am but poorly prepared. Many things have broken in on me.'

But Sheridan was not deterred by his lack of knowledge. Behind the scenes he had been working furiously to repeat his original triumph. Moore, who had access to Sheridan's papers, says that

'. . . amongst the proofs of the labour which not only of himself but of Mrs Sheridan was a large pamphlet of Mr Hastings consisting of more than two hundred pages, copied out neatly in her writing with assistance from another female hand. The industry of all around him was put into requisition for this great occasion, some busy with pen and scissors making extracts, some pasting and stitching his scattered memorandums in their places. Hardly a single member of the family could not boast of having contributed to the mechanical construction of the speech.'

The impeachment began in 1788. The managers had good time to sharpen their metaphors, and practise their oratorical strokes, while Warren Hastings doggedly collected his few supporters and defenders around him.

Westminster Hall was to be the magnificent and hallowed setting for Sheridan's crowning triumph. Into the sombre vaulted hall walked a procession of nearly two hundred scarlet robed peers, marshalled by heralds dressed in cloth of gold. This was the pageantry of power ranged before the accused.

The other side of the occasion was more frivolous. Owing to the immense acclaim which Sheridan's previous speech had received, to which the gossip in the clubs and drawing-rooms had added greater lustre, the tickets cost fifty guineas a piece. Sir Gilbert Elliott said 'the clamour for them was so great that people were almost putting their hands into one's pocket for them'.

His description of the occasion itself is vivid and racy giving that mixture of dignity and raffishness which is typical of the day, or perhaps of any day:

'The ladies are dressed and mobbing it in Palace Yard by six or half after six, and they sit from nine till twelve before business begins. The press was so terrible, that I think it possible I may have saved, if not Mrs Morrice's life at least a limb or two. I could not, however, save her cap, which perished in the attempt. Shoes are, however, the principal and most general loss. Several ladies went in barefoot; others, after losing their own, got the stray shoes of other people, and went in with one red and one yellow shoe.'

But in spite of torn tempers and torn gowns, eventually all the town were seated in their places, well dressed ladies in serried rows prepared to have their feelings harrowed by Sheridan's oratory.

Hastings himself wore a plain poppy-coloured suit of clothes with a diamond hilted sword. It was said that he was the 'most splendid delinquent that had ever appeared'. Like Garrick on a different occasion, he had dressed himself very fine for his ordeal.

Amongst the throng watching him face that ordeal were the Queen, the Prince of Wales, statesmen, lawyers, nobility, gentry – it was the most brilliant audience in the world. Miss Fanny Burney described Hastings, 'he, that, so lately, had the Eastern World nearly at his back; he under whose tyrant power princes and potentates sunk and trembled, pale looked his face, pale, ill, and altered, dreadful harrass written on his countenance'.

The sharp penned Horace Walpole was also present at a spectacle which made him afterwards exclaim that although the oration had not quite come up to his expectations yet 'Well! we are sunk and deplorable in many points, yet not absolutely gone when history and eloquence throw out such shoots! I thought I had outlived my country; I am glad not to leave it desperate.'

Burke had commenced the proceedings some months before with his usual mixture of vituperation and facts. When the molten lava of his oratory had ceased to flow over Hastings, the latter knelt and made a plea to the assembled peers, 'Save me, my lords, from these men my accusers.'

Then Sheridan's turn came, and the astonishing fact about Sheridan's second oration on the well-worn subject of the princesses of Oude was that he did not repeat himself. Some critics said that the speech was more mannered and more worked over than the previous one in the House of Commons, but as Sheridan spoke at length on four separate days June 3rd, 6th, 10th and 13th, this was not surprising. The only surprising thing is that he found new things to say and at such great length on a subject which by this time must have occupied a good deal of his time, and had perhaps become less exciting to his imaginative mind – but like the actor and playwright he was, he managed by twisting and turning the emotions of his audience to achieve an even greater triumph in Westminster Hall.

The sensibilities of his audience were given much to work on for their fifty guineas. Mrs Siddons fainted. Gainsborough, determined to hear Sheridan, went there in a delicate state of health, and contracted a fatal chill which brought on his last illness.

Sheridan was dressed in a plain dark suit of clothes, and both he and the other managers carried the voluminous notes they needed. At this time in his life Sheridan is described by Wraxall:

'His countenance and features had in them something peculiarly pleasing, indicative at once of intellect, humour and gaiety. All these characteristics played about his lips when speaking, and operated with inconceivable attraction; for they anticipated, as it were to the eye, the effect produced by his oratory on the ear, thus opening for him a sure way to the heart or the understanding.'

It was said that his voice though occasionally tending to thickness was singularly musical, vibrating to every mood that modulated it. Fox was said to 'bark' and Pitt, although stately and imposing, spoke as if 'a ball of worsted was in his mouth', but Sheridan sang his listeners into attention.

Hastings, facing his accuser, was a small spare man, upright, with a high forehead, 'with arched eyebrows overhanging, soft, sad eyes which presently flashed defiance on his accusers'. His picture gives an impression of strength and watchfulness – it could be a portrait of one of the early Puritan leaders. Accused and accuser faced one another across the background of pageantry. So Sheridan rose to snatch his triumph before the brilliant assembly.

Reading old speeches, it is difficult to recall the orator's effect – oratory and acting are both spells which vanish with the dying fall of the speaker's voice. Even the modern tape cannot recall them, for the sentiments which animated the hearers have also vanished. To listen again to the wartime speeches of Churchill, or the cosy orations of Priestley is to realize that one's own sentiments of loved ones in peril and death in the skies contributed to the speech itself. So it was with Sheridan.

It is easy to dismiss those high-flown sentiments as fustian –
they may be fustian to the modern reader, but to the listeners
in Westminster Hall, they were the here and the now. This
was the year before the storming of the Bastille, when liberty
was going to combat and defeat oppression everywhere.

Sheridan began with a compliment to Burke, 'My Lords,
the great illustration necessary to your Lordships' information
was given to you at the commencement of this business by him
alone who was equal to that task – by him to whom the world
owes the obligation of causing this embodied stand in favour of
the rights of man against man's oppression.'

In between tracing the intricacies of Indian politics Sheridan
made direct appeals to the minds and sentiments of his audience. He made the point that he had no personal malice
against the defendant, his only motive was to retrieve British
honour in India.

'I should say that it is the proud attempt to mix a variety of
lordly crimes that unsettles the prudence of the mind, and
breeds the distraction of the brain; that one master passion
domineering in the breast may win the faculties of the
understanding to advance its purpose and to direct to that
object everything that thought or human knowledge can
effect . . . these are the furies of the mind, my Lords, that
unsettle the understanding; these are the furies of the mind
that destroy the virtue, prudence; while the distracted brain
and shivered intellect proclaim the tumult that is within, and
bear their testimonies from the mouth of God himself to the
foul condition of the heart.'

To modern ears this conclusion to the first day's proceedings
sounds more like a high-flown sermon than a brief. As the days
wore on even Sheridan's strength ebbed, and at one point he
nearly fainted, and Burke had to take his place. This was not
astonishing, considering the very length and complications of
the facts and emotions which he had to draw together.

The sufferings of the Begums again caused the floods of
oratory to break the banks of emotion:

'Women there are not as in Turkey – they neither go to the

mosque nor to the bath – it is not the thin veil alone which hides them – but the utmost recesses of their Zenana. They are kept from public view by those reverenced and protected walls, held sacred even by the ruffian hand of war. To dispute with the Counsel about the original right to those treasures – their title to them is the title of a Saint to the relics upon an altar placed there by piety guarded by Holy Superstition and to be snatched from thence only by sacrilege.'

A Mr Law, unimpressed by the sufferings of the Begums, remarked later that as the treasure of the Begums included muskets, camels and elephants, he wondered how these were to be placed upon the altar. But oratory must never be subjected to the scrutiny of mere logic: it is used to stir the emotions, as a speech in a play.

When it came to the depredations of the British, and the descriptions of 'swarms of English pensioners and placemen' Sheridan's metaphors were even more fervent. He described them as

'. . . reclining on the roots and shades of that spacious tree which their predecessors had stripped branch and bough – watching with eager eyes the first budding of a future prosperity and of the opening harvest which they considered as the prey of their perseverance and rapacity. . . . Truth calls now to your Lordships, in the weak but clear tone of that Cherub Innocence whose voice is more persuasive than eloquence, more convincing than argument, whose look is supplication, whose tone is conviction, it calls upon you for redress, it calls upon you for vengeance upon the oppressor, and points its heaven-directed hand to the detested, but unrepenting author of its wrongs.'

The Cherub innocents were of a reasonable age for they were the mother and grandmother of the Rajah of Oude, but it was an attractive illustration – giving the impression of plump cupids by Boucher floating over Westminster Hall. He describes the Begum as looking for protection to the English who were 'dragging her wretched son to the walls of Fyzabad to destroy her'. This was, he said, a violation of the deepest instincts:

'And yet, my Lords, how can I support the claim of filial love by argument – much less the affection of a son to a mother – where love loses its awe, and veneration is mixed with tenderness? What can I say upon such a subject? Filial Love! The morality of instinct, the sacrament of nature and duty, or rather let me say, it is miscalled a duty, for it flows from the heart without effort, and is its delight, its indulgence, its enjoyment. It is guided, not by the slow dictates of reason, it asks no aid from memory; it is an innate, but active consciousness, having been the object of a thousand tender solicitudes, a thousand waking watchful cares, of meek anxiety and patient sacrifices, unremarked and un-requited by the object.'

These high-flown sentimental passages fall strangely from the lips of the boy neglected at Harrow, whose father had no use for him, yet so often it is the neglected child whose tears flow for the picture of the ideal mother, and the ideal father who in reality had never existed. Family life is always sweeter and nobler to those who have never experienced it.

Speaking of Hastings' deputies he said, 'They do seem to admit here, that it was not worth while to commit a massacre for the discount of a small note of hand, and to put two thousand women and children to death, in order to secure prompt payment.' But when it came to horrors, India was full of them. In 1756, in an attack in Calcutta, 146 European men and women had been squeezed into a guard room twenty feet by fourteen feet on one of the hottest nights of the year. The next morning twenty-two men and one woman remained alive. The faults and cruelties were not all on the side of the British, but Hastings bore the brunt of the roused sensibilities of Sheridan's audience. In the fervent philippics he is compared to Caligula and Nero.

On the last day, Sheridan resumed his attack in earnest, demolishing the defence:

'This is the character of all the protection ever offered to the allies of Britain under the government of Mr Hastings. They send their troops to drain the products of industry. Then they call it *protection*. Like a vulture with her harpy talons grappled in the vitals of the land, they flap away the lesser kites and then they call it protection. It is the protection of the vulture to the lamb.'

He closed with a rousing peroration:

'Let the Truth appear, and our cause is gained. It is to this I conjure your Lordships for your own honour, for the honour of the nation, for the honour of human nature, now entrusted to your care; that I, for the Commons of England speaking through us, claim this duty at your hands. They exhort you to it by everything that calls sublimely upon the heart of man, by the majesty of justice which this bold man has libelled, by the wide frame of your own renowned tribunal, by the sacred pledge which you swear in the solemn hour of decision, knowing that that decision will bring you the highest reward that ever blessed the heart of man, the consciousness of having done the greatest act of Mercy for the world, that the earth has ever yet received from any hand but Heaven.
My Lords, I have done.'

Here, overcome by the end of the ordeal which he had experienced, Sheridan faltered, and was caught in Burke's arms. The outburst of praise was as universal and heady as that which had greeted Sheridan's first speech in the House of Commons.
Eliza wrote to Lissy in Dublin:

'It is impossible, my dear woman, to convey to you the delight, the astonishment, the adoration, he has excited in the breasts of every class of people. What must my feelings be, you can imagine. To tell you the truth it is with some difficulty that I can let down my mind, as Mr Burke said afterwards, to talk or think of any other subject; but pleasure too exquisite becomes pain, and I am at this moment suffering from the delightful anxieties of last week I am a poor creature and cannot support extremes.'

Poor Eliza was also probably suffering from overwork as the hardworking amanuensis, from copying manuscripts, and supporting the nervous hero of the hour. But these were the tiresome background labours, not to be spoken about. What appeared to the world was the finished product, which was there for admiration.

Sir Gilbert Elliott recorded his emotions, as usual, remarking to his wife that there were few dry eyes in the Assembly, and he added proudly that he never remembered having cried so copiously. He added 'Burke caught him in his arms as he sat down, which was not the least affecting part of the day to my feelings. I have myself enjoyed that embrace on such an occasion and know its value.' Today such fervent embraces of achievement have passed from politicians to footballers.

Although Sheridan's sister Betsy did not attend the impeachment till the following year, she gives a vivid account of the atmosphere which seems to have approximated to a visit to a private box at Drury Lane. She echoes others in noting that Burke's manner and voice were against him, and that she disliked Fox's voice. But when her brother began to speak she felt overcome with emotion. 'I felt a thousand pulses beat as he rose and gulped down the tears that were almost choking that I might not appear too nervous.' 'Nervous' in the fashionable parlance of the day meant suffering from an excess of sensibility. Betsy, like others, comments that his voice much resembled his father's:

'I was also reminded of him by his manner which is certainly very like my father's though not an imitation. There is a calm dignity in it, yet animated to the greatest degree where the subject admits of it. His voice is uncommonly fine, and his utterance so distinct that I did not lose a syllable which is surprising as you know his general way of speaking is rather slovenly. The sight in itself is certainly fine, and from accessory ideas must strike the imagination of any person.'

The set lived up to the speaker, and set off the fine flow of his language:

'I thought of you and wished my poor neighbour Mrs Dixon quietly at home, and you in her place. When the Court adjourned we strolled about in some of the outward courts and met several of the Managers. Mr Burke came up to take care of Mrs Dixon and Irishmanlike insisted on the Young Lady as he stiled me taking his other arm, so under the care of this friend of the Begums I got through the croud.'

In spite of the paeons of admiration there were dissident voices. Gibbon at first was full of praise. 'Mr Sheridan's eloquence commanded my applause, nor could I hear without emotion the personal compliment which he paid me in the presence of the British Nation.' Sheridan had said, 'I do say, that if you search the history of the world, you will not find an act of tyranny or fraud to surpass this; if you read all past histories, peruse the annals of Tacitus, read the luminous pages Gibbon.' When questioned later Sheridan said to a brother Whig, 'I did not say luminous, I said *vo*luminous.'

But if Sheridan was not averse to a crack at Gibbon's weighty volumes – Gibbon equally found it easy to let down his mind, and his hair, when writing to Lord Sheffield:

'Yesterday the august scene was closed for this year. Sheridan surpassed himself; and though I am far from considering him as a perfect orator, there were many beautiful passages in his speech, on justice, filial love, etc; and one of the closest chains of argument I ever heard to prove that Hastings was responsible for the acts of Middleton; and a compliment, much admired, to a certain Historian of your acquaintance. Sheridan at the close of his speech sank into Burke's arms; a good actor; but I called this morning – he is perfectly well.'

Sir Gilbert Elliott was less disposed to take Sheridan's illness as sham. He says, 'Sheridan had been extremely ill the night before and had strained himself by vomiting so severely as to make it doubtful whether he would be able to speak at all.'

This sounds very much like a nervous crisis of an actor before a performance, and considering the lofty nature of the audience, and the bulk of the material to be transformed into sentiments to move the heart, it was not surprising that Sheridan suffered from nerves. So much seemed to be at stake, but the triumph was worth all the suffering. Eliza was glad that it was over. It had been for her, as she said, 'exquisite pain'.

She wrote to her sister-in-law in Dublin:

'You were perhaps alarmed by the accounts of Sheridan's illness in the papers; but I have the pleasure to assure you he is now perfectly well, and I hope by next week we shall be quietly settled in the country, and suffered to repose. We have, both of us, been in a constant state of agitation, of one kind or another, for some time back.

I am glad your father continues so well. Surely he must feel happy and proud of such a son. I take it for granted that you see the newspapers; I assure you the accounts in them are not exaggerated, and only echo the exclamation of admiration that is in everybody's mouth. I make no excuse for dwelling on this subject: I know you will not find it tedious. God bless you, I am an invalid at present and not able to write a long letter.'

The peers returned their robes to the cedar boxes, the managers folded their documents, the show was over for the year, and the principal actors went off to enjoy the sights and sounds of the countryside. Only the accused was left to face years of dogged defence.

The trial lasted, in all, seven years. At its conclusion, on April 23, 1795, Warren Hastings was acquitted upon each of the charges brought against him. He was then allowed to go free. He had paid £76,000 for his defence. It had been a Pyhrric victory for both sides. For, gradually as the trial wore on year after year, people began to realize that if Hastings' crimes were of such enormity, it was astonishing that it took so long to prove his guilt. Hastings came out of his long ordeal guiltless, and penniless.

For Sheridan the prospects which had opened out as a result of his fame seemed limitless.

CHAPTER 14

The Fatal Connection

Apart from the general blunder of having allied himself with his old enemies, Fox had other liabilities, which in turn affected Sheridan. One of these was the heir to the throne. The Prince of Wales had come of age, and Fox had always been anxious to keep in with the heir. The hope had been that when the King died, the Whig millennium would commence.

There had been a secret pact by which the Prince had been promised by Fox that he would use his influence to gain for him £100,000 a year when he came of age. Unfortunately, the coming to power of Fox and his friends and the Prince's coming of age coincided.

The ministry was supposed to be dedicated to economy and to the general elimination of place hunting. It was an awkward moment to suggest that the Prince should have a cool hundred thousand a year. As ill-luck would have it, this meant that Fox was not only at odds with his own Chancellor of the Exchequer but also with the King. The Whigs, under Fox, could hardly have great appeal for the country, if one of their banners advocated more money for the extravagant Prince. But the Prince had firmly aligned himself to the Fox Hounds amongst whom was Sheridan, whom he met for the first time at Devonshire House. It was to be a fatal connection for Sheridan.

It is easy now that so many generations have passed to dismiss the Prince of Wales as the fat lecher he afterwards became. When he first met Sheridan, Prinny was twenty-one. He was handsome, athletic, graceful, he charmed the great Whig ladies, and was popular with the mob. He sang well, rode well, shot well, danced well, and talked well. No one could bow as he could bow, and although he drank 'like a leviathan' he had perfect taste in pictures, silver – and women. It was not easy to resist either the Prince or the company he kept. At Carlton House, with a background of Italian music, he attracted the admiring glances of those favourites of Sheridan's, Mrs Crewe and the Duchess of Devonshire. It was no small thing for the poor player's son to walk with Princes.

Just as Sheridan had been dazzled by Fox, so he was overwhelmed by the Prince. It is curious that charmers are so often deceived by charm, as it is said confidence tricksters are easily taken in by other quick gentlemen of the trade. Fox had charmed Sheridan, and Sheridan was in his turn fascinated by the Prince.

Fox, although friendly towards the Prince, perhaps viewed him more as a political pawn, but to Sheridan he was a real friend. Possibly Fox, who had lived so long amongst the rich and great was not deceived by Prinny's superficial characteristics. For the Prince courted popularity, and it was said, 'He was ever too important to himself, saying finer things than his feelings prompted.' With Sheridan it was the other way round, he constantly felt fine emotions but lacked the means or influence to carry out the promptings of his heart.

But Prinny, like Edward VII, had over-reacted against his strict background, and had already in his teens become a man of expensive pleasures and sensual enjoyments. This was not an ambience which would have disturbed Sheridan. He liked the world and its pleasures too much himself.

No doubt at this point in Prinny's monetary troubles Sheridan had sympathy with him – debts were something he knew a great deal about. Added to which, Fox realized that Sheridan could prove useful to him. A certain amount of patching up had to be done, and Sheridan was a good persuader. Fox had managed to get the Prince to agree to a mere £50,000 a year, the Duchy of Cornwall, and a downpayment of £30,000.

There were other minor inconveniences such as Perdita Robinson. Mrs Robinson, who had played at Drury Lane, had the Prince's bond for £20,000. This had somehow to be prised from her grasp. Fox managed to persuade Perdita to settle for an annuity of £500 a year. It is quite possible that Sheridan could have had a hand in the negotiations, for she had acted under his management.

Meanwhile, Fox had taken Perdita into keeping, after the Prince had tired of her, somewhat like taking over and renewing the lease of a house which was on the point of coming to an end. After Fox resigned for the first time in 1782 one of his aunts wrote, 'I hear Charles saunters about the streets and brags that he has not taken a pen in hand since he was out of place. *Pour se desennuyer*, he lives with Mrs Robinson, and is all day figuring away with her.'

The great and growing bourgeoisie, however, preferred the spotless family life led by their own dear King with his enormous troop of children, however stupidly he had behaved, and Sheridan had allied himself to a party which was now fixed in some people's minds as a party of gamblers, 'turfites', and keepers of light ladies. The solid middle class was not in favour of such people.

The Prince's affairs, both monetary and female, were temporarily patched up, but the problem of the Prince himself was something which was to remain to plague Fox and Sheridan. It is difficult to sort out the complications of the relationships between Fox, Sheridan, and the Prince because, as always, posthumous memoirs written by partisans take the point of view which suits the exigencies of their political bandwagons.

Sheridan is supposed to have got to know the Prince in about 1781, but he did not become useful to him and to Fox until the troubles over Mrs Fitzherbert in 1785. There is no doubt that at one point in this well-known affair the Prince of Wales, exerting his famous charm, led Charles James Fox right down the garden path into a pond of trouble. Speaking of marriage and Mrs Fitzherbert, the prince vowed and declared: 'Make yourself easy, my dear friend; believe me the world will soon now be convinced that there not only is not, but never was any ground for these reports which have of late been so malevolently circulated.' He was in fact already planning his marriage. Ten days later he married the woman.

Fox went down to the House and denied that there ever was or ever could have been a marriage. 'The fact not only never could have happened legally, but never did happen in any way whatsoever', he stated, and the story had from the beginning been a base and malicious falsehood, adding that it was 'only fit to impose on the lower orders in the street'.

Shortly afterwards Fox went to Brooks's where a member is supposed to have said to him, 'I see by the papers, you have denied the fact of the marriage of the Prince with Mrs Fitzherbert. You have been misinformed. I was present at that marriage.' The Prince, anxious as always to have the best of both worlds, said to his beloved: 'Only conceive, Maria, what Fox did yesterday; he went down to the House, and denied that you and I were man and wife. Did you ever hear of such a thing?'

The facts constituted a cat's-cradle of legality and illegality. Although by marrying a catholic the Prince had cut himself off from the succession, yet by the Royal Marriage Act of 1772, it was no marriage at all. The House voted the Prince £160,000, but Pitt, obviously aware of the trouble, quoted from Othello, 'Villain, be sure thou prove my love a whore.'

Fox had fallen into a trap, but he refused to admit before the House that he had been duped. The Prince, caught between two fires, his genuine love for Maria Fitzherbert, and his right to succeed, fussed, fumed, and cried out, 'Well, then *Sheridan* must say something.'

It was a situation which was to tax even Sheridan's ingenuity. To soothe the Prince's feelings, to allay the suspicions of the populace about the marriage, and yet to protect the virtue of Mrs Fitzherbert was a triple bill which even the manager of Drury Lane was to find difficult. A little circumlocution with honey seemed the only answer:

'But whilst his Royal Highness's feelings had no doubt to be considered on this occasion, he must take the liberty of saying, however some might think it a subordinate consideration that there was another person entitled in every delicate and honourable mind, to the same attention – one whom he would not otherwise venture to describe or allude to, but by saying it was a name which malice or ignorance alone could attempt to injure, and whose conduct and character claimed, and were entitled to the truest respect.'

Whether this satisfied Mrs Fitzherbert is open to doubt, but the public remained happily convinced that Maria was just another of the Prince's kept ladies, while the lady herself was beginning to see the extent of the Prince's unreliability. It was over this crisis that Sheridan became deeply enmeshed with the Prince. Even Sheridan's enemies admit that he was never subservient to the Prince, that he delighted and amused him, being on terms of great friendship with him, advising and helping him, while remaining independent of him financially and morally.

The upshot of the Fitzherbert crisis was that Maria never spoke to Fox again, and his relations with the Prince were seriously strained. But as Fox saw it the Prince was merely a political asset, while to Sheridan the Prince was a friend and an achievement. Fox was not so simple-minded as Sheridan when it came to mixing with the great.

Possibly from then on both Fox and the Prince came to regard Sheridan as a useful go-between, while Sheridan saw himself as the successor to Fox in the Whig party. This was not the way Fox saw him. His lack of social position was still an insuperable barrier. He was even lampooned as a political adventurer:

'It could not happen in any country but England: that a young man, the son of a player should refuse though in very distressed circumstances to let his wife sing at a royal concert because it would degrade his character as a *gentleman* . . . that this man of fashion being so embarrassed as not to find the most common credit, and apprehensive even of fatal inconveniency to his public property, should desert the comic muse for politics, and with the last guinea of a borrowed purse, to get elected into parliament, and set up, at once, for an active politician, exclaiming against placemen and ministers, and boasting the loudest zeal for patriot integrity and public virtue.'

But in spite of his social disadvantages, when it came to the Prince's affairs, Fox found Sheridan useful, and when the King became ill for the first time in 1788, he was more useful still.

Fox had gone abroad with his current mistress, Mrs Armistead, when the King became 'mad' – according to modern medical ideas, he was suffering from the illness of porphyria, but as contemporary opinion considered him 'mad', it is perhaps simpler to report his illness in that way. The political intrigues which now surrounded the heir to the throne put the cabals and undercurrents of place-hunting in a more than usually unattractive light.

If once the principle of a Regency could be established then the Fox Hounds could be returned to power, helped by the influence of the Prince. Over the ailing body of the King, the battles were fought. The reports of the doctors on the King's health were avidly read by the contemporary politicians much as reports on bloody revolutions which could influence oil shares are scrutinized today. The atmosphere was no more edifying.

While Fox was absent abroad, the Comptroller of the Prince of Wales' Household, Admiral Payne, wrote to Sheridan, saying that Pitt had just left Windsor, having managed to get Parliament adjourned. 'The Duke of York, who is looking over me, and is just come out of the king's room bids me add that His Majesty's situation is every moment becoming worse. His pulse is weaker; and the Doctors say it is impossible to survive it long.'

Hope was rising amongst the followers of Fox, who was now coming back post-haste from Italy. The doctors were promising death rather than madness, and Admiral Payne was worried about publicity. Opposition hopes were rising with the detailed and gloomy reports from the doctors, 'cataplasms are on His Majesty's feet', and 'strong fermentations used without effect'.

The following day he seemed a little better, but the Admiral reported, 'His theme has been all this day on the subject of religion from which his physicians draw the *worst* consequences as to any hopes of amendment.'

Admiral Payne greeted the arrival of Charles James Fox in England with relief, but the intrigues went on. Betsy Sheridan in her Journal written from Sheridan's house in Bruton Street gives a domestic view of the comings and goings:

'I am here in the midst of news and politics. Mrs S. has had a constant levée, and the present situation of the King, of course, the only topic of conversation. I have been a good deal amused by their various conjectures which were all suited to their different interests. The fact is that the reports of the King's amendment relate only to his health. His mind continues in the same state it has been for some time past. Tickell and Richardson here as usual. Dick with us but so engaged in thought he hardly seemed to hear or see us.'

And when Richard was not at home, deep in thought, he was engaged in conference: 'Chère Frère has been gone since four o'clock this morning to a private conference. *He* is the head they all apply to now, and he will be, if things turn out as we have reason to expect, just what he chuzes.' The prospects were opening up, and power seemed to be almost within his grasp. 'Mrs S. has scarcely set eyes on her good gentleman', added Betsy. 'He is taken up entirely with Charles Fox and the Prince of Wales. I should tell you that the latter gentleman has more esteem and friendship for him than for any Man in England.'

It was said that during the general struggle for place over the body of the distracted King the Prince offered Sheridan the post of Chancellor of the Exchequer. If so, it was an odd choice in view of Sheridan's limited financial capacities, but he is said to have refused. Possibly it savoured too much of the counting of unhatched eggs, and Sheridan did not want to be made to look foolish later.

But already some of his friends were beginning to doubt his solidity. Georgiana, Duchess of Devonshire, wrote in her diary that Sheridan 'gave convincing evidence of his talents, but also evinc'd the danger of his character. I do not mean to accuse him of any duplicity; in fact he has stood the test of even poverty and I feel convinc'd of the honor of his political sentiments – but he cannot resist playing a sly game; he cannot resist the pleasure of acting alone.'

It was flattering to his vanity for him to feel his power, that his was the head they consulted, and his the hand that wrote the letters from the Prince of Wales. Fox, who already distrusted the Prince over the Fitzherbert marriage, now began to have doubts about Sheridan. It was a difficult tightrope which Sheridan was walking, and always behind him he heard the footsteps of the past and knew that he had to go forward in order to seize the prizes which were within his grasp. The Prince was his only hope of rising in the world, of freeing himself from the uncertainties of the theatrical scene, and above all of laying forever the evil spirits of penury, humiliation, and social stigma which had haunted his father, old Thomas Sheridan, and also to some extent himself. Had his father been a brilliant success, he might have thought and reacted differently. But Thomas's disasters shadowed the son's life. Ironically the theatre to which Sheridan devoted only a total of about five years' creative work, as against over thirty to politics, was his claim to immortality, yet it was also the one thing he longed to regard as expendable. Yet he still saw himself, rightly, as the Prince's adviser and friend, not merely as someone who waited in the wings for the royal favours.

The hopes and fears of the government and the opposition rose and fell with the conflicting medical bulletins. They make unpleasant reading. The opposition leaders were like the heirs to a fortune whose greatest joy would be to hear that the patient had passed away.

The unfortunate King had been sent to Kew and had been put into a strait-jacket. Dr Willis, presumably on the government side, delivered a note to Pitt saying that the King was much better and a perfect recovery was expected. While a rival doctor, in receipt of this news, immediately set off for Kew and found out that at the precise moment when Dr Willis was announcing the good tidings of his recovery, the King had never been worse.

Sheridan's hopes began to wane. It seemed unlikely that even if the Regency could be established it could be more than a temporary expedient. The two women of the family, Eliza and Betsy, Sheridan's sister, who was staying with them at this time, had their eyes set on practical things, and they deplored the fact that whatever the outcome it seemed unlikely that Dick would be able to bring himself to ask for any favours. Betsy remarked when writing to her sister Lissy, 'Mrs S. and I have been talking over this matter, but she says that such is Dick's shyness in applying for any personal favour, that she knows though the Regent may rejoice in the opportunity of providing for him, she has no hopes of him taking one step in the business.'

When the bad news of the King's improvement was finally confirmed, Sheridan took it with panache. His sister remarked on his 'spirit unacquainted with despondence' and says there was 'something chearing in his manner that in a great measure conquered the gloom that hung over us'.

The hopeful members of the Opposition assembled in the Sheridans' drawing-room had reason to be gloomy. Tickell was hoping for some Government appointment, Joseph Richardson was waiting to step into Tickell's shoes at the Stamp Office. With a Mr Reid and others they were all waiting at Bruton Street to hear something to their own advantage when Sheridan returned: but he remained his cheerful and sanguine self. No one had lost more than he had at that minute. He announced the news and then said, 'Let us all join in drinking His Majesty's speedy recovery.' According to some reports he had already accepted the post of Treasurer to the Navy, and had been to Somerset House to view his prospective apartments.

The disappointments ended in Anglo-Irish junketings, for the Irish Parliament had moved and carried a proposal that the Prince of Wales be made Regent of Ireland without restriction. The resolution was brought to England by the Duke of Leinster and the Earl Charlemont, but by the time they arrived to discuss the details, the celebrations for the King's recovery were on and Dick was dining with them at Carlton House.

The *Town and Country Magazine* fell over itself with pleasure at the Regent's entertainments:

'In elegance and convivial pleasure the entertainment given by the Prince of Wales to the delegates of the Irish parliament was truly enchanting. It was the Feast of Reason and the Flow of Soul such as Pythagoras and his disciples used to enjoy. Burke and Sheridan were among the guests, each with abilities to keep the table in a roar, not with gross humour but with wit of Attick polish and Attick point –

bright as the champagne they drank, and the champagne was the best the world could afford.'

The Duchess of Devonshire gave a ball at Devonshire House, and Sheridan gave a supper at Bruton Street. 'We are to have the Prince, the Duke of York, Mrs Fitzherbert – all the fine people', wrote Betsy. 'I should be very glad to give them the slip if I had any decent pretext.'

Thus the disappointments were dissipated to the sound of the popping of champagne corks, and masqucrades, galas, balls, operas and plays were launched on a wave of pseudo-patriotism. White's gave a gala which two thousand people attended at the Pantheon, and members of Brooks's naturally anxious to let everyone forget their former hopes of the King's death, put on a promenade concert supper and ball at the Opera House in the Haymarket which was 'superbly fitted up for the occasion'. Mrs Siddons, dressed as Britannia, recited a patriotic ode in her best and noblest style, and concluded the entertainment in an original, if somewhat surprising way – 'to the gratified astonishment of the spectators she sat down in the exact attitude of the figure on the pennypiece'. It was thought that this happy piece of theatre was Sheridan's idea, and Mrs Siddons was so pleased with her reception as a living coin that she repeated it on her benefit night a few weeks later.

*

In spite of the fêtes and galas, some bitterness remained in the Royal family, and no doubt there were many of Fox's enemies, and the enemies of the Prince of Wales, who were only too ready to retail to the King the behaviour of the opposition during his illness. There was more patching up to be done and again Sheridan's was the hand and head which were used, for he wrote a dignified letter for the Prince Regent to send to his father:

'Your Majesty's letter to my brother the Duke of Clarence was the first direct imitation I had ever received that my conduct and that of my brother the Duke of York, during your Majesty's late lamented illness, had brought on us the heavy misfortune of Your Majesty's displeasure. In this painful interval I have employed myself in drawing up a full statement and account of my conduct during the period alluded to, and of the motives and circumstances which influenced me.'

Nor was the Queen disposed to take a good view of her son's cabals with the opposition, for the letter refers to her: 'I cannot omit this opportunity of lamenting those appearances of a less gracious disposition in the Queen, towards my brothers and myself than we were accustomed to experience.' Queens do not like to be reminded that they can easily become dowagers.

But if the bitter aftermath remained, the balls went on. The last ball of the season was given at a mansion in Hammersmith to which Richard, Eliza and Betsy went, Eliza remarking 'that amusement was the way to banish disagreeable reflexions'.

It was a splendid affair with the entrance hall decorated with an abundance of natural flowers and lights, with transparencies of the Prince of Wales' Crest and devices representing the Army and Navy. Mrs Sheridan unmasked and received many compliments from the company. The Prince of Wales and his brothers all arrived dressed as Highland chiefs. He immediately approached Mrs Sheridan enquiring for Richard, and making sure that he sat next to Eliza at supper. Betsy remarked, 'I sat next, and le chère Frère [Richard] next to me who by the bye is always particularly civil to me in public unlike a certain sneaking puppy of our acquaintance [her brother Charles].' Mrs Fitzherbert was also at the Prince's table, dressed simply in a white dress and black veil.

When the supper was over there was music with some excellent Catch singers and immediately afterwards the Prince, who enjoyed his music, called to the Catch singers and suggested that one of them should join himself and Mrs Sheridan in singing a trio. Eliza was taken by surprise at his request and though she had not practised for months immediately agreed. They sang two or three songs and 'then gave over for fear of tiring Mrs S. He has a good voice, and being so well supported, seemed to me to sing very well.' It was a high point in high

Sheridan

summer, as Richard watched Eliza singing with the Prince in front of the grand company. He was in great spirits. He had reason to be.

After supper Richard, not anxious to leave the party, put on a disguise and 'having plagued several people sufficiently, resumed his Domino, and returned to the company pretending he had just left a party at Supper . . . after we had all unmask'd Dick walk'd about a good deal with us, and several of the masks remark'd that having such a Partner it was no wonder he kept by her – I think I never saw Mrs S. look handsomer.'

They returned to town in the dawn. Betsy ended her account: 'I have had a peep at the Raree Shew of the great world without trouble or risk, and not being young enough to have my brain turn'd, shall enjoy my broil'd bone in Cuffe Street with as much pleasure as ever.'

Broil'd bones were not for 'dear Dick', and the Raree Shew was his world. He was only thirty-seven, and if the King had unfortunately recovered his wits, Dick felt that with a beautiful wife, a great reputation, and a friend in the Prince of Wales, there was nothing that could not be achieved – 'the best way not to fail is to determine to succeed', and in some things he was determined enough.

262

CHAPTER 15

Fighting the Shadows

During the Hastings Trial, old Thomas Sheridan had been in Ireland trying to raise money for the improvement of Irish education. His idea was that some of the free schools should be suppressed, and with the funds thus made available to him, he would found a 'Lyceum' at New Geneva, near Waterford. As a plan it was not the essence of democracy, but in spite of his age and declining health, the omens seemed promising. A friend of his, Mr Orde, had the ear of the Lord Lieutenant, and he felt that soon he would see the desire of his heart accomplished.

While the trial dragged on Eliza, as always, had protected her dear Dick from the kind of gloomy news which he dreaded. She had written to Betsy who was with her father in Ireland:

'I would not show your letter to Sheridan for he has lately been so much harrassed by business, and I could not bear to give him the pain I know your letter would have occasioned. Partial as your father has always been to Charles, I am confident he never has, nor ever will feel half the duty and affection that Dick has always expressed. I know how deeply he will be afflicted if you confirm the melancholy account of his (Thomas') declining health; but I trust your next will remove my apprehensions, and make it unnecessary for me to wound his affectionate heart.'

But Thomas's health did not improve, and when his patron Mr Orde fell from his horse out hunting and killed himself, it was the final blow. He seemed to go into a decline from the moment all hope of his Academy was extinguished. Betsy brought him back to England, with the idea that he should sail for Lisbon in the hope that the sea voyage would restore his health. Betsy and Thomas made a slow journey through England in July of 1788. 'We had got into Staffordshire and the good gentlewoman of the house having learned our name, a general curiosity to look at Mr Sheridan's father had seized the whole set.'

At this moment in his career, Sheridan's fame seems to have been that of a modern pop star. In spite of his declining and frail state, old Thomas's will was still set against Richard with whom he refused to stay even for a short time. The insult of being sent away from Drury Lane had not been forgotten. Thomas was equally determined not to be impressed by his son's fame, perhaps from jealousy, but it followed him wherever he went. At their lodgings an old servant of theirs, Thompson, came to visit him, bringing new-laid eggs and good Madeira. He praised his 'dear Master Richard' saying, 'Sir, your Son is the first Man in England – you will find everyone of that opinion.' This time Thomas seemed rather pleased, which made a distinct change.

The following day Betsy went to see Dick and Eliza, accompanied by Thompson. 'Mrs Sheridan received me very kindly, but my Brother seemed very much affected. His eyes filled with tears and his voice choak'd. After embracing me very affectionately he hurried out of the room. Mrs S. said he was very nervous but would return to us soon which he did.' When Richard came into the room he enquired about his favourite sister Lissy, and spoke affectionately of his father.

This is a curious little vignette, like the picture of Sheridan watching his family from the wings at Drury Lane without being able to speak to them. It was obvious that he minded very much about his estrangement from his father. His nature was that of a man whose emotions, suppressed on so many occasions in order to appear bright and witty, often came quickly to the surface and overwhelmed him. It is easy for critics and commentators, taking a human being to pieces like the mechanism of a watch, to say that this piece is false or that unnecessary; all the pieces are necessary to produce the life which makes a human being tick. The emotions which Sheridan's orations produced on his hearers were obviously his own emotions transmuted, they were part of his make-up. The suppressed tears, the horror of tragedy, the easy sentimentality, the quick gibe, each was part of the same man.

By the end of July, the two peacemakers, Betsy and Eliza, had managed to bring the son and the father together at last. 'I must tell you we had a long visit today from Dick and his wife. All pass'd off very well. My father a little stately at first but soon thoroughly cordial with his Son who staid till near six, but could not dine with us.' Vanity Fair drew Richard away in spite of the easy tears about filial devotion. Betsy's quick vivid sketches of Dick and his wife give a very good idea of the 'bustling life' they led. Eliza, as always, comes over as sympathetic and sweet of nature – pressing the old ailing father to come and stay with them at Deepdene, which had been lent to them by the Duke of Norfolk, offering to be his nurse. 'In short everything that could flatter or induce him to comply, but he keeps his own intentions.' Old Thomas did not give up easily, not completely.

Eventually a sea voyage was decided upon. The air of Lisbon in Portugal would be good for his health. He was to travel to Margate, there to wait until he was sufficiently recovered before taking the ship to Lisbon with Betsy. Richard, 'dear Dick', had promised to lend them his coach, but it turned out that 'something had happened to it'. Possibly the livery stable bill had not been paid. But promptly, and true to his word, Richard sent 'Lord R. Spencer's. I knew my Father would not mind the livery so I said nothing of this change till we set out, and he was well satisfied.'

Betsy settled down in lodgings with her father. A parlour and two rooms was a modest setting for Thomas, a man who had started with such large ambitions. At Margate, Eliza and Richard called on the sick father. Richard declared that as soon as the election was over he and Eliza would return. 'They seem'd both tollerably [sic] tired of the election.'

As always with elections at this date, it was also 'tollerably' full of incident: 'Mrs Sheridan told me she had just given ten guineas (a collection she made) to the poor Black who at the risk of his life had step'd forward and received a cut on the head that was intended for Charles Fox. They seem'd in good spirits and quite certain of success.'

Despite the good Madeira and the sea air Thomas was not to make progress. He was attended by Mr Jarvis, 'medical gentleman of Margate', who gave a description of Thomas's illness:

'On the 10th of August 1788 I was first called on to visit Mr Sheridan who was then fast declining at his lodgings in this place, where he was in the care of his daughter. On the next day, Mr R. B. Sheridan arrived here from town, having brought with him Dr Morris of Parliament Street. I was in the bed-room with Mr Sheridan when the son arrived and witnessed an interview in which the father showed himself to be strongly impressed by his son's attention, saying, with emotion, "Oh, Dick, I give you a great deal of trouble!" and seeming to imply, by his manner, that his son had been less to blame than himself for any previous want of cordiality between them.

On my making my last call for the evening, Mr R. B. Sheridan with delicacy but much earnestness expressed his fear that the nurse in attendance on his father might not be so competent as myself to the requisite attentions, and his hope that I would consent to remain in the room for a few of the first hours of the night; as he himself, having been travelling the preceding night, required some short repose. I complied with his request, and remained at the father's bedside till relieved by the son, about three o'clock in the morning; he then insisted on taking my place. From this time he never quitted the house till his father's death.'

So died Thomas with Richard by his side. This is a picture of a man who can rise to an emergency, and who has great sensitivity, and insight into the feelings of others. There were many reasons why Richard should not have watched beside the bed of his dying father but if to know all is to forgive all, possibly Richard found in the recesses of his own nature traces of his father, and knowing him he forgave him.

The paragon son Charles stayed comfortably in Ireland. Maybe the idea of the expense of the journey deterred him: it might be a false alarm. As Lissy wrote of Richard, 'and yet it was that son, and *not* the object of his partial fondness, who at last closed his eyes'.

Thomas had expressed the desire to be buried in the parish where he died. Richard wrote to the doctor, sending him £10 and said: 'It is my desire to have the hearse and the manner of coming to town, as respectful as possible.' Richard and his brother-in-law Tickell followed the coffin to the grave.

It was typical that it was Mr Jarvis, the doctor, after waiting patiently for nearly twenty years who raised the money for old Thomas Sheridan's monument. The wording on it was more truthful than some laudatory stones of the period: 'Through some of his opinions ran a vein of singularity, mingled with the rich ore of genius. In his manners there was dignified ease; – in his spirit, invincible firmness; – and in his habits and principles unsullied integrity.' Poor Richard knew all about the invincible firmness, or what Eliza called, with more accuracy, 'damned mulish obstinacy'.

After the funeral Betsy wrote:

'I know not whether you will feel, like me, a melancholy pleasure in the reflexion that my father received the last kind offices from by brother Richard, whose conduct on this occasion must convince every one of the goodness of his heart and the truth of his filial affection. One more reflection of consolation is that nothing was omitted that could have prolonged his life or eased his latter hours.

With regard to my brother's kindness, I can scarcely express to you how great it has been. He saw my father while he was still sensible and never quitted him till the awful moment was past. His feelings have been severely tried, and I earnestly pray he may not suffer from that cause, or from the fatigue he has endured. His tenderness to me I can never forget. I had so little claim on him, that I still feel a degree of surprise mixed with my gratitude.'

Betsy was taken off to live with Eliza and Richard at Deepdene, and mingled with her gratitude and surprise, no doubt, was the contrast between the behaviour of the two brothers.

There had been other and greater tragedies in the family, for

Mary Tickell née Linley, Eliza's best loved sister, had died in 1787. She was only twenty-nine. Eliza wrote:

'In February 1787 my dear sister came to London in a bad state of health, dangerously ill of a fever which turned to a hectic that never afterwards left her.

On the 19th June we went by slow degrees to Clifton Hill, near the Hot Wells, with a faint hope that the air and waters might restore her, but after struggling with this most dreadful of all diseases [tuberculosis] and bearing with gentlest patience and resignation the various pains and horrors which mark its fatal progress, on the 27th July she ceased to suffer, and I for ever lost the friend and companion of my youth, the beloved sister of my heart, whose loss can never be replaced, whose sweet and amiable qualities endeared her to all those who were so happy to know her.'

Richard Tickell reacted hysterically to his wife's death. He was restrained from putting up a memorial to her on which was to be inscribed a vow that he would never marry again. This was just as well, for less than two years afterwards he was indeed married again – to a beautiful girl of only eighteen.

In view of his vagaries, Eliza took his children under her wing, and when Betsy came to Deepdene (which the Sheridans often call Dibden) Eliza was trying to rebuild a family life for her sister's children. She wrote: 'The dear children remained with me till that time [Tickell's marriage]. The boys were taken home by their father. The girl, the dying legacy of her ever dear and lamented mother, is still mine and constitutes all my happiness.' Eliza was trying to cling to the past and to the family. It was not easy. The Linleys had been a numerous, beautiful, and gifted brood – 'a nest of Linnets', they had been called – but like frail flowers, which bloomed too early in the year, they had dropped and died one by one.

Eliza's favourite brother, at an age when most boys would have been at school, studied music in Vienna under Mozart. He was a gifted violinist, and died uselessly in a boating accident on the Duke of Ancaster's lake at the age of twenty-two, in 1778.

Her other brother, Samuel Linley, had joined the Navy and served in the 'Thunderer'. He returned stricken with fever to his father's house in Norfolk Street where he died, nursed by Emma Lyon, later to be Lady Hamilton, who seems to have been a home-help in the Linley household. It was said that she tended the young midshipman day and night, and that when he died she was so upset that she left the family.

Maria Linley, also a beautiful singer, had died of some 'brain fever' in 1784 at the age of twenty-one. Her actual passing was dramatic. Just before she died she raised herself up from her pillows, and sang in a clear voice, 'I know that my Redeemer Liveth', and then fell back dead.

If Sheridan was alarmed by tragedy he had good reason to be, because it was all around him, and his own father's death had been merely a culmination of a series of Linley tragedies. Eliza was not recovering easily from her sister's death, and it was possibly partly to escape from this aura of sadness which so often surrounded the family that Sheridan plunged into ever more hectic activity. There are certain natures which cannot accept tragedy, who do not regard life as a continuing circle of birth, and death, decay and renewal. They seek to kill death with activity. The sight of his wife mourning the disappearance of her brothers and sisters was something from which he sought escape.

Certainly, the atmosphere at Deepdene was not conducive to escaping from the horror of reflection; besides the children, reminders of the dead sister, Eliza wore round her neck a miniature which was painted of her sister on her deathbed. Neither Tickell nor Richard was inclined to stay overlong in this gloomy family setting. Richard had plenty of excuses to stay in town and Eliza was left with her sister's children for weeks on end. She found plenty of occupations for teaching the children, reading and singing helped to fill her days. She seems to have been cultured and creative as well as beautiful and talented. The customs of the time did not make it easier to lighten a loss in the family. Not only the grown-ups but the children and the servants serving at table wore mourning garments which must have made it more difficult for a sensitive

nature like Eliza's to escape from melancholy thoughts of her
pale expiring sister.

Both Mary and Eliza had had difficult married lives.
Richard Tickell seems to have been a minor Sheridan, without
his real talents. He deputized for Sheridan at Drury Lane
Theatre and wrote several plays, including *The Carnival of
Venice* and *The Camp*, which Sheridan revised. He was also
the author of various political satires. With Joseph Richardson,
the two Richards formed a trio addicted to drinking, social
life and the complicated practical jokes of the period. To
modern eyes some of them seem either pointless or cruel, or
both.

Sheridan was notorious not only for his debts, but for his
lack of ready money. He once found himself in a coach in
which he had been driving around for several hours with no
cash to pay the driver. Looking out of the coach window he
saw his friend Joseph Richardson, and suggested taking him
part of the way. Richardson was well known for being very
argumentative. Sheridan managed to get him into a high state
of excitement on some subject about which they disagreed.
Eventually Sheridan pretended to be very angry, saying that
he could not think of staying in the same coach with a person
who could use such language. He pulled the check string of
the coach, and asked the coachman to let him out. Richardson
leaned out of the window hurling further arguments after
Sheridan, who walked happily away, leaving Richardson, of
course, to pay for the coach.

On another occasion when staying at his country house
near Osterley, one of the guests the Rev. O'Byrne has been
asked by his patron Mr Child to preach the following day.
The parson, although anxious to shine, had no sermon prepared,
and Sheridan offered very kindly to write one for him. The
following morning it was delivered neatly tied with ribbon,
the subject being 'The Abuse of Riches'. The delighted Mr
O'Byrne duly delivered the sermon in his best style in the
village church. What he did not know was that the local
squire, Mr Child, was in the congregation, and what was more
he was very unpopular in the village for prosecuting some poor
parishioners for 'carrying away garden-stuff which had been

thrown over the wall'. The clergyman could not understand why the Child family were cutting him in the village. Everyone in the church had enjoyed the sermon and its local implications except the unconscious preacher, who in order to impress his patrons had kept his eyes firmly fixed on them while he orated. The local parson then called on O'Byrne and said that Mr Child would never forgive him and added according to Sheridan 'if O'Byrne had quoted the Apostles fairly he might had been justified; but he had garbled them, in order to apply their reproaches to Mr Child'. In fact Sheridan had altered the gospels to suit his purpose.

It is a curious story, with that mixture of complicated political undermining in which Sheridan delighted. As the Rev. O'Byrne, through the patronage of Lord Fitzwilliam became Bishop of Meath, it presumably did not check his preferment; but an uneasy doubt remains. It was the action of a man who acted without thought on the spur of the moment, with no regard for the consequences.

On another occasion, when Sheridan was out riding with Tickell, Eliza and Mrs Crewe were following by carriage. Rounding a curve in the road they were confronted by the sight of Sheridan, lying on the ground apparently in the agony of death, and Tickell standing over him in an attitude of theatrical despair. The ladies, fearing Sheridan had met with some ghastly accident, gave cries of alarm which were followed by roars of laughter from Tickell and Sheridan.

This was the age of the mad squire Waterton, when setting fire to a fellow guest's bed curtains was considered a witty jape. The practical jokes of Tickell and Sheridan certainly had much of the fun and malice of schoolboys. In addition to which, again like the jokes of schoolboys, they were very elaborate and carefully prepared. 'On one occasion', it is reported, 'Sheridan having covered the floor of a dark passage, leading from the drawing-room, with all the plates and dishes of the house ranged closely together, provoked his unconscious play-fellow to pursue him into the midst of them. Having left a path for his own escape, he passed through easily, but Tickell falling at full length into the ambuscade was very much cut in several places. The next day, Lord John Townshend, on

paying a visit to the bedside of Tickell, found him covered
over with patches, and indignantly vowing vengeance against
Sheridan. In the midst of his anger, he could not help exclaiming, "But how amazingly well *done* it was!" ', a remark
of a true connoisseur.

For Sheridan, the jokes were all part of a deep sense of sheer
boyish fun. His sister-in-law once wrote: 'Oh, how I longed
for Sheridan to roll with me on the carpet.' He could be a
child romping with children who loved him. 'He is amazingly
amusing', the Duchess of Devonshire wrote when he was
staying at Chatsworth. 'He is going to Weirstay to shoot for a
silver arrow; he is such a *boy*.'

Sport of all kinds gave him great delight. He loved shooting,
although he was a bad shot. Fishing was also a passion, and
he was a member of the Walton Club, and drew up a set of
joking rules for the fishermen on the Test. But cruelty in
sports he hated, and managed to get a bill against bull-baiting
through the House of Commons.

Without violent exercise, he said, he could not exist. Perhaps
the reason for the constant activity was to dull certain thoughts,
and to drown the inner feelings of the artist which he intrinsic-
ally knew himself to be. When he wrote his early essay on the
education of impoverished gentlewomen he said, 'Reverie is
loneliness'; and on another occasion, 'Reverie is thought'; and
in Pizarro, 'Thought is silence'. Reverie, thought, silence all
added up to exploring the depths of the soul and that could be
depressing; far better to think up a practical joke, or to go
out fishing or shooting. This was the way to fight the shadows,
and to make an end of darkness.

There were other diversions, which were not so innocent.
His name was linked with that of Mrs Crewe and Mrs Bouverie.
Owing to the prudery of the period which followed Sheridan's
death, it is difficult to find the truth of his affaires. Moore
merely says Sheridan 'was the object of universal admiration,
whose vanity and passions too often led him to yield to the
temptations with which he was surrounded'. The present age
is often more concerned with a man's sexual life than it is
with his intellect and achievements. In Sheridan's day, it was
rightly regarded as an appetite, like any other, and relegated

to its proper place in the general background of life. A man is, after all, more than the secrets he tells to his psychiatrist.

Yet it is permissible to wonder whether, at the root of his sexual infidelities, there was a mixture not only of vanity and desire, but also the knowledge, and perhaps the excuse, that Eliza's constitution would not admit of too much childbearing. There was always the letter from Thomas Linley, warning him about Eliza's frail health and 'seminal weakness'. There were also undoubtedly hints that Eliza and Sheridan 'did not live as man and wife'.

In an age when actresses were regarded as little more than courtesans and playthings for anyone who might care to call around to the green-room to pay their respects, there is no evidence that Sheridan had mistresses who were actresses. Even the scandal sheets of the period never linked his name with any of the actresses at his theatre. Perdita Robinson goes to great pains to make it clear that their relations were absolutely innocent.

Sir Gilbert Elliott thought that many of Sheridan's gallantries were 'more play acting than passion'. In 1789, he wrote, 'Sheridan is a great gallant and intriguer among fine ladies. He appears to me a strange choice having a red face, and as ill a look as I ever saw. But he employs a great deal of art with a great deal of pains to gratify, not the proper passion in these affairs, but vanity; and he deals in the most intricate plotting and under-plotting like a Spanish play.'

His infidelities were known to Eliza. She wrote a long poem which her friend Mrs Canning found. Part of it ran:

> Ingrate! that now has fled these arms,
> Disdaining all those boasted charms
> That once had power to bless;
> Are then these sighs, these endless tears,
> The sad reward for all *her* cares
> Who gave thee happiness.

Betsy Sheridan, when staying at Deepdene, wrote to her sister:

'As for your questions concerning Mrs Crewe and Mrs Bouverie I cannot entirely satisfy you as I do not know the cause of their difference. That Mrs Crewe hates Mrs B. is certain. And to such a degree as to be distressed if they accidentally meet. Mrs B. neither seeks nor avoids her and by what had drop'd from Mrs Sheridan I fancy she is the injured person. Some love affair I believe to be the origin of the quarrel. You know also that Mrs Crewe among other Lovers (favored ones I mean) has had our Brother in her train. As his fame and consequence in Life have encreased her charms have diminished and, passion no longer the tie between them, his affection, esteem and attentions returned to their proper channel. And he never has seem'd or I believe never was in truth so much attached to his wife as of late, and this her *dear friend* can not bear. Mrs S. tells me that while they were at Crewe Hall she took little pains to conceal her jealousy. A strange system you will say altogether and for such people to associate and disgrace the name of friendship is truly disgusting. Yet such I am told is the universal practice of the great world.'

Although Sheridan may have temporarily repented, the effect was not to be long lasting. At the end of 1790 Sheridan's relations with Lady Duncannon had become notorious, and Sheridan was threatened with being a party to a notorious and complicated society divorce. It was said that the Duke of Devonshire managed to hush up the scandal. But he was soon in another scrape. This time he was not choosy. The disorder in his life was spreading its net wider, as Eliza's account makes clear:

'At the moment in which he was swearing and imprecating all sorts of curses on himself, on me, and his child, if ever he was led by any motive to be false to me again, he threw the whole family at Crewe into confusion and distress by playing the fool with Miss F. (little Emma's governess) and contriving so awkwardly too, as to be discovered by the whole House locked up with her in a bedchamber in an unfrequented part of the house.'

At this point Eliza apparently decided to separate from

Sheridan, but Mrs Bouverie and Charles Fox managed to patch up matters. Richard was at last frightened by her attitude, and although she forgave him she had, not surprisingly, 'lost all confidence in his professions and promises'.

Although it has to be admitted that Betsy Sheridan had no liking for the fine people, or their manners, Eliza's own point of view had been changing, for Betsy said:

> 'Mrs S. is always amiable and obliging but has adopted ideas on many subjects so very different from what mine must be that we can never converse with that freedom that minds in some sort of the same kind indulge in. She told me last night she had converted Mrs Canning who was uncommonly rigid in her notions and therefore was not without hopes of bringing me over to her way of thinking. I assured her that my opinions were as fixed as my principles and that I was now too old to change either. That I allowed other to indulge their own way of thinking and should no more quarrel with a woman for thinking differently in point of morals than I should on religious matters if she had happened to be brought up a Mahometan.'

Sheridan's sister had kept her simple middle-class way of thinking and was not to be deterred, but Eliza, no doubt, was loyally still making excuses for Dick and his friends. She probably felt that appearances had to be kept up, but even her devoted and painstaking love was beginning to crack. She had been married for nearly seventeen years, and it had been a hard struggle to keep up with the *beau monde* supported by nothing but a pile of debts. Infidelities and promises of reform added to an impossible burden.

She now plunged into hectic gaieties, spurred on perhaps not merely by Richard's own exploits, but by that desire for feverish activity which has sometimes been noted in those affected by tuberculosis. Card playing was still her weakness – although most of the time she managed to lose, as she had always done. Her voice was as beautiful and as admired as ever. She often sang at grand houses such as those of the Duke of Portland and the Duchess of Devonshire. Wilberforce said:

'She sang old English songs angelically', and Michael Kelly, the singer, who joined Drury Lane in 1787 and was familiar with all the finest singers in Europe said, 'Her voice, taste and judgement make her the *rara avis* of the day.'

There is no doubt she could have paid Richard back in his own coinage, on more than the one occasion when she did. She seems to have held out against a good many temptations. Sir Gilbert Elliott wrote:

'Mrs Sheridan is really nearer one's notion of a muse or an angel or some such preternatural or semi-divine personage than anything I have ever seen alive, and it is therefore not surprising that Mr Mundy should be very much in love with her. Sheridan it seems has taken notice of it; but there has never been the slightest suspicion of Mrs S. having listened to Mundy, or to anybody else.'

Edward Mundy was MP for Derby County and a friend of the Sheridans, and he was not the only suitor for the divine Cecilia. Charles Fox had been much taken with her, and seems to have flirted with her openly – to Sheridan's discomfiture, for it is one thing to yield to little infidelities, and give oneself absolution, it is quite another when there is the merest hint of revenge. The spirit of Faulkland in *The Rivals* was not quite dead in Sheridan's breast.

These were not Eliza's only temptations for the Duke of Clarence was a constant admirer and in her letters Eliza speaks of the necessity of being 'stout' [standing firm] and says that she must put an end to his pursuit of her. This seems to have been in the autumn of 1789, when she was living at Richmond. She wrote to Mrs Canning, known as Sister Christian, on account of her stern principles: 'The Duke of Clar. lives within a hundred yards of me and he generally pays me a visit most mornings.' No doubt she enjoyed it all. Attention, even if it remains this side of 'guilty', is soothing to the injured spirit of a beautiful and accomplished woman.

In 1790, Sheridan was again electioneering at Stafford, and Lady Palmerston wrote that Sheridan, as usual, had 'the ladies on his side, for he was attended into the town by four hundred, headed by the beautiful Miss Furnio'.

Eliza wrote to him in June of that year:

'This letter will find you, my dear Dick, encircled with honours at Stafford. I am happy to find you and my dear cub [Tom their son] are well. And now for my journal, sir, which I suppose you expect. I was at home all day busy for you, went to the Opera afterwards to Mrs St John's where I lost my money sadly, Sir, eat strawberries and cream for supper – sat between Lord Salisbury and Mr Meynell (hope you approve of that, Sir). Sunday called on Lady Julia – on the evening at Lady Hampden's lost my money again, Sir, and came home by one o'clock. I have promised to dine with Mrs Crewe who is to have a female party only, no objection to that I suppose, Sir?'

In spite of her sprightly letters, and her attempts to understand the great world and its ways, Eliza was at bottom a simple soul, and so in the end she weakened. Her lover is supposed to have been Lord Edward Fitzgerald. Some of Sheridan's late Victorian biographers, fascinated by the beauty and charm of Eliza, have denied that this could possibly have happened.

William Smyth, the tutor of Sheridan's son Tom, says:

'By outraging her feeling by the most unpardonable indulgence of his unlawful passions, Sheridan at last destroyed the patience and probably alienated the heart of this incomparable woman; and in a fatal hour, brought up as she had been and living as she still was in the gay and fashionable society, she turned to listen to Lord Edward Fitzgerald who was a perfect madman about her.'

Even prissy Mr Moore says that it was understandable that 'there should be mutual admiration between two such noble specimens of human nature, it is easy without injury to either of them to believe'.

Lord Edward Fitzgerald was a cousin of Charles James Fox,

an habitué of Devonshire House, and had recently recovered from an unsuccessful attempt to marry his cousin Lady Georgiana Lennox. Like many younger sons he was not regarded as a good match because he was not rich. This was the second time he had been rebuffed – £800 a year had not been sufficient to win the daughter of Clancarty, and it had failed in the same way with Georgiana, daughter of Lord George Lennox.

Lord Edward was an idealistic young man eight years younger than Eliza. They were perhaps the only idealistic couple in the raffish society which surrounded them, where the only moral scruple which a wife might have was that she should produce an heir before being unfaithful. Although she had hitherto held out, she had been weakening for some time, for in 1786 her sister had opened a letter addressed to Eliza at Hampton Court, and had sworn not to divulge a syllable of its contents to anyone. This, however, was different. A neglectful husband with a tendency to drink too much made a poor contrast to a handsome, attentive young man. Nor was the school of scandal-mongers averse to joining in. Eliza wrote to Mrs Canning [Sister Christian]:

'Do you know I was very near coming to spend a week with you some little time ago if I had not been afraid of my dear Sister Christian's purity bringing me and my pecadillos into a scrape that I know she would have been sorry for. Seriously, I was coming, but I thought that if I did that S. would most probably pay me a visit, and then if he should have asked a question about the anonymous letter, I felt sure that your face at least would betray me, which now that everything is blown over, would have been attended with very disagreeable consequences – and I therefore gave up a scheme which would have given us both, I hope, great pleasure. So you see what you get, or rather what you lose, by your goodness.'

Eliza was not so 'stout' as she had been. But she still looked back to the beginning, when she wrote to Sister Christian:

'I visited our old House at East Burnham the other day

and I wished for you to keep me in countenance. I wept so pitifully at the sight of all my old Haunts and ways of Happiness and Innocence. But though I have tasted the forbidden fruit since that time, I have gained the knowledge of good and evil by it.'

To Sheridan she wrote, 'Ah! *my dear Friend*, you were not *then* a Parliament Man or Member of Brooks's, and yet I question if you have *ever* known happier Hours than those we passed at East Burnham.' It was not only the Parliament man with whom Eliza had to contend, however. The ladies of Devonshire House took up a great deal of Sheridan's time. It is difficult to read letters he wrote to Lady Bessborough without feeling that a wife might have found them both nauseating and humiliating.

One extract runs: 'I must bid 'oo good night, for by the lights peeping to and fro over your room, I hope you are going to bed and to sleep happily with a hundred little cherubs fanning their white wings over you in appreciation of your goodness. Yours is the untroubled sleep of purity.'

In view of the fracas over the governess at Crewe Hall, this sentiment seems to show a remarkable imagination, as does the following, despite a more mundane ending: 'Grace shine around you with serenest beams, and whispering angels prompt your golden dreams – and yet, and yet, beware Milton will tell you that even in Paradise serpents found their way to the ear of slumbering innocence.' No doubt the broad-minded society ladies liked to see themselves guarded by sweet little cherubs, and Sheridan, as always, was ready to play to his audience. But it was not surprising that Eliza had come to the end of her patience, her understanding, and perhaps her love. The constant worry and difficulties of her lot did not improve her health.

During the time that Betsy spent with the Sheridans she was constantly ailing: 'Mrs S. really very much indisposed' . . . 'Mrs S. considerably better tho' not able to venture down.' Like the careful observer she was, Betsy noted all the comings and goings in the house. 'Dick was at home and supped with us . . . Mrs Crewe in the little room *listening* to what passed in the next.' Nor did she take a good view of the beautiful Georgiana, Duchess of Devonshire, or the entourage:

'I thought I had told you all about the Duchess of Devonshire. She cannot I think be called *fat*, but on the whole I think there is too *much* of her. She gives me the idea of being larger than life. I do not think her elegant. She was here last night and with her Lady Elizabeth Foster who lives with her and is her bosom friend but is supposed to be more particularly the friend of the Duke. Such is the system of the fine World. As to the Duchess tho' we who stand at awful distance consider her character in a respectable light, I find among her friends she is by no means supposed to be sparing of her *smiles* at least.'

Eliza, however, was still obliged to keep up with the fine people. She wrote to Mrs Canning:

'You will think I am a little touched with the Royal Malady when I tell you that I ventured to the Brooks's Ball Tuesday in spight of remonstrances – my Physician and Hairdresser met together at my Toilette in the Morning and Prescriptions and Papilottes [curl papers] went on very amicably at last – for I cd not bear to have all my Money and my pretty Dress wasted – so I tell you Justin patch'd me up, and I bore my raking better than even I expected.'

But Dr Turton noted that she had an ugly cough and 'spitting of blood in a slight degree these two days'. There are constant references to Richard either arriving home at five o'clock in the morning, or never staying two days at a time with her. It was little wonder that she sought hectic amusement to stop her thinking.

In 1791 she was pregnant. It is hard to make out whether this was by accident or design. It had been thought that tuberculosis patients benefited from becoming pregnant, perhaps on the grounds that it would stem the flow of blood from the lungs. In view of Sheridan's neglect of her at this time, it is hard to dismiss the allegation that Lord Fitzgerald was the father. Some biographers categorically state that the child was Lord Edward's. But it is difficult in view of his subsequent behaviour to suppose it was not Richard's child. It could have been the fruit of reconciliation.

Early in 1792 Eliza was at Southampton, and in March Sheridan wrote to his two 'flirts', the Duchess of Devonshire and Lady Bessborough, who were travelling in Italy, that he was

. . . 'taking Dr Bejamin Moseley of Chelsea Hospital to see E. who is much better, because I want to decide about moving her. I am just returned from a long solitary walk on the beach. Night, silence, solitude, and the sea combined will unhinge the cheerfulness of anyone, when there has been length of life enough to bring regret in reflecting on many past scenes, and to offer slender hope of anticipating the future. How many years have passed since on these unreasoning, restless waters, which this night I have been gazing at and listening to, I bore poor E., who is now so near me fading in sickness, from all her natural attachments and affections and then loved her so that, had she died, as I once thought she would in the passage, I should gladly have plunged with her body to the grave. What times and what changes have passed, what has the interval of my Life been, and what is left me but misery from memory and horror of reflexion.'

The shadows, after all, were not so easy to defeat.

Eliza was moved to London where her daughter Mary was born. 'March 30, at Cromwell House, Brompton, Mrs Sheridan of a daughter.' It was hoped that when the child was born Eliza would regain her strength, but it was not to be. Sheridan wrote to Lady Bessborough:

'I find my mind turning towards you as the only creature whom I find it a relief to think of.

I am writing to you on the Road to Bristol, while E. is in bed very, very ill – eager to get there, and sanguine of the Event. But many glaring omens have told me our Hopes will be disappointed. I have been in long and great anxiety about her – flying from my Fears and yet hoping, one event safely over, that all would be well. But this day sen'night every favourable appearance exceeded our most sanguine hopes, since [until] Friday when the infant was christened, and she has been steadily falling back. Her impatience to get to Bristol made all delay impossible.'

At Bristol Hot Wells Eliza was to take the waters which it was hoped would restore her to health. Several writers, including Smollett, have described the pale fading ghosts taking the waters in Bristol. It was here that Eliza had watched her sister die. Now in hectic hope she was to join the pale wraiths herself. Sheridan was with her: 'I was to have followed her in a week, but yesterday she was so sunk and alarmed that she begged me not to leave her, tho' before she had stipulated that I should settle my affairs in town, and I was only to come with her to Maidenhead bridge.'

He had managed to patch up Eliza's relations with the prudish Sister Christian:

'My dear Mrs Canning, you do not know the state she has been in, and how perilous and critical her state now is, or indeed you would up braid yourself for harbouring one altered thought, or even for abating in the least degree the warmest zeal of Friendship! Of such friendship as nothing in Nature could ever have prevented her heart showing you. Pray forgive my writing to you thus; but convinced as I am that there is *no chance of saving her life* but by tranquillising her mind, and knowing as I do, and as I did hope you knew, that God never form'd a better heart, and that she has no errors but what are the Faults of those whose conduct has created them in her against her nature, I feel it impossible for me not to own that the idea of unkindness or coldness towards her *from you* smote me most sensibly, as I see it does her to the soul.'

Sheridan subsequently visited Mrs Canning who made some allusion to Lord Edward, which threw Sheridan into a dark

despair. 'Oh, not a word of that kind, she is an angel if ever
there was one. It is all *my* fault. It is I, I that was the guilty
friend.' He then sank into convulsive grief. But Mrs Canning
conquered her censorious feelings, and five days later they
were all on their way to Bristol Hot Wells. 'Her friend whom
she loves best in the world', Sheridan wrote to his Duchess,
'I have prevailed on to accompany her, and she is now with
her – there never was a more friendly act than her doing so.
She has left her daughter and all her children, whom she
dotes on, for this office. Poor E. feels such a difference in her
conduct from all her worldly friendships.'

On the journey Sheridan passed by the scenes of his duel
with Mathews. It seemed a very long time ago:

'I stopt yesterday evening as we came over King's Down,
while poor E's chaise was going slowly down the Hill – and
went to the spot where my life was strangely saved once. It
is marked with a great Stone cut by the man, who, I
remember used to make a show of our broken swords and
a sleeve button of mine, and the setting of her picture which
was broke on my neck and placed where he found the blood.
At this man's cottage, I remember I got some water and I
remember many thoughts that passed in my mind, believing
as I did, that I was dying. What an interval has passed
since and scarce one promise that I then made to my own
soul have I attempted to fulfil. I looked at the carriage that
bore her down the same road, and it wrung my heart to
think over the intervals, the present and the too probably
conclusion. My nerves are shook to pieces. The irregularity
of all my Life and pursuits, the restless contriving temper
with which I have persevered in wrong Pursuits and Passions
makes reflexion worse to me than even to those who have
acted worse.'

He had left his affairs in London in ruinous confusion, but
this was nothing new, and now the press of people and affairs
was forgotten. The hopes and fears of the illness dragged on:

'She was so well on Saturday that I mean that night to

have gone to town, but in the evening she grew very ill again. She wanted to receive the Sacrament. Ever since she has been brought to bed, she has turned her head almost wholly to think and talk and read on religious subjects, and her fortitude and Calmness have astonished me. I am confident if she can recover, there never was on earth anything more perfect than she will be; and to be different, she says, to me for ever from what she has been makes her so seriously eager to live. But she cannot be deceived about the Danger of her situation. The affection and kindness of her words and manner to me make me more unhappy, and do not comfort. Last night she desired to be placed at the piano-forte. Looking like a shadow of her own Picture, she played some notes with the tears dropping on her thin arms. Her mind is become heavenly, but her mortal form is fading from my sight.'

The fluctuating condition went on from day to day. Now her pulse seemed better, now she was less feverish, now worse. She had been bled, they had applied a blister, she seemed better. But Sheridan, although he still tried to believe that she might recover, said, 'I cannot describe to you how sunk I am and how horrid the solitude of the night is to me. I now watch half the night in the expectation of being called for by some new alarm' . . . 'I exert myself in every way, and avoid remembering or reflecting as much as possible, but there are thoughts and forms and sounds that haunt my heart and will not be put away.' Not easy now to drive the shadows away with wax candles, music, wit, and practical jokes.

Deep down Eliza had not changed her mind about dear Dick's fundamental weakness of character. One of the last things she did was to write a letter which she made him sign. 'I here solemnly promise my dear Betsey never to interfere on any account with Mrs C. in the education or in any other way of my poor child. I cannot write all my wish but he knows my Heart. Swear or I shall not die in peace.'

Tom, the dear 'Cub', arrived and her family came to see her. She seemed to rally a little and the family went away. But at the end of June hope was ebbing and her family hastily came back again. Mrs Canning wrote the details to Lissy in Dublin:

'They were introduced one at a time at her bedside and were prepared as much as possible for this sad scene. The women bore it very well, but all our feelings were awakened for her poor father. The interview between him and the dear angel was afflicting and heart-breaking to the greatest degree imaginable. I was afraid she would have sunk under the cruel agitation – she said it was indeed too much for her. She gave some kind injunction to each of them, and said everything she could to comfort them under this severe trial. They then parted in the hope of seeing her again in the evening. Mr Sheridan and I sat up all that night with her, indeed he had done so for several nights before.

About four o'clock in the morning we perceived an alarming change and sent for her physician. She said to him, "If you can relieve me, do it quickly; if not, do not let me struggle, but give me some laudanum." His answer was, "Then I will give you some laudanum." Before she took it, she desired to see Tom [her son] and Betty Tickell [her niece], of whom she took a most affecting leave. Your brother behaved most wonderfully, though his heart was breaking; and at times his feelings were so violent, I feared he would have been quite ungovernable at the last. Yet he summoned up courage to kneel at the bedside, till he felt the last pulse of expiring excellence, and then withdrew. She died at five o'clock in the morning. For my part I never beheld such a scene – never suffered such a conflict – much as I have suffered on my own account.'

She was conscious till the last, and 'said she had no fear of death, and that all her concern arose from the thoughts of leaving so many dear and tender ties, and of what they would suffer from her loss'.

She had thought of others till her last breath. Now Sheridan, alone, could only think of darkness, blackness, loss, and the triumphant grin of Death. 'The loss of the breath from a beloved object, long suffering in pain and certain to die, is not so great a privation as the last loss of her beautiful remains, if they remain so. The Victory of the Grave is sharper than the Sting of Death', he wrote.

The long and pompous ceremonials of burial were not calculated to relieve his spirits. Eliza was buried at Wells Cathedral near her beloved sister Mary. Mrs Canning described how they were up at six o'clock in the morning. The funeral procession started at seven-thirty, and after two miles they then spent five hours in an inn with nothing to look at but the hearse and the coffin.

In her death Eliza was not able to protect Sheridan from gloomy thoughts as she had in life. In the evening the sad procession set off again and at seven o'clock arrived at Wells Cathedral where they made their way in solemn procession. Mrs Canning says, 'The whole scenery was to a great degree beautiful and affecting and greatly heightened by the recollection of its being the spot where her early life was spent.'

Large crowds, drawn by curiosity, thronged the Cathedral precincts, and even in the church

> 'the buzz and tumult were so great that although the Rev. Mr Leigh exerted his voice to the utmost we could hardly hear him.
>
> The coffin was then carried before us to the grave with singing as before. I thought I should have fainted with the heat and terror and agitation altogether. The crowd pressed upon us so at the grave that poor Mr Leigh was really afraid of being thrown into it.'

In life she had always been surrounded by a press of people, and with singing, and in death her situation had not altered. 'Sheridan behaved the whole time with the most astonishing resolution; at the last moment I perceived a wildness in his look, which terrified me, but it soon passed away, and we retired from the sacred spot immediately.'

The pomp and the enormous crowd grated on Sheridan's feelings, however, and one eye-witness report said that he returned later and descended into the vault and remained praying all night. It could have been a turning-point in his life if he had been willing to accept the necessity of reflection.

In July he went back to Isleworth with Mrs Canning, who left him with his children:

'He suffered a great deal in returning the same road, and was most dreadfully agitated on his arrival. His grief is deep and sincere, and I am sure will be lasting. He is in very good spirits and at times is even cheerful but the moment he is left alone he feels all the anguish of sorrow and regret. The dear little girl is the greatest comfort to him. He cannot bear to be a moment without her. Tom behaves with constant and tender attention to his father.'

But Sheridan's good spirits were assumed; Michael Kelly the singer and composer tells how in private he luxuriated in his grief:

'I never beheld more poignant grief than Mr Sheridan felt for the loss of his beloved wife; and although the world which knew him only as a public man will perhaps scarcely credit the fact that I have seen him, night after night, sit and cry like a child, while I sang to him at his desire a pathetic little song of my composition, 'They bore her to her grassy grave." '

Another friend who slept next to him when staying at a country house reported that he had heard him sobbing all night. The Parliament man and the member of Brooks's had been brought up against reality at last.

Mingled with the furious unreasoning grief which he felt were the regrets and the reflections of wasted time. East Burnham had gone forever. In verse he expressed his loss:

No more shall the spring my lost treasure restore;
Uncheered, I still wander alone,
And sunk in dejection, for ever deplore
The sweets of the days that are gone.

Each dew drop that steals from the dark eye of night
Is a tear for the bliss that is flown;
While others cull blossoms, I find but a blight,
And I sigh for the days that are gone.

'I exert myself in every way, and avoid remembering or reflecting as much as possible, but there are thoughts and forms and sounds that haunt my heart and will not be put away.' The memory of her beautiful figure and strange haunting voice was strong, and it seemed that activity would never exorcize it: nor did it.

*

Only one frail link remained, the child Mary, who reminded him of Eliza, and to whom he was devoted. He was always bringing her ribbons, dresses, and toys. Smyth, his son's tutor, remarked on his extravagance over the child's clothes, and how sometimes he would linger at the child's bed, trying to amuse her, for long periods.

With appalling suddenness even this link was cut. He had sent his children with Mrs Canning to stay at Wanstead, and here he tried to establish a new family life. In October he was somewhat recovered from his grief and was giving a party for Tom and a number of Tom's young friends. Mrs Canning wrote the epilogue to Eliza's death:

'We were all in the height of our merriment – he himself remarkably cheerful, and partaking of the amusement, when the alarm was given that the dear little angel was dying! It is impossible to describe the confusion and horror of the scene – he was quite frantic. We very soon had every possible assistance, and for a short time we had some hope that her precious life would have been spared to us – but that was soon at an end!

The dear baby never throve to my satisfaction – she was small and delicate beyond imagination. Mr Sheridan made himself very miserable at first from an apprehension that she had been neglected or mismanaged; but I trust he is perfectly convinced that this was not the case. He was severely afflicted at first. The dear babe's resemblance to her mother after her death was so much more striking, that it was impossible to see her without recalling every circumstance of that afflicting scene, and he was continually in the room indulging the sad remembrance. In this manner he indulged his feelings for four or five days; then, having indispensable business, he was obliged to go to London, from whence he returned on Sunday, apparently in good spirits and as well as usual. But however he may assume the appearance of ease or cheerfulness, his heart is not of a nature to be quickly reconciled to the loss of any thing he loves. He suffers deeply and secretly; and I dare say he will long and bitterly lament mother and child.'

He was forty-one years old. He would never recapture the past, or recover from it.

CHAPTER 16

Courtship and Contrivance

Those in whom life runs most strongly will seek to recapture a
living person to replace the dead. Within a few months of his
wife's death, Sheridan was pursuing Pamela, the beautiful
daughter of Madame la Comtesse de Genlis. Although Pamela
was officially received as Madame's adopted daughter, she was
in all probability her natural daughter by Philippe Egalité,
Duc d'Orleans, but the polite fiction that she was adopted was
kept up.

Madame's explanations of her long visit to England are
involved, and full of political complications due to the Duke's
attachment to the Jacobins. She travelled all round England
with Pamela, with her niece, and with the Duke's legitimate
daughter, to whom she refers as 'Mademoiselle'. She seems to
have been in touch with Fox and with Sheridan to seek advice
on political business, and describes how Sheridan arrived at
Bury St Edmunds, 'only staying for the necessary time to give
me advice which might be useful to me'. It was probably during
these four hours that he saw Pamela for the first time.

Later he invited the ladies to say with him at Isleworth.
Eventually the duke demanded that his daughter should be
despatched back to France, and Madame, who alleges she had
resigned as governess to Mademoiselle, was in a dilemma.
Sheridan advised her against sending her precious charge
back to France alone and consequently she decided to accompany her.

Madame says, 'Two days before our departure, M. Sheridan
made, in my presence, his declaration of love to Pamela, who,
touched by his reputation and his amiability, accepted with
pleasure the offer of his hand; and we agreed that he would
marry her on our return from France, that was to say in a
fortnight.'

There then took place according to Madame de Genlis a very curious incident. They set off for Dover, but after a roundabout journey only succeeded in arriving as far as Dartford in Kent. She said it seemed strange that the postilions should lose their way from London to Dover, and her highly dramatic and overcharged narrative of hired lackeys, and positilions who, reasonably enough, spoke only English, ended with their return to Sheridan's house where they spent another month. Later investigation allegedly brought to light the fact that some unknown gentleman had met the postilions in an inn and paid them to take this circuitous route. Although Madame's story is not corroborated, it has all the feeling of one of Sheridan's more practical practical jokes, and was a way of making it necessary for Pamela to stay longer in England. When the Duke again demanded the return of his daughter, Sheridan agreed to accompany the ladies as far as Dover, where, Madame says, 'I parted from M. Sheridan with great emotion, and he himself wept on leaving us.'

She draws a picture of Sheridan as he was then:

'This man, who was so famed for his wit and his talents, was one of the most pleasant men I have ever met. He was, at that time, forty-six [Madame adds a little to his years], he had an open countenance, and had preserved all the gaiety of youth. He was at the same time a great statesman, a great orator, and the best comedy writer in the English theatre. His mind was deep, wide ranging, and outstandingly intelligent, but his character was light, inconsequential, and lazy; although his heart was tender, and he was a charming companion.'

She adds that 'his conduct was full of disorder', which was a fair summing up on Madame's part. When she sailed for France, Pamela, according to Madame la Comtesse, regarded herself as engaged to Sheridan. If so, the romance was short-lived; for irony of ironies, Pamela married Lord Edward Fitzgerald, Eliza's former lover, at Tournai in December of 1792.

Doubt has been cast on Mme de Genlis's story that Sheridan

proposed to Pamela, in view of her subsequent marriage to Lord Edward. It appears to have been love at first sight on Lord Edward's part. He first saw Pamela in a box at a theatre in Paris. According to Madame, Pamela's resemblance to Eliza Sheridan, 'the person he regretted with so much bitterness, struck him so vividly that he immediately fell passionately in love with Pamela, and was introduced to her by a Mr Stone'.

Shortly afterwards, Madame was forced by the increasing difficulties with the revolutionaries to flee to Tournai in Belgium, taking Mademoiselle and Pamela, and it was here that her adopted daughter was married to Lord Edward. It is quite possible that the canny Madame de Genlis, realizing the difficulties of marrying off a daughter of doubtful antecedents, may have kept both suitors living in hope, in order to decide who was the best match; or possibly, in the interim after her departure, she may have weighed up the gossip about Sheridan himself. In spite of his grand house at Isleworth and his lavish entertainments, the rumours of his debts may well have reached the Countess's sharp ears. There was a certain difference between a handsome younger son of twenty-nine with a future, even if he only had £800 a year, and a widower of over forty encumbered with debts. It was not so easy to renew youth.

When Eliza's common sense and restraining influence were removed, Sheridan's affairs became more involved than ever. In the excess of his grief he had leased a new house in London, this time in Grosvenor Street. He had also rented the house at Wanstead for his children. In addition to which there was his Thames-side mansion at Isleworth, for which he was supposed to pay Mrs Keppel £400 a year. Friends remarked that judging by the size of the entertainments he was giving at his Isleworth retreat, Mrs Keppel did not stand much chance of being able to collect her rent. He himself was living at Neot's Hotel, because he could not bear to be in the London house alone.

He was notorious for not paying his rent, and whether paying rent or not, it was known to be difficult to get houses back from him once he was in residence. There is a long report from an agent of Sir Thomas Channing who was trying to regain possession of his London house. The luckless agent was constantly calling to say that Sir Thomas had decided to sell the house, but was told that Sheridan was in bed, and he should call later. When he called later he was told that Sheridan had gone out. Messages passed backwards and forwards, but Sheridan even refused to let the potential buyer into the house to look over it.

Ebdon, the agent, at length wrote to Sir Thomas: 'I am advised to go with a witness and demand, as your agent, possession of the house, if that is refused, doubled rent immediately commences and by proceeding against him he must soon quit the house.' Six months later Sheridan still held the field: 'I have called twice at Mr Sheridan's since I wrote to you, but have not seen him, and am advised to call no more.' It was said that possession was only regained when the owner stripped off the roof.

The affairs at the theatre were in no better shape. It was badly in need of repair and had been reported unsafe in 1791. In the year Eliza died it was pulled down. But the magic of Sheridan's name was such that it was easy for him to raise £150,000 for a new theatre. Unfortunately this large sum raised ideas of grandeur in the minds of the manager and the architect, and an enormous new theatre was planned. Part of the reason for this, however, was that when enlarged it would bring in £700 a night, and the company was, as always, encumbered with debt.

Michael Kelly, the opera singer, and afterwards musical director at Drury Lane, became an intimate of Sheridan about this time. He gives a vivid picture of the manager of Drury Lane and his 'contrivances'. The Company was now compelled to perform at different theatres until their new and grand abode was finished: 'The Drury Lane Company performed at the Little Theatre in the Haymarket on Tuesday and Saturday, and at the Opera House on Monday, Wednesday and Friday', and there were, of course, the usual difficulties in paying the performers.

Mr Kelly was, on one occasion, faced with a strike at the theatre. The Italian opera singers were not so disposed to be calmed with a display of charm as some of their English colleagues. Kelly says:

'I have seen many instances of Mr Sheridan's power of raising money when pushed hard; and one among the rest, I confess, even astonished me. He was once £3,000 in arrears with the performers, payment was put off from day to day, and they bore the repeated postponements with Christian patience; but at least even their docility revolted, and they resolved not to perform any longer until they were paid. As manager, I accordingly received on the Saturday morning their written declaration that not one of them would appear that night.'

The unfortunate Kelly hurried round to Messrs Morlands Banking House, where he received the dusty answer that 'not another shilling would they advance either to Mr Sheridan or the concern'. Kelley remarked that 'This was a pozer', as indeed it was. He hastened to Sheridan, in Hertford Street, who coolly remarked: 'Three thousand pounds, Kelly! – there is no such sum in nature.'

Kelly replied, 'Then, sir, there is no alternative to closing the Opera House.' Kelly was about to leave when Sheridan asked him to ring the bell and order a hackney coach, and sat down and read the newspaper, 'perfectly at his ease', till the coach arrived. They drove off to Morlands, where Kelly remained in the carriage in a state of nervous suspense but, 'in less than a quarter of an hour, to my joy and surprise, out he came with £3,000 in bank notes in his hands. He saw by my countenance the emotions of surprise and pleasure his appearance, so provided, had excited and laughing bid me take the money to the treasurer.'

As the final *coup de théâtre* Sheridan said, according to Kelly: 'Be sure to keep enough out of it to buy a barrel of native oysters, which he would come and roast that night at my house in Suffolk Street.' He had achieved the impossible, as usual, and wanted a small celebration. The rest of the debts could wait till tomorrow.

It is easy to be censorious about Sheridan's debts, and his hand-to-mouth way of living, but it is also necessary to take account of the extraordinary state of society at the time, and the fact that so many people were in debt or living on credit.

Fox's gambling debts were astronomical and he was the spoiled and darling son of a very rich man. Society and Devonshire House were disposed to be lenient to Fox's debts, however, for it was said that he only 'owed money to the Jews' and that Sheridan's debts were to small tradesmen and therefore more to be despised. It was a nice distinction.

Pitt was in debt, and the Prince of Wales was one of the biggest debtors of all. At a time when keeping a good table, entertaining lavishly, drinking deeply, and running large establishments with their accompanying servants, carriages, and display meant so much it was small wonder that Sheridan behaved in the same fashion as everyone else.

Another remarkable factor in society at this time was its fluidity – respectable aristocrats, ladies in keeping, actresses, rich Indian nabobs, raffish earls and drunken dukes all mixed together. Admittedly attempts were sometimes made to separate the sheep from the goats.

As the Pantheon masquerades flourished, growing, it was said, 'more and more degraded in their character', someone decided that no 'doubtful persons' should be admitted. But Mrs Baddeley, falling into the doubtful category, a number of members of the aristocracy, vowed that 'let who might be refused admission to the Pantheon, Mrs Baddeley should be let in'. Fifty gentlemen armed with swords closed round her chair, accompanying it in solemn procession to the Pantheon. The constables who were guarding the ballroom tried to stop the procession, and the gentlemen then drew their swords and fought a passage for her into the masquerade. Here, still armed, they demanded an apology from the Managers. Once Mrs Baddeley was admitted, Mrs Abington followed and after that no line was drawn 'between vice and virtue'.

In this metropolitan society, addicted to show and to financial uncertainty, everyone borrowed on their expectations of next week, next month, next year, and waited for fathers, uncles, and cousins to be gathered to their ancestors with financial expectations then happily falling into empty pockets. Fox counted on the indifferent health of his elder brother for a fortune to rehabilitate his ailing finances. He was unlucky.

His brother lasted just long enough to marry and father an heir before departing this mortal coil.

Sheridan had no expectations. The theatre was his sole means of support, but had he been content to foster and tend this resource it would have been possible for him to survive. His instincts and his recoil from the world of the theatre which had ruined his father drew him away. He always felt that somehow, somewhere, a political plum wound fall into his grasp and that all troubles would be solved.

Meanwhile the new Theatre Royal was opened in Lent 1794 with the usual Lenten Oratorios in which Eliza had once sung. Kelly, obviously overawed by the sheer size of the theatre, remarks, 'The Orchestra represented the interior of a Gothic cathedral and had a most sublime effect', which sounds very much as if there were a touch of the Music Room at Brighton Pavilion, in the taste of the time. Unfortunately the sublime effects had their disadvantages, and the new theatre was so large that it was impossible any longer to play the old comedies with the same intimate appeal. Asides which are shouted lose their effect, and spectators complained of being able neither to see nor to hear.

But Michael Kelly came to the rescue. He suggested putting on spectacular shows such as he had played in Naples, with processions and special effects – waterfalls, cascades, and lavish scenery. They had their successes, but they also had their critics. One of them wrote: 'The dresses, the scenes, the decorations of every kind, are, I am told, in a new style of splendour and magnificence—whether to the advantage of our dramatic taste upon the whole I very much doubt. It is a Shew and a spectacle, not a play, that is exhibited.'

There were a few reminders of the past. Eliza's harpsichord still graced the theatre, and there was also a plank from the stage on which Garrick had once delighted people with his varied talents. Another reminder of Garrick was a clock which had been wound up once a year, when the accounts were scrutinized and the profits calculated. Garrick's had been an orderly region: now the profits were not so easily calculated, and the old plays and the old players were things of the past.

Parliament, the theatre, and his social round were not enough to fill Sheridan's life. There was always the point when it was necessary to go home, and now there was no one to go home to. Moreover, a year after Eliza's death, Sheridan's boon companion Richard Tickell died. It was said that he was reading on the balcony at Hampton Court when his second wife went up to call him: he was found to have 'fallen off'. It was generally supposed that he had committed suicide, one report saying that he had fallen with such violence that his body had made a hole a foot deep in the paving below. Sheridan, when speaking to Hobhouse, pronounced a curious epitaph on Tickell: 'He was a wicked fellow and loved mischief for mischief's sake – solitary mischief. Tickell's last exploit was throwing himself off the roof of a house.'

They were a curious trio, Sheridan, Richardson and Tickell – all clever, all high spirited, and all given to childish practical jokes. Obviously, like Sheridan, Tickell had his streak of melancholy, like Sheridan he had early lost his first wife: perhaps the past haunted him and so he had destroyed himself.

Richardson also had a streak of darkness in his character. From an inn in Tunbridge Wells he wrote to Sheridan. 'After you had been gone an hour or two I got moped damnably. It is damned foolish for ladies to leave their scissors about – the frail thread of a worthless life is soon snipped.'

If men are to be judged by their companions, Sheridan's intimates were witty, melancholy, funny, despairing, and in some ways mirrors of himself. The death of Tickell removed another prop from under Sheridan's feet, another link with the past had gone, and he did not like making new acquaintances. He felt more comfortable with his old friends who took him for granted and understood him. It was yet another tragic blow.

*

During the three years following Eliza's death, he was constantly speaking in Parliament. Like Fox he spoke in favour of the French revolution, which at the outset he saw as the dawn of liberty and a chance for men to achieve that equality which he always regarded as desirable. As one to whom place had not been granted as of right, he was strongly in favour of any system which could remove the disadvantages of those who had their way to make in the world.

It was on this subject that he and Burke fell out, for Burke, with all the vehemence of his nature, had now turned against the revolutionaries, and directed his invective against France. He was as immoderate in condemning the French as he had once been in condemning Hastings. With Burke there were no half measures, and when he crossed over to the side of Pitt, he cut himself off from his former colleagues. But if in Parliament old friends fell out, at Brooks's the betting and the drinking went on:

'29th January 1793. Mr S. Bets Mr Boothby Clopton five hundred guineas that there is a Reform in the Representation of the people of England within three years from the date hereof.'

'18th March 1793. Mr S. Bets Lord Titchfield two hundred guineas that the D. of Portland is at the head of an Administration on or before the 18th of March 1796: Mr Fox to decide whether any place the Duke may then fill shall *bona fide* come within the meaning of this bet.'

And Sheridan of course felt the effects of the mornings after:

'Sir, I am very sorry that I have been so circumstanced as to have been obliged to disappoint you respecting the payment of the five hundred guineas: when I gave the draughts on Lord X I had every reason to be assured he would accept them. The circumstances I mean, however discreditable the plea, is the total inebriety of some of the party, particularly of myself, when I made this preposterous bet.'

Disorder now surrounded Sheridan on all sides, and surely the best way to combat disorder was to marry again. Sheridan is supposed to have met his second wife, Esther Ogle, then aged twenty, at a party at Devonshire House. He was forty-three, and was said to have lost his former good looks: 'his forehead was fine and his eyes brilliant in the extreme, but the lower

298

part of his face was coarse and disagreeable: he looked like the "old lion" Hector in the Tower of London'. Furthermore, his many years of drinking had not improved his complexion.

Smyth, Tom's tutor, like many other acquaintances of Sheridan, took great exception to the idea of Eliza being replaced. Apparently Esther Ogle – so curiously named, like a character in a Sheridan play – was a smart young lady who liked to make provocative remarks, and when she met Sheridan she told him to go away calling him 'Fright' and 'Terrible creature'. Smyth says:

'By this silly woman, this silly man was thus unfortunately piqued. In an evil moment he resolved that she should feel his power, and after some little contrivance, she admitted that though a monster he was clever, and though ugly he was agreeable, and then she realised forcibly that he was one of the most celebrated men in the kingdom.'

Smyth was not a disinterested witness, because Sheridan was constantly leaving him in lodgings with Tom, with no money and no salary. Smyth acidly describes how Sheridan once rode into Chichester 'at the head of a cavalcade impressing the inhabitants with his fine horses, fine ladies, his grooms and himself, adding one feather more to the plume of his renown'.

At the time of his courtship of Esther, he seems to have lived in a feverish pitch of excitement. On one occasion he sent a letter to his son Tom telling him to meet him at Guildford, then forgot all about him and thundered straight through Guildford, his coach heading towards London and his heart high with hope. From the incoherent state of his father's correspondence, Tom even had some idea that it was *he* who was to be married off. Then he had a message from his father, that it was not the son but the father who contemplated wedlock. During all these comings and goings, Smyth, the tutor, was sitting in Bognor with no money, for 'sea gulls and sounding shores could not interest Sheridan for long'.

Esther Ogle was the daughter of the Dean of Winchester. The dean was canny about money, and Esther had a modest

dowry of £5,000 – so her father insisted that the future bridegroom should settle £15,000 on her. Somehow or other,
Sheridan managed to raise the money, much to the irritation
of the Dean who thought he had found an effective way of
stopping his daughter's contemplated marriage. When the
money was produced, and lodged at the bankers, according to
Smyth, 'the two youngsters, for Sheridan now appeared in this
capacity, laughed at the old ones, feeling that they had out-
witted them. They forgot that it was themselves they had out-
witted.' Sheridan, in his usual charming way, persuaded Tom
that his marriage was the most sensible thing which could be
in the world.

The *Gentleman's Magazine* for 1795 reported: '27th April at
Winchester Collegiate Church, Richard Brinsley Sheridan,
Esqre, MP for Stafford to Miss Ogle, only daughter of the Dean
of Winchester.' It was an announcement which was typical of
Sheridan's attitude towards himself. His plays and the theatre
were forgotten. He was an Esqre and the MP for Stafford. As
for money, that could be disregarded, his wife's dowry was
£5,000, and he had raised the £15,000 demanded by the Dean.

Meanwhile he happily borrowed Wanstead back from his
son, because it was wanted for the honeymoon, and it was said
by those who knew him well at this period that they had
seldom seen his spirits in a state of 'more buoyant vivacity'.

He spent much of his time at the house of the Dean near
Southampton, and sailed in a small boat he called the *Phaedra*
after the magic boat in Spenser's *Faerie Queene*, a typical sentimental Sheridan touch. A friend of his, a Mr Bowles, wrote
some suitable verse to the pleasure of the lapping water and the
soft landscape which surrounded the bridegroom and his
bride:

> Smooth went our boat upon the summer seas,
> Leaving (for so it seem'd) the world behind,
> Its cares, its sounds, its shadows; we reclin'd
> Upon the sunny deck, heard but the breeze . . .

It was light verse which could easily have been written by
Sheridan himself. It reflected his mood: the desire to escape
from reality, the ability to forget about the theatre which was

his living, the tragedies of his former life, the debts and duns which were his constant shadows. Sailing at Southampton had many affinities with walking in the woods at East Burnham. But this time the roles were reversed: it was now Sheridan who did all the letter writing, and from him came reproaches for the lack of replies. His letters to Esther are full of sentimental extravagances and baby talk, typical of a character who has never quite grown up, and who likes to think of himself as a figure on a Grecian urn 'forever will he love and she be fair'.

His pet name for Esther was Hecca, and she called him her Dan. His letters to Hecca were decorated with extravagant beginnings, 'My sweet beloved', 'My only delight in life', 'My own Gypsey', 'My darling Wench', 'My own dear bit of brown Holland', and 'prettiest of all that my eyes ever thought pretty, dearest of all that ever was dear to my heart'. The endings to his letters are equally sweet toothed: 'Bless your bones, bless your low forehead and your round plump elbows and your flowing tresses.' He was particularly taken with her green eyes to which he constantly refers: 'as for your emeralds, I will guarantee them' and again 'By Jove I will see my emeralds on Friday.' 'Now you are fast asleep, your green eyes closed and your arm round one of your rosy cheeks – I will kiss your green beads on Saturday.'

On January 14, 1796, Sheridan's second son was born, his only child by Esther. He was christened Charles Brinsley, though Sheridan refers to the baby as Robin:

'My beloved. Forgive Dan that again he has only a moment for a single Line. Nurse my angel, and make her stout and fat again, scold her for the cold in her head. I can't think of Robin if anything is the matter with her. Little Beast will take care of himself but it should be the duty of forty Angels to Guard Hecca.

Oh Ma'am, Dan is Lemoncholy as a yew-tree in a Church Yard, all alone no sweet Hecca near him.'

Having wooed and won and fathered a new family, the next thing to do was to become a landed proprietor. Sheridan had raised the £15,000 demanded by the Dean, Esther's father by – as usual – pledging the shares of Drury Lane. This money was then in its turn used to purchase Polesden Lacy in Surrey. But unfortunately for Sheridan, although the money had been spent on the estate, he could not pledge the estate. The money which he had raised and sunk into Polesden Lacy was irrevocably tied up on their child Charles.

Meanwhile the sun still shone and creditors could be forgotten in the pleasures of the moment:

'Sweet Hecca shall have a house after her own Fancy, and it shall be the Seat of Health and Happiness – where she shall chirp like a bird, bound like a Fawn and grow fat as a little pig, and will get rid of all the nasty servants and have all good and do all good round us. The thought and Plan of this is my Hope and Happiness, and puts all dismal thoughts from me. I can never visit Bath without laying in a store of them. O me it is a Place where every spot in it and round it leads to some interesting and melancholy recollection. But you, my angel, you and you only could have done it, have brought Peace and chearfulness to a restless and harrass'd Heart.'

In spite of the 'peace and chearfulness' that she managed to bring him, there were disadvantages in this marriage to a young girl. Putting pen to paper was something she found hard to do, she would rather be out riding. Typical of his reproaches is: 'Gracious God! Not a single line. If a voice from Heaven had told me that any human being should have treated me thus, I should not have believed it.' Eliza doubtless thought the same in her time.

Unfortunately for Sheridan, Esther, unlike Eliza, was not in the least interested in politics and regarded the theatre simply as a place which could or should produce money when desired. This was again in complete contrast to Eliza, who had been brought up to entertain, was an accomplished artist herself, and who even when Sheridan was away, was constantly sending him bulletins about the state of public opinion and attempting to get his affairs at the theatre into some sort of order. Marriage builds up a pattern of threads spun together to form a solid web. Eliza had grown up with the threads of Sheridan's life, Hecca for all his sudden and frantic love for her, had neither the interest nor the acute intelligence of Eliza. She represented youth, energy, and escape, that was all.

It is difficult to avoid the conclusion that Sheridan was far better at making honeymoons memorable, than in keeping his wives happy once he had won them. For soon he was drawn back into his usual pursuits and writing the usual excuses to his new wife:

'My soul's beloved, my Heart's Hecca, I find the nasty House of Commons will not let me see your lovely eyes so soon as I hope – and me thinks of you so that I must send to get a line from you to tell me that you are well and that you don't depise [*sic*] Dan.'

The letters are difficult to reconcile with the character of the wit who kept the House of Commons amused night after night.

By the autumn of his marriage year, he was writing his normal frantic notes to Richard Peake at Drury Lane: 'I am exceedingly disappointed at not hearing from you to Day – surely Hammersely [his banker] cannot have refused to advance if he has you must pay him the £600 and we *must* use the receipts.' Drury Lane was still the constant source of funds:

'I have not a shilling at this place and the bills are all un-paid. I have been obliged to give Mrs Sheridan a Draught on Hammersly's for £30. Do not fail on any account to take £30 from tonights that it may be paid tomorrow when it will be presented. To prevent mistakes I enclose a Draught in the Proprietors Name for £50.'

Peake later wrote on the draft: 'This was intended as a gift but I never got the Money.'

Sheridan's hand was still heavily in the till, and the actors were still being so unfriendly as to demand their money regu-larly. By this time Sheridan had Joseph Richardson and John Grubb as co-managers at Drury Lane and, ever optimistic, was writing to Grubb in October saying that he saw the 'prospect of future prosperity clear and certain'. This was a surprising assessment because the theatre's finances had never been in worse shape. About this time Mrs Siddons wrote that she was acting again but 'how much difficulty to get my money. Our theatre is going on to the astonishment of everybody. Very few of the actors are paid, and all are vowing to withdraw themselves: yet still we go on.' A year or two later she wrote, 'I can get no money from the theatre. My precious two thousand pounds are swallowed up in that drowning gulf, from which no plea of right or justice can save its victims.'

Money was not Sheridan's only trouble. In 1795, the year of his second marriage, a writer called Ireland alleged he had discovered a new tragedy by Shakespeare, called *Vortigern and Rowena*, and sent it to Sheridan. Sheridan had been procrastinating, as usual, but procrastinating with compliments. In June he was still 'putting off the pleasure of having *Vortigern* read'. Meanwhile Covent Garden were bidding for the privilege of staging this seemingly certain success. It is impossible to decide whether Sheridan actually read the play with attention, whether he was taken in by it, or whether he simply looked on it as a certain box office sensation, and decided to risk its authenticity.

Ireland himself said in his own defence that Sheridan did not rate Shakespeare 'so high as to inspire him with a very watchful fastidiousness of judgement'. Poor old Thomas Sheridan's passion for Shakespeare could have been a deterrent. When he had been in Ireland, he had bored the Dublin audience with the Bard – 'A Groan for Shakespeare' the lampoon had said. Possibly his son felt the same way as the lampoon writer.

The probable truth is that he was trying to do too many things at once, and the addition of a young, expensive and heedless wife, however fascinating her emerald eyes, had added one more complication to his burdens. It is said that Sheridan only read a few pages of this alleged masterpiece. Before signing the agreement which was to give Ireland £300, and half the profits for sixty nights, however, he did finally glance at the play and came across a line which he said 'was not strictly poetic'. He turned to Ireland's father and said, 'This is rather strange; for though you are acquainted with my opinion as to Shakespeare, yet, be it as it may, he certainly always wrote poetry'. His snap judgment was that, though the ideas seemed crude, they must have been written by Shakespeare when he was a young man and that 'as the papers bore undoubted marks of age, the contents must be genuine'.

Kemble, better acquainted with the music of Shakespeare's words, did not believe the play to be authentic, but those seeking financial success in the theatre will cling to any sensational spar, and the production went on. Naturally, there were the usual backstage delays. In November, Sheridan was writing to the scene painter at Drury Lane, 'I wish you to forward the Scenery of *Vortigern* as speedily as possible, it is certain to be represented at D. L. Theatre and that without delay.' But the scenery was not forthcoming until the following year, for the scene painter said that 'consistently with the orders from the house he could not pay it any attention'. He probably had not been paid either.

Then Ireland, like the author in *The Critic*, became difficult: 'You carefully avoid mentioning the name of Shakespeare in your advertisement. This is an injury to my property.' Possibly Sheridan was hedging his bets on this point. Nor were the actors on his side: 'I now hear that at rehearsal several passages were sneered at.' And Mrs Siddons' health, as it turned out, was not up to *Vortigern*. She sent her compliments to Mr Ireland and begged to assure him that she was very sorry that the weak state of her health, after almost six weeks of indisposition, rendered her incapable of even going to the necessary rehearsals. The prospect of a flop has been known to bring on bouts of sickness in the theatre.

The first night of *Vortigern and Rowena* took place at Drury Lane on April 2, 1789. The theatre was besieged with eager playgoers. At first all seemed to be going fairly well, and after two acts Mrs Jordan even congratulated Ireland on the production and reception, and on his astuteness in rescuing the tragedy from oblivion. But the quiet in the pit was not to last. There is always a risk that at some point a chance phrase will amuse an audience, and the sympathy between audience and actors will break down. As Kemble, playing Vortigern, said,

'And when this solemn mockery is ended', the most discordant howl 'that ever assailed the organs of hearing' came from the pit.

The Hiss was on, and the curtain was rung down, never to be rung up again on this entirely new Shakespeare play. The takings for the night were £550, the surplus being £206, which was divided between Sheridan and Ireland's father. Young Ireland, the happy forger, got a mere £30 for his pains.

In the new large theatre it was absolutely necessary to follow sensation with sensation. Mrs Siddons remarked that she would never have made her name had she commenced her career in the new Drury Lane. It was not a theatre for intimate acting. Forcedly spectacles were now the order of the day, with burning buildings, rescues, battles, and *The Caravan* – in which a performing dog called Carlo jumped nightly into a pool to rescue a child from drowning. The dog was the sensation of the season.

The author, Reynolds, described how after the first performance, Sheridan, sensing success, rushed behind the scenes and called out, 'Where is my Preserver?' Reynolds modestly came forward to accept the manager's congratulations. 'Pooh, not you, but the *dog*,' said Sheridan. On another occasion, when one of the principals told Sheridan that something terrible had happened – he was afraid he could not go on because he had lost his voice – Sheridan, much relieved, remarked, 'Oh, is that all? I thought something had happened to the dog!' No doubt these were funny cracks at the time, but they were not calculated to amuse touchy actors or authors, especially when the profits from benefits were hard to come by.

In 1799, Sheridan's last play, *Pizarro*, was produced. This was a concoction from the German *Der Spanier in Peru*, by Kotzebue. A German called Constantine Gesweiler brought Sheridan the rough translation of this play. With his sure instinct for a piece of 'theatre' Sheridan at once bought it for £100, and in his usual impetuous way immediately announced in the Drury Lane playbills 'a grand new drama from the German of Kotzebue is in preparation'.

There were the usual theatrical complications about the piece. Although the title was kept secret, one of the hopeful authors haunting the green-room found out about it, and told Sheridan that *he* was translating *The Spaniards in Peru,* and unless he was paid £100, he intended to publish it. Sheridan paid up and after some delay received three acts.

Another character then appeared in the Peruvian drama, a lady called Anna Plumtree, who published *The Virgin of the Sun* and announced that it would be followed by her further translation of *The Spaniards in Peru.* Sheridan, by now thoroughly jumpy, sent an intermediary round to implore Mrs Plumtree to hold up her splendid book until after the first night. She agreed to hold it up for six weeks. Naturally, she received no reply from Sheridan: a month went by so she gave her translation to the printer. Two days before the publication, Sheridan appeared on Mrs Plumtree's doorstep – full of apologies for his delay. Her letter had been put in the bottomless pit of his letter bag, and now Sheridan again implored her to hold up the publication date. Eventually Sheridan had to go round to the printer, who after receiving £50, agreed to postponement. Sheridan *en passant* also managed to get a free copy of the book. The play was not staged for another two months, and indeed Sheridan only just managed to get it on before the theatre closed for the summer, for there were fearsome delays.

Poor Kelly describes the backstage confusion of himself and the actors. When every seat in the house was already sold for *Pizarro* Sheridan had neither finished the play nor given Kelly the words for his music. 'I attended on Mr Sheridan, representing that time was flying; and that nothing was done for me. His answer uniformly was "Depend upon it, my dear Mic, you shall have plenty of matter to go on with tomorrow."' But tomorrow and tomorrow came, and Kelly had nothing to work on. He declared that this drove him 'half crazy', which is not surprising since his name was advertised as the composer of the music.

Kelly describes a strange episode when Sheridan burst in on a dinner party, and said that Kelly must come down to the theatre with him at once, that it was essential to the success of the piece. When they arrived Kelly 'found the stage and house lighted up, as it would have been for a public performance; not a human being there, except ourselves, the painters and the carpenters, and all this preparation was merely that he might see two scenes, those of Pizarro's tent and the Temple of the Sun.'

Sheridan sat in the centre of the pit, with a large bowl of punch in front of him, and contemplated the beauty of the scenes which his imagination had painted for him, and which the scene painters had caused to come to life. It was the action of a man who appreciated the smell and feel of the theatre, and had it in his blood, whether he willed it or no. The charm of the large empty theatre, and the scenes unfolding before his eyes gave him a sense of power. At that moment the play was his, the theatre was his, and once the audience filled the pit and boxes, the illusion would be gone.

Kelly, the practical musical director and singer, had no time for illusions. He was angry that he had been taken away from his dinner party just to see the scenery and machinery. As he rightly pointed out, he was not a stage carpenter or a machinist. Sheridan simply replied that he wished him 'to see the Temple of the Sun, in which the chorusses and marches were to come over the platform. "Tomorrow I promise I will come and take a cutlet with you and tell you all you have to do. My dear Mic, you know you can depend on *me*, and I know that I can depend on *you*; but these bunglers of carpenters require looking after."' With these delicately oiled compliments the Manager kept Kelly sweet. They went back to Kelly's house and the party did not break up till five o'clock in the morning. Kelly remarks: 'At this period, Mr Sheridan was getting largely in my debt; I myself was not keeping out of debt, and my wine bills were very large; the purple tide flowed by day and I never stopped it, for then I took the drunkard for a god.' Kelly was no more able to get money from Sheridan than anyone else. 'Tomorrow was always his favourite pay day; but like the trust-day at a French inn', Kelly remarked it never arrived.

Eventually Sheridan kept his promise about the music for *Pizarro*. He arrived punctually at Kelly's for dinner and they got to work.

'My aim', said Kelly, 'was to discover the situations of the different choruses and the marches, and Mr Sheridan's ideas on the subject.'

'In the Temple of the Sun', said Sheridan, 'I want the virgins of the Sun and their high priest to chant a solemn invocation to their deity.'

Kelly gives a very vivid picture of Sheridan's power of communicating his ideas and inspiring others to carry out his thoughts:

'I sang two or three bars of music to him, which I thought corresponded with what he wished and marked them down. He then made a sort of rumbling noise with his voice (for he had not the slightest idea of turning a tune) resembling a deep gruff bow, wow, wow; but though there was not the slightest resemblance of an air in the noise he made, yet so clear were his ideas of effect that I perfectly understood his meaning though conveyed through the medium of a bow, wow, wow.'

Although Sheridan turned a verse or two, Kelly had to find a poor literary gentleman to write some words to match the bow wow wows, and these, said the ever optimistic Kelly, were 'well enough to answer my purpose.'

These were not the only troubles with *Pizarro*. If Kelly had not received the words for his music, Mrs Siddons and Charles Kemble, until the eleventh hour, had no speeches at all for the last act. Upstairs in the prompter's room Sheridan frantically finished off the play, bringing the dialogue down little by little and passing it to the actors – 'abusing himself and his negligence, and making a thousand winning and soothing apologies for having kept the performers so long in such painful suspense'.

Kelly's view of this was that Sheridan liked to keep the performers keyed up, as he felt they would then give of their best, and that as they were all very quick studies 'he could trust them to be perfect in what they had to say, even at half an hour's notice'.

In the event, the spectacle of *Pizarro* was an enormous success, with its processions to the Temple of the Sun, the chanting priests, the music, the processions of soldiers, the wars, and the alarums. Several discordant voices, including Pitt's, found it a piece of mummery put together from old scraps of Sheridan's speeches against Warren Hastings. But Sheridan himself felt it to be his masterpiece and he took it with intense seriousness, beating out the rhythm of the actors' speeches with his fingers, like a music master, and declaiming against the slightest slip in emphasis made by Mrs Jordan or Mrs Siddons. Kemble, as Rolla, he approved because no doubt his principal actor took the play in the spirit in which it was written, and declaimed in the fashionable 'noble' style. There was a touch of old Thomas in the tragedy, and in the interpretation.

The play came at the right patriotic moment when England was at war, and what may seem to be boring and exaggerated language on the printed page struck a chord in the audience. It is easy to sneer at old plays, but it is often forgotten that it takes three to make a play – the author, the actors, and the audience, and to this play the audience brought their hatred of revolutionary France, their fears of invasion, and the enthusiasm of the militia drilling on village greens.

Kemble, as Rolla, was called for night after night to repeat his famous speech to the Peruvians: 'My brave associates . . . your generous spirit has compared, as mine has, the motives which in a war like this can animate their minds and ours. *They* follow an adventurer whom they fear, and obey a power which they hate; *we* serve a monarch whom we love – a God whom we adore. When'er they move in anger, desolation mourns their friendship.' Then Rolla launches into a piece from the Warren Hastings speech: 'They offer us their protection: yes, such protection as vultures give to lambs – covering and devouring them! Tell your invaders this, and tell them, too, we seek no change, and least of all such change as they would bring us.'

The stage directions then are: *A solemn procession commences, the Priests and Virgins arrange themselves on either side of the altar which the High Priest approached and the solemnity begins. The innovation of the High Priest is followed by the chorus of the priests and virgins. Fire from above lights upon the altar. The assembly rise, and join in the thanksgiving*: 'Our offering is accepted. Now to Arms, my friends; prepared for battle!'

All this, plus: 'The scenery, dresses and decorations entirely

New. The Music, Air, Chorusses and Marches incidental to the Piece, compos'd by Mr Kelly. The scenery designed and executed by Messrs Marinari, Greenwood, Demara, Banks, the Machinery under the direction of Mr Johnston and the Finale Dresses designed and executed by Miss Reis.' What more could the Pit desire?

Rolla's speech was encored night after night. It was the encoring of such a speech which had caused the destruction of the Smock Alley Theatre, and Sheridan's father's finances. But Richard had better political timing in his theatre business than Thomas, and the spectacles, the play, the author, the players and the sentiments, had all come at the right time to bring the money flowing back into the box office.

When the play was printed it was dedicated proudly to Hecca, 'To Her, whose approbation of this drama and whose peculiar delight in the applause it has received from the Public, have been to me the higheat gratification its success has produced.' He had given Eliza *The Rivals* as a belated wedding present, and to Hecca he gave *Pizarro*. The difference is that the play of his wit, his youth, and his high spirits has endured for nearly two hundred years, and *Pizarro* has been thrown into the dusty corners of libraries amongst other fustian dramas which once had the power to move an audience.

But there was something of Sheridan even in the fustian tragedy. Critics sneered at the fact that the thunder and lightning were suddenly hushed to enable Cora to croon to her child. But her line spoken to her child, 'Mild innocence, what will become of thee?' has an echo of Eliza's dying concern for her infant daughter. Sheridan, like others, was the prisoner of his character, and of his past. If he was sneered at for provoking the easy tear from his audiences with *Pizarro*, he shed easy tears for himself.

In spite of the occasional smash hit, the theatre had its ups and downs and was becoming increasingly expensive and difficult to run. Sheridan's double harness began to creak, and in 1802, the blow fell.

Under an order of the Court of Chancery, in favour of Hammersley, the funds were impounded. The bankers were put in charge of the cash which was taken at the doors, so that Sheridan's one means of pouching ready money was dried up at the source. The profits were to be put aside to pay the shareholders and the creditors. Sheridan decided to appear in Court in his own defence. It was a courageous decision, and his impassioned defence concentrated on the fact that the box office receipts were needed to pay the working actors. It might be thought that an obvious rider to this was that they were also needed to keep the Sheridan family afloat.

The prosecuting counsel, Mr Mansfield, denounced Sheridan pitilessly and exposed the enormous waste which had been going on at the theatre. While huge sums poured in at the box office, there was no money for canvas to make scenery, and the actors whose cause Sheridan was so eloquently pleading, were, and always had been, on the point of rebellion.

The Duke of Bedford, the ground landlord, was owed £8,000, and the furniture and fittings at the theatre were in danger of being seized. Sheridan announced that he had already made a proposal to pay £10 from each night's takings to the agent of the Duke of Bedford. This agreement was never carried out, because, said Sheridan, the agent had never answered his letter. The agent's reply, quite naturally, was found at the bottom of Sheridan's letter bag, his version of a modern Mount Pleasant Post Office. It was unopened after a year.

Grubb, one of the co-managers, had by this time also turned against Sheridan, and his Counsel complained that of an immense sum of money received, nearly £300,000, only a third had been accounted for. Holland, the architect, pointed out that £80,000 was supposed to have been available to him, but it was not forthcoming. Sheridan skated lightly and easily over the financial facts. Money was an irrelevance to him.

Mr Charles Butler, the eminent lawyer, was concerned in this case, and was greatly impressed by the display of Sheridan's powers of pleading:

'The court was crowded; Sheridan spoke during two hours, with amazing shrewdness of observation, force of argument, and splendour of eloquence, and, as he spoke from strong feeling, he introduced little of the wit and prettiness with which his oratorical displays were generally filled. While his speech lasted, a pin might be heard to drop. But it did not prevent Mr Mansfield from making a most powerful reply. He exposed, in the strongest terms, the irregularity of Mr Sheridan's conduct as manager of the theatre; and the injuries done by it to the proprietors and creditors.'

Orpheus was singing with his lute as sweetly as ever, but bankers are not so easily beguiled as wives, theatre audiences, or even the House of Commons. The Chancellor summed up and decided against Sheridan, and added insult to injury by quoting to Sheridan the words which Dr Johnson had written in the conclusion of his life of the poet, Richard Savage: 'Those who, in the confidence of superior capacities or attainments, disregard the common maxims of life, will be reminded that nothing will supply the want of prudence; and that negligence and irregularity long continued, will make knowledge useless, wit ridiculous, and genius contemptible.'

But Kelly, always ready to take a rosy view of his fellow Irishman, said: 'He left the place amidst the loud congratulations of his friends, and the envy and discomfiture of his enemies. He walked with me to my house in Pall Mall where he dined, and told me that he should have spoken better if I had not kept him up so late the night before.'

The purple tide was still flowing, and Kelly and Sheridan swam in it, but the actors were not so beguiled. Acting is a chancy, uncomfortable, and precarious profession, and successful actors like to be paid. The theatre is a hard task mistress, and a theatre run with disorder finds actors uncertain, coy, and hard to please.

'He has now', wrote one of the actresses, 'with only one short speech – but I am told appropriate both in sense and address, as if delivered by Milton's devil – so infatuated all the Court of Chancery, and the whole town along with them that everybody is raving against poor Hammersley – the banker and companion of Sheridan; *all except his most intimate friends who know all particulars; they shake their heads and sigh! Kemble, unable to get even £500 out of £4,000* packed up his boxes, gave a parting supper to his friends, and ordered his chaise at seven o'clock the next morning. As they were sitting down to supper, pop! he comes, like the catastrophe Mr Sheridan was announced; Kemble and he withdrew to the study, and the next morning I heard all was settled.'

The cracks were papered. The house lights were lit. The singer was ready to sing his song again.

CHAPTER 17

Friends and Enemies

Parallel with marrying a young wife, running a theatre, and coping with high and low finance, Sheridan was also on his feet orating night after night in the House of Commons. During the years after the Fall of the Bastille, and all through the Revolutionary Wars with France, the Whig party, or rather the Fox Hounds, were in disarray. Fox with his impetuosity and determination, and his knowledge of France and the French, had hailed the advent of the French Revolution with enthusiasm: 'How much the greatest event it is that ever happened in the world! and how much the best!'

Burke, who was given to studying things in depth, and examining the long term effects of every event, was not so enthusiastic about either the lines of French thought, 'the philosophy of vanity', or the French, who in his opinion had thrown off the yoke of law and morals along with their political servitude. His view seemed sound: 'I must delay my congratulations on your acquisition of liberty. You have made a revolution, but not a reformation. You may have subverted monarchy but not recovered freedom.' He also pointed out that 'the tyranny of a multitude is but a multiplied tyranny'. Nor was Burke the only one to see the other side of the coin.

Michael Kelly was in Paris when the unfortunate King Louis XVI and Marie Antoinette were brought back to Paris as prisoners, execrated and spat on by the crowd. 'The Queen wore a black bonnet covered with dust,' said Kelly, who happened to be near Tom Paine when this melancholy procession was wending its way through Paris. He mentions 'the delight of that caitiff Tom Paine, his Bardolph face blazed with delight and Governor Wall vociferated curses on their heads'. Thomas Paine, author of *The Rights of Man*, had forgotten what he had written about Burke: 'He pities the plumage but forgets the dying bird.'

Fox and Burke parted company over the French Revolution, and they parted company in public, in the House of Commons, with Fox bursting into tears, saying it was 'not the end of friendship', and Burke saying uncompromisingly that it was. The spectacle of the two friends, who had kept one another afloat for so many years, and had in some senses formed two necessary arms of the party, quarrelling so bitterly was unfortunate.

Sheridan, as usual, was caught in the cross-fire between the two opponents. At first he had supported the French Revolution and was among the many who had seen the Revolution and the downfall of the Bourbons as the dawn of a new era, misjudging the nature of the tyranny of man over man, and ignorant of the Corsican awaiting his opportunity.

After the dramatic split between Fox and Burke, the split between Fox and Sheridan was a slow parting, like a boat which had slipped its moorings and gradually drifted from sight of the shore. There are many reasons given by different people for the cooling of the friendship. It has been said that apart from his usefulness as a go-between, Fox never considered Sheridan to be his social equal, and although Richard considered that he himself was second-in-command of the Whig party, Fox never looked on him in that light. Sheridan was disqualified by his lack of family background and moral stamina. Fox was said to have spoken on occasions to Sheridan 'as if he were talking to a swindler'. It was true that in certain respects Sheridan lacked stamina, but when it came to acting without thought, and speaking before thinking, Sheridan made less mistakes than Fox, for he had more to lose.

Another important facet of life had come between the two men – their women. Fox had been devoted to Eliza Sheridan; in fact, many people thought he had tried to seduce her, but there is no evidence for this. After Eliza's death, presumably he had less interest in Hecca, a pert little wife of twenty, beneath his own intellectual level.

At the opening of the new century when Fox was happily settled down with Mrs Armistead, Sheridan's debts both at home and in the theatre had become too public to be ignored. People are often happy to be entertained on credit, but once the debtor is branded publicly, their consciences become more delicate. Sheridan's debts had the disadvantage of being made public. Even in his debts Fox was in a happier position than Sheridan. When his hopes of inheritance were disappointed, Fox's own debts were paid by a whip-round among the great Whig families. In fact, the incomparable Charley's friends contributed no less than £70,000 and an annuity which combined with Mrs Armistead's property from her former protectors enabled the couple to be comfortably settled.

The bloom of Sheridan's honeymoon with Fox and the Whigs was long ago. The clubbable fellows were growing old. There was now a closed ring against Richard, and his gradual split with Fox enabled the latter to add fuel to the calumnies. Sheridan was no longer regarded as good ministerial material, not even for Ireland. Lord Fitzwilliam, the Viceroy, gave voice to this view: 'He might have a lucrative office, but never could be admitted to one of confidence.'

It is easy to pass a man over if it is generally accepted that he is a light weight. He can be used as a smoother-over of difficulties, as Sheridan was, or as an entertainer. A wit in the party can be an asset in the House, but he can be ignored when it comes to the sharing out of office. Steadier men are more deserving of reward.

Admittedly Sheridan was drinking very heavily by the beginning of the century, but Fox was well known for this vice, and even the admirable Pitt was sick behind the Speaker's chair. Sheridan cannot be judged by modern standards either for his debts or his drinking. The bitterness of Sheridan's feelings occasionally broke through in his speeches. In a long diatribe attacking the administration at the time of the French War in 1794, he contrasts the tub thumping patriotic speeches demanding self-sacrifice from the populace with the way in which the place hunters were benefiting themselves and lining their own pockets:

'Nay, even from those who seem to have no direct object of office or profit, what is the language which their actions speak? The Throne is in danger! – we will support the Throne; but let us share the smiles of Royalty; the order of

Nobility is in danger! – "I will fight for Nobility", says the Viscount, "but my Zeal would be much greater if I were made an Earl." "Rouse all the Marquis within me", exclaims the Earl, "and the peerage will never turn forth a more undaunted champion in its cause than I shall prove." What are the people to think of our sincerity? – What credit are they to give to our professions? – Is this system to be persevered in? Is there nothing that whispers to that Right Honourable Gentleman [Lord Mornington] that the crisis is too big, that the times are too gigantic, to be ruled by the little hackneyed and every-day means of *ordinary* corruption?'

Sheridan at least preserved himself from that, and if Fox had fallen out with him it was as much because Richard liked to preserve his independence of Fox as he did with the Prince of Wales. He was no sycophant. Sometimes he voted with Fox and sometimes against him, and Fox could not stomach independence from someone he found his social inferior. Fox found Sheridan's conduct 'intolerable', his erstwhile companion had become 'past praying for' and 'mad with vanity and folly'.

As most of the political follies and misjudgements, including the fatal coalition with Lord North, had been those of Fox himself, it was hard that Sheridan should be held solely responsible for the disasters. In many instances, Sheridan had shown greater tact and delicacy than Fox, but this was often regarded as underhand. Even the Duchess of Devonshire was writing in her diary: 'He [Sheridan] cannot resist the pleasure of acting alone, and added to his natural want of judgement and his dislike of consultation this frequently has made him commit his friends and himself.'

In December of 1802, when Sheridan had made one of his finest speches, Fox wrote to Lord Holland: 'Sheridan made a foolish speech, if a speech so full of wit can with propriety be so-called, upon the Army Estimates, of which all who wish him well, are vexed at it. He will, however, I have no doubt, still be right in the end.'

There is something a little pussy in this letter. A damning with faint praise on the part of Creevey's 'incomparable Charley'. Fox liked people to follow him and admire him absolutely, as did Creevey who wrote of him in fervent admiration. 'In addition to the correctness of his views and delineations, he was all fire and simplicity and sweet temper.' Charley was still allowed to have all the cream, as he had been when a child, and now Fox, as he got older, was surrounded by younger admirers, and what was more to his taste, admirers who belonged to families which were known to him. Maybe in his heart he thought it had perhaps been a mistake to get too intimate with a person with a theatrical background.

*

In the short peace between the two wars with France, Fox, Lord Holland and Lord Grey had been to France and were received by Napoleon, then First Counsul, receiving that attention which important visiting foreigners find gratifying from a head of state. As a result, Fox was unwilling to believe in the hostile intentions of France, or the First Consul. There is often the feeling amongst distinguished persons that because other distinguished persons show them normal respect, then there can be no malice in them. Fox, for one, was no exception. During these happy visits, Sheridan stayed at home, and did not have the opportunity to be beguiled by the Emperor.

In 1803, although the warlike intentions of France were becoming obvious, Fox was still suggesting that preparations for war were premature. Sheridan adopted a different and more robust attitude and supported the summoning of the militia and volunteers, saying that if war were inevitable then, 'by the exertions of a loyal united and patriotic people, we shall look with perfect confidence to the issue, and we are justified in a well-founded hope that we shall be able to convince not only the First Consul of France, but all Europe, of our capability, even single-handed to meet all and triumph over the dangers, however great and imminent, which threaten us with the renewal of hostilities'.

The hostilities were not only abroad. Although Creevey drank a bumper to 'Devotion to Fox', Sheridan was becoming disillusioned. It was becoming a two-way switch, Creevey remarked. 'For the last three months he has been damning Fox in the midst of his enemies and in his drunken and un-

319

guarded moments has not spared him even in the circles of his most devoted admirers.' This was not good enough for Fox. He was prepared to submit to admiration from Sheridan, he was not prepared to stomach independence amounting to impertinence and downright hostility.

Nor was Sheridan's new-found patriotism as evinced in *Pizarro* to Fox's taste. The King had commanded a special performance of this epic. It was the first play he had seen for years. Sheridan's attitude of loyalty to the Crown was much caricatured at the time, and in May 1800, during a review in Hyde Park, a soldier had discharged his musket – it was thought by accident – when the King was only a few yards away. That same evening, when he was at Drury Lane with the Queen and the whole Royal family, just as George III was bowing to the audience a man in the pit, Hadfield, stood up and fired a horse-pistol at him. The King, showing great courage, went to the front of the box and bowed, to the acclamations of the audience. He also insisted on staying to see the play.

Sheridan acted with as much calm as the King. He sent a quick message to the Princesses to say that there was no need for alarm – it was just a scuffle in the pit. He cross-questioned Hadfield in the Manager's room and then, quick to take advantage of a theatrical sensation, wrote a new verse to 'God Save the King', in the interval, which was as quickly passed to his musical director, Kelly.

> From every latent foe,
> From the assassin's blow
> God Save the King.
> O'er him Thine arm extend,
> For Britain's sake defend,
> Our father, Prince and friend,
> God save the King.

It was not great verse, but Sheridan always had that quick theatrical eye for taking advantage of a situation, like an actor who can fit a joke to the current news. The verses were cheered to the echo and repeated – but this kind of showy theatrical patriotism was hardly likely to appeal to Charles James Fox or the Whig Party.

14   *Left*:   Sheridan. *Portrait by Reynolds*   *Right*:   Esther Ogle, Sheridan's second wife.

View of the HUSTINGS in Covent Garden. — Vide. The Wesminster Election, Nov.ʳ 1806

Published Dec.ʳ 15ᵗʰ 1806 by H. Humphrey 27 St. James's Street. J. Budd. Pall-Mall & R. Bagshaw, Bridges Street.

15 *a:* Gillray's view of Sheridan in his decline. *b:* Gillray's view of Sheridan and the Duke of Norfolk leaving Brooks's

PILLARS of the CONSTITUTION.
— Three o'Clock in a Cloudy M.

CHAPTER *18*

'Young Tom'

Sheridan was devoted to his son. He was constantly and neurotically worried about his health, which was not surprising in view of the boy's blood, and the fact that he was the sole survivor of Sheridan's first and happy marriage.

When young, Tom had been kept much at home, or else coached by tutors, and Smyth, the main tutor, tells a story of how Sheridan had set off one day in his coach, only to return a quarter of an hour later – 'his eyes shining brighter than the lamps of the coach' – to demand a firm promise from Symth that Tom should not be allowed to skate. The tutor dismissed such anxiety as ridiculous, and other friends suggested to Sheridan that he should keep Tom under a glass case. But like many parents Sheridan was trying to give Tom the one thing which he had most missed himself when young, a feeling that his family were near him.

Tom was regarded by everyone as an engaging lad, and Angelo said of him: 'He was a great favourite of my mother. We have often had him for days with us. He could not have been more than eight years old, yet his manners were so insinuating that everybody was pleased with him. After his mother's death, we seldom saw him.'

In the end, he had an erratic childhood, and an erratic schooling. Smyth describes him on one occasion: 'The son appeared after dinner, a fine lad with sallow complexion and dark hair, with a quick intelligent look and lively manner; but he was impatient to shoot swallows that were seen flitting about the river, and he soon left us.' His tutor went with him to Cambridge, but Tom does not seem to have done much work:

'There was, alas! only great expense, and the destruction

L   321

of all my schemes for his instruction. He was the idol of the young men, who pronounced him the cleverest fellow in the place, as in point of fun and humour he certainly was. I no longer saw him in the evenings. I made out how often he had been in Hall by the number of times he had been fined; for like his father, he was always too late. As a pupil he was from the first a constant source of alternate hope and disappointment "equal to all things, for all things unfit".'

It was not surprising that Tom lacked concentration. He had been a spoilt child, he had lost his mother, and the disorder of his father's life spilled over into his. 'Don't I allow you £800 a year?' 'Allow it, yes,' said Tom once, 'but it is never paid.'

Tom was offered a place by the Government Registrar of the Admiralty Court, at Malta. Sheridan was afraid that if accepted it would compromise the independent reputation which he had built up in the House of Commons. If his father's ambitions did not wreck Tom's only chances, his father's fierce independence did not improve them.

Everyone loved Tom Sheridan, and even his young stepmother, Esther, had a particular affection for him. She wrote to Dan: 'I trust that you will be able to do someting *positive* for Tom about money. I am willing to make any sacrifice in the world for that purpose, or to live in any way whatever. Whatever he has now ought to be certain, or how will he know how to regulate his expenses?' No one who had anything to do with Sheridan was ever able to know how to regulate either his expenses or his life. His son was to be no exception to the rule.

But Sheridan still had one link with his happy past, his friend Joseph Richardson. He was not only an admirable companion and drinking partner, but he had become the go-between for Sheridan with his wife. The fervent early letters – 'My beloved I miss you more than I should my eyes'. 'Heart of mine – I have only a moment to say bless you – and again to beg no risk – I am now frighten'd at your account of Pantaloon [her horse]' – had by 1801 given way to a different form of correspondence. He was always absent, his affairs were always in disorder, and for his young wife, who liked to make a splash in the world, to receive letters from Woburn describing parties from which women were excluded was hardly encouraging: 'The party here consists of The Duke of Bedford, The Duke of Devonshire, Fox, Lord John Townshend, Grey, Lord John Russell, Lord W. Russell, Francis, Lord R. Spencer, and of course Sheridan and his friend Richardson. It was also tactless, and, adding to her sense of isolation, to tell his wife happily: 'I dare say you live almost in the wood like three gypsies with two Bratts.' But in all the differences with his wife, Joseph Richardson had stood by Sheridan.

On June 9, 1803, Richardson died. Sheridan lamented that 'there was now nobody who could enter into his domestic cares and be a confidential agent, when occasion might require between himself and Mrs Sheridan'. His last prop from the past was gone.

The day of the funeral found Sheridan encompassed with business, and just as he was starting out he was delayed by the Duke of Bedford. Corpses can wait, but Dukes cannot. When the funeral party arrived late to pay their last respects, another unfortunate circumstance had occurred: the chief undertaker, unlike Sheridan, was a punctual man, and he had hustled off to another funeral. So when the mourners arrived the obsequies were already over. The whole incident trembled on the verge of farce, because Sheridan was wearing a mourning cape much too short for him, and a friend who accompanied him was in a cape which was much too long. When the comic mourners tottered late into the churchyard, and found the undertakers gone, the vicar was made aware of what had occurred. He permitted his son, the curate, to repeat the service, and this 'gave a sort of mournful exultation to Mr Sheridan'. He now felt he could face people without being reproached for not being present when his best friend was buried.

On the way back, the belated funeral party dined at Bedfont, and a Mr Taylor who was an eye witness, says: 'Mr Sheridan entered into a eulogium on his deceased friend, of whom he spoke with sincere emotion and affecting eloquence.' When Sheridan arrived in London he showed further great emotion, 'and in the agony of his feelings struck his head against the door of the nearest house, exclaiming that he had lost his dearest friend, and there was nobody who could enter into his domestic cares'.

Yet in public he showed a different face, for when Lord Thanet consoled him on the loss of his friend, he said, 'Yes, very provoking, indeed; and all owing that curst brandy and water, which he *would* drink.' Like the death of his mother so long ago, the loss of his friend was a disagreeable fact, and he refused to think about it. When it came to his relations with his wife, he had indeed lost his needed advocate. By the end of June, he was writing to her: 'By my life and soul if you talk of leaving me now you will destroy me. I am wholly unwell – I neither sleep nor eat. You are before my eyes Night and Day. I will contrive that you shall go to the North at all events, but don't leave me to myself.' Naturally the crisis was known to his friends. His erstwhile intimate Lady Bessborough wrote: 'S. is is never sober for a moment and his affairs worse than ever – *pour comble* he has quarrelled with Mrs S. A sort of separation took place, but I believe it is partly made up again, at least they live in the same house again, but not very good friends.'

The same month he wrote desperately to poor Richard Peake, the treasurer at Drury Lane: 'Dear Peake, Give my £31 10s od [his salary from Drury Lane] to J. Edwards before you sleep for God's sake. I return with Mrs S. Tuesday, and then will work like a Horse for the Theatre. Yours R. B. S. Get £10 from some damn'd Tenant or other and give it to Mrs Richardson.'

The split was patched up, but Hecca's view of her hero, like his first wife's, had changed. She had married a Member of Parliament, a prominent and eminent man, and had expected her marriage to be a brilliant success. She had not anticipated the debts, the shifts, and the frantic search for ready money. She upbraided him and accused him of having deceived her about his financial position. The truth was that he equally deceived himself. A month later he was writing: 'I am now going about business and to get my wench a *mot* of money!'

But he was not entirely deceived about Esther's attitude to him. 'I dined yesterday at Guildhall, where I met Lord Charles Somerset. They drank Dan's Health and it was so received as would have gratified Hecca's heart, who endeavours to perswade [sic] that heart that it can distinguish its devotion to Sheridan's Fame and honour from affection to him – – ' The fame and honour were undeniable, but the money to back them up was a more fluctuating commodity. Since the agreement after the Court case, he was no longer able to manipulate the theatre finances as if they had been his own. Nor was Fox's attitude more friendly than his wife's. Fox told Grey that Sheridan was undependable and added, 'many will follow Sheridan whom we should be sorry to lose'. The bloom had definitely departed from the Sheridan rose. The good fellows were good comrades no more.

If Sheridan's affairs were not prospering the affairs of the country as a whole were in no better shape. Napoleon's victory at Ulm and Nelson's death at Trafalgar followed swiftly, one on the heels of the other. After these two blows, which broke Pitt's health, he made his immortal remark: 'England has saved herself by her exertions, and will as I trust save Europe by her example.' Fox took a more partisan view, and said the victory of Trafalgar 'far more compensates for the temporary succour which it will certainly afford to Pitt in his distress. I am very sorry for poor Nelson, for though his conduct at Naples was atrocious, I believe he was at bottom a good man.' Pots and kettles were at it, of course, and which was pot and which kettle was anybody's guess. At the beginning of the following year came the news of Austerlitz. Pitt went home to die.

After more than twenty years Fox was now in power. Two of the first things he had to do were to bury the former Prime Minister, Pitt, and to pay Pitt's debts. Although Fox was quite willing to pay the debts, he refused to put up a memorial to his most deadly rival. Pride adopted an ungenerous attitude to the dead. Meanwhile there was business to be done, power to be savoured, a ministry to be formed.

When the spoils of office were being shared out in the 'Ministry of All the Talents', Fox was still uncertain of Sheridan's drinking habits and his alleged unreliability, and advised him to accept a 'patent place' worth £2,000 a year for life. The plums, of course, had gone to the scions of the Whig families. Sheridan refused this, but accepted the office of Treasurer of the Navy, without a seat in the Cabinet. In

seventeen years he had made no progress, and he wrote somewhat bitterly to Fox about the defraying of his expenses as a
Member of Parliament, saying:

'I thought the prosposition perfectly reasonable, but that as
to myself it being understood that I would spend no more of
my own money at Stafford I rely on you that my seat should
be properly managed.

But being on the chapter of grievance which, believe me
Dear Fox, with you is a very hateful discussion to me, I will
unpack my mind at once and once for all. I am allotted a place
to which I think there is allotted a Duty if a part is to be
fairly supported, I mean of reciving and entertaining members whom the Cabinet cannot open their houses to – of
course if I mean to serve you fairly out of my office I cannot
save one guinea. I tell you frankly that I take that office
without the slightest feeling of obligation to anyone living,
perhaps I might say more – it is seventeen years since when
you professed to me that I should not be content to accept
that alone – I come directly to my point – and that is *my
Son* – I will not recapitulate to you the motives that indepen-
dently of the dear affection I bear him influence me on this
subject. In the King's last illness, when perhaps I was deemed
of more use than the present famed administration may
estimate, I had a very distinct pledge from you that Tom
should be taken care of. All our *mutual friends Men and Women*
cried out Tom must be provided for – how does it end? You
turn me over with a note to Lord Grenville which ends by a
letter from him to ask a place from me for a friend of his,
meaning no doubt to inform me that he had no patronage
that could serve my son. In one word, if nothing can be
done for my Son, the Grenville administration are perfectly
welcome to dispose of my office.'

Harsh words, and Fox was apparently very angry at Sheridan's letter. He said that he had every intention of doing
something for Tom, but had 'no hopes of doing it instantane-
ously'.

Sheridan had never been inclined to ask for rewards; now

he was over fifty and disillusioned, and it was even harder to be obliged to solicit favours for his son. Others took Sheridan's decline more lightly:

> 'Sheridan is very little consulted at present, and it is said will not have a seat in the Cabinet. This is a distressing necessity. His habits of daily intoxication are probably considered as unfitting him for trust. The little that has been confided to him he has been running about to tell. At a dinner at Lord Cowper's on Sunday, where the Prince was, he got drunk as usual and began to speak slightingly of Fox. From what grudge this behaviour proceeds I have not learned. The whole fact is one to investigate with candour, and with a full remembrance of Sheridan's great services, in the worst times, to the principles of Liberty.'

Though few of his former companions were prepared to remember Sheridan's services, he did manage to obtain a post for Tom as 'Muster Master General in Ireland'. He could no longer afford to refuse even the smallest benefits, but it was humiliating to have to accept them after so many years.

However, Sheridan's new post now gave him splendid apartments in Somerset House. He celebrated this new office by giving a fête, but like so many of Sheridan's grand gestures, the fête had its touch of bathos.

When Kelly arrived, presumably to direct the music from *Macbeth*, which was to be part of the entertainment, he found Sheridan in despair because he had no cheese for the feast. Kelly says: 'What was to be done? Sunday, all shops shut – without cheese his dinner would be incomplete. I told him I thought some of the Italians would be prevailed upon to open their doors and supply him; and off we went together *cheese hunting* at six o'clock on a Sunday afternoon – the dinner hour being seven.'

The brilliant dinner was described in all the newspapers – but the furniture had been brought in from the theatre because Sheridan was unable to hire any in case it was seized by his creditors, and there were not sufficient servants. In the end a happy compromise was reached: spear carriers from Drury

Lane, and visiting bailiffs were dressed in livery to serve the guests. All Sheridan's houses were built on sand – but now the cracks in the foundations were beginning to show in earnest.

It has been generally thought that, like Fox, the Prince of Wales acted with more reserve towards Sheridan as he got older. However, he did not entirely forget his debt to Sheridan over the various crises which had arisen when the King was 'mad'. At the first opportunity he offered him a lucrative 'place'. When Lord Elliott died, the Prince had the gift of the Receiver-Generalship of the Duchy of Cornwall to dispose of. There had been no vacancy for this appointment for forty-five years. On February 20, 1804, the Prince wrote:

'Dear Sheridan,
    You well know that I never forget my old friends. The death of Lord Elliott affords me the opportunity of offering you a trifling proof of that sincere friendship I have always profess'd and felt for you through a long series of years. I wish to God it was better worth your acceptance.
                                    Ever affectionately yours,
                                              George P.'

Sheridan immediately wrote to Addington, the Prime Minister, informing him of the appointment, saying:

'I do not regard it to be an impertinent intrusion to inform you that the Prince has in the most gracious manner, and wholly unsolicited, been pleased to appoint me to the late Lord Elliot's situation in the Dutchy of Cornwall. I feel a desire to communicate this to you myself because I feel a confidence that you will be glad of it. – It is has been my Pride and Pleasure to have exerted my humble efforts to serve the Prince without ever accepting the slightest obligation from him. But in the present case and under the present circumstances I think it would have been really False Pride and apparently mischievous affectation to have declined this Mark of His Royal Highness's confidence and Favour. I will not disguise that at this peculiar crisis I do feel greatly gratified at this event. Had it been the result of a mean and subservient Devotion to the Prince's every wish and object I could neither have respected the Gift, the Giver or myself. But when I consider how recently it was my misfortune to find myself compell'd by a sense of Duty stronger than my attachment to him wholly to risk the situation I held in his confidence and favour and that upon a subject on which his feelings were so eager and irritable.'

Sheridan is referring to the fact that the Prince wanted to serve as an active commander in the Army and Sheridan had sided with Addington against the Prince. He continues:

'I cannot but regard the increased attention with which he has since honor'd me as a most gratifying Demonstration that he has clearness of Judgment and firmness of Spirit to distinguish the real Friends to his true Glory and Interest from the mean and mercenary Sycophants, who fear and abhor that such Friends should be near him.'

In the same month in which he was offered this appointment, the King again became ill, the idea of a Regency was revived, and once more Sheridan was used as the connecting link between Carlton House and the Government.

On February 27th, Sheridan is again excusing himself to Hecca: 'Do not think it neglectful that I do not write more to you – if you saw the worry I live in and the *really unavoidable* bad hours I keep you would rather wonder that I can write at all.' Referring to the King's illness he says:

'There never was known before anything equal to the agitation of People's minds at this moment, and the Prince, just recovered from an illness in which his Life was despair'd of for two Days, is so nervous and anxious that it is not easy to thwart him tho' he runs a great risk of making himself ill again. I now see him openly, but till lately Never saw him till after twelve at Night, and He has often kept me till 5 in the morning not supping, or with a drop of wine, in his bedroom.'

Sheridan was apparently being seen *en cachette*, for at the
same time Mrs Fitzherbert, who ought to have known, was
saying that the Prince had seen no one except Addington and
Lord Thurlow. Doubtless that was the Prince's story: he was
never known to be a trustworthy person.

A brief note to the long suffering Peake was written, about
the same time, from Carlton House: 'Most Confidential –
Come to the Door in the Park – and shew this card – and then
come in at the side door – not the great Porch. R. B. S. .' Was
the wretched Peake bringing money? Staving off creditors?
Being used for other purposes? Why was he wanted in such a
hurry at Carlton House? Why the side door? We do not know.
The whole of these various operations were obviously carried
out in a most secret manner: Fox and his friends were prepared
to use Sheridan in their negotiations with the Prince, but
they were not anxious to be seen to use him, and the Prince
too, wanted secrecy.

The alarms of the Prince were due to the fact that it had
been suggested that the Regency should be shared by the
Queen and the Duke of York as well as the Prince of Wales.
Mrs Fitzherbert and the Prince, understandably, were
thoroughly upset at this rumour, and Fox asked Sheridan 'to
tranquillize their minds on this point'. But once the crisis
about the King was again over, Sheridan sank back into his
usual state of unreliability in the eyes of the ruling party. Nor
was that the only cross he had to bear, for the appointment of
Receiver Generalship for the Duchy of Cornwall, for which he
had been so grateful, now seemed in peril.

At the time of his marriage the Prince had granted the
reversion of the office, which he had given to Sheridan, to
Major-General Gerard Lake, who had been one of his equerries;
subsequently the Major-General had been appointed com-
mander-in-chief of the forces in India, and the Prince thought
that in view of his new and splendid appointment, and his
absence from the country, the offer could be considered invalid,
in which happy thought he was to be disappointed. The
General's brother suddenly appeared like the Demon King,
and demanded that the income should be received by him as
his brother's deputy. It was carefully pointed out that as his

brother was not able to carry out his duties, such as collecting the rents, or overseeing the annual audit, it seemed odd that he should expect the income from the office. There was no doubt that the General had been promised the appointment but whether it had been legally withdrawn is difficult to judge. Sheridan's son, Tom, said the reason the Prince had given the appointment away a second time was because, 'Lake has behaved so ill to the Prince'.

Be that as it may, Sheridan bristled loyally and immediately wrote to the Prince's Secretary, saying that, 'Nothing on earth shall make me wish the possibility for a single scurrilous Fool's presuming to hint even that He had in the slightest manner departed from the slightest engagement. The Prince's right in point of Law and Justice on the present occasion to recall the appointment given, I hold to be incontestible.'

The affair was patched up. Sheridan agreed to forgo the income as soon as General Lake returned to England. Sheridan did, in fact, enjoy the income, but in his usual complicated way, eighteen months after accepting it, tried to get the money transferred to his son Tom. Even a piece of good fortune became a cat's-cradle in Sheridan's hands. The reason he wanted the money transferred to his son was that, in June 1805, Tom had eloped with one Charlotte Callander, and Sheridan was desperately anxious to make some solid provision for him. For this reason he went down to the Pavilion at Brighton to to try to enlist the Prince's support. He failed. Creevey draws a quick snapshot of their relations at this time:

'I was curious to see him and the Prince daily in this way, considering the very great intimacy that had been between them for so many years. Nothing certainly could be more creditable to both parties than their conduct. I never saw Sheridan during the period of three weeks (I think it was) take the least more liberty in the Prince's presence than if it had been the first day he had ever seen him. On the other hand the Prince always showed by his manner that he thought Sheridan a man that any prince might be proud of as his friend.'

He goes on to speculate, somewhat cynically, about the

reasons for Sheridan unsuccessfully trying to get the appointment for his son:

> 'What Sheridan's object in this was, cannot be exactly made out; whether it really was affection for Tom or whether it was to keep the profit of the office out of the reach of his creditors, or whether it was to have a young life in the patent instead of his own. Whichever of these objects he had in view, he pursued it with the greatest vehemence; so much so, that I saw him *cry bitterly* one night in making his supplication to the Prince. The latter, however, was not to be shaken.'

The Prince took the view that 'Sheridan's reputation was such, that it made it not only justifiable, but most honourable to him, the Prince, to make such a selection.' For three years Sheridan drew the income from the appointment, and when General Lord Lake returned to England, in 1807, the appointment was duly transferred to him 'for life'. This did not prove to be very long, for he died the following year and Sheridan was appointed for his own life.

Thomas Coutts, the Banker, was appointed to supervise the business. This was probably just as well, for Creevey tells the story that when Sheridan called for £10 at Coutts Bank, in the Strand, he was told that there was £1,300 in his account, paid in by the Duchy of Cornwall:

> 'Sheridan was of course very much set up with this, and on the very next day upon leaving us, he took a house at Barnes Terrace where he spent all his £1,300 ... Yet he was as full of his fun during those two months as ever he could be – gave dinners perpetually and was always on the road between Barnes and London, or Barnes and Oatlands [the Duke of York's house] in a large job coach upon which he would have his family arms painted.'

The Sheridans did not change. Their claims to gentility were still something to be prized. According to Sheridan they were descended from the Kings of Ireland, and their rightful name was O'Sheridan. Tom sardonically remarked that this was quite correct – for they owed everybody, and were to continue to do so.

*

In his relations with Sheridan the Prince had, by and large, been more patient than he would have been with lesser men. Michael Kelly speaks of what he tactfully calls Sheridan's 'neglect for his own interest', and then goes on to tell a story of Sheridan arriving at his house saying 'My dear Mic, I am going to Windsor with the Prince, the day after tomorrow; I must be with him at 11 o'olock in the morning, to a moment and to be in readiness at that early hour, you must give me a bed at your house.'

Kelly, accommodating as always gave him his own bed and went to sleep out of town. When Kelly arrived back later the following day Sheridan was still upstairs asleep after drinking five bottles of port, two of madeira and a bottle of brandy with two friends, as 'accompaniment to a piece of mutton'. Kelly remarks, 'It was easy to account for his drowsiness in the morning.' Sheridan never got to Windsor, although messengers had been sent from Carlton House for him several times. But Kelly had a soft spot for Sheridan: 'It would be hard indeed to find his equal as a companion. That he had his failings, who will deny; but then, who amongst us has not? One thing I may safely affirm, that he was as great an enemy to himself as to anybody else.'

Although the Prince had been patient, he was finally beginning to find Sheridan's aberrations less amusing: his unreliability in keeping appointments was fast becoming a social and political calamity. It is more difficult to accept such faults in a middle-aged man: while Fox and his friends paid lip service to their erstwhile supporter, behind his back they did not hesitate to state their uncomplimentary views of him. In 1806 Fox followed Pitt to the grave. It was said that when Fox was dying a message was received to say that Sheridan wished to see him, and that he replied that 'he could come if he wished'.

The long intimacy of the two men had been at an end for some time, but when it came to planning the public funeral this was Sheridan's task. The Whigs found him reliable enough for that. Sheridan followed the cortège to the Abbey, where Charles James Fox, with all his faults and failings, had at last found a spot free from political complications. Mrs Armistead had been his wife for some time, and as he was dying he said: 'It don't signify, my dearest, dearest Liz', which is, perhaps, a good enough comment on most careers in politics. As for Sheridan, he had remained devoted to the easy-going Charles James Fox nearly to the end, but the friendship had finally predeceased the friend.

His ambition now was to become member for Westminster, Charles's old constituency. Unfortunately Sheridan had reached the age of an elder statesman without the steadiness which the rôle demanded. As a middle-aged man he was miscast. The sudden bursts of furious energy, interspersed with lassitude, were not what the rôle demanded. Nevertheless, he took it for granted that he would get the chance of replacing Fox. But as might have been expected, the Whigs suddenly produced their own well-born candidate, Lord Percy, son of the Duke of Northumberland. The Whigs were a nice self-enclosed little bunch, and over all the years Sheridan had never really succeeded in penetrating their inner enclaves. For decency's sake a general smoke screen was raised round the dealings over this seat, and it was intimated, first, that no one thought that Sheridan wanted to succeed Fox, and secondly that it was a good idea to save Sheridan the expense. Even the good-natured Sheridan was shocked, and wrote to Richard Wilson, the Duke of Northumberland's solicitor and confidential man of business, on September 14, 1806:

'You must have seen by my manner yesterday, how much I was surprised and hurt at learning for the first time, that Lord Grenville had many days previous to Mr Fox's death, decided to support Lord Percy on the unexpected vacancy for Westminster, and that you had since been the active Agent in the Canvas already commenced.'

Sheridan, of course, had to withdraw and decline the offer of support which 'many of the electors still pressed upon him'.

His address to the electors was a valedictory comment on his
lifelong friendship with Fox:

'It is true there have been occasions upon which I have
differed with him – painful recollection of the most painful
moments of my political life! Nor were there wanting those
who endeavoured to represent these differences as a departure from the homage which his superior mind, though
unclaimed by him, was entitled to and from the allegiance
of friendship which our hearts all swore to him. But never
was the genuine and confiding texture of his soul more mani-
fest than on such occasions: he knew that nothing on earth
could detach me from him; and he resented insinuations
against the sincerity and integrity of a friend, which he
would not have noticed had they been pointed against
himself.'

He concluded by saying:

'While the slightest aspiration of breath passed those lips,
now closed for ever – while one drop of life's blood beat in
that heart, now cold for ever – I could not, I ought not, to
have acted otherwise than I did. – I now come with a very
embarrassed feeling to that declaration which I yet think
you must have expected from me, but which I make with
reluctance, because, from the marked approbation I have
experienced from you, I fear that with reluctance you will
receive it, – I feel myself under the necessity of retiring from
this contest.'

Three weeks later Parliament was dissolved, Lord Percy withdrew, and Sheridan became the candidate for Westminster.

It was a hard-fought contest in the old Hogarthian style.
Against Sheridan and Sir Samuel Hood, a Mr James Paull
presented himself. He had made a fortune in India, and had
come back to England trying to bring charges against the
Marquis Wellesley's administration. This was an echo of
ironical comment on Sheridan's past, and Paull had some time
previously to the election been trying to get both Fox and

335

Sheridan on his side, until they began to suspect his evidence. But now Paull was backed up by Horne Tooke, Cobbett, and 'some other demagoges of similar complexion'.

Sheridan was forced to go to the hustings accompanied by men carrying bludgeons, and wearing his colours. He found it impossible to make himself heard, and the first words he uttered were, 'Gentlemen, I wish to know whether you want an election or a riot?' Theatrical touches were not absent. Sir Samuel Hood appeared in full-dress naval uniform – with medals and orders, and an empty sleeve drawing attention to 'our much lamented hero, Lord Nelson'. On leaving the hustings, Sheridan was assaulted by a butcher who struck him on the back with a marrow bone.

Soon an elector's coalition was formed between 'the Friends of Hood' and the 'Friends of Sheridan'. Their manœuvres would have done credit to Drury Lane. The Admiral's friends proceeded to the hustings with platoons of seamen wearing his colours, with laurel branches in their hands, and with pipes and drums playing 'Hearts of Oak' and 'Rule Britannia'. Sheridan's supporters were described as 'a posse of Hibernians from the purlieus of St Giles's [a slum] armed with cudgels, roaring "Sheridan for ever!"'

Nor did the mob itself spare Paull's feelings. His father had been a tailor, so the parade against him also included a man dressed as an ape holding a pair of tailor's scissors, and a man dressed up as a French revolutionary wearing Paull's colours; in one hand he held a truncheon on which was written 'Liberty, Protection, and Peace'.

Sheridan's origins were not forgotten. After thirty years the same gibes appeared in the scurrilous pamphlets:

'*To the Independent Electors of Westminster* Who is asking to be one of your Representatives? The Son of an obscure Irish player, a profession formerly proscribed by our laws; and its followers by various statutes stigmatised as *incorrigible rogues and vagabonds.* – Possesser of a considerable portion of Ribaldry, disgusting obscenity, and dissolutenes of manner, this *Harlequin Son* of a *Mountebank Father* was indulged by some few of the depraved Nobility of the age with admission

into their society, as a kind of *hired Jester*, whose grossness of
of conversation was calculated to stimulate their already too
luxuriant debauchery.

.... And Gentlemen, will you be represented by a depen-
dent and a slave of the Grenvilles? Forbid it Justice! Forbid
it Virtue! Forbid it Freedom!!!

A Calm Observer.'

A public subscription was raised to defray Sheridan's
expenses, and the Marquess of Queensberry gave a thousand
guineas. But Sheridan's reputation was confirmed by the mob
who were singing:

> Oh, Sherry! red Sherry!
> You'd make us all merry.
> With your drolls, your stage tricks and curvets;
> But don't, on old Davy
> Draw drafts for the Navy:
> Nor pay 'em as you pay your debts.

At the bitter end of the insults and the parades, the result was
Hood 5478, Sheridan 4758, and Paull 4481.

Sheridan and Hood proceeded to mount their victory car.
This had been made at Drury Lane. It was twelve feet long
with a lower deck for their principal supporters. Above them,
on a raised platform, sat Sheridan and Hood, on two state
chairs upholstered in scarlet velvet and richly gilded, and in
front of them a huge reproduction of the Royal Arms, below
which was written 'George Rex'. Six horses drew this emblem
of Roman triumph, and the horses, and the men leading them,
were profusely decorated with ribbons and cockades in Sheridan's colours of blue and orange.

Cobbett, not surprisingly, was highly contemptuous:

'The car which had been constructed by the people of Drury
Lane, was surrounded by beadles, constables, police officers,
and police magistrates, and as even their own venal prints
inform us, by the numerous officers of the Thames Police.
The people consisted of the play actors, scene-shifters,

candles snuffers, and mutes of the theatre, aided by a pretty numerous bevy of those unfortunate females who are in some sort inmates of that mansion, so that altogether the procession bore a very strong resemblance to that of Blue Beard.'

In spite of the triumphal car and the successful conclusion to the election, it had not been a popular move on Sheridan's part. He had sat for Stafford for over a quarter of a century, and they were understandably hurt at his desertion of them. He tried to make up for it by sending Tom to stand for the seat, but the young man was ignominiously defeated.

Lord Holland said that Sheridan had always envied Fox, and that in putting himself up for Westminster he had tried to set himself in Fox's place. Holland also said that Sheridan had tried to get Fox to resign his seat to Sheridan long before he died. Holland wrote:

'On the General Election and the retirement of Lord Percy, he again stood for Westminster against the advice of his friends and without the concurrence of a government to which he belonged. He, through his inordinate vanity, thought that he might defy the Court, the Aristocracy, and the Reformers, and such was his confidence in his own personal popularity that he not only neglected, but derided and insulted the clubs and committees through whose agency Mr Fox's elections had been generally secured. He was bitterly deceived.'

Perhaps Sheridan had been bitterly deceived about his true political potentialities from the beginning. It was many years since he had stolen away, on being elected for Stafford, and had felt it to be the happiest moment of his life.

Georgiana Duchess of Devonshire died the same year that Sheridan was elected for Westminster. She had been the means by which Eliza and Richard had penetrated the Whig stronghold. Eliza's songs had opened the doors, and Richard's wit had held them open. But it was all a long time ago.

Sheridan now held a 'place' from the Prince of Wales, and

his son was also a 'placeman'. It had been a hard struggle to retain independence, and in the end that also was lost.

Sheridan's triumph at Westminster was short-lived, and the following year he was defeated by Lord Cochrane. Fortunately he had at least had the prudence to make sure of another seat – at Ilchester, which enabled him to get back into Parliament. It was said that the Prince of Wales paid Sheridan's election expenses. All the props by which he had upheld his pride were being taken away. He could no longer say that he had done everything himself, or that he was no man's paid lackey.

It must have been hard to accept this.

CHAPTER *19*

Fire!

When the new Drury Lane Theatre was opened on April 24, 1794, a special epilogue was written by James Boaden, the biographer of Sarah Siddons, which drew attention to the marvellous fire precautions. It was spoken by Miss Pope, the original Mrs Candour:

> The very ravages of fire we scout,
> For we have wherewithal to put it out;
> In ample reservoirs, our firm reliance
> Whose streams set conflagrations at defiance.
> Panic alone avoid, let none begin it –
> Should the flame spread, sit still, there nothing in it,
> We'll undertake to drown you all in half a minute.

The stage directions then said: '*Scene rises and discovers water.*' There was, in fact, a great deal of water. For an eye witness reported:

'On the curtain being raised another burst of applause rang from every quarter on the exhibition of a cascade of water rushing down from tanks with which the roof had been supplied, roaring into a huge basin prepared for its reception; dashing, splashing, tumbling over artificial rocks but leaving no doubt of its own reality, and clearly showing that in such an awful event as that of fire, they could not only extinguish the flames upon the instant from whatever quarter it could originate, but actually drown the theatre.'

The iron curtain was lowered, and 'struck with heavy hammers in order to prove that it was something more than stage iron, which by its clang reverberated throughout the

340

house, mingling with the uproarious clamour of a delighted audience'.

Fire was a constant hazard in theatres lit by candles and lamps: with flimsy stage dresses, and equally flimsy scenery, it took only the carelessness of a drunken scene shifter to cause a swift disaster. To audiences hemmed in like sardines, even the idea of a fire was alarming. Another hazard was the 'panic' mentioned by Boaden in his verse.

On one occasion the scenery at Drury Lane did catch fire, and somebody rushed upstairs to Sheridan to tell him that the fire was extinguished and that he would go and tell the house. Sheridan, much more sensitive to audience reaction, replied, 'You fool, don't mention the word fire, run down and tell them that we have water enough to drown them and make a face.'

On February 24, 1809, Sheridan was in the House of Commons. Hansard reported: 'A cry of Fire! fire! frequently interrupted the latter part of the Right Hon. Secretary's speech, and Mr Sheridan in a low voice, stated across the table, that the Drury Lane Theatre was on fire.'

Lord Temple suggested that the House should adjourn. It was a kind gesture, but Sheridan 'said with much calmness that whatever might be the extent of the calamity, he did not consider it of a nature worthy to interrupt their proceedings on so great a national question'. It was a sentence born of courage and panache, but at least the fire happened in Lent, when the theatre was empty, and there was no audience to panic. Kelly records the tragedy:

'On the 24th February 1809, Mr Richard Wilson gave a dinner to the principal actors and officers of the Drury Lane Theatre at his house in Lincoln's Inn Fields. All was mirth and glee; it was about eleven o'clock, when Mr Wilson rose and drank "Prosperity and Success to Drury Lane Theatre", we filled a bumper to the toast, and at the very moment we were raising the glasses to our lips, repeating "Success to Drury Lane Theatre", in rushed the younger Miss Wilson and screamed out, that "Drury Lane Theatre was in flames!" We ran into the square and saw the dreadful sight; the fire raged with such fury that it perfectly illuminated Lincoln's Inn Fields with the brightness of day. We proceeded to the scene of destruction.'

Poor, harassed Richard Peake, recipient of so many letters demanding the swift despatch of money, dashed up the stairs with his fellow treasurer, Dunn. At the hazard of their lives, they rescued the iron chest in which was stored the patent of the theatre, the foundation of Sheridan's original piece of good fortune, and with the aid of two firemen they managed to get the chest into the street. Little else was saved. Eliza's harpsichord, the boards on which Garrick had once acted, his clock, which had been solemnly wound up once a year, the scenery, the dresses, the water tanks which were to have saved the theatre – nothing now remained.

Boaden was there when the great statue of Apollo which crowned the façade of the theatre collapsed into the flames. He wrote:

'In less than a quarter of an hour the fire spread in one unbroken flame over the whole of the immense pile, extending from Brydges Street to Drury Lane; so that the pillar of fire was not less than 450 feet in breadth. In a very few minutes all that part of the theatre, together with the front row of boxes was on fire, and the rapidity of the flames was such, that before twelve o'clock the whole of the interior was one blaze. The appearance was tremendously *grand*. Never before did I behold so immense a body of flame; and the occasional explosions that took place were awful beyond description. The interior was completely destroyed by one o'clock.'

When Sheridan eventually left the House he went to Drury Lane, and sat in the Piazza Coffee House, which had been the scene of so many celebrations, watching his theatre burn. Kelly watched the scene of so many of his successes, and all the operas he had composed, burned to ashes, but Sheridan watched his past go up in the flames. Someone remarked on his composure, and he said with his usual humour and courage: 'A man may surely take a glass of wine by his own fireside.'

There was some muttering about incendiarism, but it was generally thought that plumbers who had been repairing the roof had gone away and left their fire burning, or else that a fire grate had been moved while the coals were still hot.

The following day there was a conference, and Wroughton, the stage manager, and some of the principal actors sent a message to Sheridan to meet them for dinner in Gower Street. On this occasion, Sheridan was punctual, sensitive, and sensible. 'The first consideration', he said, 'was to find a place where he would perform under the Drury Lane patent, for though the theatre was destroyed, the patent was not, and he would make every effort in his power to forward the interests and wishes of the company.' Now, at the eleventh hour, he became the son of his father. He asked the actors if they would try to keep the company together. He said he realized that 'many of the principal performers may get profitable engagements at the different provincial theatres, but what then would become of the inferior ones, some of whom have large families? Heaven forbid that they should be deserted!' It was a belated echo of his father's sentiments when the mob had destroyed the interior of the Smock Alley Theatre, Dublin.

About this time he also remarked: 'There are but three things that should try a man's temper, the loss of what was the dearest object of his affections – that I have suffered; bodily pain, which, however philosophers may affect to despise it, is a serious evil – that I have suffered; but *the worst of all is self reproach – that, thank God, I never suffered!*' This has been cited as an instance of self-delusion, but has more the ring of defiance. For he had certainly neglected the theatre, and he was aware of this, and in the latter years at Drury Lane he had not been popular. His mounting difficulties, and the feeling that the whole of his life had taken a wrong turning, had depressed him and where the theatre was concerned he had seemingly lost interest and confidence.

Mathews, who joined the company at Drury Lane in the latter days, was struck by the heaviness of Sheridan's speech at a dinner given in his honour, and remarked:

'He was seldom agreeable in the presence of actors. He

always entered his own theatre as if stealthily and unwillingly, and his appearance amongst his performers never failed to act like a dark cloud. I perfectly well remember one particular afternoon, when Miss de Camp, after a somewhat *animated* colloquy with him, closed it by telling him "that the performers were all very happy before he entered the room, and that he never came but to make everybody uncomfortable." '

Sir Walter Scott, too, reported:

'Mathews assured me that Sheridan was generally very dull in society, and sat sullen and silent swallowing glass after glass, rather a hindrance than a help, but there was a time when he broke out with a resumption of what had been going on, done with great force, and generally attacking some persons in the company, and some opinions which they had expressed.'

Nor was he only difficult on social occasions. One night the company were acting *The School for Scandal*, that brilliant piece of his past. Later, Sheridan went into the green-room after the performance and asked what play it was. He had been drunk all through the performance. The stage manager told him it was his own *School for Scandal*.

'And who was it that acted the old fellow – Sir Peter what-d'ye call'm?'

'Mathews, sir.'

'Never let him play it again; he looks like an old pastry cook.'

'I am sorry, Mr S., to say that we seldom see you here, and you never come but to find fault', retorted the stage manager.

Now there was nothing to find fault with. The scene of the triumphs and the failures had been struck. He was at last an actor amongst actors, and he reacted like one, saying: 'Let us make a long pull, a strong pull, and a pull altogether, and above all, make the general good our sole consideration. Elect yourselves into a committee; but keep in your remembrance even the poor sweepers of the stage, who, with their children must starve, if not protected by your fostering care.'

He had shunned the theatre for so long, but now it had gone with all its memories, its past challenges, and the echoes of old applause. The slow work of reconstruction was not easy and Sheridan, though a man who could rise to a sudden emergency, was not the man for the job. Nor was it possible now to raise money for the rebuilding on his name alone, as it had been at the height of his reputation.

Esther, Sheridan's wife, had an old friend, the brewer Mr Samuel Whitbread, and he took on the task of trying to get the theatre's affairs into some sort of shape. This had to be done before the re-building could begin.

In fact the enterprise was completely bankrupt. The arrears of interest to shareholders amounted to £200,000 alone. The total amount of everybody's interest in the ashes of Drury Lane was £436,000. The theatre had only been insured for a tenth part of its value. The situation was dismal indeed, for if all the shareholders and creditors held out for their rights, the theatre could never be built. Finally the whole of the debts were consolidated at a hundred thousand pounds. Sheridan's share was to be £24,000, but out of this he had to pay the Linleys, who had suffered real financial hardship over the years from their original share in the enterprise, and had not often been paid their annuities.

Unfortunately for 'old Sherry', he had fallen into the hands of a very neat, careful businessman in Samuel Whitbread, who was reluctant to hand over any ready money to Sheridan in case his other debtors should manage to get hold of the cash. Now there were no resources, and no possibility of desperate letters to Richard Peake asking for thirty pounds. All that was left to him was the sinecure from the Prince of Wales.

Nor were his relations with his wife any safer than his financial affairs. 'Nothing shall ever induce me to utter an unkind or even an expostulatory expression towards you', he wrote to her. 'I ask your Pardon for every embarrassment and distress you have suffer'd in respect to the matters your Letter refers to.' Esther had been begging Peake to send her money to pay her washerwoman. 'No one can be in the smaller affairs of the world of a more negligent forgetful and pro-crastinating habit of mind than I am, united at the same time

345

with a most unfortunately sanguine temper, and a rash confidence that I am capable of exertions equal to any difficulty whenever extremity may call for them. To this Frame and Temper of mind you may trace the ground of everything you complain of, and not one atom of it to intentional neglect or indifference to your Comfort and Happiness.'

Esther seems to have been living apart from him at this time, and he writes at great length, going over the past, explaining about the marriage settlement, which he had made and which he was unable to touch until the £15,000 had amounted to £40,000. This was indeed true because their son Charles Brinsley inherited this money.

His worries for Tom's health come breaking through. Tom had been sent to Sicily for his health, but it had not improved, for he had inherited his mother's delicate constitution. Sheridan ends his letter to Esther with a self-revealing sentence: 'I could say more but were I to pour out all that is in my mind I should never close. I repeat again that you do not know me, nor can you be fairly apprised of the real tests and trials which in my former Life would, more than any observations you have had the means of making, have explain'd to you my character.'

The twenty-three years between them had made a breach, and it was hard to make a woman understand who had never known him in his struggling youth, who had never known his father, and all the difficulties which he had had to fight against. It is facile to say that most of his troubles were compounded of neglect and of certain things coming soo easily to him. Fox was forgiven much – Sheridan was not.

Shortly afterwards, he writes to the long-suffering Peake, 'Dear Peake, I sent all you sent me to Mrs Sheridan and so am peniless again – a supply by bearer.' But cash supplies were difficult to come by, for both Sheridan and his son's money due from the theatre was to be paid out in shares, so that until the theatre was built there was to be no interest. The worst blow of all was that Samuel Whitbread insisted that Sheridan should have nothing to do with the direction of the theatre. The door had been slammed in his face.

The only slender hope left now was Sheridan's friendship

with the Prince of Wales. In 1811, George III, after so many
false alarms, succumbed finally to disease, and yet again the
old question of the Regency cropped up. Like some worn
refrain, the politicians began to sing their usual songs. The
Whigs saw the final eclipse of the King into 'madness' as their
golden opportunity, and the Lords Grey and Grenville formed
the impression that power should be immediately transferred
to them. Spencer Perceval, the Prime Minister, was a King's
friend, and they, on the other hand, had constituted themselves
the Prince's friends. The same haggles cropped up, the same
restrictions were to be placed on the Regent, and the same
bedchamber plots were hatched with the Queen.

Suddenly the Regent changed his mind. He decided to ask
Perceval to continue in office. The débâcle was blamed
entirely on Sheridan, who was still in the Prince's counsels,
and writing his letters for him. It is difficult and tedious to
sort out the charges and counter charges of perfidy, double
dealing, and general mayhem of which the politicians accused
one another. Moore says:

'By the death of Mr Fox the chief *personal* tie that connected
the Heir Apparent with the party of that statesman was
broken. Immediately after the death of Mr Fox, His Royal
Highness made known his intentions of withdrawing from
all personal interference in politics; and, though still continuing his sanction to the remaining Ministry, expressed
himself as no longer desirous of being considered a "party
man".'

This is probably true. Although Sheridan may have been
suspected of double dealing, the Prince can by no means be
considered the soul of honour.

But the Lords Grey and Grenville, whatever they may have
felt themselves to be, were not in fact ministers, and there
was no doubt that they resented Sheridan's influence with the
Prince. He was forced to write a long and involved explanation
of his conduct to Lord Holland, which was marked, 'Read
and approved by the Prince, January 20, 1811.'

It did Sheridan little good with the party. It was generally

347

thought that Sheridan might have been motivated by revenge for the treatment which had been meted out to him over the years. Moore says:

'His anxiety that the Prince should not be dictated to by others was at least equalled by his vanity in showing that he could govern him himself. But, whatever were the precise views that impelled him to this trial of strength, the victory which he gained in it was far more extensive than he himself had either foreseen or wished. He had meant the party to *feel* his power, not to sink under it. . . . He had, therefore, in the ardour of undermining, carried the ground from beneath his own feet. There remained to him now, for the residue of his days, but that frailest of all sublunary treasures, a Prince's friendship.'

The *Morning Chronicle* was not disposed to be kind:

'The actors in the plot have been various, and those who have played the most prominent parts have been farthest from the real secret of the drama, the manager and contriver of which has hitherto kept himself in the back ground; and if his vanity would have allowed him to be silent, the piece might have gone off successfully without any one suspecting who was its author. SLY BOOTS is a "notable contriver" but he has the misfortune to be leaky in his cups, and when overtaken, confirms the old adage, *in vino veritas*.'

There were other worries. There always were. The threat of a third theatre loomed large again, but this time at least there were people in the House who wanted to do something for 'old Sherry'. General Tarleton 'appealed to the feelings of the House, and called on them to consider the immortal works of Mr Sheridan and the stoical philosophy with which, in that House, he had witnessed the destruction of his property. Surely some indulgence was due such merit?'

Sheridan, delighted, wrote triumphantly to Esther:

'I have but one moment to tell you in one word the good

news that the Council have unanimously decided in our favour on the patent right question, and now I shall get my affairs right, and you shall never know a plague again; otherwise irretrievable ruin must have been the consequence to me and poor Tom and his family. It was going against us till I spoke on Monday and is decided entirely on the ground I put the question on. I spoke for nearly two hours.'

But Whitbread was standing on the letter of the law. Everything was to be handled by him. Sheridan was even to be excluded from the designing of the theatre, and Mrs Sheridan wrote to Lord Holland:

'Whatever reasons I may have had to complain of Sheridan, and however my comfort and happiness may have been thrown away, I never can see him as *deeply wounded*, as I have seen him lately, without feeling the full extent of my regard for him. What is most distressing to me is that Whitbread has urged me to employ all my influence to bring S. "to Reason", when I confess that my whole heart and soul is *with* Sheridan.'

It was very hard not to be kind to Sheridan, as Mrs Tickell had once pointed out.

*

The fluctuating affairs of Tories and Whigs were not to be decided entirely by their own actions. For unlucky and tragic Spencer Perceval, the safe man, was not to prove so safe after all. Fitzgerald gives a graphic description of the incident which ended many hopes:

'On the 11th of May, a Member burst into the House, and said, "Mr Perceval is shot".

Mr Jerdan said, "I saw a small curling wreath of smoke rise above his head, as if the breath of a cigar; I saw him reel back, and I heard him exclaim, 'O my God!' and then making an impulsive rush, as it were to reach the entrance of the House on the opposite side for safety, I saw him totter forward, not half-way and drop dead between the four pillars which stood there in the centre of the space, with a slight trace of blood issuing from his lips."

One of the clerks of the House called out, "That is the murderer." Jerden then seized him by the collar.

Someone coming out of the adjoining room said to him, "Mr. Perceval is dead! Villain, how could you destroy so good a man and make a family of twelve children orphans?" To which he almost mournfully replied, "I am very sorry for it."

Whilst his language was cool, the agonies which shook his frame were actually terrible.'

The assassin was put on trial and hanged within a few days. He was not allowed to bring witnesses as to his mental state.

A dissolution of Parliament then became a certainty, and caught Sheridan between two fires. He did not want to stand again for Ilchester, for he wished to be free to support Catholic Emancipation, and a seat in the gift of the Prince would have tied his hands. He decided to return to Stafford.

The last time he spoke in Parliament was on his own motion to the Overtures of Peace from France:

'Yet, after the general subjugation and ruin of Europe should there ever exist an independent historian to record the awful events that produced this universal calamity, let that historian have to say "Great Britain fell, and with her fell all the best securities for the charities of human life, for the power and honour, the fame, the glory, and the liberties not only of herself, but of the whole civilised world." '

The voice and the sentiments rang as true as ever whatever had happened to the man, and in the autumn of 1812 he went off hopefully to do battle in Stafford. He had written to Mr Perkins, one of his supporters:

'I pant for my own independent seat. You are a sportsman and, as all lovers of fields sports must be, more or less friendly to poetry, I may refer you to Goldsmith:

And as hare whom hounds and horns pursue
Pants to the goal from whence at first she flew,
I still have hopes, my long vexations past
There to return and die at home at last.

Political death, mind, I mean. But even before that I trust
that we and the few surviving old friends may yet spend
some pleasant days together.'

But the surviving friends at Stafford were not numerous
enough, and Sheridan was defeated.

There are a good many different versions of Sheridan's fialn
eclipse from the House of Commons. Speaking to Croker many
years afterwards, the Prince Regent, then George IV, gave
his version. 'He came to explain to me his failure at Stafford,
of which he laid all the blame upon Whitbread, of whom he
spoke with perfect fury, and called him a *scoundrel!*'

Sheridan's story was that Whitbread was afraid of him, that
Whitbread was involved in intrigues with Princess Charlotte,
and was determined to keep him out of the House of Commons.
The Prince added that he had remarked at the time, that it
was Sheridan's own indolence and indecision, and his being
neither on one side nor the other which had kept him out.

Lord Moira apparently interceded with the Prince for
Sheridan, who agreed that he would help. The Duke of
Norfolk was apparently ready to cut the price of a seat belonging
to him from £4,000 to £3,000, but the Prince cannily remarked
that this was not so great a gift as it appeared, because Sheridan
would still have to vote with Norfolk. Eventually, the Prince
agreed to pay £3,000. Sheridan then came forward with an
entirely new plan for buying an independent seat at Wootton
Bassett from an un-named young man. The money was
produced – 'not that we advanced the sum to Sheridan',
declared the Prince, 'we knew him too well for that; but the
money was lodged in the hands of Mr Cocker, a respectable
solicitor named by Sheridan, who was to pay it over to the
young man in question when the transfer of the seat should be
made. Sheridan took a world of trouble to convince MacMahon
[the Prince's secretary] that all this transaction was *bona fide*,'

as well he might, since he was engaged in a real confidence trick.

Apparently Sheridan eventually indicated that he was setting off for Wootton Basset, and would MacMahon call round at eight in the morning, as he had forgotten to say something to him. MacMahon thought this very amusing, as Sheridan never got up early, but he had some suspicions about the whole transaction, and so went round to find Sheridan's carriage at the door, and the servants packing the boxes in.

Sheridan alleged that he was awaiting the mysterious Mr X, owner of the seat. The money was duly paid over to Mr Cocker and the Prince expected to hear some news of Sheridan's progress towards clinching his new seat in Parliament. Three days later, however, the Prince said he was on horseback in the Oxford Road and thought he saw Sheridan at a distance. 'The person, whoever he was, turned down into Poland Street, or one of those streets as if to avoid me.'

There were further Sheridanesque complications with missing letters from Brooks's alleged not to have been delivered. MacMahon then became very worried about the £3,000, and when he went round to the lawyer, Mr Cocker, 'he answered that the question of a seat in Parliament was quite new to him; that Mr Sheridan when he desired him to receive the money never hinted at any such object, that it was paid to him on Mr Sheridan's account, and that he had disposed of it according to Mr Sheridan's directions, viz. to pay certain pressing debts'. As some of these debts were due to Mr Cocker, the money had fallen into the wrong hands.

The Prince went on:

'I was, as I told you, obliged to repay this money [i.e. give it to the owner of the Parliamentary seat] but I never saw Sheridan, to speak to after, not that it was much worse in principle than other things of his, nor that I had given orders to exclude him, but it was felt by Sheridan himself to be so gross a violation of confidence – such a want of respect and such a series of lies and fraud, that he did not venture to approach me, and in fact, he never came near me again.'

Several biographers have taken the view that this story was
a fabrication on the Prince's part, but taking into account all
Sheridan's mysterious contrivances, it has the air of truth. It
would be pointless and difficult to make up so many details
so long after the event. The whole story has the vividness of
accurate reporting.

Sheridan did, in fact, make one attempt to patch matters
up and contacted MacMahon, the Prince's secretary, laying
all the blame on Whitbread. According to the Prince the scene
went as follows:

'In short, said Sheridan, throwing off the air of shame and
contrition with which he began the conversation and taking
up a kind of theatrical tone and manner, "in short" said
he, "I went to see that scoundrel Whitbread, and it was like
the scene of Peachum and Lockit. I told him that I came to
tell him that I did not want his assistance, that I retracted
the intreaties which my necessities had obliged me to make
to him, that I could wait for the £2,000 which he had
refused to let me have to get into Parliament, for that I
had got £2,000 without being under any obligation to him,
and that I should be in Parliament next week."

"My dear Sheridan," replied Whitbread, "it is true that
I would not give you £2,000 to get into Parliament, and in
your circumstances, I am sure I acted the part of a true
friend, but did I ever refuse you £2,000 *to stay out* of Parliament?" In short, he paid me my £2,000 on condition I
should *not come in* and when I came to ask for the £3,000
which you, my dear friend, had advanced, for the purpose
of returning it to you I found that that fellow Cocker had
chosen to apply it to his own debt, and that it was not
forthcoming.'

The Prince concluded: 'MacMahon listened to all this, but
with no good-will towards Sheridan, and came immediately to
report it to me, but after that Sheridan never came near
either of us.'

The last bastion had fallen.

*

Swift had remarked about Richard's grandfather, 'He was a generous, honest, good-natured man, but his perpetual want of discretion and judgment made him act as if he were neither generous, honest or good-natured.' This could have been said of the grandson.

Admittedly Richard Sheridan was unreliable, but there were worse men who had been better served, and mediocrities who had been better rewarded. He had suffered many disappointments – he had given devotion to his first political friend, Georgiana, Duchess of Devonshire, who had finally cold-shouldered him, he remained ever devoted to Lord Holland, who in his decline belittled him, and Charles Fox, another devoted friend, had before his death sown the seeds of distrust in the Whig party against him. And in the last eight years of his political life, he was ostracized by even the nonentities of his own party.

That he was a lover of intrigue is undeniable, and yet to read old memoirs is to see that most of the politicians were intriguers. As Dr Johnson said to William Windham on entering politics 'Don't be afraid sir, you will soon make a very pretty rascal.' Sheridan cannot be said to have been more given to intrigue than most of them. He did not always take his fellow politicians seriously, and some of his jokes hit them very hard. They did not forget his witticisms at their expense over Catholic Emancipation difficulties – that he 'had known many men knock their heads against a wall, but he had never before heard of a man collecting bricks and building a wall for the express purpose of knocking out his own brains against it'. Politicians, on the whole, do not like jokes; nor do they feel safe with men who make them.

Yet Sheridan was the man who had always defended the cause of liberty. He defended the Irish against the Union which had destroyed the heart of the country: 'In fine, I think the situation of Ireland a paramount consideration. If they were to be the last words I should ever utter in this House, I should say "Be just to Ireland, as you value your own honour; be just to Ireland as you value your own peace." '

When Charles Fox was still putting up a case for Napoleon, Sheridan had adopted a patriotic viewpoint. Sheridan's speeches fill several volumes, and they were always witty, and pertinent to the cause he fostered. Some of his witticisms in the House could be used with good effect even today.

Speaking about a bill which had been badly worded he said: 'This is the House that Jack Built. There is a bill imposing a tax, then comes in a bill to amend that bill for imposing a tax, and then comes a bill to explain the bill that amended the bill, next a bill to remedy the defect of the bill, for explaining the bill that amended the bill, and so on *ad infinitum.*' He had a great ability to make fun of pomposity in the extraordinary requirements of certain tax bills:

'The Horse tax bill required a stamp to be placed not on the animal but on some part of the accoutrements. Then it was said names and numbers of all horses in each parish should be affixed to the church door. Churchwardens also required to return lists of windows in their districts.

Now if the horses were in the habit of looking out at windows, this might possibly have been a wise and judicious regulation . . . but there was some little wonder how such ideas came to be associated in the minds of those who framed the bill.'

For him, the twin supports of his life, the theatre and the House of Commons, had collapsed, and like Samson he was buried in the ruins.

It is hard to withhold admiration from a man like Sheridan and to realize how much of his life was given to the House. Against the background of the great events of Europe he seems a small figure, and in the history books is merely set down by the single word 'orator'. Yet in his own day, he was considered a great figure, both by his own party and by his opponents.

If Sheridan was careless and behindhand with his plays, his speeches were carefully worked over, because in the House of Commons, he found a careful and critical audience. There are in his speeches many instances of great prescience, as when he warned England to be just to Ireland. It could be said that it was England's injustice and stupidities in Irish policy which partly caused the bitterness with which she was long regarded in America. About the English character he also showed great insight:

'Never was there any country in which there was so much absence of public principle, and at the same time so many instances of private worth. Never was there so much charity and humanity towards the poor and distressed. When Great Britain falls she will fall with a people full of private worth and virtue; she will be ruined by the profligacy of the governors, and the security of her inhabitants – the consequence of those pernicious doctrines which have taught her to place a false confidence on her strength and freedom, and not to look with distrust and apprehension to the misconduct and corruption to whom she has trusted the management of her resources.'

Moore quotes this passage and adds that the reasons for the downfall of the English will be 'the love of ease that luxury brings along with it, the selfish and compromising spirit in which the members of a polished society countenance each other, and which reverses the principle of patriotism, by sacrificing public interests to private ones, the substitution of intellectual for moral excitement, and the repression of enthusiasm by fastidiousness and ridicule, these are among the causes that undermine a people . . . and the period in which their rights are best understood may be that in which they most easily surrender them . . . till at last, deceiving themselves with the semblance of rights gone by, and refining upon the forms of their institutions after they have lost the substance, they smoothly sink into slavery with the lessons of liberty on their lips.' The whole passage has a distressingly contemporary ring.

Now, after over thirty years, he was out of Parliament which would remain unenlivened by his wit, and Whitbread would not let him have any share in the reconstruction of the Theatre Royal, Drury Lane. Shut out of the House of Commons he could no longer rely on the protection of being an MP, and was at the mercy of his creditors. He could now be arrested for debt.

Gradually everything was slipping away, even the furniture of the house – the gilded books which his friends had given him, the silver cup from the electors of Stafford, pictures by Gainsborough and Morland, even the portrait of his first wife by Reynolds. And in the spring of 1814 he was arrested and taken to the spunging house. He wrote furiously to Whitbread from Tooke's Court, Cursitor Street:

'Whitbread, putting all false professions of friendship and feeling out of the question, you have no right to keep me here! – for it is in truth *your* act – if you had not forcibly withheld from me the twelve thousand pounds, in consequence of a threatening letter from a miserable swindler, whose claim you in particular knew *to be a lie* I should at least have been out of reach of *this* state of miserable insult, for that, and that only lost me my seat in Parliament. . . . Oh God! with what mad confidence have I trusted your word – I ask justice from you, and no boon.'

His spirits however were still not daunted and when Whitbread went down to get him released from Tooke's Court, Sheridan was calculating the odds on the Westminster Election. But when he got home to his wife he burst into a fit of long passionate sobbing 'at the profanation which his person had suffered'.

Now husband and wife were closer – grim circumstances created the need to trust and love one another. He was Dan again, writing to Hecca: 'Never again let one harsh word pass between us, during the period which may not perhaps be long, that we are in this world together, and life, however clouded to me, is mutually spared to us.' But there were other torments to his spirit which were not spared. His son Tom had been ill for some time, and in the end a post at the Cape of Good Hope had been engineered for him. In 1813 Sheridan wrote to him:

'McMahon informed me of your application to the Prince respecting some situation at the Cape. I think you were right, and right also in not saying anything to me about it. However reliance on the Prince we can have none, and it has

357

so turn'd out that I have effected your object in a way and with a Quarter which I think will be infinitely more grateful to you. I have the Duke of York's solemn word and pledge that your desire shall be immediately accomplish'd.'

He adds that Tom will owe nothing to the Prince or his Ministers.

Later that year Sheridan wrote to his wife:

'It would half break your heart to see how he [Tom] is changed. I spend all the time with him I can as he seems to wish it, but he so reminds me of his mother, and his feeble, gasping way of speaking affects and deprives me of all hope. He tries to suppress the irritability of his temper in a very amiable way which makes me fear he thinks ill of himself . . .'

Tom set sail with his family, but by the end of 1814 Sheridan wrote to Esther:

'I have endeavoured to escape from despairing of Tom as long as my sanguine heart would hold a hope – it is a heavy stroke and the long postponing of it led to a habit of irrational confidence on the subject, for his malady seem'd to have become a part of his constitution and unable to conquer Life. Yet heavy as the affliction will be the anxiety with which I look to your Health and Life almost extinguishes what I ought to feel on the occasion. But if you were well I would go to him tho' the scene would crack what nerves I have left.'

He had always battled with the two sides of his conflicting character, and the high spirits and airy nonchalance which went hand in hand with his wit, were often a shield to protect the deep inner darkness of his soul. Now the darkness was again overshadowing those he loved best in life.

To Esther he also wrote: 'I can safely swear that I never pass a day or an hour almost, without having present to my mind the probability of one's last hour being nearer than the accomplishment of the most immediate object of our hopes and pursuits.' Underneath his stoic calm and quick quips there lay an unhappy soul which had never tried to attain self-knowledge. 'But then comes the silent hour that asks how long will you want expanse of space on earth?' While he lived his space of earth was always coloured by the flowers of his wit, and there were still cheerful moments when he knew he was appreciated.

Since the opening of the new theatre in Drury Lane he had not been down to see it. When it opened the management was deluged with poems, all making allusion to the Phoenix rising on the ashes of the old. Even Samuel Whitbread had joined in this carnival of verse. Of his efforts Sheridan said with a flash of his old wit, 'But Whitbread made *more* of this bird than any of them; and he entered into particulars, and described its wings, beak, tail etc; in short it was a Poulterer's description of a Phenix.'

In the end Sheridan was tempted to visit the theatre he had avoided for so long. Lord Essex persuaded him to dine with him, and go to Drury Lane to see Kean, who, at the beginning of Kelly's reign had played 'one of the imps' in *Macbeth* and been sacked for creating confusion behind the scenes, but was now the rising star.

Once in the theatre the old atmosphere of the past came stealing over him, and during the entr'acte Lord Essex missed him. 'He found him installed in the Green Room with all the actors around him, welcoming him back to the old region of his glory, with a sort of filial cordiality. Wine was immediately ordered, and a bumper to the health of Mr Sheridan was drank by all present, with the expression of many a hearty wish that he would often, *very* often, re-appear among them.' The old actor had come home and he was among his own people – the people who understood him, and whom he understood despite his long fight to rise above the world of the theatre. He went home in a state of euphoria. All was not lost after all.

Yet on parting with Lord Essex at his front door in Savile Row he turned triumphantly to him and said: 'The World would soon hear of him, for the Duke of Norfolk was about to bring him into Parliament.' There was no mention of the theatre. Parliament was the rock on which his life had been split, but his gaze was still set upon it.

Sheridan had been friendly with Dr Johnson in the days when his fame as a playwright first astonished the town. In his declining days he met Byron. 'What a wreck is that man', wrote Byron, 'and all from bad pilotage; for no one had ever better gales, though now and then a little too squally. Poor dear Sherry! I shall never forget the day he and Rogers and Moore and I passed together; when *he* talked and we listened, without one yawn, from six till one in the morning.'

Byron had an intense admiration for what he called 'the ladies and gentlemen of the old school'. Yet even he was astonished at the oddness of Sheridan's shifts of sentiment. 'Lord Holland told me a curious piece of sentimentality in Sheridan. The other night we were all delivering our respective opinions on him and other *hommes marquans* and mine was this:

"Whatever Sheridan has done or chosen to do has been par excellence the *best* of its kind. He has written the *best* comedy (*School for Scandal*), the best opera (*The Duenna*) (In my mind far before that St Giles's lampoon the *Beggar's Opera*), the best farce (*The Critic*), it is only too good for a farce, and the best address (*The Monologue on Garrick*) and to crown all delivered the best Oration (the famous Begum Speech) ever conceived or heard in this country."

Somebody told S. this the next day, and on hearing it he burst into tears! Poor Brinsley! if they were tears of pleasure, I would rather have said these few, but most sincere, words than have written the Iliad or made his own celebrated Philippic.'

Although Byron was drawn to Sheridan he was not unaware of his faults, or deceived about his appearance: 'The upper part of his face that of a god, while below he showed the satyr.' Or Sheridan's sudden changes of mood when he would even abuse his own writings. 'One day I saw him take up his own Monody on Garrick. He lighted upon the dedication to the Dowager Lady Spencer: on seeing it he flew into a rage, and exclaimed "that it must be a forgery – that he had never dedicated anything of his to such a damned canting bitch".'

But Byron considered him a great man and a great orator:

'I heard Sheridan only once, and that briefly; but I liked his voice, his manner, and his wit; he is the only one of them I ever wished to hear at greater length. In society I have met him frequently; he was superb! He had a sort of liking for me, and never attacked me – at least to my face, and he did everybody else – high names, and wits. . . . I have seen him quiz Mme de Stael. Poor fellow! he got drunk very thoroughly and very soon. It occasionally fell to my lot to convoy him home – no sinecure, for he was so tipsy that I was obliged to put on his cock'd hat for him: to be sure it tumbled off again, and I was not myself so sober as to be able to pick it up again.'

In October of 1815 Byron described a convivial party:

'Yesterday I dined out with a large-ish party, where were Sheridan and Colman [a dramatist from Covent Garden].

Like other parties of the kind, it was first silent, then talky, then argumentative, then disputatious, then unintelligible, then altogether, then inarticulate, and then drunk. When we had reached the last step of this glorious ladder, it was difficult to get down again without stumbling; and, to crown all, Kinnaird and I had to conduct Sheridan down a damned corkscrew staircase, which had certainly been constructed before the discovery of fermented liquors, and to which no legs, however crooked, could possibly accommodate themselves. We deposited him safe at home, where his man evidently used to the business, waited to receive him in the hall.'

Perhaps the manservant receiving the sad fuddled man agreed with Lord Byron who said: 'Poor fellow, *his* very dregs are better than the first sprightly runnings of others.'

Writing to Thomas Moore, Byron says, 'Perhaps you heard of a late answer of Sheridan to the watchman who found him bereft of that divine particle of air called reason. The Watchman, who found Sherry in the street, fuddled and bewildered:

"Who are you, sir?" No answer. "What's your name?" A hiccup. "What's your name?" Answer, in a slow, deliberate, and impassive tone: "Wilberforce!"'

But in spite of all his drunken aberrations and changes of mood, Byron pitied him. "I don't know why, but I hate to see the *old* ones lose; particularly Sheridan, notwithstanding all his *mechancété*.' It was a salute from the rising star to the falling, burned-out comet.

Over the last few years of his life Sheridan had been dropped by many of his friends, and even if the Prince's story of the final break with Sheridan is discounted, there was little doubt that the Prince had put up with a great deal from Sheridan. Whatever charity may dictate, it is very difficult to remain friendly with a man who has been completely overtaken by the vagaries of the drunkard. Some friends did rally round him, and although, curiously, he had never borrowed money, in the end he was forced to do so.

His house at Polesden Lacy was let, but he still had two farms there and his nephew describes one of his visits to Surrey. 'During the few days we remained there, he rose early, and after breakfast proceeded in his barouche to his estate, over a portion of which he walked each day, making minute inquiries relating to his affairs, over which he seemed very anxious.'

He writes to his son Charles saying that he had walked over his farms, but did not like to look at the house. It was too reminiscent of the past. Yet when he brought himself to write to Samuel Whitbread he said: 'I have a hatful of Polesden violets on the table while I write and three samples of lambs wool.' There was always another spring.

But three months after Sheridan wrote to Whitbread about his hatful of violets, Whitbread, overcome it was said by the debts and difficulties of Drury Lane, cut his own throat. When a post-mortem was carried out, 'part of the skull and brain were found in such a state that it is impossible he could have kept his senses'.

In the Spring of 1816 Byron wrote that he regretted he would not be able to 'wait upon Mr Sheridan'. Driven away by the scandals about Augusta Leigh, he never returned to England, and he never saw 'old Sherry' again. Already, in

March of 1816, Sheridan's health was breaking up. His body, long much abused, was giving way at last. On March 17th he was obliged to send an excuse about the St Patrick's Day dinner to the Duke of Kent. The contents of this letter were communicated to the company, and the Duke of Kent (father of Queen Victoria) wrote to Sheridan from Kensington Palace saying, 'I have been so hurried ever since St Patrick's day, as to be unable earlier to thank you for your letter, which I received while presiding at the festive board.' The Duke said he had explained that Sheridan was ill and 'the company expressed, in a manner that could not be *misunderstood*, their continued affection for the writer of it'.

This was a balm to the sick man's soul. For his distresses were many. Two months later he was writing to Samuel Rogers:

'I find things settled so that £150 will remove all difficulties. I am absolutely undone and broken-hearted. I shall negotiate for the Plays successfully in the course of a week, when all shall be returned. . . . They are going to put the carpets out of the window, and break into Mrs S's room and *take me*. – for God's sake let me see you. R. B. S.'

It is hard to find out the facts about Sheridan's last days. There seems to be some truth in the view that he was in physical poverty, although most of his old friends managed to put up a smoke screen about it. Apparently Samuel Rogers and Thomas Moore went down to Savile Row to try to do something. The house was locked up but a servant peering out of the basement told them that all was safe for the night, but that bills of sale were going to be posted on the house the following day.

The next morning Moore and Rogers turned up with a draft for £150. Sheridan, said Moore, was as good-natured and cordial as ever, though both his wife and himself were extremely ill, and the house was described as being almost bare, with Sheridan lying covered with nothing but an old blanket. By a curious twist of fate Dr Bain, who was attending him, was the same man who had tended Eliza and comforted

Sheridan at the Hot Wells, Bristol, so long ago when she had died.

His sister Lissy had also written to him, comforting him and comparing him to her own son, Tom, and saying, 'I am persuaded had you not too early been thrown upon the world, and alienated from your family, you would have been equally good as a private character. Do, dear brother, send me one line to tell me you are better. Most affectionately, Yours, Alicia Lefanu.' Alicia knew the deprivations of his childhood, for she had been a partner in them, and now on the edge of his dissolution she sent him love and an excuse for failure.

It was said that Sheridan was deserted by all his friends, but Croker says: 'Sheridan – a self immolated victim to his own lamentable and shameful weaknesses – had hidden himself from their [his friends] Society.' It was, Lord Holland told Moore, a peculiarity of Sheridan's disposition, that he had all his life endeavoured to put a false face on his difficulties, and to conceal his private embarrassments and wants. He was still living – nominally at least – in his usual respectable four-storied residence at 17 Savile Row; beyond that circumstance, everything about him had long been obscure. No one knew or suspected the extremities to which he was reduced.

When the Regent heard the truth he sent an agent round to enquire what he could do. Croker gives the story which he had from the Regent himself:

'The last time that I saw Sheridan was in the neighbourhood of Leatherhead on the 17th August 1815. I know the day from this circumstances that I had gone to pay my brother a visit at Oatlands on his birthday. I saw in the road near Leatherhead old Sheridan coming along the pathway. I see him now in the black stockings and the blue coat with metal buttons. I said to Bloomfield "There's Sheridan" but as I spoke he turned off into a lane when we were within thirty yards of him, and walked off without looking behind him.'

The Regent then described how 'Colonel MacMahon came in to say that Vaughan, who we called Hat Vaughan, had called to say that Sheridan was dangerously ill, and really in great distress and want. I think no one who ever knew me will doubt that I immediately said that his illness and want made me forget his faults, and that he must be taken care of. He asked me to name a sum.' The Regent was a little hazy about how much, but he thought it was £500, but in his own defence said, 'I set no limit to the sum, nor did I say or hear a word about the mode in which it was to be applied.' The Regent was cagey. He did not want it to be known that he was sending the money, for he said that Sheridan's debts were 'la mer à boire.' He might be asked for more. Eventually Vaughan agreed to accept £200, but later came back and said that only £130 was wanted.

'He said that he found him and Mrs Sheridan both in their beds, both apparently dying, and both starving! It is stated in Mr Moore's book that Mrs Sheridan attended her husband in his last illness; it is not true. She was too ill to leave her own bed, and was in fact already suffering from the disease [cancer of the womb] of which she died a couple of years after. They had hardly a servant left. Mrs Sheridan's maid she was about to send away, but they could not collect a guinea or two to pay the woman's wages. When Mr Vaughan entered the house, he found all the reception rooms bare, and the whole house in a state of filth and stench that was quite intolerable. Sheridan himself he found in a truckle bed in a garret with a coarse blue and red coverlet, such as one sees as horse-cloths over him; out of this bed he had not moved for a week, not even for the occasions of nature, and in this state the unhappy man had been allowed to wallow, nor could Vaughan discover that anyone had taken any notice of him, except one lady, whose name I hardly know whether I am authorised to repeat, Lady Bessborough, who sent £20.'

There is a nice touch of irony in the fact that Croker adds 'Some ice and currant water were sent from Holland House – an odd contribution, for if it was known that he wanted these little matters, they might have been had at the confectioners'. Yet, notwithstanding all this misery, Sheridan on seeing Mr

Vaughan appeared to revive; he said he was quite well, talked of paying off all his debts, and, though he had not eaten a morsel for a week he spoke with a certain degree of alacrity and hope. Mr Vaughan saw that this was a kind of bravado, and that he was in a fainting state, and he immediately procured him a little spiced wine and toast, which was the first thing (except brandy) that he has tasted for some days.

'Mr Vaughan lost no time in buying a bed and bed clothes, half a dozen shirts, some basons, towels, etc. He had Sheridan taken up, and put into the new bed; he had the rooms cleaned and fumigated; he discharged, I believe, some immediately pressing demands; and, in short, provided for the care and comfort, not only of Sheridan, but of Mrs Sheridan.'

This narrative of the squalor of Sheridan's house is borne out by Tom's tutor, Smyth: 'Nothing could be more deplorable than the look of everything wherever I turned my eyes. There were strange-looking people in the hall; the parlour seemed dismantled. A crumpled piece of paper on the table proved to be a prescription by Sir H. Halford.'

Two days later the Regent's money was sent back. Vaughan came to MacMahon, says Croker, 'with an air of mortification, and stated that he was come to return the £200. "The £200!" said MacMahon, with surprise. "Why, you had spent three forths of it the day before yesterday!"' Vaughan said that this was true 'but some of those who left these poor people in misery have now insisted on their returning this money, which they suspect has come from the Prince. Where they got the money I know not; but they have given me the amount with a message that *Mrs* Sheridan's friends have taken care that Mr Sheridan wanted for nothing. I could only say that this assistance came rather late', added Mr Vaughan, 'for that three days ago I was enabled by his Royal Highness's bounty, to relieve him and her from the lowest state of misery and debasement in which I had ever seen human beings.'

It is alleged that the Regent was remembering with advantages what he had done, but there is no doubt that he offered money, and that once he had done this it revived some humanity in the ice-and-currant-water brigade.

At one point the bailiffs did break into the house, and were about to take Sheridan and carry him away in blankets, but the ever-faithful Dr Bain threatened them with an indictment for murder if they carried out their threat.

Moore and Rae both deny these stories of misery. Moore did not like the Regent, and was not disposed to give him the benefit of the doubt, and Rae was writing in 1896 under the aegis of the respectable great-grandson of Sheridan, the Marquess of Dufferin and Ava. The descriptions have the ring of truth and the immediacy of events observed.

The final help came from a fellow Irishman, a Mr Dennis O'Bryan, who put a notice in the newspaper which included the words, 'Oh, delay not to draw aside the curtain within which the proud spirit hides its sufferings! Prefer ministering in the chamber of sickness to ministering at the splendid sorrows that adorn the hearse.' After this a spate of help and callers burst forth. The newspapers recorded the names of 'persons of the highest distinction' who visited Sheridan – including the Duke of York, Lord Wellesley, and the Countess of Jersey.

But, it was getting late for social calls. Mrs Sheridan was ill in a separate room and Sheridan wrote her little notes. In one he asked her to send their son Charles to him: 'The sight of me may do him good.'

His solicitor was sent for and Sheridan remarked 'There he comes with his damned will-making face.' Typically, he never made a will. His charm held true to the last for he won the heart of the old woman installed by his creditors who seemingly contracted an attachment for him as strong as if she had attended him from his childhood.

These were the last sparks from a dying fire, and when Lady Bessborough called three days before he died, he asked her what she thought of his looks. She said his eyes were brilliant still.

'He then made some frightful answer about their being fixed for eternity. He took her hand and gripped it hard, and then he told her that he gave her that token to assure her that, if possible, he would come to her after he was dead. Lady Bessborough was frightened, and said that he had persecuted her all his life and would now carry his persecution into death. Why should he do so? "Because", said Sheridan, "I am resolved you shall remember me." He said more frightful things, and she withdrew in great terror.'

Tragedy and death had caught up with the young man who with airy wit had remarked that it 'would be snug lying in the Abbey', and he now spoke with his own Mr Justice Credulous: 'I won't die Bridget, I don't like death.'

He sent a last message to Lady Bessborough that his eyes would look up to the coffin lid with the same brilliancy as ever. But when he realized he was really dying his wife said she had never seen such awe on the face of anyone. There were no more jokes and no contrivances.

The Bishop of London was sent for, but by the time he arrived Sheridan was unconscious, although it was given out that he had joined in the prayers with the Bishop. Appearances had to be kept up.

He died on July 7, 1816, at midday. He was nearly sixty-five.

*

The funeral was splendid and the coffin was followed by everyone from the royal dukes down to the players of Drury Lane. The pall-bearers were Lord Holland, the Duke of Bedford, and Lords Lauderdale and Spencer.

Sheridan wanted to be buried next to Charles Fox. Moore said, 'He disliked any allusion to his being a dramatic writer. He would if he could have spoken out when they were burying him, have protested loudly against the place where they laid him, as the Poet's Corner was his aversion.' But posterity has chosen to put him in his rightful place near Garrick. If in life he chose the wrong road, in death he was set in his right context. He had, after all, been what he most determined not to be, a writer and a player.

Yet, in one of his darker moments he said that he did not regret the failure of his political career but he did regret 'not having devoted himself to the Muses', and added: 'I have thrown myself away.' Nothing remained but the eulogies, the monodies, the posthumous praise, 'the last of the giants', 'the last of the luminaries', 'a mighty spirit is eclipsed'.

The Regent in grief, shut himself up in his room. The friend of his youth had proved the mortality of the liveliest wits, but when Prinny spoke to Moore about Sheridan he spoke with feeling and with sincerity. All the bitterness of the past had been forgotten.

'He was a great man, Mr Moore, but in the simplicity of his nature he never knew his own greatness.'

And then, perhaps thinking of his own chicaneries, the Regent said: 'He had an abounding confidence in every man; and although his pen indicated a knowledge of human nature, yet that knowledge was confined to his pen alone, for in all his acts he rendered himself the dupe of the fool and the designing knave. He was a proud man, sir, a very proud man.'

Sheridan was survived by Captain Mathews, his erstwhile rival and duelling opponent, who lived to a comfortable and respected old age in Bath. He was popular because of his prowess at whist, about which he had written a successful book.

In his character Sheridan had the twin strains of the foolish prodigality of his grandfather, and the stubborn pride of his father. For worldly success, they were to prove a fatal combination. Yet in spite of all the misery and anguish, when his debts were examined, they amounted to only £5,000. The following year Esther died, leaving £40,000, the sum which Sheridan had caused to accumulate under her settlement.

Once Sheridan was safely buried busy pens got to work. Before she died, Esther asked Moore to write his life, and Moore remarked that what she wanted was that 'I should praise him through thick and thin.' But before the book was under weigh Esther died. In 1817, Tom died, from tuberculosis, the disease which had killed his mother, and when the book finally came out, the only people whom Moore had to keep his eye on were his political and aristocratic friends. Byron gave Moore good down to earth advice:

'I do not know any good model for a life of Sheridan but

that of Savage.[1] Recollect, however, that the life of such
a man may be made far more amusing than if he had been a
Wilberforce; – and this without offending the living, or
insulting the dead. The Whigs abuse him; however, he
never left them. As for his creditors, remember, Sheridan
never had a shilling and was thrown, with great powers and
passions, into the thick of the world, and placed upon the
pinnacle of success, with no other external means to support
him in his election. Did Fox pay his debts? – or did Sheridan
take a subscription? Was the **'s drunkenness more excusable
than his? Were his intrigues more notorious than those of
all his contemporaries? and is his memory to be blasted, and
theirs respected? Don't let yourself be led away by clamour
but compare him with the coalitioner Fox, and the pensioner
Burke as a man of principle, and with ten hundred thousand
in personal views, and with none in talent, for he beat them
all *out* and out. Without means, without connexion, without
character (which might be false at first, and make him mad
afterwards from desperation) he beat them all, in all he ever
attempted. In writing the Life of Sheridan, never mind the
angry lies of the humbug Whigs. Recollect that he was an
Irishman and a clever fellow, and that *we* have had some
very pleasant days with him.'

Byron wrote the best epitaph on Sheridan: 'Alas, poor
human nature.'

*

The concluding ironies in the story of the Sheridans were
written by their descendants. Tom, who died in 1817, left

[1] Richard Savage (1697–1743), playwright and poet, was claimed to be the
illegitimate son of the Countess of Macclesfield and Earl Rivers. His life reads
like an eighteenth-century romance of unfaithful wives, violent husbands, and
missing heirs put out to nurse. His claims seem to have been accepted by some
members of his family, but his immoderate behaviour in the end alienated his
family and his patrons, who included Queen Caroline (wife of George II) and
Ann Oldfield, the actress. At one point in his career he did achieve a certain
affluence. Johnson, in his life of Savage, says: 'This was the golden part of Mr
Savage's life, his appearance was splended, his expences large, and his acquaintance extensive.' Savage was noted for his charm and witty conversation, but
eventually died in penury. Richard Sheridan wrote a prologue to Savage's play
Sir Thomas Overbury when it was produced at Drury Lane.

seven children. His daughters married into the great families who had considered their grandfather socially inferior. The oddest circumstance of all was that Sheridan's great grandson, the teetotal Victorian Marquess of Dufferin and Ava, became Viceroy of India, occupying the exalted throne whose foundations had been built by Warren Hastings.

All the pride, resentment, and frustrated ambitions of the player and playwright Sheridans came to fruition in an eminent Victorian. It was the final joke.

SELECT BIBLIOGRAPHY

Aldington, Richard. *The Strange Life of Charles Waterton*
Appleton, William W. *Charles Macklin*
d'Arblay, Madame. *Diary and Letters*
Barton, Margaret. *Garrick*
Boaden, James. *Memoirs of the Life of John Philip Kemble.*
   Memoirs of Mrs Siddons.
Boswell, James. *London Journals.*
   The Ominous Years.
Burnim, Kalman A. *David Garrick, Director.*
Butler, E. M. *Sheridan, a Ghost Story.*
Clark, William Smith. *The Early Irish Stage.*
Creevey Papers, The.
Croker, Rt. Hon. John Wilson. *Correspondence and Diaries.*
Darlington, W. A. *Sheridan.*
Davies, A. Mervyn. *Warren Hastings.*
Davies, C. Collin. *Warren Hastings and Oudh.*
Davies, Thomas. *Life of David Garrick.*
Dulck, Jean. *Comédies de R. B. Sheridan.*
Ehrman, John. *The Younger Pitt, the Years of Acclaim.*
Elliott, Sir Gilbert. *Life and Letters.*
Fitzgerald, P. H. *Lives of the Sheridans*
Genlis, Mme de. *Mémoirs inédits.*
Gibbs, Lewis. *Sheridan.*
Gibson, Edward. *Pitt.*
Grier, Sydney C. (ed.). *Letters of Warren Hastings to his Wife.*
Hobhouse, Christopher. *Fox.*
Hobhouse, John Cam. *Recollections of a Long Life.*
Hogan, Charles Beecher. *London Stage 1776–1800.*
Holland, Lord. *Memoirs of the Whig Party.*
Johnson, Dr Samuel. *The Life of Mr Richard Savage, son of the
   Earl of Rivers.*
Kelly, Michael. *Reminiscences of the King's Theatre and the
   Theatre Royal, Drury Lane.*
Laski, Harold (ed.). *Burke's Letters.*
Le Fanu, Alicia. *Memoirs of the Life and Writings of
   Mrs Frances Sheridan.*
Le Fanu, William (ed.). *Betsy Sheridan's Journal, Letters from
   Sheridan's Sister.*
Little (D. M.) and Kahrl (G. K.) (ed.). *Letters of David Garrick.*
Longford, Elizabeth. *Wellington, the Years of the Sword.*

Magnus, Sir Philip. *Edmund Burke.*

Manvell, Roger. *Sarah Siddons.*

Moore, Thomas. *Letters and Journal.*

  Memoirs of the Life of the Rt. Hon. R. B. Sheridan.

Murray, K. L. *Beloved Marion, Social History of Mr and Mrs Warren Hastings.*

Oliphant, Mrs. *Sheridan.*

Playfair, Nigel. *The Prodigy (Strange Life of Master Betty).*

Pope, W. Macqueen. *Theatre Royal Drury Lane.*

Price, Cecil (ed.). *Letters of Richard Brinsley Sheridan.*

Quennell, Peter. *Byron, in Italy.*

  Byron, the Years of Fame.

Quennell, Peter (ed.). *Byron, Letters and Diaries.*

  Memoirs of William Hickey.

Rae, W. Fraser. *Sheridan.*

Reid, Loren. *Charles James Fox.*

Rhodes, E. Crompton. *Harlequin Sheridan.*

Rhodes, E. Crompton (ed.). *Poems and Plays of Richard Brinsley Sheridan.*

Robinson, Mrs. *Memoirs of the Late Mrs Robinson, written by herself.*

Russell, W. Clark. *Representative Actors.*

Sheldon, Esther Keck. *Thomas Sheridan of Smock Alley.*

Sheridan, Frances. *The Dupe. The Discovery [Comedies.]*

Sheridan, R. B. *Speeches.*

Sheridan, Thomas. *Pamphlets of:*

  A Full vindication of the Conduct of the Manager of the Theatre Royal, Dublin 1747.

  Oration on Elocution.

  An Humble Appeal to the Publick together with some considerations on the present critical and dangerous state of the stage in Ireland, Dublin 1758.

  The Playhouse Prorogued, Dublin 1754 (Satire against Thomas Sheridan).

Sheridan and His Times. By an Octogenarian.

Sheridan, Modern Orator.

Sheridiana. (Table Talk and Bon Mots 1826)

Sherwin, Oscar. *Uncorking Old Sherry.*

Sichel, Walter. *Sheridan.*

Store, George Winchester. Jr. *London Stage, 1747–1776.*

Strong, L. A. G. *The Minstrel Boy (Life of Thomas Moore).*

Tracy, Clarence. *The Artificial Bastard (A Life of Savage).*

Walpole, Horace. *Life and Letters.*
Watkins, J. *Memoirs of the Public and Private Life of Richard Brinsley Sheridan.*
Weitzman, Sophia. *Warren Hastings and Philip Francis.*
White, Beatrice. *Cast of Ravens (The Strange Case of Sir Thomas Overbury).*
Wilson, Harriette. *Memoirs.*
Windham Papers
Wraxall, Sir Nathaniel. *Memoirs.*

BACKGROUND MATERIAL

Anonymous: *The Secret History of the Green Room* (Containing Authentic Entertaining Memoirs of the Actors and Actresses in the Three Theatres Royal).

The Bets Book at Brooks's

Bovill, E. W. *English Country Life 1780–1830*.
Bryant, Arthur. *The Age of Elegance*.
  The Years of Endurance.
Clerk, Thomas. *The Works of Hogarth*.
Craig, Maurice. *Dublin 1660–1860*.
Cullen, L. M. *Life in Ireland*.
Edwards (R.) and Ramsey (L. G. G.) (ed.). *Connoisseur Guides to the Early Georgian, Late Georgian and Regency Periods*.
Falk, Bernard. *Thomas Rowlandson, His Life and Art*.
Herold, J. Christopher. *The Age of Napoleon*.
Kemble, J. P. *The Prompt Books of John Philip*.
Memoirs of Brooks's, 1907
Nettles, Curtis P. *George Washington and American Independence*.
New Bath Guides for 1771 and 1773.
Nicholson, Harold. *The Age of Reason*.
Nicoll, Allardyce. *Eighteenth Century Drama*.
Priestley, J. B. *Prince of Pleasure*.
Quennell, Peter. *Hogarth's Progress*.
Rudé, George. *Hanoverian London, 1714–1808*.
Thackeray, W. M. *The Four Georges*.
Thomas, P. D. G. *The House of Commons in the Eighteenth Century*.
White, T. H. *The Age of Scandal*.
Willey, Basil. *Eighteenth Century Background*.
Wood, John. *A Description of Bath 1765*.

INDEX

RBS has been used as an abbreviation for Richard Brinsley
Sheridan throughout.

Index

379